Prentice Hall

LITERATURE

PENGUIN  EDITION

Reader's Notebook

Grade Eight

PEARSON

Upper Saddle River, New Jersey
Boston, Massachusetts
Chandler, Arizona
Glenview, Illinois

ISBN-13: 978-0-13-366676-2
ISBN-10: 0-13-366676-X
10 V011 17 16 15 14 13 12

ACKNOWLEDGMENTS

Grateful acknowledgment is made to the following for copyrighted material:

Arte Publico Press
From *My Own True Name* by Pat Mora. Copyright © 2000 Arte Publico Press—University of Houston. Published by Arte Publico Press. "Baseball" by Lionel G. Garcia from *I Can Hear the Cowbells Ring* (Houston: Arte Publico Press—University of Houston, 1994). Used by permission.

Ashabranner, Brent
"Always to Remember: The Vision of Maya Ying Lin" by Brent Ashabranner from *Always to Remember.* Copyright © 1988. Used by permission of Brent Ashabranner.

Black Issues Book Review
"Zora Neale Hurston: A Life in Letters, Book Review" by Zakia Carter from *Black Issues Book Review, Nov–Dec 2002;* www.bibookreview.com. Used by permission.

Curtis Brown London
"Who Can Replace a Man" by Brian Aldiss from *Masterpieces: The Best Science Fiction of the Century.* Copyright © 1966 by Brian Aldiss. Reproduced with permission of Curtis Brown Group Ltd, London on behalf of Brian Aldiss.

Child Health Association of Sewickley, Inc.
"Thumbprint Cookies" from *Three Rivers Cookbook.* Copyright © Child Health Association of Sewickley, Inc. Used by permission.

Copper Canyon Press c/o The Permissions Company
"Snake on the Etowah" by David Bottoms from *Armored Hearts: Selected and New Poems.* Copyright © 1995 by David Bottoms. Used by the permission of Copper Canyon Press, www.coppercanyonpress.org. All rights reserved.

Gary N. DaSilva for Neil Simon
"The Governess" from *The Good Doctor* © 1974 by Neil Simon. Copyright renewed © 2002 by Neil Simon. Used by permission. CAUTION: Professionals and amateurs are hereby warned that *The Good Doctor* is fully protected under the Berne Convention and the Universal Copyright Convention and is subject to royalty. All rights, including without limitation professional, amateur, motion picture, television, radio, recitation, lecturing, public reading and foreign translation rights, computer media rights and the right of reproduction, and electronic storage or retrieval, in whole or in part and in any form, are strictly reserved and none of these rights can be exercised or used without written permission from the copyright owner. Inquiries for stock and amateur performances should be addressed to Samuel French, Inc., 45 West 25th Street, New York, NY 10010. All other inquiries should be addressed to Gary N. DaSilva, 111 N. Sepulveda Blvd., Suite 250, Manhattan Beach, CA 90266-6850.

(Acknowledgments continue on page V71)

CONTENTS

PART 1

UNIT 1 Fiction and Nonfiction

CONTENTS

CONTENTS

UNIT 3 Types of Nonfiction

CONTENTS

UNIT 5 Drama

UNIT 6 Themes in American Stories

As you read your hardcover student edition of *Prentice Hall Literature* use the ***Reader's Notebook*** to guide you in learning and practicing the skills presented. In addition, many selections in your student edition are presented here in an interactive format. The notes and instruction will guide you in applying reading and literary skills and in thinking about the selection. The examples on these pages show you how to use the notes as a companion when you read.

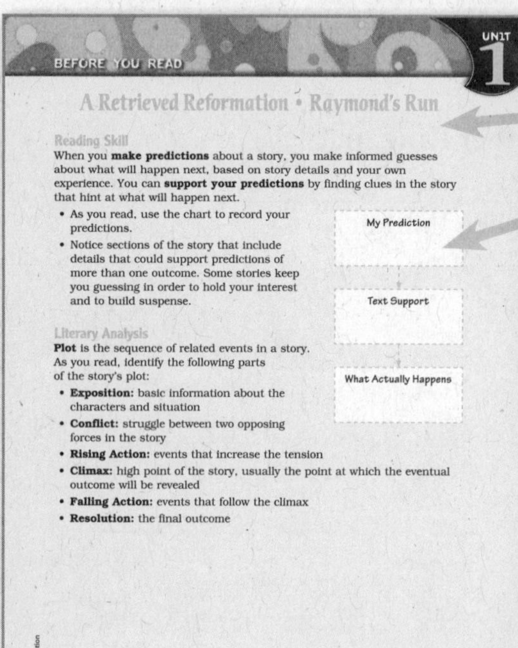

BEFORE YOU READ — UNIT 1

A Retrieved Reformation • Raymond's Run

Reading Skill

When you **make predictions** about a story, you make informed guesses about what will happen next, based on story details and your own experience. You can **support your predictions** by finding clues in the story that hint at what will happen next.

- As you read, use the chart to record your predictions.
- Notice sections of the story that include details that could support predictions of more than one outcome. Some stories keep you guessing in order to hold your interest and to build suspense.

My Prediction

Text Support

What Actually Happens

Literary Analysis

Plot is the sequence of related events in a story. As you read, identify the following parts of the story's plot:

- **Exposition:** basic information about the characters and situation
- **Conflict:** struggle between two opposing forces in the story
- **Rising Action:** events that increase the tension
- **Climax:** high point of the story, usually the point at which the eventual outcome will be revealed
- **Falling Action:** events that follow the climax
- **Resolution:** the final outcome

© Pearson Education

Get Ready to Learn

Use the *Before You Read* page to learn about the Reading Skill and Literary Analysis you will be studying.

To practice the skills, you can write directly in the graphic organizer as you read.

Get the Big Idea

A *Making Connections* page for every selection presents a selection summary, which lets you know what the selection is about before you read.

MAKING CONNECTIONS

Raymond's Run

Toni Cade Bambara

Summary Squeaky is the fastest runner in her class. She cares for her "not quite right" brother Raymond. She protects him from teasing and from getting hurt. During the annual May Day races, Squeaky learns lessons about herself, a runner named Gretchen, and Raymond.

Writing About the Big Question

Is the truth the same for everyone? In "Raymond's Run," the narrator discovers that winning a race is not the most important thing in her life. Complete this sentence:

Before ________ happened, I used to think that ________ was important. After it happened, I observed that ________

Note-taking Guide

Use this chart to record the order of the four most important events in the story.

Beginning Event			Final Outcome
Squeaky and her brother Raymond run into a group of girls whom Squeaky does not like.			

© Pearson Education

20 Reader's Notebook

Make a Big Question Connection

Sentence starters help you think about the Big Question.

Be an Active Reader

A *Note-taking Guide* helps you organize the main ideas of the selection. Complete the guide as you read to track your understanding.

TAKE NOTES

Raymond's Run

Toni Cade Bambara

I don't have much work to do around the house like some girls. My mother does that. And I don't have to earn my pocket money by hustling; George runs errands for the big boys and sells Christmas cards. And anything else that's got to get done, my father does. All I have to do in life is mind my brother Raymond, which is enough.

Sometimes I slip and say my little brother Raymond. But as any fool can see he's much bigger and he's older too. But a lot of people call him my little brother cause he needs looking after cause he's not quite right. And a lot of smart mouths got lots to say about that too, especially when George was minding him. But now, if anybody has anything to say to Raymond, anything to say about his big head, they have to come by me. And I don't play the dozens[1] or believe in standing around with somebody in my face doing a lot of talking. I much rather just knock you down and take my chances even if I am a little girl with skinny arms and a squeaky voice, which is how I got the name Squeaky. And if things get too rough, I run. And as anybody can tell you, I'm the fastest thing on two feet.

There is no track meet that I don't win the first-place medal. I used to win the twenty-yard dash when I was a little kid in kindergarten. Nowadays, it's the fifty-yard dash. And tomorrow I'm subject to run the quarter-mile relay all by myself and come in first, second, and third. The big kids call me Mercury[2] cause I'm the swiftest thing in the neighborhood. Everybody knows that—except two people who know better, my father and me.

He can beat me to Amsterdam Avenue with me having a two fire-hydrant headstart and him running with his hands in his pockets and whistling. But that's private information. Cause can you imagine some thirty-five-year-old man stuffing himself into

Activate Prior Knowledge
Tell about a time when you practiced very hard for something.

Literary Analysis
Plot is the order of related events in a story. **Exposition** is the part of plot that gives basic information about the characters and the situation. The **conflict** is the struggle between two forces in the story. Read the bracketed passage. Is this passage part of the exposition or part of the conflict? Explain your answer.

Reading Check
What is Squeaky's special talent? Circle the text that tells you.

1. **the dozens** game in which the players insult one another; the first to show anger loses.
2. **Mercury** in Roman mythology, the messenger of the gods, known for great speed.

Take Notes

Side-column questions accompany the selections that appear in the Reader's Notebooks. These questions are a built-in tutor to help you practice the skills and understand what you read.

Mark the Text

Use write-on lines to answer questions in the side column. You may also want to use the lines for your own notes.

When you see a pencil, you should underline, circle, or mark the text as indicated.

AFTER YOU READ

Raymond's Run

1. **Respond:** Which parts of Squeaky's personality would make you want to be her friend? Which parts would make you not want to be her friend?
2. **Analyze:** How does Squeaky feel about taking care of Raymond?

...ns you made as you read "Raymond's ... for each?

... **plot** chart below. Write in two events ... event from the **falling action**.

...aky crosses the

Event:

Event: Squeaky and Gretchen exchange smiles.

Falling Action

Resolution:

Raymond's Run 31

Check Your Understanding

Questions after every selection help you think about the selection. You can use the write-on lines and charts to answer the questions. Then, share your ideas in class discussions.

SUPPORT FOR WRITING AND EXTEND YOUR LEARNING

Writing: New Ending

Imagine the ending of the story if Gretchen had won the race. Write a **new ending** to show how Squeaky might react to losing. Use your notes as you write your new ending.

Does Squeaky go through a change at the end of the story? If so, how would this change affect the way she would feel about losing? Explain.

Squeaky is proud, bold, and loyal. What other adjectives describe her?

Listening and Speaking: Radio Broadcast

Use the following statements to help you prepare for your **radio broadcast.** Use action verbs so that listeners will feel the rising tension and the excitement of the race.

1. Describe Squeaky's appearance.
2. Describe Gretchen's appearance.
3. Describe how Squeaky acts.
4. Describe how Gretchen acts.
5. Describe what happens as Squeaky and Gretchen approach the finish line.

32 Reader's Notebook

Go Beyond the Selection

This page provides step-by-step guidance for completing the Writing and Extend Your Learning activities presented in your student edition.

Selections and Skills Support

The pages in your ***Reader's Notebook*** go with the pages in the hardcover student edition. The pages in the ***Reader's Notebook*** allow you to participate in class instruction and take notes on the concepts and selections.

Before You Read

Build Skills Follow along in your ***Reader's Notebook*** as your teacher introduces the **Reading Skill** and **Literary Analysis** instruction. The graphic organizer is provided on this page so that you can take notes right in your ***Reader's Notebook.***

Preview Use this page for the selection your teacher assigns.

- The **Summary** gives you an outline of the selection.
- Use the **Reading-Writing Connection** to understand the big idea of the selection and join in the class discussion about the ideas.
- Use the **Note-taking Guide** while you read the story. This will help you organize and remember information you will need to answer questions about the story later.

While You Read

Selection Text and Sidenotes You can read the full text of one selection in each pair in your ***Reader's Notebook.***

- You can write in the ***Reader's Notebook.*** Underline important details to help you find them later.
- Use the **Take Notes** column to jot down your reactions, ideas, and answers to questions about the text. If your assigned selection is not the one that is included in the ***Reader's Notebook,*** use sticky notes to make your own **Take Notes** section in the side column as you read the selection in the hardcover student edition.

After You Read

Apply the Skills Use this page to answer questions about the selection right in your ***Reader's Notebook.*** For example, you can complete the graphic organizer that is in the hardcover student edition right on the page in your ***Reader's Notebook.***

Support for Writing and Extend Your Learning Use this page to help you jot down notes and ideas as you prepare to do one or more of the projects assigned with the selection.

Other Features in the *Reader's Notebook* You will also find note-taking opportunities for these features:

- Learning About the Genre
- Support for the Model Selection
- Support for Reading Informational Materials

from The Baker Heater League

Nonfiction differs from fiction in these ways:

- Nonfiction deals with real people, events, or ideas.
- Nonfiction is told from the **point of view**, or perspective, of the author.

Many things affect the outcome of nonfiction writing. Two examples are these:

- **Mood:** the overall feeling the reader gets from the work
- **Author's style:** all of the different ways that a writer uses language. Rhythm, language, and methods of organization are all part of the author's individual style.

Purpose	Mission	Examples
To persuade	• written to convince audiences of a certain idea or opinion	• speeches • editorials
To inform	• written to present facts and information	• articles • reference books • historical essays • research papers
To entertain	• written for the enjoyment of the audience	• autobiographies • biographies • travel narratives

The 11:59

Fiction is a story created from the author's imagination. It tells about characters and events. Fiction has these basic elements:

- **Setting:** the time and place of the story
- **Plot:** the order of events that moves the reader through the story. The plot includes a **conflict**, or problem, at the beginning of the story. The **resolution**, or conclusion, appears at the end of the story.
- **Characters:** the people or animals that take part in the action in a story. The **character's traits**, or qualities, can affect his or her thoughts and actions.
- **Point of view:** the view from which the story is told to the reader. **First-person point of view** is used when the story is told from the view of a character. **Third-person point of view** is used when the story is told from the view of a narrator outside the story.
- **Theme:** a message about life that the story tries to show

Type	Description	Characteristics
Short stories	short works that can usually be read in one sitting	• contain plot, characters, setting, point of view, and theme • usually focus on one main plot around one conflict
Novels	longer works	• contain plot, characters, conflict, and setting • may also contain **subplots**, independent stories or conflicts related to the main plot
Novellas	shorter than novels, but longer than short stories	• may contain characteristics of short stories and novels
Historical fiction	works of fiction that take place in a real historical setting	• uses information about real people and events to tell invented stories

from The Baker Heater League

Patricia C. McKissack and
Fredrick McKissack

Summary This nonfiction selection explains how railroad workers called *porters* shared tales with one another. The porters would gather around a potbellied stove, called a Baker heater, to tell their stories. Legends such as those of Casey Jones and John Henry grew out of these stories.

Note-taking Guide

Use the chart below to record the different facts and legends you learned while reading "The Baker Heater League."

Facts	Lengends
About 1870, John Henry joined a steel-driving team for the C & O Railroad.	John Henry was so strong that he could drive steel with a hammer in each hand.

from The Baker Heater League

Patricia C. and Fredrick McKissack

Porters developed a language and history that grew out of their common experiences. And they shared their experiences from coast to coast, north and south. Singing and telling stories helped to pass the time while waiting for an assignment, and it took the edge off being away from home and their loved ones.

Train stations provided quarters for porters called "porter houses." Sitting around a Baker heater, a large pot-bellied stove, the first porters told tales, jokes, and real-life stories that, in time, developed into a communication network peculiar to themselves. For example, if something happened in New York on Friday, porters in every state would know about it on Sunday. Political news, a good joke, style changes, even a girl's telephone number could be passed from New York to Chicago to Los Angeles, or from Minneapolis to St. Louis to New Orleans. This special brotherhood became known as "The Baker Heater League."

As older porters died or retired, their stories became a part of railroad lore, and their legacy helped to reshape and mold new heroes and legends. Just as lumberjacks created their superhero, Paul Bunyan, and cowboys sang about wily Pecos Bill, railroaders had Casey Jones and John Henry.

John Luther Jones, better known as Casey Jones, was an engineer on Cannonball Number 382. On the evening of April 29, 1900, Casey and his black fireman, Sim Webb, prepared to take the Cannonball from Memphis to Canton. The scheduled engineer was out ill. The train left at 12:50 A.M., an hour and thirty minutes late. Casey was determined to make up the lost time. Through a series of mishaps and miscommunications, Casey's train crashed. Although

Vocabulary Development

lore (lawr) *n.* knowledge and traditions that people learn from other people rather than from books

mishaps (MIS haps) *n.* unfortunate or unlucky accidents

TAKE NOTES

Activate Prior Knowledge 

What lessons could you learn from family members who tell stories about jobs they have done?

____

____

____

Nonfiction 

One purpose of nonfiction is **to inform,** or to present facts and information to the reader. Read the bracketed paragraph. What do the details describe?

Reading Check 

What cities do the porters visit? Circle the names in the bracketed text.

TAKE NOTES

Nonfiction

Mood is the feeling that a work stirs in the reader. Read the first bracketed passage about Casey Jones. What mood do you think the author is trying to create? Explain.

Nonfiction

The **author's style** consists of all the different ways that the author uses language. Why do you think the author chose to put songs in this piece? What does this tell you about the author's style?

Stop to Reflect

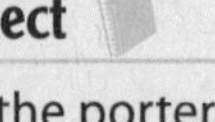

Why would the porters have looked up to Daddy Joe as a hero?

Reading Check

What did John Henry tell his father? Circle the text that tells you.

the brave engineer could have jumped to safety, he stayed with the train and saved many lives at the cost of his own. Casey Jones became a railroad hero, and many songs were written about him:

Fireman jumped but Casey stayed on;
He was a good engineer, but he's dead
and gon'.

Legend tells us in another song that:

When John Henry was a little boy,
He was sitting on his papa's knee;
He was looking down on a piece of steel,
Say's "A steel-drivin' man I'll be, Lord, Lord.
A steel-drivin' man I'll be."

The real John Henry, believed to be a newly freed slave from North Carolina, joined the West Virginia steel-driving team hired to dig out the Big Bend Tunnel for the C & O Railroad, circa 1870. Many stories detail the life and adventures of this two hundred-pound, six-foot man who was so strong he could drive steel with a hammer in each hand. John Henry's death occurred after competing with a steam drill, winning and then dying.

The steam drill set on the right-hand side,
John Henry was on the left.
He said, "I will beat that steam drill down
Or hammer my fool self to death."

Casey Jones and John Henry belonged to all railroaders, but the Pullman[1] porters had their very own hero in Daddy Joe.

Daddy Joe was a real person, but like most legends, his exploits were greatly exaggerated. One story establishes in legend, if not in fact, that Daddy Joe was the "first Pullman porter." He was said to have stood so tall and to have large hands so powerful that he could walk flat-footed down the aisle and let the upper berths down on each side.

1. **Pullman** cars featured special seats, which were converted to sleeping berths at night. The porters who readied the berths for sleeping also helped the train passengers during the day.

Whenever a storyteller wanted to make a point about courtesy, honesty, or an outstanding job performance, he used a Daddy Joe story. And a tale about him usually began with: "The most terrific Pullman porter who ever made down a berth was Daddy Joe." Then the teller would tell a story like this one:

Hostile Indians were said to have attacked a train at a water tank. The all-white passengers were terrified. But Daddy Joe, with no regard for Pullman rules or his own safety, climbed on top of the train and spoke to the Indians in their own language. Afterwards Daddy Joe threw a Pullman blanket to each member of the attacking party and added a blessing at the end. The Indians let the train pass safely.

Whether he was facing hurricanes, high water, fires, robbers, or Indians, Daddy Joe always masterfully dealt with the situation. Legend has it that he even thwarted one of Jesse James's[2] attempted robberies. Daddy Joe got so many tips from grateful passengers, he was said to be "burdened down with silver and gold."

The first porters, who created Daddy Joe in their own image, were proud of him. He represented the qualities they valued—unquestionable loyalty and dedication to the job.

New railroad employees were always the source of a good laugh, too. This new-brakeman story—or one like it—was a porter house favorite.

It began with a young college graduate who got a yearning to work on the railroad. So, he traded in his suit and tie for the rusty railroad blues. Right away he was hired as a brakeman on the Knox & Lincoln Line. On his first run, the engineer was having a very hard time getting the freight up a steep hill. After getting the train over, the engineer called out, "I was afraid she'd stall and the train would roll backward!"

Vocabulary Development

burdened (BER duhnd) *adj.* weighted down by work, duty, or sorrow

2. **Jesse James** (1847–1882) and his brother Frank roamed the American West after the Civil War, robbing trains and banks.

TAKE NOTES

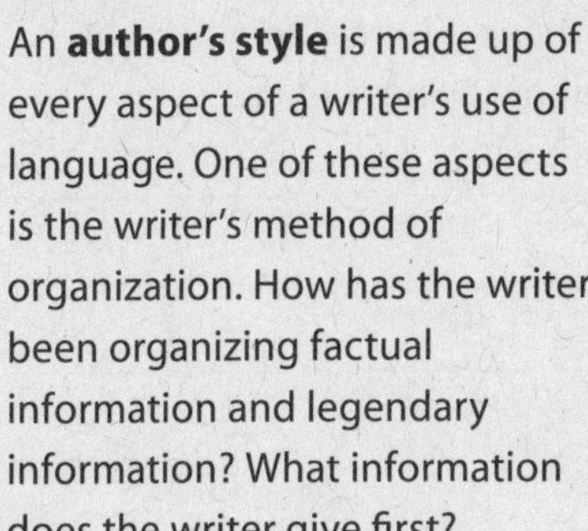

Nonfiction

An **author's style** is made up of every aspect of a writer's use of language. One of these aspects is the writer's method of organization. How has the writer been organizing factual information and legendary information? What information does the writer give first?

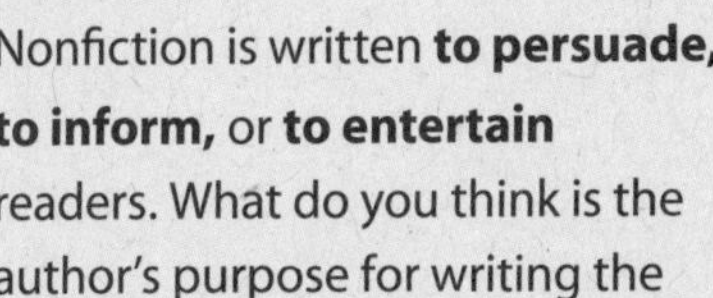

Nonfiction

Nonfiction is written **to persuade, to inform,** or **to entertain** readers. What do you think is the author's purpose for writing the bracketed paragraph about Daddy Joe?

Stop to Reflect

Why do you think the porters liked to tell one another funny stories about new railroad employees?

TAKE NOTES

Stop to Reflect 

What is a funny story that you enjoy telling friends?

______

______

______

______

______

Reading Check

How did the porters' tales stay fresh and original over time? Underline the text that tells you.

The new brakeman smiled broadly and assured the engineer. "No chance of that happening," he said, beaming with pride, "because before we started, I went back and set the brakes."

Amid thigh-slapping laughter, another tale would begin with: "Did you hear the story about the flagman?" Of course they'd all heard the story a hundred times. But each teller added or subtracted something until the tale was his own. That's how the tales stayed fresh and original.

Reader's Response: What parts of the writing did you enjoy most? Did you enjoy the factual information or the fictional tales of the railroad legends better? Explain your answer.

______

______

______

The 11:59

Patricia C. McKissack

Summary Lester Simmons, a retired porter, hangs out every night at the porter house, telling stories to the other railroad employees. One night, he tells the young porters about the mysterious 11:59 Death Train. Lester's story becomes real. He tries to escape the train.

Note-taking Guide

Use this web to recall the different stories that Lester tells.

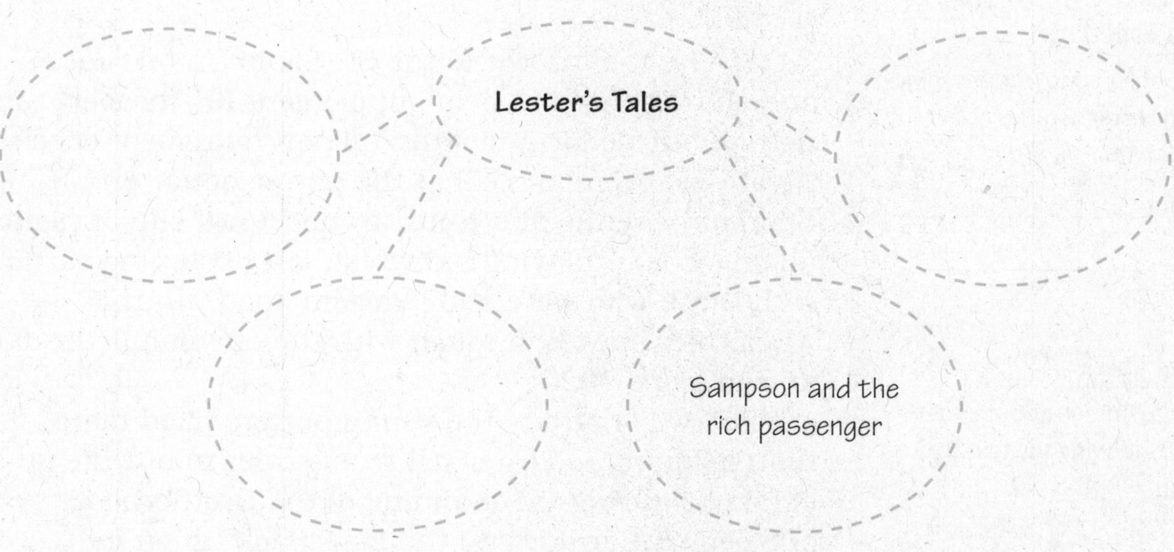

TAKE NOTES

The 11:59

Patricia C. McKissack

From 1880 to 1960—a time known as the golden age of train travel—George Pullman's luxury sleeping cars provided passengers with comfortable accommodations during an overnight trip. The men who changed the riding seats into well-made-up beds and attended to the individual needs of each passenger were called Pullman car porters. For decades all the porters were African Americans, so when they organized the Brotherhood of Sleeping Car Porters in 1926, theirs was the first all-black union in the United States. Like most groups, the porters had their own language and a network of stories. The phantom Death Train, known in railroad language as the 11:59, is an example of the kind of story the porters often shared.

Lester Simmons was a thirty-year retired Pullman car porter—had his gold watch to prove it. "Keeps perfect train time," he often bragged. "Good to the second."

Daily he went down to the St. Louis Union Station and shined shoes to help supplement his meager twenty-four-dollar-a-month Pullman retirement check. He ate his evening meal at the porter house on Compton Avenue and hung around until late at night talking union, playing bid whist,[1] and spinning yarns with those who were still "travelin' men." In this way Lester stayed in touch with the only family he'd known since 1920.

There was nothing the young porters liked more than listening to Lester tell true stories about the old days, during the founding of the Brotherhood of Sleeping Car Porters, the first black union in the United States. He knew the president, A. Philip Randolph,[2] personally, and proudly boasted that it was Randolph who'd signed him up as a union man back in 1926. He passed his original card around for inspection. "I knew all the founding brothers. Take Brother E. J. Bradley. We hunted many a day together, not for the sport of it but for something to

Activate Prior Knowledge 

Think of some scary stories that you know. What makes a story scary?

Fiction 

Setting is the time and place of a story. Underline words in the bracketed paragraph that tell you about the setting.

Stop to Reflect 

Why do the young porters enjoy hearing Lester's stories about the old days?

Reading Check 

What was unique about Lester's union? Underline the text that tells you.

1. **bid whist** (hwist) *n.* card game for four players that developed into bridge.
2. **A. Philip Randolph** (1889–1979) president of the Brotherhood of Sleeping Car Porters, the first black union. Randolph gave the opening speech at the historic March on Washington in 1963.

eat. Those were hard times, starting up the union. But we hung in there so you youngsters might have the benefits you enjoy now."

The rookie porters always liked hearing about the thirteen-year struggle between the Brotherhood and the powerful Pullman Company, and how, against all odds, the fledgling union had won recognition and better working conditions.

Everybody enjoyed it too when Lester told tall tales about Daddy Joe, the porters' larger-than-life hero. "Now y'all know the first thing a good Pullman man is expected to do is make up the top and lower berths for the passengers each night."

"Come on, Lester," one of his listeners chided. "You don't need to describe our jobs for us."

"Some of you, maybe not. But some of you, well—" he said, looking over the top of his glasses and raising an eyebrow at a few of the younger porters. "I was just setting the stage." He smiled good-naturedly and went on with his story. "They tell me Daddy Joe could walk flatfooted down the center of the coach and let down berths on both sides of the aisle."

Hearty laughter filled the room, because everyone knew that to accomplish such a feat, Daddy Joe would have to have been superhuman. But that was it: To the men who worked the sleeping cars, Daddy Joe was no less a hero than Paul Bunyan was to the lumberjacks of the Northwestern forests.

"And when the 11:59 pulled up to his door, as big and strong as Daddy Joe was . . ." Lester continued solemnly. "Well, in the end even he couldn't escape the 11:59." The old storyteller eyed one of the rookie porters he knew had never heard the frightening tale about the porters' Death Train. Lester took joy in mesmerizing[3] his young listeners with all the details.

"Any porter who hears the whistle of the 11:59 has got exactly twenty-four hours to clear up earthly matters. He better be ready when the train comes the next night . . ." In his creakiest voice, Lester drove home the point. "All us porters got to board that train one day. Ain't no way to escape the final ride on the 11:59."

Silence.

3. **mesmerizing** (MEZ muh ryz ing) *n.* fascinating; amazing.

TAKE NOTES

Fiction 

Point of view is the view from which a story is told to the reader. **First-person point of view** is used when the story is told from the view of a character. **Third-person point of view** is used when the story is told from the view of a narrator outside the story. From which point of view is this story told? Explain.

______

______

______

Fiction 

Characters are the people in a story. What character is Lester telling the porters about? Underline the character's name in the bracketed paragraph.

Stop to Reflect 

Why does Lester use his "creakiest voice" when he tells the porters about the 11:59 train?

______

______

______

TAKE NOTES

Reading Check 

What did the female passenger have with her when she boarded the train? Circle the text that tells you.

Stop to Reflect 

Lester's friend Sampson thinks that the woman on the train will give him a big tip. Why does he think this?

____

____

____

____

Fiction 

A **plot** is the order of events that moves the reader through a story. A story sometimes has a **theme,** or message about life. What is a possible theme of the story of Tip Sampson?

____

____

____

____

____

"Lester," a young porter asked, "you know anybody who ever heard the whistle of the 11:59 and lived to tell—"

"Not a living soul!"

Laughter.

"Well," began one of the men, "wonder will we have to make up berths on *that* train?"

"If it's an overnight trip to heaven, you can best be believing there's bound to be a few of us making up the berths," another answered.

"Shucks," a card player stopped to put in. "They say even up in heaven *we* the ones gon' be keeping all that gold and silver polished."

"Speaking of gold and silver," Lester said, remembering. "That reminds me of how I gave Tip Sampson his nickname. Y'all know Tip?"

There were plenty of nods and smiles.

The memory made Lester chuckle. He shifted in his seat to find a more comfortable spot. Then he began. "A woman got on board the *Silver Arrow* in Chicago going to Los Angeles. She was dripping in finery—had on all kinds of gold and diamond jewelry, carried twelve bags. Sampson knocked me down getting to wait on her, figuring she was sure for a big tip. That lady was worrisome! Ooowee! 'Come do this. Go do that. Bring me this.' Sampson was running over himself trying to keep that lady happy. When we reached L.A., my passengers all tipped me two or three dollars, as was customary back then.

"When Sampson's Big Money lady got off, she reached into her purse and placed a dime in his outstretched hand. A *dime*! Can you imagine? *Ow*! You should have seen his face. And I didn't make it no better. Never did let him forget it. I teased him so—went to calling him Tip, and the nickname stuck."

Laughter.

"I haven't heard from ol' Tip in a while. Anybody know anything?"

Vocabulary Development

finery (FYN uhr ee) *n.* fancy clothing and accessories

worrisome (WER ee suhm) *adj.* causing worry or anxiety

"You haven't got word, Lester? Tip boarded the 11:59 over in Kansas City about a month ago."

"Sorry to hear that. That just leaves me and Willie Beavers, the last of the old, old-timers here in St. Louis."

Lester looked at his watch—it was a little before midnight. The talkfest[4] had lasted later than usual. He said his goodbyes and left, taking his usual route across the Eighteenth Street bridge behind the station.

In the darkness, Lester looked over the yard, picking out familiar shapes—the *Hummingbird*, the *Zephyr*.[5] He'd worked on them both. Train travel wasn't anything like it used to be in the old days—not since people had begun to ride airplanes. "Progress," he scoffed. "Those contraptions will never take the place of a train. No sir!"

Suddenly he felt a sharp pain in his chest. At exactly the same moment he heard the mournful sound of a train whistle, which the wind seemed to carry from some faraway place. Ignoring his pain, Lester looked at the old station. He knew nothing was scheduled to come in or out till early morning. Nervously he lit a match to check the time. 11:59!

"No," he said into the darkness. "I'm not ready. I've got plenty of living yet."

Fear quickened his step. Reaching his small apartment, he hurried up the steps. His heart pounded in his ear, and his left arm tingled. He had an idea, and there wasn't a moment to waste. But his own words haunted him. *Ain't no way to escape the final ride on the 11:59.*

"But I'm gon' try!" Lester spent the rest of the night plotting his escape from fate.

"I won't eat or drink anything all day," he talked himself through his plan. "That way I can't choke, die of food poisoning, or cause a cooking fire."

Lester shut off the space heater to avoid an explosion, nailed shut all doors and windows to keep out intruders, and unplugged every electrical appliance. Good weather was predicted, but just in case a freak storm came and blew out a window, shooting deadly glass shards in his direction, he

4. **talkfest** (TAWK fest) *n.* informal gathering for discussion.

5. ***Zephyr*** (ZEF uhr) *n.* soft, gentle breeze, named for the Greek god of the west wind.

TAKE NOTES

Fiction 

Lester makes his way home. Circle the words in the first bracketed paragraphs that describe the **setting**.

Stop to Reflect 

What do you think Lester would say about travel today?

____

____

____

____

Fiction 

A **conflict** is a problem that a character faces. What conflict does Lester face in the second bracketed passage?

____

____

Reading Check

What happens at exactly 11:59? Underline the text that tells you.

TAKE NOTES

Fiction

Fiction can be a **short story, novel, novella,** or **historical fiction.** What type of fiction do you think this story is? Explain.

____

____

____

Fiction

A **theme** is a message about life that a story attempts to show. Read the bracketed passage. What is a possible theme of Lester's story?

____

____

Stop to Reflect 

Why does thinking about the past make Lester smile?

____

____

____

moved a straight-backed chair into a far corner, making sure nothing was overhead to fall on him.

"I'll survive," he said, smiling at the prospect of beating Death. "Won't that be a wonderful story to tell at the porter house?" He rubbed his left arm. It felt numb again.

Lester sat silently in his chair all day, too afraid to move. At noon someone knocked on his door. He couldn't answer it. Foot-steps . . . another knock. He didn't answer.

A parade of minutes passed by, equally measured, one behind the other, ticking . . . ticking . . . away . . . The dull pain in his chest returned. He nervously checked his watch every few minutes.

Ticktock, ticktock.

Time had always been on his side. Now it was his enemy. Where had the years gone? Lester reviewed the thirty years he'd spent riding the rails. How different would his life have been if he'd married Louise Henderson and had a gallon of children? What if he'd taken that job at the mill down in Opelika?[6] What if he'd followed his brother to Philly?[7] How different?

Ticktock, ticktock.

So much living had passed so quickly. Lester decided if he had to do it all over again, he'd stand by his choices. His had been a good life. No regrets. No major changes for him.

Ticktock, ticktock.

The times he'd had—both good and bad—what memories. His first and only love had been traveling, and she was a jealous companion. Wonder whatever happened to that girl up in Minneapolis? Thinking about her made him smile. Then he laughed. That *girl* must be close to seventy years old by now.

Ticktock, ticktock.

Daylight was fading quickly. Lester drifted off to sleep, then woke from a nightmare in which, like Jonah, he'd been swallowed by an enormous beast. Even awake he could still hear its heart beating . . . *ticktock, ticktock* . . . But then he realized he was hearing his own heartbeat.

6. Opelika city in Alabama.

7. Philly informal name for Philadelphia, Pennsylvania.

Lester couldn't see his watch, but he guessed no more than half an hour had passed. Sleep had overtaken him with such little resistance. Would Death, that shapeless shadow, slip in that easily? Where was he lurking? *Yea, though I walk through the valley of the shadow of death, I will fear no evil . . .* The Twenty-third Psalm was the only prayer Lester knew, and he repeated it over and over, hoping it would comfort him.

Lester rubbed his tingling arm. He could hear the blood rushing past his ear and up the side of his head. He longed to know what time it was, but that meant he had to light a match—too risky. What if there was a gas leak? The match would set off an explosion. "I'm too smart for that, Death," he said.

Ticktock, ticktock.

It was late. He could feel it. Stiffness seized his legs and made them tremble. How much longer? he wondered. Was he close to winning?

Then in the fearful silence he heard a train whistle. His ears strained to identify the sound, making sure it *was* a whistle. No mistake. It came again, the same as the night before. Lester answered it with a groan.

Ticktock, ticktock.

He could hear Time ticking away in his head. Gas leak or not, he had to see his watch. Striking a match, Lester quickly checked the time. 11:57.

Although there was no gas explosion, a tiny explosion erupted in his heart.

Ticktock, ticktock.

Just a little more time. The whistle sounded again. Closer than before. Lester struggled to move, but he felt fastened to the chair. Now he could hear the engine puffing, pulling a heavy load. It was hard for him to breathe, too, and the pain in his chest weighed heavier and heavier.

Ticktock, ticktock.

Time had run out! Lester's mind reached for an explanation that made sense. But reason failed when a glowing phantom dressed in the porters'

TAKE NOTES

Stop to Reflect

Read the underlined sentence. Why do you think Lester talks to Death as though he were talking to a person?

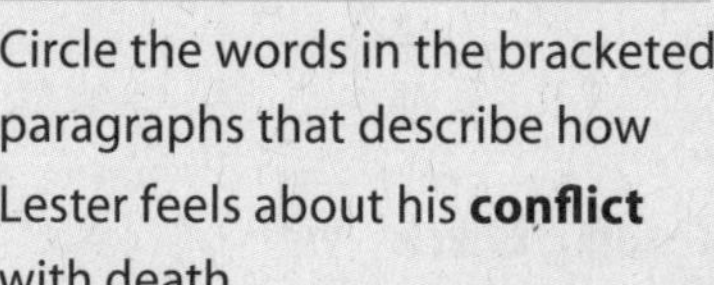

Fiction

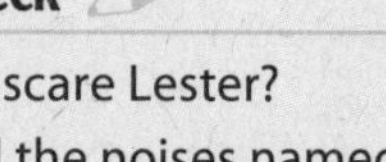

Circle the words in the bracketed paragraphs that describe how Lester feels about his **conflict** with death.

Reading Check

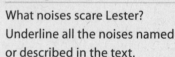

What noises scare Lester? Underline all the noises named or described in the text.

Vocabulary Development

lurking (LERK ing) *v.* waiting to spring out or attack; existing undiscovered

Fiction 

Which two **characters** are talking to each other? Circle both of their names.

Fiction

The **resolution** of a **plot** is often its conclusion. What is the resolution of Lester's story?

____

____

Reading Check 

Why does Tip visit Lester? Underline the text that tells you.

blue uniform stepped out of the grayness of Lester's confusion.

"It's *your* time, good brother." The specter spoke in a thousand familiar voices.

Freed of any restraint now, Lester stood, bathed in a peaceful calm that had its own glow. "Is that you, Tip?" he asked, squinting to focus on his old friend standing in the strange light.

"It's me, ol' partner. Come to remind you that none of us can escape the last ride on the 11:59."

"I know. I know," Lester said, chuckling. "But man, I had to try."

Tip smiled. "I can dig it. So did I."

"That'll just leave Willie, won't it?"

"Not for long."

"I'm ready."

Lester saw the great beam of the single headlight and heard the deafening whistle blast one last time before the engine tore through the front of the apartment, shattering glass and splintering wood, collapsing everything in its path, including Lester's heart.

When Lester didn't show up at the shoeshine stand two days running, friends went over to his place and found him on the floor. His eyes were fixed on something quite amazing—his gold watch, stopped at exactly 11:59.

Reader's Response: Did the story end the way you thought it would? Explain your answer.

____

____

____

Nonfiction and Fiction

1. **Interpret:** What causes Lester's death in "The 11:59"?

2. **Classify:** Use the chart below to record information about the railroad figures mentioned in "The Baker Heater League." List the heroes. Write the facts and legends that are given about each one.

Railroad Heroes	Fact	Legend/Fiction

3. **Nonfiction: Nonfiction** writers often use fictional elements in their work. Why does the author include tales about well-known railroad figures in "The Baker Heater League"?

4. **Fiction:** What details in the **setting** make the "The 11:59" seem believable?

Talk Show

Present a **talk show**. The following tips will help you create your show.

- Read some of the authors' works. Patricia and Fredrick McKissack's books include *Christmas in the Big House, Christmas in the Quarters; Bugs!; Martin Luther King, Jr.: Man of Peace; Rebels Against Slavery: American Slave Revolts;* and *Let My People Go.*

  What I learned from the McKissacks' writing:

  ____

  ____

  ____

  ____

- Search the Internet: Use words and phrases such as "Patricia McKissack article."

  What I learned about Patricia and Fredrick McKissack:

  ____

  ____

  ____

  ____

- Watch the video interview with Patricia McKissack. Add what you learn from the video to what you have already learned about the author and her husband.

  Additional information learned about the authors:

  ____

  ____

  ____

  ____

Use your notes to write your talk show.

A Retrieved Reformation • Raymond's Run

Reading Skill

When you **make predictions** about a story, you make informed guesses about what will happen next, based on story details and your own experience. You can **support your predictions** by finding clues in the story that hint at what will happen next.

- As you read, use the chart to record your predictions.
- Notice sections of the story that include details that could support predictions of more than one outcome. Some stories keep you guessing in order to hold your interest and to build suspense.

My Prediction

Text Support

What Actually Happens

Literary Analysis

Plot is the sequence of related events in a story. As you read, identify the following parts of the story's plot:

- **Exposition:** basic information about the characters and situation
- **Conflict:** struggle between two opposing forces in the story
- **Rising Action:** events that increase the tension
- **Climax:** high point of the story, usually the point at which the eventual outcome will be revealed
- **Falling Action:** events that follow the climax
- **Resolution:** the final outcome

Raymond's Run

Toni Cade Bambara

Summary Squeaky is the fastest runner in her class. She cares for her "not quite right" brother Raymond. She protects him from teasing and from getting hurt. During the annual May Day races, Squeaky learns lessons about herself, a runner named Gretchen, and Raymond.

Writing About the Big Question

Is the truth the same for everyone? In "Raymond's Run," the narrator discovers that winning a race is not the most important thing in her life. Complete this sentence:

Before ____________________________ happened, I used to think that ____ was important. After it happened, I observed that ____.

Note-taking Guide

Use this chart to record the order of the four most important events in the story.

Beginning Event	→		→		→	Final Outcome
Squeaky and her brother Raymond run into a group of girls whom Squeaky does not like.						

Raymond's Run

Toni Cade Bambara

I don't have much work to do around the house like some girls. My mother does that. And I don't have to earn my pocket money by hustling; George runs errands for the big boys and sells Christmas cards. And anything else that's got to get done, my father does. All I have to do in life is mind my brother Raymond, which is enough.

Sometimes I slip and say my little brother Raymond. But as any fool can see he's much bigger and he's older too. But a lot of people call him my little brother cause he needs looking after cause he's not quite right. And a lot of smart mouths got lots to say about that too, especially when George was minding him. But now, if anybody has anything to say to Raymond, anything to say about his big head, they have to come by me. And I don't play the dozens[1] or believe in standing around with somebody in my face doing a lot of talking. I much rather just knock you down and take my chances even if I am a little girl with skinny arms and a squeaky voice, which is how I got the name Squeaky. And if things get too rough, I run. And as anybody can tell you, I'm the fastest thing on two feet.

There is no track meet that I don't win the first-place medal. I used to win the twenty-yard dash when I was a little kid in kindergarten. Nowadays, it's the fifty-yard dash. And tomorrow I'm subject to run the quarter-mile relay all by myself and come in first, second, and third. The big kids call me Mercury[2] cause I'm the swiftest thing in the neighborhood. Everybody knows that—except two people who know better, my father and me.

He can beat me to Amsterdam Avenue with me having a two fire-hydrant headstart and him running with his hands in his pockets and whistling. But that's private information. Cause can you imagine some thirty-five-year-old man stuffing himself into

1. **the dozens** game in which the players insult one another; the first to show anger loses.

2. **Mercury** in Roman mythology, the messenger of the gods, known for great speed.

TAKE NOTES

Activate Prior Knowledge 

Tell about a time when you practiced very hard for something.

Literary Analysis 

Plot is the order of related events in a story. **Exposition** is the part of plot that gives basic information about the characters and the situation. The **conflict** is the struggle between two forces in the story. Read the bracketed passage. Is this passage part of the exposition or part of the conflict? Explain your answer.

Reading Check 

What is Squeaky's special talent? Circle the text that tells you.

TAKE NOTES

Literary Analysis

The first bracketed passage contains **exposition** that helps you learn about the way Raymond acts. Circle information you learn about Raymond from this passage.

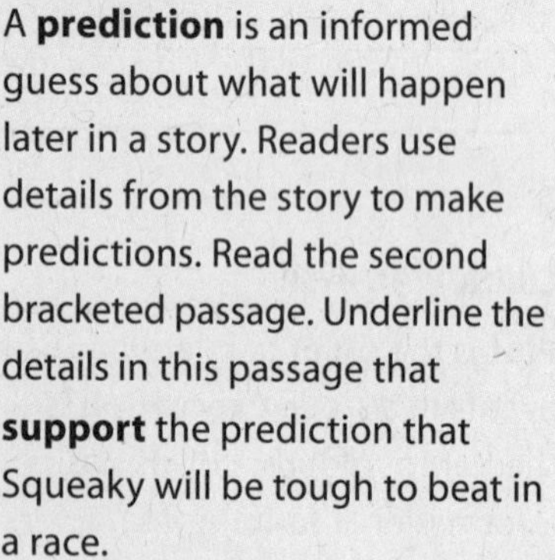

Reading Skill

A **prediction** is an informed guess about what will happen later in a story. Readers use details from the story to make predictions. Read the second bracketed passage. Underline the details in this passage that **support** the prediction that Squeaky will be tough to beat in a race.

Stop to Reflect

Do you think that it is hard for Squeaky to take care of Raymond? Explain your answer.

PAL[3] shorts to race little kids? So as far as everyone's concerned, I'm the fastest and that goes for Gretchen, too, who has put out the tale that she is going to win the first-place medal this year. Ridiculous. In the second place, she's got short legs. In the third place, she's got freckles. In the first place, no one can beat me and that's all there is to it.

I'm standing on the corner admiring the weather and about to take a stroll down Broadway so I can practice my breathing exercises, and I've got Raymond walking on the inside close to the buildings, cause he's subject to fits of fantasy and starts thinking he's a circus performer and that the curb is a tightrope strung high in the air. And sometimes after a rain he likes to step down off his tightrope right into the gutter and slosh around getting his shoes and cuffs wet. Or sometimes if you don't watch him he'll dash across traffic to the island in the middle of Broadway and give the pigeons a fit. Then I have to go behind him apologizing to all the old people sitting around trying to get some sun and getting all upset with the pigeons fluttering around them, scattering their newspapers and upsetting the waxpaper lunches in their laps. So I keep Raymond on the inside of me, and he plays like he's driving a stage coach, which is O.K. by me so long as he doesn't run me over or interrupt my breathing exercises, which I have to do on account of I'm serious about my running, and I don't care who knows it.

Now some people like to act like things come easy to them, won't let on that they practice. Not me. I'll high prance down 34th Street like a rodeo pony to keep my knees strong even if it does get my mother uptight so that she walks ahead like she's not with me, don't know me, is all by herself on a shopping trip, and I am somebody else's crazy child.

Now you take Cynthia Procter for instance. She's just the opposite. If there's a test tomorrow, she'll say something like, "Oh, I guess I'll play handball this afternoon and watch television tonight," just to let you know she ain't thinking about the test. Or like last week when she won the spelling bee for the millionth time, "A good thing you got 'receive,' Squeaky, cause

3. **PAL** Police Athletic League.

I would have got it wrong. I completely forgot about the spelling bee." And she'll clutch the lace on her blouse like it was a narrow escape. Oh, brother.

But of course when I pass her house on my early morning trots around the block, she is practicing the scales on the piano over and over and over and over. Then in music class she always lets herself get bumped around so she falls accidently on purpose onto the piano stool and is so surprised to find herself sitting there that she decides just for fun to try out the ole keys and what do you know—Chopin's[4] waltzes just spring out of her fingertips and she's the most surprised thing in the world. A regular prodigy. I could kill people like that.

I stay up all night studying the words for the spelling bee. And you can see me any time of day practicing running. I never walk if I can trot, and shame on Raymond if he can't keep up. But of course he does, cause if he hangs back someone's liable to walk up to him and get smart, or take his allowance from him, or ask him where he got that great big pumpkin head. People are so stupid sometimes.

So I'm strolling down Broadway breathing out and breathing in on counts of seven, which is my lucky number, and here comes Gretchen and her sidekicks—Mary Louise who used to be a friend of mine when she first moved to Harlem from Baltimore and got beat up by everybody till I took up for her on account of her mother and my mother used to sing in the same choir when they were young girls, but people ain't grateful, so now she hangs out with the new girl Gretchen and talks about me like a dog; and Rosie who is as fat as I am skinny and has a big mouth where Raymond is concerned and is too stupid to know that there is not a big deal of difference between herself and Raymond and that she can't afford to throw stones. So they are steady coming up Broadway and I see right away that it's going to

Vocabulary Development

prodigy (PRAHD uh jee) *n.* a wonder; an unusually talented person

4. **Chopin** (SHOH pan) Frédéric François Chopin (1810–1849), highly regarded Polish composer and pianist, known for his challenging piano compositions.

TAKE NOTES

Stop to Reflect

Squeaky studies hard and practices her running. What do these actions tell you about her character?

Reading Check

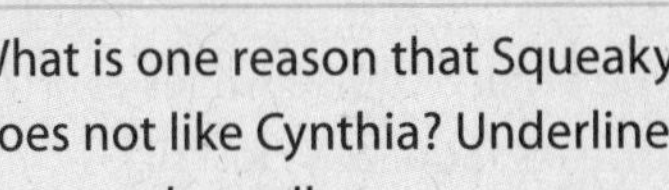

What is one reason that Squeaky does not like Cynthia? Underline the text that tells you.

TAKE NOTES

Reading Skill 

Read the underlined sentence. What can you **predict** will happen if the girls tease Raymond?

Circle the text that **supports your prediction**.

Stop to Reflect 

When Mary Louise smiles at Squeaky, Squeaky describes her smile as "not a smile at all." What does Squeaky mean by saying this?

Literary Analysis

Rising action refers to events that increase tension. Read the bracketed passage. Is this passage part of the story's rising action? Explain.

be one of those Dodge City[5] scenes cause the street ain't that big and they're close to the buildings just as we are. First I think I'll step into the candy store and look over the new comics and let them pass. But that's chicken and I've got a reputation to consider. So then I think I'll just walk straight on through them or even over them if necessary. But as they get to me, they slow down. I'm ready to fight, cause like I said I don't feature a whole lot of chit-chat, I much prefer to just knock you down right from the jump and save everybody a lotta precious time.

"You signing up for the May Day races?" smiles Mary Louise, only it's not a smile at all.

A dumb question like that doesn't deserve an answer. Besides, there's just me and Gretchen standing there really, so no use wasting my breath talking to shadows.

"I don't think you're going to win this time," says Rosie, trying to signify with her hands on her hips all salty, completely forgetting that I have whupped her many times for less salt than that.

"I always win cause I'm the best," I say straight at Gretchen who is, as far as I'm concerned, the only one talking in this ventriloquist-dummy routine.[6]

Gretchen smiles, but it's not a smile, and I'm thinking that girls never really smile at each other because they don't know how and don't want to know how and there's probably no one to teach us how cause grown-up girls don't know either. Then they all look at Raymond who has just brought his mule team to a standstill. And they're about to see what trouble they can get into through him.

"What grade you in now, Raymond?"

"You got anything to say to my brother, you say it to me, Mary Louise Williams of Raggedy Town, Baltimore."

Vocabulary Development

reputation (rep yoo TAY shuhn) *n.* widely-held opinion about a person, whether good or bad

5. **Dodge City** location of the television program *Gunsmoke,* which often presented a gunfight between the sheriff and an outlaw.

6. **ventriloquist** (ven TRIL uh kwist)-**dummy routine** a comedy act in which the performer speaks through a puppet called a "dummy."

"What are you, his mother?" sasses Rosie.

"That's right, Fatso. And the next word out of anybody and I'll be *their* mother too." So they just stand there and Gretchen shifts from one leg to the other and so do they. Then Gretchen puts her hands on her hips and is about to say something with her freckle-face self but doesn't. Then she walks around me looking me up and down but keeps walking up Broadway, and her sidekicks follow her. So me and Raymond smile at each other and he says, "Gidyap" to his team and I continue with my breathing exercises, strolling down Broadway toward the ice man on 145th with not a care in the world cause I am Miss Quicksilver herself.

I take my time getting to the park on May Day because the track meet is the last thing on the program. The biggest thing on the program is the May Pole dancing, which I can do without, thank you, even if my mother thinks it's a shame I don't take part and act like a girl for a change. You'd think my mother'd be grateful not to have to make me a white organdy dress with a big satin sash and buy me new white baby-doll shoes that can't be taken out of the box till the big day. You'd think she'd be glad her daughter ain't out there prancing around a May Pole getting the new clothes all dirty and sweaty and trying to act like a fairy or a flower or whatever you're supposed to be when you should be trying to be yourself, whatever that is, which is, as far as I am concerned, a poor black girl who really can't afford to buy shoes and a new dress you only wear once a lifetime cause it won't fit next year.

I was once a strawberry in a Hansel and Gretel pageant when I was in nursery school and didn't have no better sense than to dance on tiptoe with my arms in a circle over my head doing umbrella steps and being a perfect fool just so my mother and father could come dressed up and clap. You'd think they'd know better than to encourage that kind of nonsense. I am not a strawberry. I do not dance on my toes.

Vocabulary Development

organdy (AWR guhn dee) *n.* sheer and crisp cotton fabric

TAKE NOTES

Literary Analysis

Read the bracketed passage. Who is Squeaky's main rival in this **conflict**? Circle clues in the passage that helped you find the answer.

___

Stop to Reflect

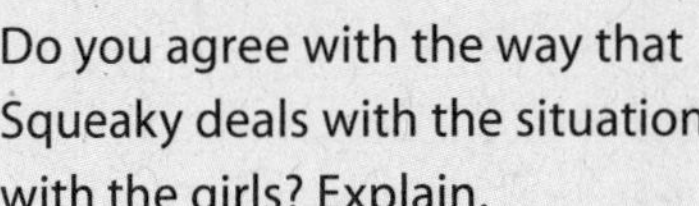

Do you agree with the way that Squeaky deals with the situation with the girls? Explain.

___

___

___

___

Reading Check

What would Squeaky's mother prefer that Squeaky do on May Day? Underline the text that tells you.

TAKE NOTES

Reading Skill 

Do you **predict** that Gretchen will come and race? Explain your answer.

____

____

____

Stop to Reflect 

Read the bracketed passage. What does the dialogue reveal about Squeaky?

____

____

____

Reading Check 

What is the nickname that Squeaky and the other children have for Mr. Pearson? Underline the text that tells you.

I run. That is what I am all about. So I always come late to the May Day program, just in time to get my number pinned on and lay in the grass till they announce the fifty-yard dash.

I put Raymond in the little swings, which is a tight squeeze this year and will be impossible next year. Then I look around for Mr. Pearson, who pins the numbers on. I'm really looking for Gretchen if you want to know the truth, but she's not around. The park is jam-packed. Parents in hats and corsages and breast-pocket handkerchiefs peeking up. Kids in white dresses and light-blue suits. The parkees unfolding chairs and chasing the rowdy kids from Lenox as if they had no right to be there. The big guys with their caps on backwards, leaning against the fence swirling the basketballs on the tips of their fingers, waiting for all these crazy people to clear out the park so they can play. Most of the kids in my class are carrying bass drums and glockenspiels[7] and flutes. You'd think they'd put in a few bongos or something for real like that.

Then here comes Mr. Pearson with his clipboard and his cards and pencils and whistles and safety pins and fifty million other things he's always dropping all over the place with his clumsy self. He sticks out in a crowd because he's on stilts. We used to call him Jack and the Beanstalk to get him mad. But I'm the only one that can outrun him and get away, and I'm too grown for that silliness now.

"Well, Squeaky," he says, checking my name off the list and handing me number seven and two pins. And I'm thinking he's got no right to call me Squeaky, if I can't call him Beanstalk.

"Hazel Elizabeth Deborah Parker," I correct him and tell him to write it down on his board.

"Well, Hazel Elizabeth Deborah Parker, going to give someone else a break this year?" I squint at him real hard to see if he is seriously thinking I should lose the race on purpose just to give someone else a break. "Only six girls running this time," he continues, shaking his head sadly like it's my fault all of New York didn't turn out in sneakers. "That new girl

7. **glockenspiels** (GLAHK uhn speelz) *n.* musical instruments with flat metal bars that make bell-like tones when struck with small hammers.

should give you a run for your money." He looks around the park for Gretchen like a periscope[8] in a submarine movie. "Wouldn't it be a nice gesture if you were . . . to ahhh . . ."

I give him such a look he couldn't finish putting that idea into words. Grownups got a lot of nerve sometimes. I pin number seven to myself and stomp away, I'm so burnt. And I go straight for the track and stretch out on the grass while the band winds up with "Oh, the Monkey Wrapped His Tail Around the Flag Pole," which my teacher calls by some other name. The man on the loudspeaker is calling everyone over to the track and I'm on my back looking at the sky, trying to pretend I'm in the country, but I can't, because even grass in the city feels hard as sidewalk, and there's just no pretending you are anywhere but in a "concrete jungle" as my grandfather says.

The twenty-yard dash takes all of two minutes cause most of the little kids don't know no better than to run off the track or run the wrong way or run smack into the fence and fall down and cry. One little kid, though, has got the good sense to run straight for the white ribbon up ahead, so he wins. Then the second-graders line up for the thirty-yard dash and I don't even bother to turn my head to watch cause Raphael Perez always wins. He wins before he even begins by psyching the runners, telling them they're going to trip on their shoelaces and fall on their faces or lose their shorts or something, which he doesn't really have to do since he is very fast, almost as fast as I am. After that is the forty-yard dash which I use to run when I was in first grade. Raymond is hollering from the swings cause he knows I'm about to do my thing cause the man on the loudspeaker has just announced the fifty-yard dash, although he might just as well be giving a recipe for angel food cake cause you can hardly make out what he's saying for the static. I get up and slip off my sweat pants and then I see Gretchen standing at the starting line, kicking her legs out like a pro. Then as I get into place I see that ole Raymond is on line on the other side of the fence,

8. **periscope** (PER uh skohp) *n.* instrument on a submarine that can be raised to show objects on the water's surface.

TAKE NOTES

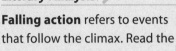

Literary Analysis

Falling action refers to events that follow the climax. Read the bracketed passage. Is this part of the falling action or the **rising action**? Explain.

___

___

___

Stop to Reflect

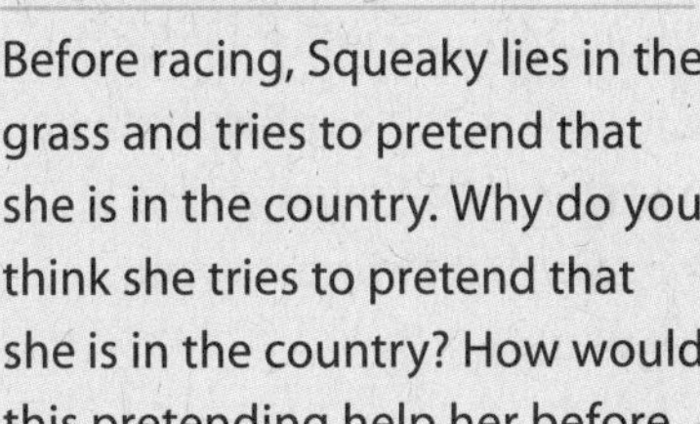

Before racing, Squeaky lies in the grass and tries to pretend that she is in the country. Why do you think she tries to pretend that she is in the country? How would this pretending help her before the race?

___

___

___

___

Reading Skill

Who do you **predict** will win the race in which Squeaky and Gretchen are competing?

___

Underline the details that **support your prediction**.

___

___

TAKE NOTES

Literary Analysis

Summarize the major events of the story's **plot** so far.

Reading Skill 

What do you **predict** will be the outcome of the **conflict** between Gretchen and Squeaky? Circle the text that **supports your prediction**.

Reading Check

What does Squeaky tell herself just before she runs a race? Underline the text that tells you.

bending down with his fingers on the ground just like he knew what he was doing. I was going to yell at him but then I didn't. It burns up your energy to holler.

Every time, just before I take off in a race, I always feel like I'm in a dream, the kind of dream you have when you're sick with fever and feel all hot and weightless. I dream I'm flying over a sandy beach in the early morning sun, kissing the leaves of the trees as I fly by. And there's always the smell of apples, just like in the country when I was little and used to think I was a choo-choo train, running through the fields of corn and chugging up the hill to the orchard. And all the time I'm dreaming this, I get lighter and lighter until I'm flying over the beach again, getting blown through the sky like a feather that weighs nothing at all. But once I spread my fingers in the dirt and crouch over the Get on Your Mark, the dream goes and I am solid again and am telling myself, Squeaky you must win, you must win, you are the fastest thing in the world, you can even beat your father up Amsterdam if you really try. And then I feel my weight coming back just behind my knees then down to my feet then into the earth and the pistol shot explodes in my blood and I am off and weightless again, flying past the other runners, my arms pumping up and down and the whole world is quiet except for the crunch as I zoom over the gravel in the track. I glance to my left and there is no one. To the right a blurred Gretchen, who's got her chin jutting out as if it would win the race all by itself. And on the other side of the fence is Raymond with his arms down to his side and the palms tucked up behind him, running in his very own style, and it's the first time I ever saw that and I almost stop to watch my brother Raymond on his first run. But the white ribbon is bouncing toward me and I tear past it, racing into the distance till my feet with a mind of their own start digging up footfuls of dirt and brake me short. Then all the kids standing on the side pile on me, banging me on the back and slapping my head with their May Day programs, for I have won again and everybody on 151st Street can walk tall for another year.

"In first place . . ." the man on the loudspeaker is clear as a bell now. But then he pauses and the loudspeaker starts to whine. Then static. And I lean down to catch my breath and here comes Gretchen walking back, for she's overshot the finish line too, huffing and puffing with her hands on her hips taking it slow, breathing in steady time like a real pro and I sort of like her a little for the first time. "In first place . . ." and then three or four voices get all mixed up on the loudspeaker and I dig my sneaker into the grass and stare at Gretchen who's staring back, we both wondering just who did win. I can hear old Beanstalk arguing with the man on the loudspeaker and then a few others running their mouths about what the stopwatches say. Then I hear Raymond yanking at the fence to call me and I wave to shush him, but he keeps rattling the fence like a gorilla in a cage like in them gorilla movies, but then like a dancer or something he starts climbing up nice and easy but very fast. And it occurs to me, watching how smoothly he climbs hand over hand and remembering how he looked running with his arms down to his side and with the wind pulling his mouth back and his teeth showing and all, it occurred to me that Raymond would make a very fine runner. Doesn't he always keep up with me on my trots? And he surely knows how to breathe in counts of seven cause he's always doing it at the dinner table, which drives my brother George up the wall. And I'm smiling to beat the band cause if I've lost this race, or if me and Gretchen tied, or even if I've won, I can always retire as a runner and begin a whole new career as a coach with Raymond as my champion. After all, with a little more study I can beat Cynthia and her phony self at the spelling bee. And if I bugged my mother, I could get piano lessons and become a star. And I have a big rep as the baddest thing around. And I've got a roomful of ribbons and medals and awards. But what has Raymond got to call his own?

So I stand there with my new plans, laughing out loud by this time as Raymond jumps down from the fence and runs over with his teeth showing and his arms down to the side, which no one before him has

TAKE NOTES

Literary Analysis 

The **climax** is the high point of the story, when the outcome is revealed. Read the underlined sentences. Do you think this is the climax? Explain your answer.

Reading Skill 

Read the second sentence that is underlined. If Squeaky loses the race, do you **predict** that she will be very upset or not? What details in the underlined sentence support your prediction?

Reading Check 

After the race, Squeaky thinks that her brother may have a special talent. What talent is this? Underline the sentence that tells the answer.

TAKE NOTES

Literary Analysis

After running the race, Squeaky is thinking more about her brother than she is thinking about the race. How does Raymond affect the story's **conflict**?

____

____

____

____

Reading Check 

After racing, does Squeaky feel differently about Gretchen? Circle the sentence that tells you the answer.

Stop to Reflect 

Read the last sentence in the story. What do you think Squeaky means by this sentence?

____

____

____

____

quite mastered as a running style. And by the time he comes over I'm jumping up and down so glad to see him—my brother Raymond, a great runner in the family tradition. But of course everyone thinks I'm jumping up and down because the men on the loudspeaker have finally gotten themselves together and compared notes and are announcing "In first place—Miss Hazel Elizabeth Deborah Parker." (Dig that.) "In second place—Miss Gretchen P. Lewis." And I look over at Gretchen wondering what the "P" stands for. And I smile. Cause she's good, no doubt about it. Maybe she'd like to help me coach Raymond; she obviously is serious about running, as any fool can see. And she nods to congratulate me and then she smiles. And I smile. We stand there with this big smile of respect between us. It's about as real a smile as girls can do for each other, considering we don't practice real smiling every day, you know, cause maybe we too busy being flowers or fairies or strawberries instead of something honest and worthy of respect . . . you know . . . like being people.

Reader's Response: What did you like about the story? What did you dislike? Would you change any events of the plot?

____

____

____

Raymond's Run

1. **Respond:** Which parts of Squeaky's personality would make you want to be her friend? Which parts would make you not want to be her friend?

2. **Analyze:** How does Squeaky feel about taking care of Raymond?

3. **Reading Skill:** List two predictions you made as you read "Raymond's Run." What support did you have for each?

4. **Literary Analysis:** Complete the **plot** chart below. Write in two events from the **rising action** and one event from the **falling action**.

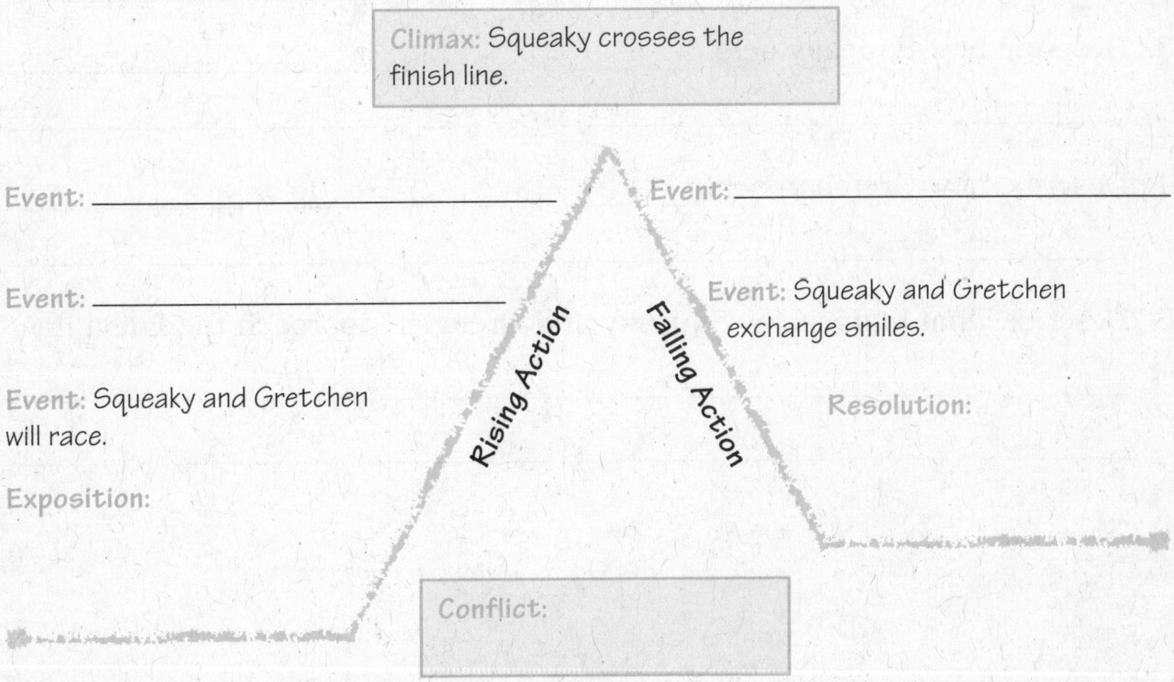

Climax: Squeaky crosses the finish line.

Rising Action

Event:

Event:

Event: Squeaky and Gretchen will race.

Exposition:

Conflict:

Falling Action

Event:

Event: Squeaky and Gretchen exchange smiles.

Resolution:

Writing: New Ending

Imagine the ending of the story if Gretchen had won the race. Write a **new ending** to show how Squeaky might react to losing. Use your notes as you write your new ending.

Does Squeaky go through a change at the end of the story? If so, how would this change affect the way she would feel about losing? Explain.

Squeaky is proud, bold, and loyal. What other adjectives describe her?

Listening and Speaking: Radio Broadcast

Use the following statements to help you prepare for your **radio broadcast.** Use action verbs so that listeners will feel the rising tension and the excitement of the race.

1. Describe Squeaky's appearance.
2. Describe Gretchen's appearance.
3. Describe how Squeaky acts.
4. Describe how Gretchen acts.
5. Describe what happens as Squeaky and Gretchen approach the finish line.

A Retrieved Reformation

O. Henry

Summary Jimmy Valentine leaves prison and plans to go back to robbing safes. But he falls in love and decides to become honest. He changes his name and opens a store. A detective shows up to arrest Jimmy for recent robberies. However, Jimmy's actions show that he has changed.

Writing About the Big Question

Is truth the same for everyone? In "A Retrieved Reformation," a former thief tries to reinvent the truth about his life. Complete this sentence:

People form opinions of others based on ______________________________

____.

Note-taking Guide

Use this character web to describe Jimmy Valentine's character.

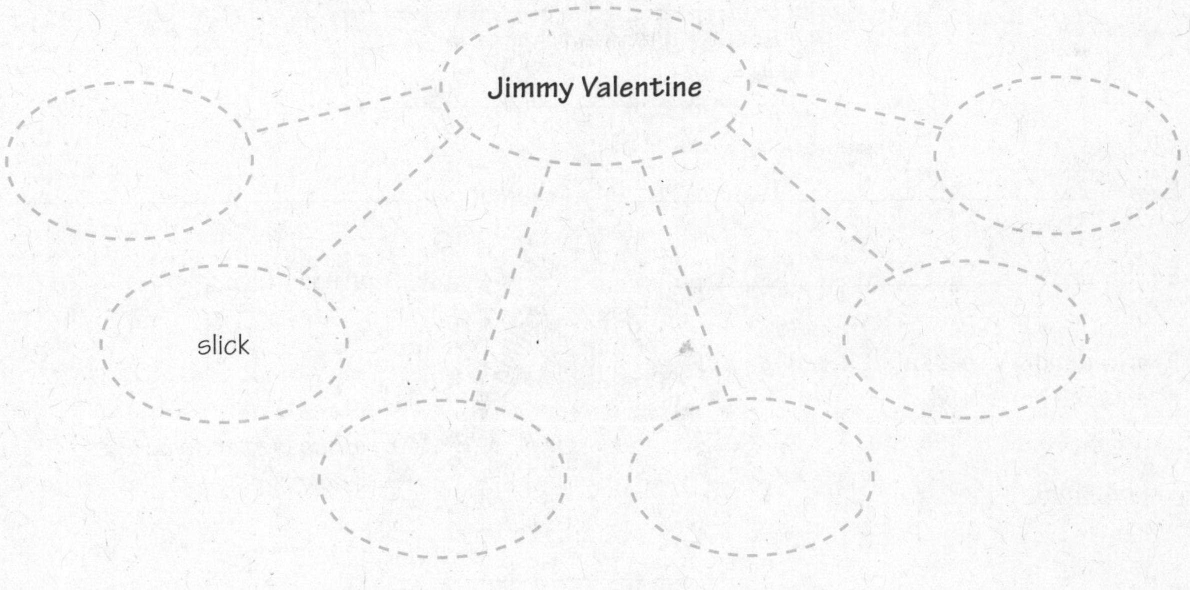

A Retrieved Reformation

1. **Deduce:** How does seeing Annabel Adams cause Valentine to have a change of heart?

____

2. **Make a Judgment:** Is it possible for people like Jimmy to reform themselves? Explain.

____

____

3. **Reading Skill:** What **support** can you find in the story for a **prediction** that Ben Price will arrest Jimmy?

____

____

4. **Literary Analysis:** A **plot** chart shows the parts of a story. In the chart below, add the missing parts.

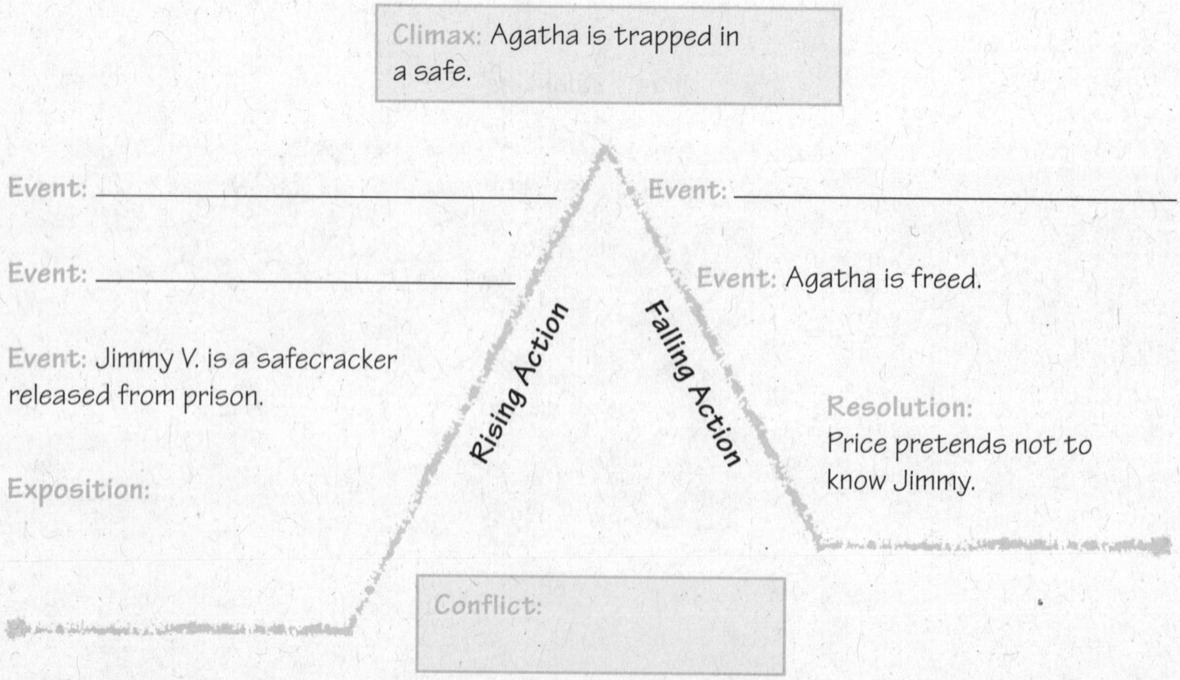

Climax: Agatha is trapped in a safe.

Event: _______________

Event: _______________

Event: Jimmy V. is a safecracker released from prison.

Exposition:

Rising Action

Falling Action

Event: _______________

Event: Agatha is freed.

Resolution: Price pretends not to know Jimmy.

Conflict:

Writing: New Ending

Write a **new ending** to the story. How would the story be different if Ben Price had arrested Jimmy? Use this chart to show how Jimmy's arrest would have changed these people's lives:

Jimmy	Annabel Adams	Ben Price

Use your notes to write your new ending for the story.

Listening and Speaking: Radio Broadcast

Write and perform a **radio broadcast** of Jimmy's rescue of Agatha. What would each of the following people say and do?

- Jimmy ____
- Annabel ____
- Agatha ____
- Agatha's mother ____
- Mr. Adams ____

Use your notes to write your radio broadcast.

Gentleman of Río en Medio • Cub Pilot on the Mississippi

Reading Skill

When you **make predictions**, use the details in what you read to make logical, informed guesses about what will happen later in a story. **Reading ahead to confirm or correct predictions** helps you remain focused on the connections between events. Follow these steps:

- As you read, look for details that suggest a certain outcome.
- Make a prediction about what will happen next.
- Use this chart to record your prediction. Then, read ahead to see whether your prediction is correct. Use new details to confirm or correct your original prediction.

Detail: Character sees a fin in the water. **Prediction:** A shark will attack.	Read Ahead →	**New Details:** The fin turns out to belong to a dolphin. **Prediction:** The dolphin will help the character get to land.

Literary Analysis

Conflict is the struggle between two opposing forces.

- **External conflict** occurs when a character struggles against another character, natural forces, or some aspect of society.
- **Internal conflict** is a struggle between competing feelings, beliefs, needs, or desires within a single character. For example, a character might struggle with feelings of guilt.

In the **resolution** of a story, problems are worked out in a way that eliminates the conflict.

Gentleman of Río en Medio

Juan A. A. Sedillo

Summary Don Anselmo is honest and proud. He sells his land to new American owners. They later have trouble with the village children. The new owners work with Don Anselmo to solve the problem with the children.

Writing About the Big Question

Is truth the same for everyone? In "Gentleman of Río en Medio," an old man becomes involved in a dispute over the value of property. Complete this sentence:

A person selling a house may be biased about his or her property because ____

____.

Note-taking Guide

Use this chart to record details about the traits of Don Anselmo.

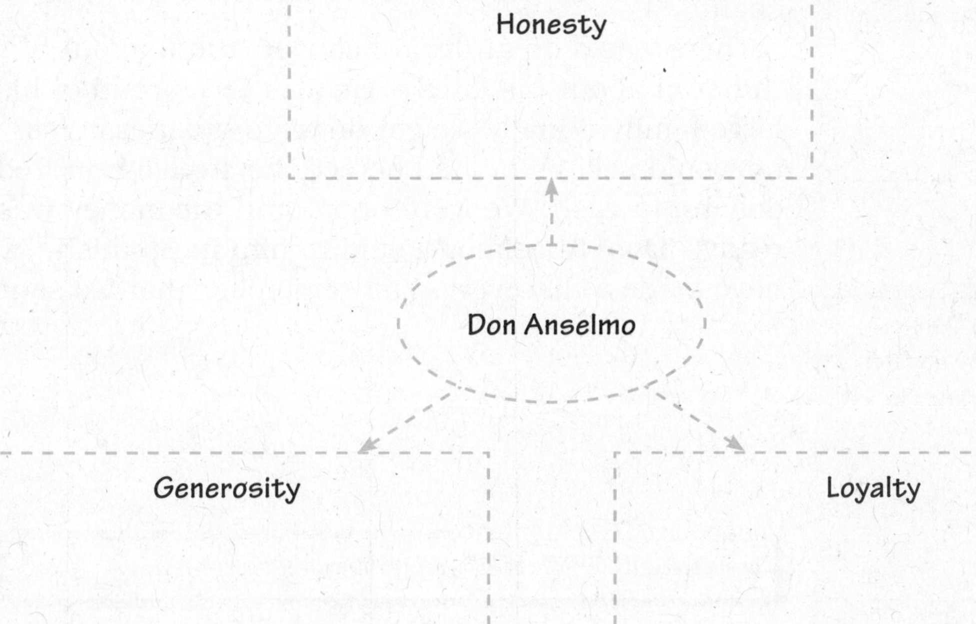

TAKE NOTES

Gentleman of Río en Medio

Juan A. A. Sedillo

Activate Prior Knowledge

When you buy something, you believe that you and the seller agree to certain things. Someone is selling a bicycle. List the terms, or main points, to which the buyer and seller might agree.

____

____

____

____

Reading Skill

One way to follow the events of a story is to **predict,** or guess, what is going to happen. What kind of meeting do you predict that Don Anselmo is about to have? What details support your prediction?

____

____

____

____

____

Reading Check

What agreement does Don Anselmo make with the narrator and his friends? Underline the sentence that tells you.

It took months of negotiation to come to an understanding with the old man. He was in no hurry. What he had the most of was time. He lived up in Río en Medio, where his people had been for hundreds of years. He tilled the same land they had tilled. His house was small and wretched, but quaint. The little creek ran through his land. His orchard was gnarled and beautiful.

The day of the sale he came into the office. His coat was old, green and faded. I thought of Senator Catron,[1] who had been such a power with these people up there in the mountains. Perhaps it was one of his old Prince Alberts.[2] He also wore gloves. They were old and torn and his fingertips showed through them. He carried a cane, but it was only the skeleton of a worn-out umbrella. Behind him walked one of his innumerable kin—a dark young man with eyes like a gazelle.

The old man bowed to all of us in the room. Then he removed his hat and gloves, slowly and carefully. Chaplin[3] once did that in a picture, in a bank—he was the janitor. Then he handed his things to the boy, who stood obediently behind the old man's chair.

There was a great deal of conversation, about rain and about his family. He was very proud of his large family. Finally we got down to business. Yes, he would sell, as he had agreed, for twelve hundred dollars, in cash. We would buy, and the money was ready. "Don[4] Anselmo," I said to him in Spanish, "we have made a discovery. You remember that we sent

Vocabulary Development

innumerable (i NOO muhr uh buhl) *adj.* too many to be counted

1. **Senator Catron** Thomas Benton Catron, U.S. senator from New Mexico, 1912–1917.
2. **Prince Alberts** long, old-fashioned coats worn on formal occasions.
3. **Chaplin** Charlie Chaplin (1889–1977), actor and producer of silent films in the United States.
4. **Don** (dohn) Spanish title of respect, similar to "sir" in English.

that surveyor, that engineer, up there to survey your land so as to make the deed. Well, he finds that you own more than eight acres. He tells us that your land extends across the river and that you own almost twice as much as you thought." He didn't know that. "And now, Don Anselmo," I added, "these Americans are *buena gente*,[5] they are good people, and they are willing to pay you for the additional land as well, at the same rate per acre, so that instead of twelve hundred dollars you will get almost twice as much, and the money is here for you."

The old man hung his head for a moment in thought. Then he stood up and stared at me. "Friend," he said, "I do not like to have you speak to me in that manner." I kept still and let him have his say. "I know these Americans are good people, and that is why I have agreed to sell to them. But I do not care to be insulted. I have agreed to sell my house and land for twelve hundred dollars and that is the price."

I argued with him but it was useless. Finally he signed the deed and took the money but refused to take more than the amount agreed upon. Then he shook hands all around, put on his ragged gloves, took his stick and walked out with the boy behind him.

A month later my friends had moved into Río en Medio. They had replastered the old adobe house, pruned the trees, patched the fence, and moved in for the summer. One day they came back to the office to complain. The children of the village were overrunning their property. They came every day and played under the trees, built little play fences around them, and took blossoms. When they were spoken to they only laughed and talked back good-naturedly in Spanish.

I sent a messenger up to the mountains for Don Anselmo. It took a week to arrange another meeting. When he arrived he repeated his previous preliminary

TAKE NOTES

Reading Skill

Read the underlined passage. How do you **predict** Don Anselmo will react to the offer? Explain your **prediction**.

Literary Analysis

A **conflict** is a struggle between two opposing forces. A conflict in a story usually leads to a **resolution,** or a solution. Read the bracketed passage. What is the **conflict**? How is this conflict **resolved**?

Reading Skill

Underline the details that **confirm or correct your prediction** about how Don Anselmo would react to the offer for his land.

Vocabulary Development

preliminary (pri LIM uh ner ee) *adj.* introductory; preparatory

5. ***buena gente*** (BWAY nah HAYN tay) Spanish for "good people."

TAKE NOTES

Literary Analysis

An **external conflict** happens when characters struggle against other characters. Circle the sentence that describes the external conflict between the American owners and the children of the village.

Reading Skill

Read the bracketed passage. Make a **prediction** about how the narrator will react to Don Anselmo's explanation about the trees.

Stop to Reflect

How are Don Anselmo's ideas about owning land different from those of the narrator and his friends?

performance. He wore the same faded cutaway,[6] carried the same stick and was accompanied by the boy again. He shook hands all around, sat down with the boy behind his chair, and talked about the weather. Finally I broached the subject. "Don Anselmo, about the ranch you sold to these people. They are good people and want to be your friends and neighbors always. When you sold to them you signed a document, a deed, and in that deed you agreed to several things. One thing was that they were to have the complete possession of the property. Now, Don Anselmo, it seems that every day the children of the village overrun the orchard and spend most of their time there. We would like to know if you, as the most respected man in the village, could not stop them from doing so in order that these people may enjoy their new home more in peace."

Don Anselmo stood up. "We have all learned to love these Americans," he said, "because they are good people and good neighbors. I sold them my property because I knew they were good people, but I did not sell them the trees in the orchard."

This was bad. "Don Anselmo," I pleaded, "when one signs a deed and sells real property one sells also everything that grows on the land, and those trees, every one of them, are on the land and inside the boundaries of what you sold."

"Yes, I admit that," he said. "You know," he added, "I am the oldest man in the village. Almost everyone there is my relative and all the children of Río en Medio are my *sobrinos* and *nietos*,[7] my descendants. Every time a child has been born in Río en Medio since I took possession of that house from my mother I have planted a tree for that child. The trees in that orchard are not mine, *Señor*, they belong to the children of the village. Every person in Río en Medio born since the railroad came to Santa Fe owns a tree in that orchard. I did not sell the trees because I could not. They are not mine."

6. **cutaway** *n.* coat worn by men for formal daytime occasions; it is cut in the front and curves to long tails in the back.

7. ***sobrinos*** (soh BREE nohs) and ***nietos*** (NYAY tohs) Spanish for "nephews" and "grandsons"; used here to include nieces and granddaughters as well.

There was nothing we could do. Legally we owned the trees but the old man had been so generous, refusing what amounted to a fortune for him. It took most of the following winter to buy the trees, individually, from the descendants of Don Anselmo in the valley of Río en Medio.

Reader's Response: If you had bought Don Anselmo's property, how would you feel after hearing his explanation of why he had not sold you the orchard trees? Give reasons for your answer.

____

____

____

____

____

Vocabulary Development

descendants (di SEN duhnts) *n.* children, grandchildren, and continuing generations

TAKE NOTES

Literary Analysis 

How do the narrator and his friends resolve the **conflict** about the trees?

____

____

____

Reading Check 

Why do the narrator's friends choose to buy the trees from Don Anselmo's descendants? Underline the sentence that tells you.

Gentleman of Río en Medio

1. **Respond:** Were you surprised by Don Anselmo's responses in his first meeting with the narrator? Explain your answer.

2. **Analyze:** How does the way the narrator behaves toward Don Anselmo affect the outcome of the story?

3. **Reading Skill:** What **prediction** did you make about the outcome of the story? Was your prediction correct? Explain.

4. **Literary Analysis:** Use this graphic organizer to describe the **conflict** in the story about the land sale.

How the conflict develops

Don Anselmo → vs. ←

How the conflict is resolved

Writing: Letter

Write a **letter** to Don Anselmo. Thank him for trying to protect the right of the children to play in the orchard. Use the sentence starters to help you write your letter.

Dear Don Anselmo,

Thank you for ______________________________.

I know that you care most about ______________________________.

You have given the children of our village ______________________________.

You have benefited the children by ______________________________.

Listening and Speaking: Role Play

Role play the story's conflict. One person will play Don Anselmo. Another person will play the narrator. Answer these questions to help you create your role play.

1. How does Don Anselmo feel about the children playing in the orchard?

____

____

2. How does the narrator feel about the children playing in the orchard?

____

____

3. What solutions might be acceptable to both parties?

____

____

Cub Pilot on the Mississippi

Mark Twain

Summary Mark Twain describes his experience as a cub pilot working on a Mississippi steamboat. He tries to please his boss, but nothing works. The conflict between them grows. Twain cannot control his anger.

Writing About the Big Question

Is the truth the same for everyone? In "Cub Pilot on the Mississippi," a young man gets into a violent dispute with his boss over who is telling the truth. Complete this sentence:

If a young person and an adult were to contradict each other in an argument, I would believe ______________________ is telling the truth because ____.

Note-taking Guide

Use this chart to note the differences between the two pilots in the story.

	Pilot Brown	Pilot Ealer
With which cub pilot does he work?	Mark Twain	
How does he treat cub pilots during work hours?		
How does each cub pilot react to his treatment?		

Cub Pilot on the Mississippi

1. **Infer:** Why were cub pilots assigned to work with experienced pilots?

2. **Draw Conclusions:** What are the captain's feelings about Brown? How do you know?

3. **Reading Skill:** What **predictions** did you make about the outcome of the conflict between Twain and Brown? Which clues led to your predictions?

4. **Literary Analysis:** Use the chart below to analyze the **conflict** between Twain and Brown.

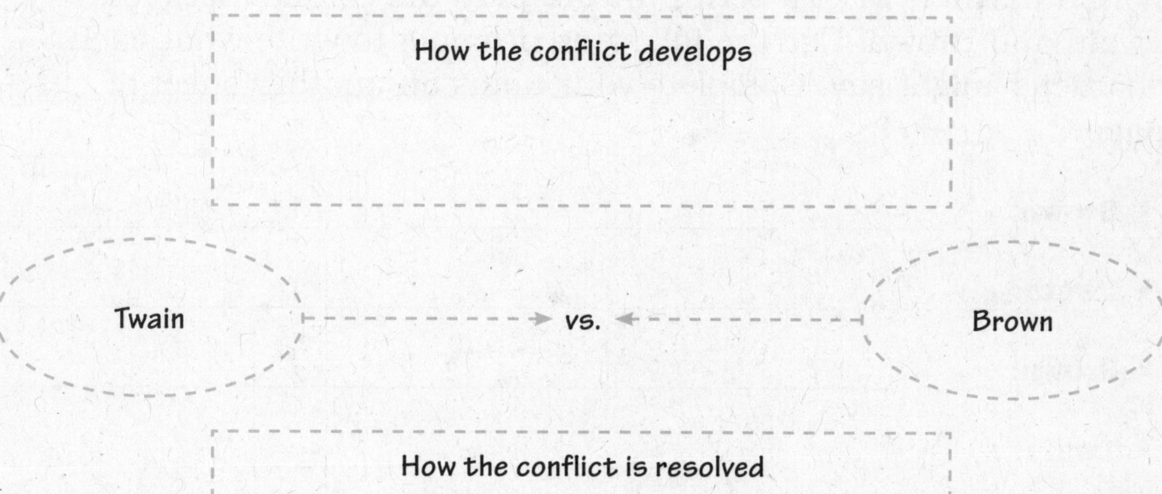

Writing: Letter

Imagine that you are Twain. Write a **letter** to your best friend, describing your first days as a cub pilot. Use the following sentence starters to think through some of your feelings.

1. When I first went on the boat, I felt __________

2. When I see Pilot Brown, I feel __________

3. When I see Pilot Ealer and George Ritchie together, I feel __________

4. When I am alone in bed at night, I feel __________

Listening and Speaking: Role Play

With a partner, write a script to **role-play** the conflict between Twain and Brown. Use the following prompts to write what each character might say. Complete your notes on another sheet of paper.

- **Brown:** __________
- **Twain:** __________
- **Brown:** __________
- **Twain:** __________
- **Brown:** __________
- **Twain:** __________

Consumer Documents: Schedules

About Schedules

Schedules help people get where they want to go.

- Schedules list arrival and departure times.

Schedules are **consumer documents.**

- Consumer documents help you buy or use a product or service.
- Other consumer documents include brochures, labels, loan applications, assembly instructions, and warranties.

Reading Skill

Reading transportation schedules is different from reading other materials. You can **use the information to solve a problem,** such as which routes to take and what time to arrive at the station or dock. The information in a schedule is organized in rows and columns to help you find what you need. Look at the chart. It shows some common features of a transportation schedule.

Features of a Schedule	
Headings	Show where to find departure and arrival times
Rows and columns	Allow easy scanning of arrival and departure times across and down the page
Special type and asterisks	Indicate exceptions, such as ferries that do not run on Sundays

Savannah Belles Ferry System

Features:

- consumer information
- details and information in lists, charts, tables, and other graphics
- text that helps the reader purchase or use a product or service
- for a specific audience

City Hall Landing To:	
Trade Center Landing Westin	
7:00 AM	3:40 PM
7:20 AM	4:00 PM
7:40 AM	4:20 PM
8:00 AM	4:40 PM
8:20 AM	5:00 PM
*	5:20 PM
9:00 AM	*
9:20 AM	6:00 PM
9:40 AM	6:20 PM
10:00 AM	6:40 PM
10:20 AM	7:00 PM
*	7:20 PM
11:00 AM	7:40 PM
11:20 AM	8:00 PM
11:40 AM	8:20 PM
12:00 PM	*
12:20 PM	9:00 PM
12:40 PM	9:20 PM
1:00 PM	9:40 PM
1:20 PM	10:00 PM
1:40 PM	10:20 PM
2:00 PM	10:40 PM
2:20 PM	11:00 PM
2:40 PM	11:20 PM
3:00 PM	11:40 PM
3:20 PM	12:00 AM
3:40 PM	*

Trade Center Landing To:		
City Hall Landing / Hyatt		Waving Girl Landing/Marriott
7:10 AM	3:50 PM	8:15 AM
7:30 AM	4:10 PM	8:45 AM
7:50 AM	4:30 PM	9:15 AM
8:10 AM	4:50 PM	9:45 AM
*	5:10 PM	10:15 AM
8:50 AM	*	10:45 AM
9:10 AM	5:50 PM	11:15 AM
9:30 AM	6:10 PM	11:45 AM
9:50 AM	6:30 PM	12:15 PM
10:10 AM	6:50 PM	12:45 PM
*	7:10 PM	1:15 PM
10:50 AM	7:30 PM	1:45 PM
11:10 AM	7:50 PM	2:15 PM
11:30 AM	8:10 PM	2:45 PM
11:50 AM	*	3:15 PM
12:10 PM	8:50 PM	3:45 PM
12:30 PM	9:10 PM	4:15 PM
12:50 PM	9:30 PM	4:45 PM
1:10 PM	9:50 PM	5:15 PM
1:30 PM	10:10 PM	5:45 PM
1:50 PM	10:30 PM	*
2:10 PM	10:50 PM	
2:30 AM	11:10 PM	
2:50 PM	11:30 PM	
3:10 PM	11:50 PM	
3:30 PM	*	

Waving Girl To:
Trade Center Landing/Westin
8:00 AM
8:30 AM
9:00 AM
9:30 AM
10:00 AM
10:30 AM
11:00 AM
11:30 AM
12:00 PM
12:30 PM
1:00 PM
1:30 PM
2:00 PM
2:30 PM
3:00 PM
3:30 PM
4:00 PM
4:30 PM
5:00 PM
5:30 PM
6:00 PM

Revised 5/23/2007

The list of ferry times allows riders to plan their schedules.

Year-Around Schedule

The Savannah Belles Ferry System operates daily, year-around, except Thanksgiving Day, Christmas Day and New Year's Day

Service Interruption

This heading helps consumers plan for times when the ferry is delayed.

The ferry may occasionally be delayed briefly by weather or visibility, or by larger vessels. We appreciate your patience.

Service Locations

TRADE CENTER LANDING--North Bank Riverwalk, between Trade Center and Westin

CITY HALL LANDING--River Street at City Hall, next to Hyatt

WAVING GIRL LANDING--South Bank Riverwalk, next to Marriott

It's Free! The Savannah Belles Ferry System is operated by Chatham Area Transit Authority (CAT) free of charge to visitors and residents. Thanks for riding with us!

www.catchacat.org, (912) 236-2111

THE BIG ?

Is truth the same for everyone?

(a) What section of the schedule explains that the details on the schedule may not always be true? **(b)** Why is it important to include this information?

Consumer Document

Features:

- purposeful reading, used to locate specific information
- details presented in lists, charts, tables, and other graphics
- text that helps readers purchase or use a product or service

Baylink

Travel the Easy Way

Vallejo - San Francisco Ferry Bldg
Vallejo - San Francisco Pier 41

Effective September 1 - December 1, 2006

Vallejo-S.F. Ferry Bldg • MON-FRI

BUS OR FERRY	VALLEJO FERRY BLDG DEPART	SF FERRY BUILDING DEPART	FISHERMAN'S WHARF PIER 41 ARRIVE	FISHERMAN'S WHARF PIER 41 DEPART
Bus	5:00 a	6:05 a		
Ferry	**5:30 a**	**6:35 a**		
Bus	5:50 a	6:55 a		
Bus	6:20 a	7:20 a		
Ferry	**6:30 a**	**7:35 a**		
Bus	6:45 a	7:50 a		
Ferry	**7:00 a**	**8:10 a**		
Bus	7:22 a	8:30 a		
Ferry	**7:45 a**	**8:55 a**		
Ferry	**8:45 a**	**9:55 a**		
Ferry	**10:00 a#**	**11:10 a#**	**11:20 a#**	**11:30 a#**
Ferry	**11:30 a**	**12:40 p**		
Ferry	**1:00 p**	**2:10 p**		
Ferry	**2:00 p***	**3:30 p***	**3:00 p***	**3:10 p***

This heading shows readers where to locate fare information.

Fare Schedule • All Routes

TICKETS REQUIRED TO BOARD FERRIES & BUSES

Adult One-Way.......................... $11.50
Senior/Disabled/Medicare One-Way (65+/disabled)*.......................... $5.75
Youth One-Way (6-12 years)................ $5.75
Baylink DayPass.......................... $19.25
Napa/Solano DayPass.................... $20.75
Reduced Fare DayPass*.................. $11.50
10-Ride Punch Card...................... $89.75
Reduced Fare 10-Ride Punch Card*....... $57.50
Monthly Pass.......................... $247.25
Monthly Pass w/MUNI.................. $287.25
Fairfield/Vacaville Monthly Pass............ $300
Fairfield/Vacaville Monthly Pass w/MUNI.... $340

Up to two children under 6 years of age travel free with each fare-paying adult. Bicycles are also free, subject to capacity limitations. First come, first served; vessel capacity 300 passengers.

** Bay Area Regional Transit Connection Discount Cards and Medicare Cards with Photo ID are accepted for senior and disabled fares.*

Vallejo-S.F. Ferry Bldg • SAT-SUN

BUS OR FERRY	VALLEJO FERRY BLDG DEPART	SF FERRY BUILDING DEPART	FISHERMAN'S WHARF PIER 41 ARRIVE	FISHERMAN'S WHARF PIER 41 DEPART
Bus	7:00 a	8:10 a		
Ferry	**8:45 a**	**9:55 a**		
Ferry	**10:00 a#**	**11:10 a#**	**11:20 a#**	**11:30 a#**
Ferry	**11:30 a**	**12:40 p**		
Ferry	**1:00 p**	**2:10 p**		
Bus	2:00 p	3:10 p		
Ferry	**3:[illegible] p***	**4:30 [illegible]***	**[illegible]:00 [illegible]**	**4:1[illegible] p***

Arrival and departure times are organized in rows and columns.

Is truth the same for everyone?
What section or sections of this document help you understand the amounts different people pay for tickets?

Water Taxi™

SERVICE SCHEDULE & FARES

Effective
December 17, 2007

Times listed in grey and white run every day.	Times listed in yellow run Friday, Saturday, Sunday and Monday

North End		Fort Lauderdale Beach			South End			Downtown / New River		
1 Shooters	**2** Gallery One	**3** Seville Street	**4** Beach Place	**5** Bahia Mar	**6** Pier 66	**7** Convention Center	**8** 15th Street Fisheries	**9** SE 9th Avenue	**10** Downtowner Saloon	**11** Las Olas Riverfront
9:30	Express to Las Olas Riverfront									10:00
9:30	Express to Beach Place		9:59	10:12	10:27	10:30	10:32	10:49	10:54	11:00
10:00	10:17	10:25	10:29	10:42	10:57	11:00	11:02	11:19	11:24	11:30
10:30	10:47	10:55	10:59	11:12	11:27	11:30	11:32	11:49	11:54	12:00
11:00	11:17	11:25	11:29	11:42	11:57	12:00	12:02	12:19	12:24	12:30
11:30	11:47	11:55	11:59	12:12	12:27	12:30	12:32	12:49	12:54	1:00
12:30	12:47	12:55	12:59	1:12	1:27	1:30	1:32	1:49	1:54	2:00
1:00	1:17	1:25	1:29	1:42	1:57	2:00	2:02	2:19	2:24	2:30
1:30	1:47	1:55	1:59	2:12	2:27	2:30	2:32	2:49	2:54	3:00
2:00	2:17	2:25	2:29	2:42	2:57	3:00	3:02	3:19	3:24	3:30
2:30	2:47	2:55	2:59	3:12	3:27	3:3	3:3	3:49	3:54	4:00

Read across to locate the columns that have the information you need.

These notes give additional information about riding the Water Bus and about reading this schedule.

Downtown / New River			South End			Fort Lauderdale Beach			North End	
11 Las Olas Riverfront	**10** Downtowner Saloon	**9** SE 9th Avenue	**8** 15th Street Fisheries	**7** Convention Center	**6** Pier 66	**5** Bahia Mar	**4** Beach Place	**3** Seville Street	**2** Gallery One	**1** Shooters
				9:55	9:58	10:15	10:28	10:32	10:40	11:00
10:00	10:01	10:07	10:23	10:25	10:28	10:45	10:58	11:02	11:10	11:30
11:00	11:01	11:07	11:23	11:25	11:28	11:45	11:58	12:02	12:10	12:30
11:30	11:31	11:37	11:53	11:55	11:58	12:15	12:28	12:32	12:40	1:00
12:00	12:01	12:07	12:23	12:25	12:28	12:45	12:58	1:02	1:10	1:30
12:30	12:31	12:37	12:53	12:55	12:58	1:15	1:28	1:32	1:40	2:00
1:00	1:01	1:07	1:23	1:25	1:28	1	1:5	2:02	:10	2:30

One table shows the schedule of stops when traveling Inbound, or from north to south. The other shows the schedule of stops when the Water Bus travels from south to north.

Read down to see all of the times the Water Bus stops at a location.

Adult.....................$12.00
Children (under 12).....$9.00
Seniors (over 65)........$9.00
After 7:00 PM........$7.00
Family Pack.........$42.00
Valid for 2 adults and 3 children/seniors

Consumer Document

Features:

- purposeful reading, scanned for specific needed information
- contains details and information in lists, charts, tables, and other graphics
- helps the reader purchase or use a product or service
- for a specific audience

THE BIG ?

Is truth the same for everyone?
How might Fort Lauderdale's popularity as a vacation spot affect the choice to name most of the stops along the Water Bus route according to the restaurants and other attractions at each location, rather than naming the stops with geographical information, such as addresses or intersections?

Thinking About the Schedule

1. In what situation would a schedule be useful?

2. Explain how you can figure out what time a ferry will arrive.

Reading Skill

3. What time does the earliest ferry depart from the San Francisco Ferry Building on Monday morning?

4. Why is each stop on the Water Bus schedule listed twice?

WRITE ABOUT IT Timed Writing: Itinerary (20 minutes)

An **itinerary** is a written document that includes dates, times, and locations for a trip. Plan a round-trip itinerary. Use the Savannah Belles ferry schedule. Use this chart to help you make plans.

Place you will go	Departure time	Arrival time

The Adventure of the Speckled Band • from An American Childhood

Reading Skill

The **author's purpose** is his or her reason for writing. Learn to **recognize details that indicate the author's purpose.** Look for these types of details:

- To *inform*, an author might use facts and technical language. Read closely: Pause frequently and take notes.
- To *persuade*, an author might include reasons that lead readers to agree with an opinion. Read critically: Question and evaluate the author's statements and check facts.
- To *entertain*, an author might use facts that amuse, intrigue, horrify, or fascinate readers. Read for enjoyment: Respond to images, ideas, and characters.

Frequently, the author has both a specific purpose and a general purpose in mind. As you read, use this chart to identify both types of purposes.

Types of Details	General Purpose	Specific Purpose
Surprising event; unique characters	To entertain	To capture a particular feeling or insight

Literary Analysis

Mood, or atmosphere, is the overall feeling that a literary work creates for the reader. The mood of a work might be serious, humorous, or sad. A variety of elements contributes to mood.

- Words, such as *grumpy* or *gleeful.*
- Images, such as *a starlit night.*
- Setting, such as *a dark, shadowy room.*
- Events, such as *heavy storm clouds lifting.*

from An American Childhood

Annie Dillard

Summary The author shares an experience that scared her as a young child. She thinks there is a "presence" that will harm her if it reaches her. She figures out what it is. She realizes that her inside world is connected to the outside world.

Writing About the Big Question

Is the truth the same for everyone? In *An American Childhood,* Annie Dillard's perception of the world around her is influenced by her youthful imagination. Complete this sentence:

Small children may draw illogical conclusions about the world around them because ____

____.

Note-taking Guide

Use this chart to help you summarize the story.

Event
The author is frightened by mysterious, moving lights that she sees in her bedroom at night.
Cause
Main Idea

TAKE NOTES

from An American Childhood

Annie Dillard

Activate Prior Knowledge

Tell about a time in childhood when you made an important discovery. For example, perhaps you discovered that you could float more easily in salt water than in fresh water.

____

____

____

Reading Skill

The **author's purpose** is his or her main reason for writing. One purpose could be to entertain. Read the bracketed passage. What details describe the author's sister? Circle the details in the text.

Reading Check

What did Dillard see in her room each night when she was five? Underline the sentence that describes what Dillard saw.

When I was five, growing up in Pittsburgh in 1950, I would not go to bed willingly because something came into my room. This was a private matter between me and it. If I spoke of it, it would kill me.

Who could breathe as this thing searched for me over the very corners of the room? Who could ever breathe freely again? I lay in the dark.

My sister Amy, two years old, was asleep in the other bed. What did she know? She was innocent of evil. Even at two she composed herself attractively for sleep. She folded the top sheet tidily under her prettily outstretched arm; she laid her perfect head lightly on an unwrinkled pillow, where her thick curls spread evenly in rays like petals. All night long she slept smoothly in a series of pleasant and serene, if artificial-looking, positions, a faint smile on her closed lips, as if she were posing for an ad for sheets. There was no messiness in her, no roughness for things to cling to, only a charming and charmed innocence that seemed then to protect her, an innocence I needed but couldn't muster. Since Amy was asleep, furthermore, and since when I needed someone most I was afraid to stir enough to wake her, she was useless.

I lay alone and was almost asleep when the thing entered the room by flattening itself against the open door and sliding in. It was a transparent, luminous oblong.[1] I could see the door whiten at its touch; I could see the blue wall turn pale where it raced over it, and see the maple headboard of Amy's bed glow. It was a swift spirit; it was an awareness. It made noise. It had two joined parts, a head and a tail, like a Chinese dragon. It found the door, wall, and

Vocabulary Development

serene (suh REEN) *adj.* not disturbed or troubled; calm

luminous (LOO muh nuhs) *adj.* giving off light; shining; bright

1. **oblong** (AHB lawng) *n.* shape that is longer than it is broad.

headboard; and it swiped them, charging them with its luminous glance. After its fleet, searching passage, things looked the same, but weren't.

I dared not blink or breathe; I tried to hush my whooping blood. If it found another awareness, it would destroy it.

Every night before it got to me it gave up. It hit my wall's corner and couldn't get past. It shrank completely into itself and vanished like a cobra down a hole. I heard the rising roar it made when it died or left. I still couldn't breathe. I knew—it was the worst fact I knew, a very hard fact—that it could return again alive that same night.

Sometimes it came back, sometimes it didn't. Most often, restless, it came back. The light stripe slipped in the door, ran searching over Amy's wall, stopped, stretched lunatic at the first corner, raced wailing toward my wall, and vanished into the second corner with a cry. So I wouldn't go to bed.

It was a passing car whose windshield reflected the corner streetlight outside. I figured it out one night.

Figuring it out was as memorable as the oblong itself. Figuring it out was a long and forced ascent to the very rim of being, to the membrane of skin that both separates and connects the inner life and the outer world. I climbed deliberately from the depths like a diver who releases the monster in his arms and hauls himself hand over hand up an anchor chain till he meets the ocean's sparkling membrane and bursts through it; he sights the sunlit, becalmed hull of his boat, which had bulked so ominously from below.

I recognized the noise it made when it left. That is, the noise it made called to mind, at last, my daytime sensations when a car passed—the sight and noise together. A car came roaring down hushed Edgerton Avenue in front of our house, stopped at the corner stop sign, and passed on shrieking as its engine shifted up the gears. What, precisely, came into the bedroom? A reflection from the car's oblong windshield. Why did it travel in two parts? The window sash split the light and cast a shadow.

Night after night I labored up the same long chain of reasoning, as night after night the thing burst into

TAKE NOTES

Reading Skill

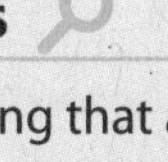

Learn to **recognize details that indicate the author's purpose.** Sometimes authors use details to entertain the reader. Read the first bracketed passage. Underline three words or phrases that make what Dillard fears seem to be alive.

Literary Analysis

Mood is the feeling that a literary work creates for the reader. Read the second bracketed passage. Underline a sentence or phrase that tells you the mood of the story is about to change from fear to something else.

Stop to Reflect

How do Dillard's senses help her discover what the "thing" really is?

____

____

____

the room where I lay awake and Amy slept prettily and my loud heart thrashed and I froze.

There was a world outside my window and contiguous[2] to it. If I was so all-fired bright, as my parents, who had patently no basis for comparison, seemed to think, why did I have to keep learning this same thing over and over? For I had learned it a summer ago, when men with jackhammers broke up Edgerton Avenue. I had watched them from the yard; the street came up in jagged slabs like floes. When I lay to nap, I listened. One restless afternoon I connected the new noise in my bedroom with the jackhammer men I had been seeing outside. I understood abruptly that these worlds met, the outside and the inside. I traveled the route in my mind: You walked downstairs from here, and outside from downstairs. "Outside," then, was conceivably just beyond my windows. It was the same world I reached by going out the front or the back door. I forced my imagination yet again over this route.

The world did not have me in mind; it had no mind. It was a coincidental collection of things and people, of items, and I myself was one such item—a child walking up the sidewalk, whom anyone could see or ignore. The things in the world did not necessarily cause my overwhelming feelings; the feelings were inside me, beneath my skin, behind my ribs, within my skull. They were even, to some extent, under my control.

I could be connected to the outer world by reason, if I chose, or I could yield to what amounted to a narrative fiction, to a tale of terror whispered to me by the blood in my ears, a show in light projected on the room's blue walls. As time passed, I learned to amuse myself in bed in the darkened room by entering the fiction deliberately and replacing it by reason deliberately.

TAKE NOTES

Stop to Reflect

Why do you think Dillard never previously connected the sound of the jackhammers outside with the sounds she was hearing inside?

Literary Analysis

The **mood** in the piece shifts from fear to confidence. Identify some of the words Dillard uses to show her new feeling of confidence. Look in the bracketed passage.

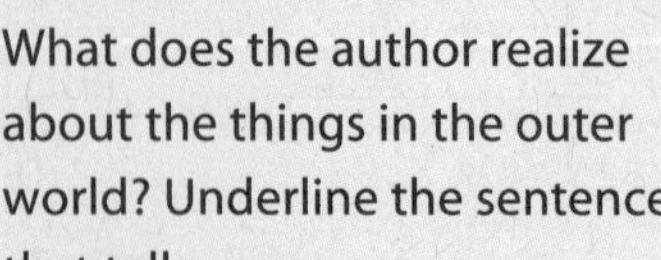

Reading Check

What does the author realize about the things in the outer world? Underline the sentence that tells you.

Vocabulary Development

conceivably (kuhn SEEV uh blee) *adv.* in an imaginable or believable fashion

2. **contiguous** (kuhn TIG yoo uhs) *adj.* in physical contact; near or next to.

When the low roar drew nigh and the oblong slid in the door, I threw my own switches for pleasure. It's coming after me; it's a car outside. It's after me. It's a car. It raced over the wall, lighting it blue wherever it ran; it bumped over Amy's maple headboard in a rush, paused, slithered elongate[3] over the corner, shrank, flew my way, and vanished into itself with a wail. It was a car.

Reader's Response: Can you relate to Dillard's childhood fears? Explain.

TAKE NOTES

Reading Skill

What is the **author's purpose** in repeating the phrase "It's a car"?

3. **elongate** (i LAWN gayt) *adv.* in a way that emphasizes length and narrowness.

from An American Childhood

1. **Contrast:** The author's sister is in the room when the mysterious event happens. Why does her sister fail to react in the same way that Dillard does?

2. **Infer:** After solving the mystery, Dillard sometimes pretends that she does not know the solution. Why does she do this?

3. **Reading Skill:** How does the author's description of the object that she is afraid of contribute to her general **purpose**?

4. Before Dillard realizes what the light really is, her **mood** is one of fear. Use this chart to list words, phrases, and images that contribute to this mood.

Words	Phrases	Images

Writing: Personal Narrative

Write a **personal narrative** about an important childhood insight. Fill in the chart with clues that eventually led to the new understanding. Then, write what each clue turned out to mean.

Clue	What the Clue Meant

Use your notes to help you write your personal narrative.

Research and Technology

Write a brief **report** about an important scientific puzzle. Use the questions to help you write your report.

- Why is the puzzle important?

  ____

- What new knowledge was gained from the solution?

  ____

  ____

- What has been the impact of the new knowledge?

  ____

  ____

The Adventure of the Speckled Band

Sir Arthur Conan Doyle

Summary Sherlock Holmes, a great detective, meets Miss Helen Stoner. She needs his help. Miss Stoner wants to know who killed her sister. She also fears for her own life. Holmes follows the clues to find the murderer.

Writing About the Big Question

Is the truth the same for everyone? In *The Adventure of the Speckled Band,* a detective determines that the truth about a young woman's mysterious death is not what people had previously believed. Complete this sentence:

To prove a theory about a crime scene, a detective can ________________

____.

Note-taking Guide

Use this graphic organizer to note details about Dr. Grimesby Roylott's actions.

How are Dr. Roylott and Miss Stoner related?	Why doesn't Dr. Roylott work as a doctor?	How does Dr. Roylott support himself?	How will Dr. Roylott's life change if the sisters marry?

The Adventure of the Speckled Band

1. **Compare:** In what three ways is Helen's situation when she visits Holmes similar to Julia's just before Julia dies?

____

____

2. **Speculate:** What do you think would have happened if Helen had not consulted Holmes?

____

____

3. **Reading Skill:** In the first paragraph of the story, Dr. Watson provides details about Holmes's cases. What do these details indicate is the author's general **purpose**?

____

____

____

4. **Literary Analysis:** Helen Stoner describes the night her sister died. The **mood** is one of terror and mystery. Use the chart below to list words, phrases, and images that contribute to this mood.

Words	Phrases	Images

Writing: Personal Narrative

Write a **personal narrative** about a time that you used logic, or reasoning, to solve a problem. Record various problems and solutions. Decide which you will write about. Use your notes to write your personal narrative.

Problem	Solution
1.	1.
2.	2.
3.	3.

Research and Technology: Report

Use the following questions to help you gather information for your **report** on the solving of a real-life crime.

- What type of crime did the case involve?

____

____

- Who solved the case?

____

____

- What clues did the detectives use?

____

____

- What was the big break through in the case?

____

____

from Steinbeck: A Life in Letters • from Travels With Charley • The American Dream

Reading Skill

An **author's purpose** is the reason he or she has for writing, such as to persuade, to entertain, or to provide information. The author's purpose influences the kinds of details he or she includes. As you read, use the chart below to **evaluate whether the author achieves his or her purpose**. Keep in mind that sometimes an author wants to achieve more than one purpose.

Author's Purpose	What details does the author use to support the purpose?	Evaluation

Literary Analysis

An **author's style** is his or her particular way of writing. Elements that factor into an author's style include these:

- word choice
- length and rhythm of sentences
- tone—the author's attitude toward the subject and audience

Some writers write informally, using everyday language and simple, straightforward sentences. Other writers use formal words and longer, more complicated sentences. As you read, notice a writer's unique style.

from Steinbeck: A Life in Letters • from Travels With Charley

John Steinbeck

Summary John Steinbeck sets out across the United States to see the country and meet people. His dog, Charley, travels with him. These excerpts tell about his experiences in Maine, Wisconsin, and in the Badlands of North Dakota.

Writing About the Big Question

Is the truth the same for everyone? In the excerpts from *Steinbeck: A Life in Letters* and *Travels with Charley,* Steinbeck tours the country to refresh his memory about what Americans are really like. Complete this sentence:

The objective truth about America and Americans is ______________________

____.

Note-taking Guide

Use this chart to recall the highlights of Steinbeck's writings.

What does Steinbeck see in Maine and Wisconsin?	How does Charley react to life on the road?	How are day and night different in the Badlands?

from Steinbeck: A Life in Letters • from Travels With Charley

1. **Infer:** What attitude toward travel do Steinbeck's letters show?

____

____

2. **Contrast:** How do Steinbeck's feelings about the Badlands change as night falls?

____

____

3. **Reading Skill:** Explain Steinbeck's **purpose** in writing this essay.

____

____

4. **Literary Analysis:** Fill in the chart below to analyze the **author's style**. In each oval, write a word to describe that element of Steinbeck's writing, and give an example.

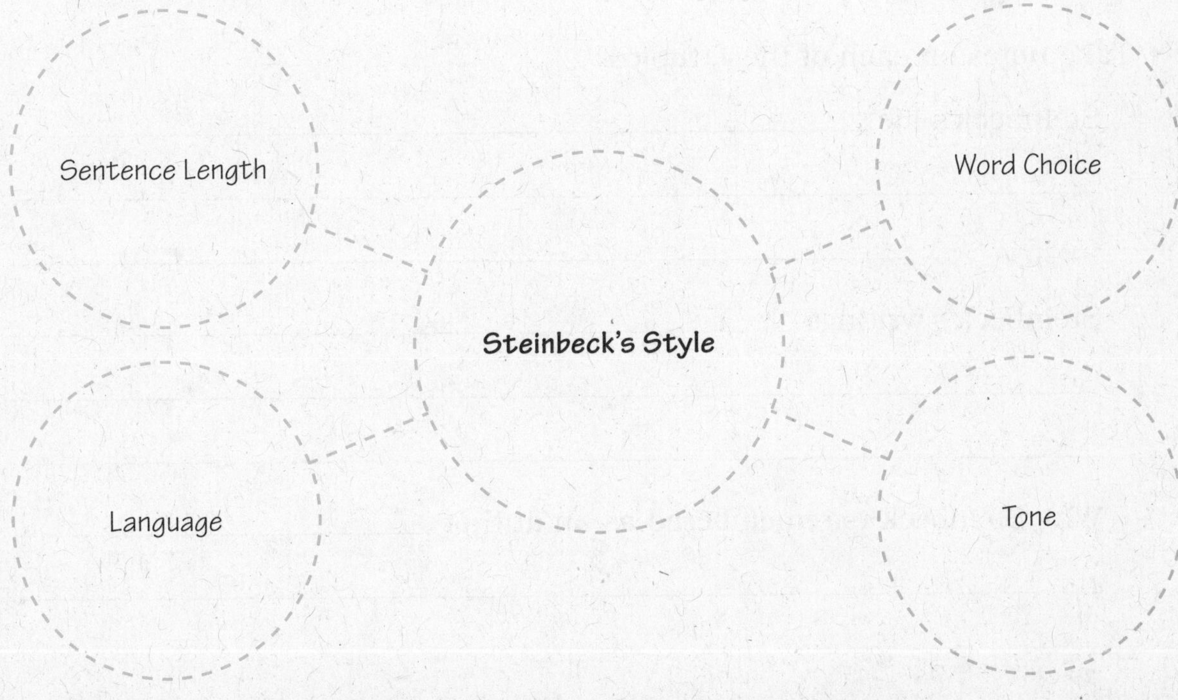

Writing: Observations Journal

Write an entry for an **observations journal** about a favorite place you have visited. Choose a place about which to write by identifying places you have visited in the chart below.

Favorite Places	
Near Home	On Trips

Listening and Speaking: Oral Presentation

Use library and Internet resources to research the life and work of John Steinbeck. Then, using your findings, prepare and deliver an **oral presentation** on Steinbeck.

- List three resources you checked for information. ______

  ______

- Take notes on each of these topics:

  Steinbeck's life ______

  ______

  ______

  Steinbeck's writings ______

  ______

  ______

  Why Steinbeck is remembered as an author ______

  ______

The American Dream

Martin Luther King, Jr.

Summary In this speech, Martin Luther King, Jr. describes his dream for America. He says that America does not make it possible for everyone to share in the dream. He discusses ways that Americans can help make his dream a reality.

Writing About the Big Question

Is the truth the same for everyone? In "The American Dream," Martin Luther King, Jr. quotes from the Declaration of Independence that "all men are created equal." Complete this sentence:

In America today, the promise of full equality is confirmed by

____.

Note-taking Guide

Use this web to record King's ideas about the American dream.

TAKE NOTES

Activate Prior Knowledge 

Think about the way your family lives. You go to school. You choose your friends. Your adult family members can vote. At one time, not everyone had the same rights. On the lines below, finish the statement: "I am thankful that in America I can…"

___

___

___

Reading Skill 

An **author's purpose** is the reason he or she has for writing. An author uses details to tell you what that purpose is. Read the bracketed passage. What does it suggest as the author's purpose for writing this speech?

___

___

___

Reading Check 

What does King believe is one of the first and most important things about the American dream? Underline the sentence that tells you.

The American Dream

Martin Luther King, Jr.

America is essentially a dream, a dream as yet unfulfilled. It is a dream of a land where men of all races, of all nationalities and of all creeds[1] can live together as brothers. The substance of the dream is expressed in these sublime words, words lifted to cosmic proportions: "We hold these truths to be self-evident, that all men are created equal, that they are endowed by their Creator with certain unalienable rights, that among these are life, liberty, and pursuit of happiness."[2] This is the dream.

One of the first things we notice in this dream is an amazing universalism. It does not say some men, but it says all men. It does not say all white men, but it says all men, which includes black men. It does not say all Gentiles, but it says all men, which includes Jews. It does not say all Protestants, but it says all men, which includes Catholics.

And there is another thing we see in this dream that ultimately distinguishes democracy and our form of government from all of the totalitarian regimes[3] that emerge in history. It says that each individual has certain basic rights that are neither conferred by nor derived from the state. To discover where they came from it is necessary to move back behind the dim mist of eternity, for they are God-given. Very seldom if ever in the history of the world has a sociopolitical document expressed in such profoundly eloquent and unequivocal language the dignity and the worth of human personality. The American dream reminds us that every man is heir to the legacy of worthiness.

Vocabulary Development

unequivocal (un i KWIV uh kuhl) *adj.* clear; plainly understood

1. **creeds** (kreedz) *n.* systems of belief.
2. **"We hold these truths . . . pursuit of happiness."** opening words of the Declaration of Independence, which asserted the American colonies' independence from Great Britain in 1776.
3. **totalitarian** (toh tal uh TER ee uhn) **regimes** (ruh ZHEEMZ) countries in which those in power control every aspect of citizens' lives.

Ever since the Founding Fathers of our nation dreamed this noble dream, America has been something of a schizophrenic[4] personality, tragically divided against herself. On the one hand we have proudly professed the principles of democracy, and on the other hand we have sadly practiced the very antithesis of those principles. Indeed slavery and segregation have been strange paradoxes in a nation founded on the principle that all men are created equal. This is what the Swedish sociologist, Gunnar Myrdal, referred to as the American dilemma.

But the shape of the world today does not permit us the luxury of an anemic democracy. The price America must pay for the continued exploitation of the Negro and other minority groups is the price of its own destruction. The hour is late; the clock of destiny is ticking out. It is trite, but urgently true, that if America is to remain a first-class nation she can no longer have second-class citizens. Now, more than ever before, America is challenged to bring her noble dream into reality, and those who are working to implement the American dream are the true saviors of democracy.

Now may I suggest some of the things we must do if we are to make the American dream a reality. First I think all of us must develop a world perspective if we are to survive. The American dream will not become a reality devoid of the larger dream of a world of brotherhood and peace and good will. The world in which we live is a world of geographical oneness and we are challenged now to make it spiritually one.

Man's specific genius and technological ingenuity has dwarfed distance and placed time in chains. Jet

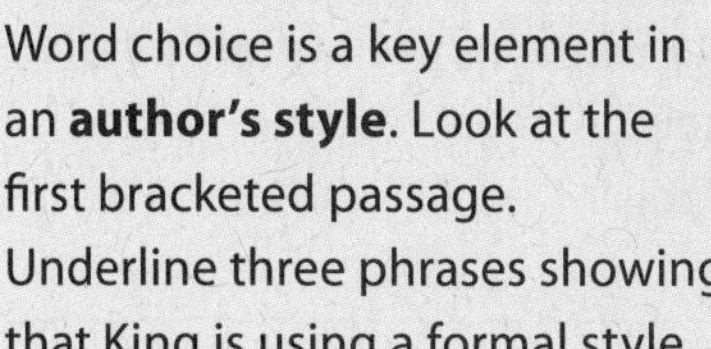

Literary Analysis

Word choice is a key element in an **author's style**. Look at the first bracketed passage. Underline three phrases showing that King is using a formal style.

Reading Skill

Read the second bracketed passage. Is the **author's purpose** to persuade, entertain, or give information? Explain.

Stop to Reflect

What does King think will happen to America if its people cannot make the changes he suggests?

Reading Check

According to King, what is one of the most important ways to make the American dream a reality? Underline the answer.

Vocabulary Development

antithesis (an TITH uh sis) *n.* direct opposite
paradoxes (PER uh dahks iz) *n.* two things that seem directly at odds
exploitation (eks ploy TAY shuhn) *n.* the act of using another person for selfish purposes

4. **schizophrenic** (skit suh FREN ik) *adj.* characterized by a separation between the thought processes and emotions, often changing from one attitude and opinion to another.

planes have compressed into minutes distances that once took days and months to cover. It is not common for a preacher to be quoting Bob Hope, but I think he has aptly described this jet age in which we live. If, on taking off on a nonstop flight from Los Angeles to New York City, you develop hiccups, he said, you will hic in Los Angeles and cup in New York City. That is really moving. If you take a flight from Tokyo, Japan, on Sunday morning, you will arrive in Seattle, Washington, on the preceding Saturday night. When your friends meet you at the airport and ask you when you left Tokyo, you will have to say, "I left tomorrow." This is the kind of world in which we live. Now this is a bit humorous but I am trying to laugh a basic fact into all of us: the world in which we live has become a single neighborhood.

Through our scientific genius we have made of this world a neighborhood; now through our moral and spiritual development we must make of it a brotherhood. In a real sense, we must all learn to live together as brothers, or we will all perish together as fools. We must come to see that no individual can live alone; no nation can live alone. We must all live together; we must all be concerned about each other.

Reader's Response: Do you think King's suggestions would help make America a better place to live? Explain.

____

____

____

____

____

____

TAKE NOTES

Literary Analysis

Do you think the **author's style** helps him get his point across? Explain.

____

____

____

____

Reading Skill

Read the underlined sentence. Is the **author's purpose** specific in saying what he wants his audience to do? Explain.

____

____

____

____

Reading Check 

How does King think Americans should learn to live? Underline the sentence that states this.

The American Dream

1. **Infer:** Why does King quote lines from the Declaration of Independence in his speech?

____

____

2. **Generalize:** According to King, what steps must Americans take to make the American dream a reality?

____

____

3. **Reading Skill:** What is King's **purpose** in writing this speech? Support your answer.

____

____

4. **Literary Analysis:** Use this chart to look at elements of the **author's style**. In each oval, tell how King uses the element. Write a word or phrase from the text that gives an example of each element.

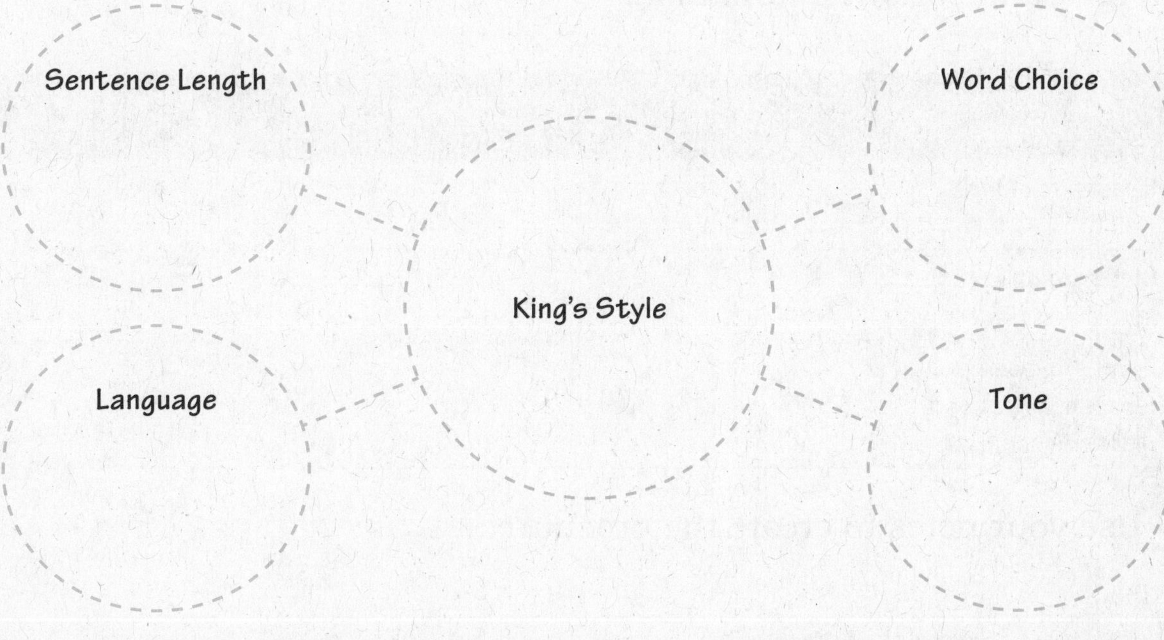

Writing: Observations Journal

Write an entry for an **observations journal**. Record your thoughts about an aspect of today's society that could be improved.

- What could be improved in your school or community?

____

____

- What could be improved in your country?

____

____

- What could be improved in the world?

____

____

Use your notes to write your observations journal.

Research and Technology: Brochure

People use **brochures** to get information about a place that they may want to visit. The information should be clear, accurate, and to the point. As you search for historical sites, use the following chart to record important information.

Information for Brochure	Site 1:	Site 2:	Site 3:
Reason for King's visit?			
Message delivered			
Form of message (speech, act of civil disobedience)			

Use your notes to create the brochure.

Magazine Articles

About Magazine Articles

A **magazine article** is a piece of nonfiction. A magazine article is usually short. Magazine articles can tell you about subjects such as these:

- Interesting people
- Animal behavior
- New technology

Magazine articles often have these parts:

- Drawings or photos that go with the text
- Captions, or words that explain the drawings or photos (refer to *captions*, as in box below)
- Sidebars with extra information

Reading Skill

You will see articles when you look through a magazine. You can **preview to determine your purpose for reading**. This means that you look over an article to decide whether you want to read it and why. When you preview an article, look at

- the title.
- the pictures or photographs.
- one paragraph.

These steps will give you an idea of the author's purpose for writing the article. Then, you can decide what purpose you have for reading it. You may decide that you have no reason to read the article. Use the questions below to help you look at parts of an article.

Questions to Help You Preview an Article

- ❑ What is the tone, or attitude, of the author?
- ❑ Are the pictures and captions designed to provide information or to entertain?
- ❑ As I skim the text, do I see statistics, quotations from experts, and facts?
- ❑ Do the first sentences of paragraphs introduce facts, opinions, or anecdotes?

TAKE NOTES

Text Structure

Look at the pictures in this article. Do they add information, or are they just for fun? Explain.

Vocabulary Builder

Multiple-Meaning Words The verb *sweep* has more than one meaning. *Sweep* can mean "clean dirt from the ground or floor with a broom." It can also mean "move quickly." What does *sweep* mean in the first paragraph?

Fluency Builder 

Read the last paragraph on this page slowly and silently. As you read, circle the punctuation. Remember that a comma (,) indicates a short pause and a period (.) indicates a full stop. Underline any words that you have difficulty pronouncing, and practice saying each word. Then, read aloud the paragraph to a partner.

Sun Suckers and Moon Cursers

Richard and Joyce Wolkomir

Night is falling. It is getting dark. You can barely see. But now . . . lights come on. Car headlights sweep the road. Windows light up. Neon signs glow red and green. Street lamps shine, bright as noon. So who cares if it is night?

But what if you are camping in a forest? Or a storm blows down power lines? Then the night would be inky. To see, you would have only star twinkle, or the moon's pale shine. Until about 1900, when electric power networks began spreading, that is how nights were: dark.

Roger Ekirch, an historian at Virginia Tech, studies those long-ago dark nights. For light, our ancestors had only candles, hearth fires, torches, walnut-oil lamps. And that made their nights different than ours.

"It used to be, when it got dark, people felt edgy," Ekirch says. He studies the years from about 1500 to 1830, when mostly only the wealthy could afford even candles. "People talked about being 'shut in' by the night," he says. Our ancestors imagined werewolves roaming at night, and demons. In their minds, they populated the darkness with witches, fairies and elves, and malignant spirits. Night had real dangers, too—robbers and murderers, but also ditches and ponds you could fall into.

What was it like, when nights were so dark?

To find out, Roger Ekirch has combed through old newspapers, diaries, letters, everything from court records to sermons. He has pondered modern scientific research, too. He has found that, before the invention of electric lights, our ancestors considered night a different "season." At night, they were nearly blind. And so, to them, day and night seemed as different as summer and winter.

They even had special words for night. Some people called the last rays of the setting sun "sun suckers." Nighttime travelers, who relied on the moon called it the "parish lantern." But robbers, who liked to lurk in darkness, hated the moon. They called it "the tattler." And those darkness-loving criminals? They were "moon cursers."

Cities were so dark that people needing to find their way at night hired boys to carry torches, or "links." Such torchbearers were called "linkboys."

Country people tried to stay indoors at night, unless the moon was out. On moonless nights, people groping in the darkness frequently fell into ponds and ravines.[1] Horses, also blinded by darkness, often threw riders.

If you were traveling at night, you would wear light-colored clothing, so your friends could see you. You might ride a white horse. You might mark your route in advance by stripping away tree bark, exposing the white inner wood. In southern England, where the soil is chalky white, people planning night trips mounded up white chalk along their route during the day, to guide them later, in the moonlight.

It was dark inside houses, too. To dress in the darkness, people learned to fold their clothes just so. Swedish homeowners, Roger Ekirch says, pushed parlor furniture against walls at night, so they could walk through the room without tripping.

1. **ravines** (ruh VEENZ) *n.* long, deep hollows in Earth's surface.

TAKE NOTES

Vocabulary Builder

Multiple-Meaning Words The verb *combed* has more than one meaning. *Combed* can mean "searched thoroughly." It can also mean "made your hair neat." What does *combed* mean in the bracketed paragraph?

____

Text Structure

Look at the first sentence in each paragraph on this page. Do these sentences begin with facts, opinions, or events? Explain.

____

____

____

____

Vocabulary Builder

Idioms The idiom *just so* means "in a careful manner." Complete the following sentence:

When nights were dark, people learned to fold their clothes *just so* in order to _______________

____

_______________.

TAKE NOTES

Text Structure 

Skim the text. Underline any facts or quotations from experts. How does this help you **preview** the article? Does it change **your purpose for reading?**

____

____

____

Vocabulary Builder 

Adjectives One or more adjectives can describe the same noun. In the paragraph that begins "At night, evildoers came out . . .", both *wealthy* and *young* describe *aristocrats.* Circle four more adjectives in the paragraph, and underline the noun that each adjective describes.

Comprehension Builder 

Read the bracketed paragraph. Summarize the ways that people might have protected themselves when they walked at night.

____

____

____

____

People began as children to memorize their local terrain—ditches, fences, cisterns, bogs.[2] They learned the magical terrain, too, spots where ghosts and other imaginary nighttime frights lurked. "In some places, you never whistled at night, because that invited the devil," says Ekirch.

One reason people feared nightfall was they thought night actually did "fall." At night, they believed, malignant air descended. To ward off that sickly air, sleepers wore nightcaps. They also pulled curtains around their beds. In the 1600s, one London man tied his hands inside his bed at night so they would not flop outside the curtains and expose him to night air. . . .

At night, evildoers came out. Virtually every major European city had criminal gangs. Sometimes those gangs included wealthy young aristocrats who assaulted people just for the thrill. . . .

If you were law-abiding, you might clang your sword on the pavement while walking down a dark nighttime street to warn robbers you were armed. Or you might hold your sword upright in the moonlight. You tried to walk in groups. You walked down the street's middle, to prevent robbers from lunging at you from doorways or alleys. Robbers depended so much on darkness that a British criminal who attacked his victim in broad daylight was acquitted—jurors decided he must be insane.

Many whose days were blighted by poverty or ill treatment sought escape at night. Slaves in the American South, for instance, sneaked out at night to dances and parties. Or they stumbled through the darkness to other plantations, to visit their wives or children. After the Civil War, says Roger Ekirch, former slaveholders worried that their freed slaves might attack them. And so they rode out at night disguised as ghosts, to frighten onetime slaves into staying indoors.

2. **cisterns** (SIS ternz), **bogs** Cisterns are large underground areas for storing water; bogs are small marshes or swamps in which footing is treacherous.

"At night, many servants felt beyond supervision, and they would often leave directly after their employers fell asleep," Ekirch adds. When they did sleep, it was fitfully, because of rumbling carts and watchmen's cries. And so Ekirch believes many workers got much too little sleep. "That explains why so many slaveowners and employers complained about their workers falling asleep during the day," he said.

Our ancestors had one overriding—and entirely real—nighttime fear: fire. Blazes were common because houses, often with thatched roofs,[3] ignited easily. At night, open flames flickered everywhere. Passersby carrying torches might set your roof ablaze. Also, householders commonly complained about servants forgetting to bank fires or snuff out candles. Roger Ekirch believes one reason night watchmen bellowed out each hour, to the irritation of sleepers, was precisely to keep everyone half awake, to be ready when fires erupted. . . .

Electricity changed the night. One electric bulb, Ekirch calculates, provided 100 times more light than a gas lamp. Night was becoming what it is today—an artificially illuminated extension of the day. Night has lost its spookiness.

Still, says Roger Ekirch, even in the electric age, his children sometimes fear the dark: "I tell them, 'Your daddy is an expert on night, and he knows a lot about the history of the night, and he can tell you there is nothing to be afraid of!' "

He shrugs. "It doesn't work well," he says.

3. **thatched** (thatchd) **roofs** roofs made of materials such as straw or rushes.

TAKE NOTES

Text Structure

How does the picture support the information in the **magazine article?** Explain.

Vocabulary Builder

Adverbs An adverb describes a verb, an adjective, or another adverb. On the lines below, write six adverbs that appear in the second paragraph on this page. Next to each adverb, write the word it describes and the word's part of speech.

Comprehension Builder 

How has electricity changed the way that people think about nighttime?

Thinking About the Magazine Article

1. Name three reasons why people were afraid of the night.

____

2. People were more afraid of fire at night than in the day. Why?

____

Reading Skill

3. What is the author's main purpose in writing this article?

____

4. What item on the first page gives you the best clue to the subject of the article?

____

WRITE ABOUT IT Timed Writing: Description (20 minutes)

Suppose that you live in seventeenth-century Europe. Write a letter explaining why people should travel in the daytime. Record your ideas in the chart below.

Being safe from criminals	
Being safe from fire	
Being able to see where you are going	

An Hour With Abuelo

Adventures, mysteries, science fiction, and animal fables are a few types of short stories. Short stories share certain elements.

Conflict is a struggle between opposing forces. There are two types of conflict:

- **Internal conflict:** takes place in the mind of a character.
- **External conflict:** takes place when a character struggles with another person or an outside force.

Plot is the sequence of events in a story. It is usually divided into five parts:

- **Exposition:** introduces the **setting**—the time and place of the story—the characters, and the situation.
- **Rising action** introduces the **conflict**, or problem.
- **Climax** is the turning point of a story.
- **Falling action** is the part of the story when the conflict lessens.
- **Resolution** is the story's conclusion.
- A **subplot** is a secondary story line that adds depth to the main plot.

Setting is the time and place of the action in a story. Sometimes it may act as a backdrop for the story's action. Setting can also be the source of the story's conflict. It can create the **mood**, or feeling, of the story.

Characters are the people or animals that take part in the action.

- **Character traits** are the qualities and attitudes that a character possesses. Examples are dependability and intelligence.
- **Character's motives** are the reasons for a character's actions. Motives can come from internal causes, such as loneliness, or external causes, such as danger.

Theme is the main message expressed in a story. It may be directly stated or implied.

- A **stated theme** is expressed directly by the author of the story.
- An **implied theme** is suggested by what happens to the characters.
- A **universal theme** is a repeating message about life that is expressed regularly across time and cultures.

Tools that writers use to enhance their writing are called **literary devices**. Examples of literary devices are in the chart below.

Literary Device	Description
Point of View	• the perspective from which a story is told • **First-person point of view:** presents the story from the perspective of a character in the story • **Third-person point of view:** tells the story from the perspective of a narrator outside the story. An **omniscient** third-person narrator is someone who knows everything that happens. He or she can tell the reader what each character thinks and feels. A **limited** third-person narrator is someone who can reveal the thoughts and feelings of only one character.
Foreshadowing	• the use of clues to hint at events yet to come in a story
Flashback	• the use of scenes that interrupt the time order of a story to reveal past events
Irony	• the contrast between an actual outcome and what a reader or a character expects to happen

An Hour With Abuelo

Judith Ortiz Cofer

Summary Arturo is sent to a nursing home to spend an hour with his grandfather. Arturo is not excited about the visit. Arturo finds his grandfather writing his life story. Arturo listens to his grandfather's story. He loses all track of time.

Note-taking Guide

Use the character wheel below to record what Arturo says, thinks, and does.

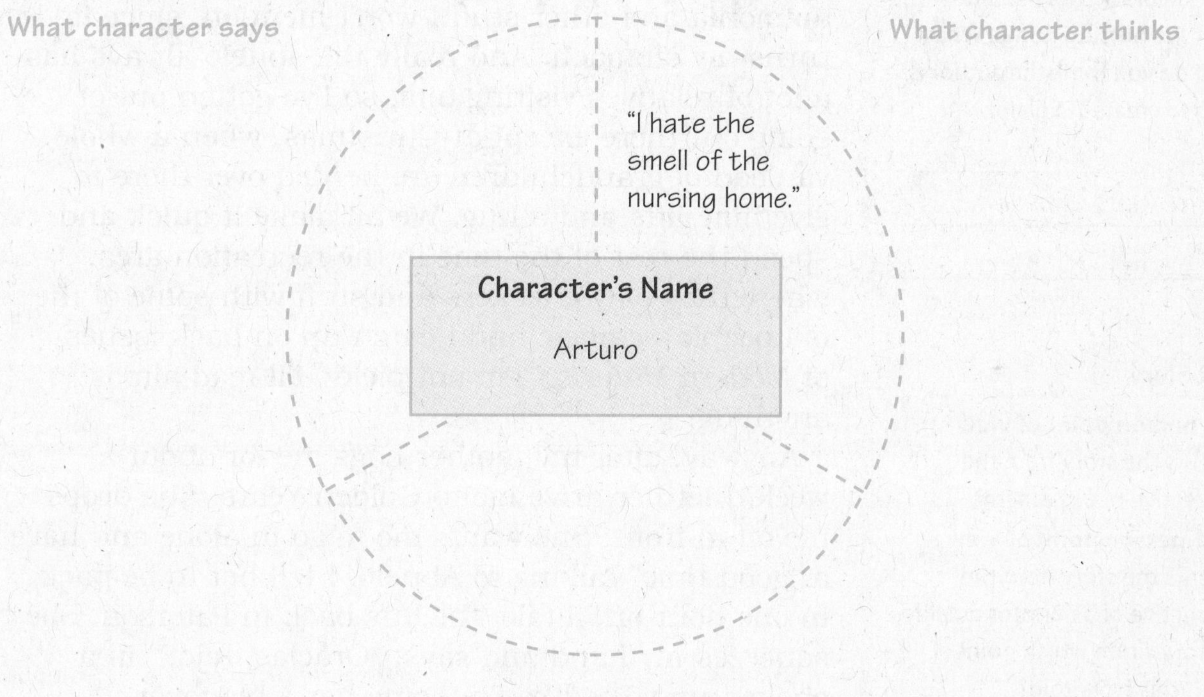

TAKE NOTES

Activate Prior Knowledge

What could you learn by spending time with older relatives?

____

____

____

Short Story

Mood is the emotional feeling that a story creates in a reader. Read the bracketed passage about the nursing home. What mood do you think the author is trying to create? Explain.

____

____

____

Short Story

First-person point of view presents the story from the perspective of a character. **Third-person point of view** presents the story from the perspective of a narrator outside the story. From which point of view is this story told?

____

Reading Check

Where does the narrator's grandfather live? Circle the text that tells you.

An Hour With Abuelo

Judith Ortiz Cofer

"Just one hour, una hora, is all I'm asking of you, son." My grandfather is in a nursing home in Brooklyn, and my mother wants me to spend some time with him, since the doctors say that he doesn't have too long to go now. I don't have much time left of my summer vacation, and there's a stack of books next to my bed I've got to read if I'm going to get into the AP English class I want. I'm going stupid in some of my classes, and Mr. Williams, the principal at Central, said that if I passed some reading tests, he'd let me move up.

Besides, I hate the place, the old people's home, especially the way it smells like industrial-strength ammonia and other stuff I won't mention, since it turns my stomach. And really the abuelo always has a lot of relatives visiting him, so I've gotten out of going out there except at Christmas, when a whole vanload of grandchildren are herded over there to give him gifts and a hug. We all make it quick and spend the rest of the time in the recreation area, where they play checkers and stuff with some of the old people's games, and I catch up on back issues of *Modern Maturity*. I'm not picky, I'll read almost anything.

Anyway, after my mother nags me for about a week, I let her drive me to Golden Years. She drops me off in front. She wants me to go in alone and have a "good time" talking to Abuelo. I tell her to be back in one hour or I'll take the bus back to Paterson. She squeezes my hand and says, "Gracias, hijo,"[1] in a choked-up voice like I'm doing her a big favor.

I get depressed the minute I walk into the place. They line up the old people in wheelchairs in the hallway as if they were about to be raced to the finish line by orderlies who don't even look at them when they push them here and there. I walk fast to room 10, Abuelo's "suite." He is sitting up in his bed writing with a pencil in one of those old-fashioned

1. **"Gracias** (GRAH see ahs), **hijo** (EE hoh)" Spanish for "Thank you, son." *Hijo* also means "child."

black hardback notebooks. It has the outline of the island of Puerto Rico on it. I slide into the hard vinyl chair by his bed. He sort of smiles and the lines on his face get deeper, but he doesn't say anything. Since I'm supposed to talk to him, I say, "What are you doing, Abuelo, writing the story of your life?"

It's supposed to be a joke, but he answers, "Sí, how did you know, Arturo?"

His name is Arturo too. I was named after him. I don't really know my grandfather. His children, including my mother, came to New York and New Jersey (where I was born) and he stayed on the Island until my grandmother died. Then he got sick, and since nobody could leave their jobs to go take care of him, they brought him to this nursing home in Brooklyn. I see him a couple of times a year, but he's always surrounded by his sons and daughters. My mother tells me that Don Arturo had once been a teacher back in Puerto Rico, but had lost his job after the war. Then he became a farmer. She's always saying in a sad voice, "Ay, bendito![2] What a waste of a fine mind." Then she usually shrugs her shoulders and says, "Así es la vida." That's the way life is. It sometimes makes me mad that the adults I know just accept whatever is thrown at them because "that's the way things are." Not for me. I go after what I want.

Anyway, Abuelo is looking at me like he was trying to see into my head, but he doesn't say anything. Since I like stories, I decide I may as well ask him if he'll read me what he wrote.

I look at my watch: I've already used up twenty minutes of the hour I promised my mother.

Abuelo starts talking in his slow way. He speaks what my mother calls book English. He taught himself from a dictionary, and his words sound stiff, like he's sounding them out in his head before he says them. With his children he speaks Spanish, and that funny book English with us grandchildren. I'm surprised that he's still so sharp, because his body is shrinking like a crumpled-up brown paper sack with some bones in it. But I can see from looking into his eyes that the light is still on in there.

2. **bendito** (ven DEE toh) Spanish for "blessed."

TAKE NOTES

Short Story 

The **exposition** introduces the time and place, characters, and situation within a story. Read the bracketed passage. What are some details you learn about Abuelo? Circle them in the text.

Short Story 

Character traits are a character's qualities and attitudes. Read the underlined passage. What character traits do you think Arturo has?

____

____

Stop to Reflect 

Why do you think that Abuelo is writing his life story?

____

____

____

TAKE NOTES

"It is a short story, Arturo. The story of my life. It will not take very much time to read it."

"I have time, Abuelo." I'm a little embarrassed that he saw me looking at my watch.

"Yes, *hijo*. You have spoken the truth. *La verdad*. You have much time."

Abuelo reads: " 'I loved words from the beginning of my life. In the campo[3] where I was born one of seven sons, there were few books. My mother read them to us over and over: the Bible, the stories of Spanish conquistadors and of pirates that she had read as a child and brought with her from the city of Mayaguez; that was before she married my father, a coffee bean farmer; and she taught us words from the newspaper that a boy on a horse brought every week to her. She taught each of us how to write on a slate with chalks that she ordered by mail every year. We used those chalks until they were so small that you lost them between your fingers.

" 'I always wanted to be a writer and a teacher. With my heart and my soul I knew that I wanted to be around books all of my life. And so against the wishes of my father, who wanted all his sons to help him on the land, she sent me to high school in Mayaguez. For four years I boarded with a couple she knew. I paid my rent in labor, and I ate vegetables I grew myself. I wore my clothes until they were thin as parchment. But I graduated at the top of my class! My whole family came to see me that day. My mother brought me a beautiful guayabera, a white shirt made of the finest cotton and embroidered by her own hands. I was a happy young man.

" 'In those days you could teach in a country school with a high school diploma. So I went back to my mountain village and got a job teaching all grades in a little classroom built by the parents of my students.

" 'I had books sent to me by the government. I felt like a rich man although the pay was very small. I had books. All the books I wanted! I taught my students how to read poetry and plays, and how to write them. We made up songs and put on shows for the parents. It was a beautiful time for me.

3. **campo** (KAHM poh) Spanish for "open country."

Short Story

A **character's motives** are the reasons for his or her actions. Read the underlined sentence. What is Arturo's reason for looking at his watch?

Short Story

Read the bracketed passage from Abuelo's life story. What **character traits** do you think Abuelo has?

Reading Check

How did Abuelo learn to read and write? Underline the part of the text that tells you.

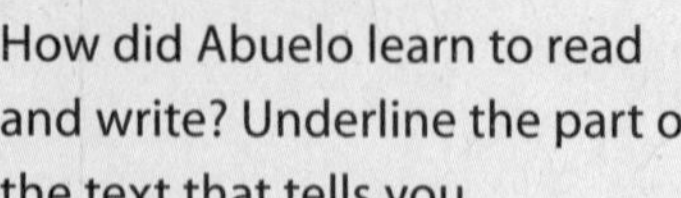

"'Then the war came,[4] and the American President said that all Puerto Rican men would be drafted. I wrote to our governor and explained that I was the only teacher in the mountain village. I told him that the children would go back to the fields and grow up ignorant if I could not teach them their letters. I said that I thought I was a better teacher than a soldier. The governor did not answer my letter. I went into the U.S. Army.

"'I told my sergeant that I could be a teacher in the army. I could teach all the farm boys their letters so that they could read the instructions on the ammunition boxes and not blow themselves up. The sergeant said I was too smart for my own good, and gave me a job cleaning latrines. He said to me there is reading material for you there, scholar. Read the writing on the walls. I spent the war mopping floors and cleaning toilets.

"'When I came back to the Island, things had changed. You had to have a college degree to teach school, even the lower grades. My parents were sick, two of my brothers had been killed in the war, the others had stayed in Nueva York. I was the only one left to help the old people. I became a farmer. I married a good woman who gave me many good children. I taught them all how to read and write before they started school.'"

Abuelo then puts the notebook down on his lap and closes his eyes.

"Así es la vida is the title of my book," he says in a whisper, almost to himself. Maybe he's forgotten that I'm there.

For a long time he doesn't say anything else. I think that he's sleeping, but then I see that he's watching me through half-closed lids, maybe waiting for my opinion of his writing. I'm trying to think of something nice to say. I liked it and all, but not the title. And I think that he could've been a teacher if he had wanted to bad enough. Nobody is going to stop me from doing what I want with my life. I'm not going to let la vida get in my way. I want to discuss this with him, but the words are not coming into my head

4. **"Then the war came, . . ."** The United States entered World War II in 1941, after the bombing of Pearl Harbor.

TAKE NOTES

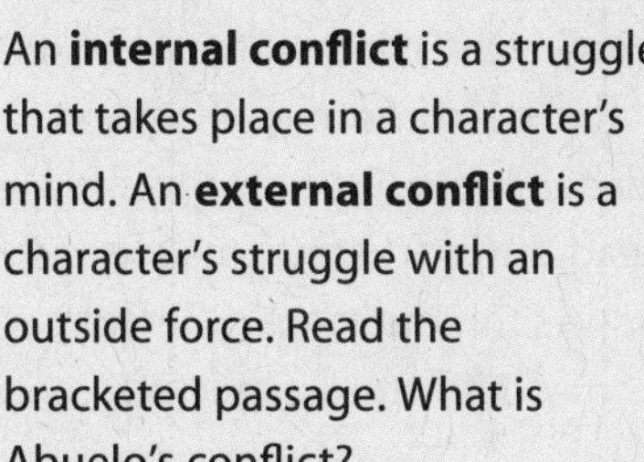

Short Story

An **internal conflict** is a struggle that takes place in a character's mind. An **external conflict** is a character's struggle with an outside force. Read the bracketed passage. What is Abuelo's conflict?

Is it an internal or external conflict?

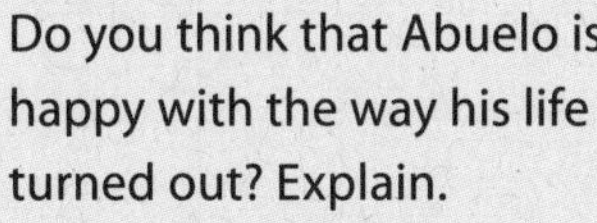

Stop to Reflect

Do you think that Abuelo is happy with the way his life turned out? Explain.

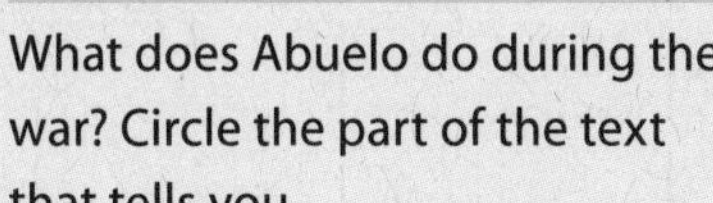

Reading Check

What does Abuelo do during the war? Circle the part of the text that tells you.

TAKE NOTES

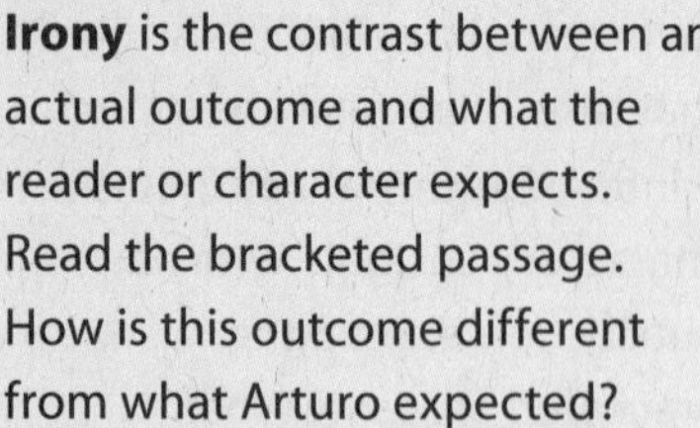

Short Story

Irony is the contrast between an actual outcome and what the reader or character expects. Read the bracketed passage. How is this outcome different from what Arturo expected?

____

____

____

____

Short Story

Resolution is the story's conclusion. What is the resolution of Arturo's story?

____

____

____

____

____

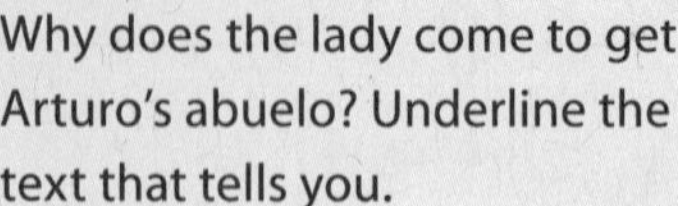

Reading Check

Why does the lady come to get Arturo's abuelo? Underline the text that tells you.

in Spanish just yet. I'm about to ask him why he didn't keep fighting to make his dream come true, when an old lady in hot-pink running shoes sort of appears at the door.

She is wearing a pink jogging outfit too. The world's oldest marathoner, I say to myself. She calls out to my grandfather in a flirty voice, "Yoo-hoo, Arturo, remember what day this is? It's poetry-reading day in the rec room! You promised us you'd read your new one today."

I see my abuelo perking up almost immediately. He points to his wheelchair, which is hanging like a huge metal bat in the open closet. He makes it obvious that he wants me to get it. I put it together, and with Mrs. Pink Running Shoes's help, we get him in it. Then he says in a strong deep voice I hardly recognize, "Arturo, get that notebook from the table, please."

I hand him another map-of-the-Island notebook—this one is red. On it in big letters it says, POEMAS DE ARTURO.

I start to push him toward the rec room, but he shakes his finger at me.

"Arturo, look at your watch now. I believe your time is over." He gives me a wicked smile.

Then with her pushing the wheelchair—maybe a little too fast—they roll down the hall. He is already reading from his notebook, and she's making bird noises. I look at my watch and the hour is up, to the minute. I can't help but think that my abuelo has been timing me. It cracks me up. I walk slowly down the hall toward the exit sign. I want my mother to have to wait a little. I don't want her to think that I'm in a hurry or anything.

Reader's Response: What did Arturo learn about his grandfather? Do you think his opinion of his grandfather has changed?

____

____

____

Short Stories

1. **Respond:** On the basis of the story, would you enjoy visiting Arturo's grandfather? Explain.

2. **Interpret:** Do you think that Abuelo has found a new purpose in life? Explain your answer.

3. **Short Story:** What is the main **conflict** in this story?

4. **Short Story:** Use the diagram below to compare and contrast the **characters** in the story.

Arturo's Unique Qualities

Shared Qualities

Abuelo's Qualities

Audio-cassette

Prepare an **audio-cassette** about Judith Ortiz Cofer. The following tips will help prepare you to create the cassette.

- Read some of the author's works. Judith Ortiz Cofer's books include *The Line of the Sun, The Meaning of Consuelo,* and *Call Me Maria.* Her short stories include "Catch the Moon," "Grandmother's Room," and "Lessons of Love."

  What I learned from Cofer's writing:

  ____

  ____

  ____

  ____

- Search the Internet: Use words and phrases such as "Judith Ortiz Cofer article."

  What I learned about Judith Ortiz Cofer:

  ____

  ____

  ____

  ____

  ____

- Watch the video interview with Judith Ortiz Cofer. Add what you learn from the video to what you have already learned about the author.

  Additional information learned about the author:

  ____

  ____

  ____

  ____

Use your notes to write and record your audio-cassette.

Who Can Replace a Man? • Tears of Autumn

Reading Skill

A **comparison** tells how two or more things are alike. A **contrast** tells how two or more things are different. **Asking questions to compare and contrast** helps you notice similarities and differences in characters, settings, moods, and ideas. It also enriches your understanding of a work. Ask questions like those shown in the chart. Fill in the answers as you read.

How is one character different from another?

?

How is this story similar to another that I have read?

?

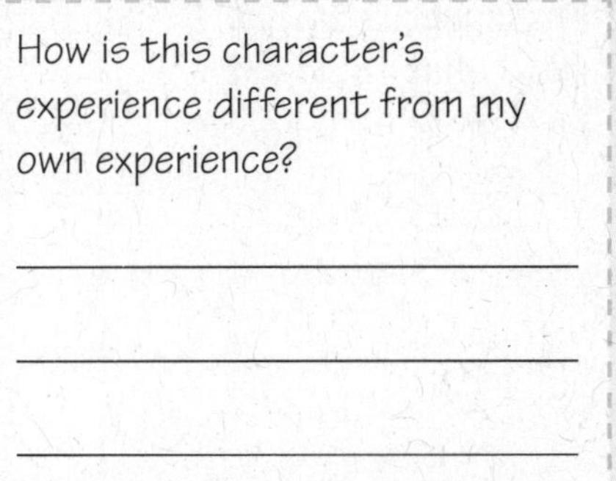

How is this character's experience different from my own experience?

Literary Analysis

The **setting** is the time and place of a story's action. A setting can create an emotional atmosphere, or *mood*. It can also give the reader the sensation of living in a different place and time. As you read, notice details like the following that make up the setting:

- the customs and beliefs of the characters
- the physical features of the land
- the weather or season of the year
- the historical era in which the action takes place

Who Can Replace a Man?

Brian Aldiss

Summary A group of machines does not receive orders as usual. The machines are programmed with different levels of intelligence. The smarter machines find out that all men have died. They try to figure out what to do.

Writing About the Big Question

Can all conflicts be resolved? In "Who Can Replace a Man?" machines in a futuristic world start to fight when their human masters disappear. Complete this sentence:

A stalemate is likely to occur in an argument when ______________________

____.

Note-taking Guide

Use this diagram to describe the problem the machines face, their solution, and its result.

Problem	Solution	Result
The machines do not know what to do when all men die.		

Who Can Replace a Man?

Brian Aldiss

Morning filtered into the sky, lending it the gray tone of the ground below.

The field-minder finished turning the topsoil of a three-thousand-acre field. When it had turned the last furrow it climbed onto the highway and looked back at its work. The work was good. Only the land was bad. Like the ground all over Earth, it was vitiated by over-cropping. By rights, it ought now to lie fallow[1] for a while, but the field-minder had other orders.

It went slowly down the road, taking its time. It was intelligent enough to appreciate the neatness all about it. Nothing worried it, beyond a loose inspection plate above its nuclear pile which ought to be attended to. Thirty feet tall, it yielded no highlights to the dull air.

No other machines passed on its way back to the Agricultural Station. The field-minder noted the fact without comment. In the station yard it saw several other machines that it recognized; most of them should have been out about their tasks now. Instead, some were inactive and some careered round the yard in a strange fashion, shouting or hooting.

Steering carefully past them, the field-minder moved over to Warehouse Three and spoke to the seed-distributor, which stood idly outside.

"I have a requirement for seed potatoes," it said to the distributor, and with a quick internal motion punched out an order card specifying quantity, field number and several other details. It ejected the card and handed it to the distributor.

The distributor held the card close to its eye and then said, "The requirement is in order, but the store is not yet unlocked. The required seed potatoes are in the store. Therefore I cannot produce the requirement."

Increasingly of late there had been breakdowns in the complex system of machine labor, but this

1. **vitiated** (VISH ee ayt id) **by over-cropping . . . lie fallow** (FAL oh) The soil has been spoiled by repeated plantings that have drawn out its nutrients. Letting the field lie fallow by not planting it would help renourish the soil.

TAKE NOTES

Activate Prior Knowledge

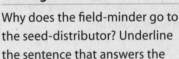

What machines do you depend on every day?

Literary Analysis

The **setting** is the time and place of a story's action. What details at the beginning show that the story is set in the future?

Reading Check

Why does the field-minder go to the seed-distributor? Underline the sentence that answers the question.

TAKE NOTES

Reading Skill 

A **contrast** tells how two or more things are different. Contrast the brain of the seed-distributor and the brain of the field-minder.

Stop to Reflect 

What problems does the field-minder have this morning? What do you think is the cause of these problems?

Reading Skill 

A **comparison** tells how two or more things are alike. How are the machines in the story similar to machines in your daily life? Give an example.

particular hitch had not occurred before. The field-minder thought, then it said, "Why is the store not yet unlocked?"

"Because Supply Operative Type P has not come this morning. Supply Operative Type P is the unlocker."

The field-minder looked squarely at the seed-distributor, whose exterior chutes and scales and grabs were so vastly different from the field-minder's own limbs.

"What class brain do you have, seed-distributor?" it asked.

"I have a Class Five brain."

"I have a Class Three brain. Therefore I am superior to you. Therefore I will go and see why the unlocker has not come this morning."

Leaving the distributor, the field-minder set off across the great yard. More machines were in random motion now; one or two had crashed together and argued about it coldly and logically. Ignoring them, the field-minder pushed through sliding doors into the echoing confines of the station itself.

Most of the machines here were clerical, and consequently small. They stood about in little groups, eyeing each other, not conversing. Among so many non-differentiated types, the unlocker was easy to find. It had fifty arms, most of them with more than one finger, each finger tipped by a key; it looked like a pincushion full of variegated[2] hat pins.

The field-minder approached it.

"I can do no more work until Warehouse Three is unlocked," it told the unlocker. "Your duty is to unlock the warehouse every morning. Why have you not unlocked the warehouse this morning?"

"I had no orders this morning," replied the unlocker. "I have to have orders every morning. When I have orders I unlock the warehouse."

"None of us have had any orders this morning," a pen-propeller said, sliding towards them.

Vocabulary Development

consequently (KAHN suh kwent lee) *adv.* as a result

2. **variegated** (VER ee uh gayt id) *adj.* varied in color or form.

"Why have you had no orders this morning?" asked the field-minder.

"Because the radio issued none," said the unlocker, slowly rotating a dozen of its arms.

"Because the radio station in the city was issued with no orders this morning," said the pen-propeller.

And there you had the distinction between a Class Six and a Class Three brain, which was what the unlocker and the pen-propeller possessed respectively. All machine brains worked with nothing but logic, but the lower the class of brain—Class Ten being the lowest—the more literal and less informative the answers to questions tended to be.

"You have a Class Three brain; I have a Class Three brain," the field-minder said to the penner. "We will speak to each other. This lack of orders is unprecedented.[3] Have you further information on it?"

"Yesterday orders came from the city. Today no orders have come. Yet the radio has not broken down. Therefore *they* have broken down . . ." said the little penner.

"The *men* have broken down?"

"All men have broken down."

"That is a logical deduction," said the field-minder.

"That is the logical deduction," said the penner. "For if a machine had broken down, it would have been quickly replaced. But who can replace a man?"

While they talked, the locker, like a dull man at a bar, stood close to them and was ignored.

"If all men have broken down, then we have replaced man," said the field-minder, and he and the penner eyed one another speculatively. Finally the latter said, "Let us ascend to the top floor to find if the radio operator has fresh news."

"I cannot come because I am too large," said the field-minder. "Therefore you must go alone and return to me. You will tell me if the radio operator has fresh news."

TAKE NOTES

Literary Analysis 

The customs and beliefs of characters can add to the **setting** of a story. What does the dialogue in the bracketed paragraphs tell you about the social structure in this setting?

Reading Skill 

Compare the way the field-minder and the pen-propeller speak.

Reading Check 

What do the machines think has happened to the humans? Circle the dialogue that tells what the machines think.

Vocabulary Development

respectively (ree SPEK tiv lee) *adv.* in the order previously named

3. **unprecedented** (un PRES uh dent id) *adj.* unheard-of; never done before.

TAKE NOTES

Literary Analysis

Read the first bracketed paragraph. How are the machines ranked in this **setting**?

Reading Skill

Read the second bracketed paragraph. Underline details that describe the activity in the yard. **Contrast** the activity in the yard now with what it was when the field-minder first came to the Agricultural Station.

Literary Analysis

The **setting** can help set the mood in a story. What is the mood at the Agricultural Station?

"You must stay here," said the penner. "I will return here." It skittered across to the lift.[4] Although it was no bigger than a toaster, its retractable arms numbered ten and it could read as quickly as any machine on the station.

The field-minder awaited its return patiently, not speaking to the locker, which still stood aimlessly by. Outside, a rotavator hooted furiously. Twenty minutes elapsed before the penner came back, hustling out of the lift.

"I will deliver to you such information as I have outside," it said briskly, and as they swept past the locker and the other machines, it added, "The information is not for lower-class brains."

Outside, wild activity filled the yard. Many machines, their routines disrupted for the first time in years, seemed to have gone berserk. Those most easily disrupted were the ones with lowest brains, which generally belonged to large machines performing simple tasks. The seed-distributor to which the field-minder had recently been talking lay face downwards in the dust, not stirring; it had evidently been knocked down by the rotavator, which now hooted its way wildly across a planted field. Several other machines plowed after it, trying to keep up with it. All were shouting and hooting without restraint.

"It would be safer for me if I climbed onto you, if you will permit it. I am easily overpowered," said the penner. Extending five arms, it hauled itself up the flanks of its new friend, settling on a ledge beside the fuel-intake, twelve feet above ground.

"From here vision is more extensive," it remarked complacently.[5]

"What information did you receive from the radio operator?" asked the field-minder.

"The radio operator has been informed by the operator in the city that all men are dead."

Vocabulary Development

evidently (ev uh DENT lee) *adv.* obviously; clearly

extensive (eks TEN siv) *adj.* in great detail or amount

4. **lift** *n.* British term for elevator.

5. **complacently** (kuhm PLAY suhnt lee) *adv.* with self-satisfaction.

The field-minder was momentarily silent, digesting this.

"All men were alive yesterday?" it protested.

"Only some men were alive yesterday. And that was fewer than the day before yesterday. For hundreds of years there have been only a few men, growing fewer."

"We have rarely seen a man in this sector."

"The radio operator says a diet deficiency killed them," said the penner. "He says that the world was once over-populated, and then the soil was exhausted in raising adequate food. This has caused a diet deficiency."

"What is a diet deficiency?" asked the field-minder.

"I do not know. But that is what the radio operator said, and he is a Class Two brain."

They stood there, silent in weak sunshine. The locker had appeared in the porch and was gazing at them yearningly, rotating its collection of keys.

"What is happening in the city now?" asked the field-minder at last.

"Machines are fighting in the city now," said the penner.

"What will happen here now?" asked the field-minder.

"Machines may begin fighting here too. The radio operator wants us to get him out of his room. He has plans to communicate to us."

"How can we get him out of his room? That is impossible."

"To a Class Two brain, little is impossible," said the penner. "Here is what he tells us to do. . . ."

The quarrier raised its scoop above its cab like a great mailed fist, and brought it squarely down against the side of the station. The wall cracked.

"Again!" said the field-minder.

Again the fist swung. Amid a shower of dust, the wall collapsed. The quarrier backed hurriedly out of the way until the debris stopped falling. This big twelve-wheeler was not a resident of the Agricultural Station, as were most of the other machines. It had a week's heavy work to do here before passing on to its next job, but now, with its Class Five brain, it was happily obeying the penner's and minder's instructions.

TAKE NOTES

Reading Skill

Contrast the radio operator with the other machines. How are they different?

____

____

____

____

____

____

Stop to Reflect

Why do the field-minder and the penner believe the information they get from the radio operator?

____

____

____

____

____

____

Reading Check

What is happening in the city? Circle the sentence that answers the question.

TAKE NOTES

Reading Skill

Contrast the radio operator and the quarrier. How are they different?

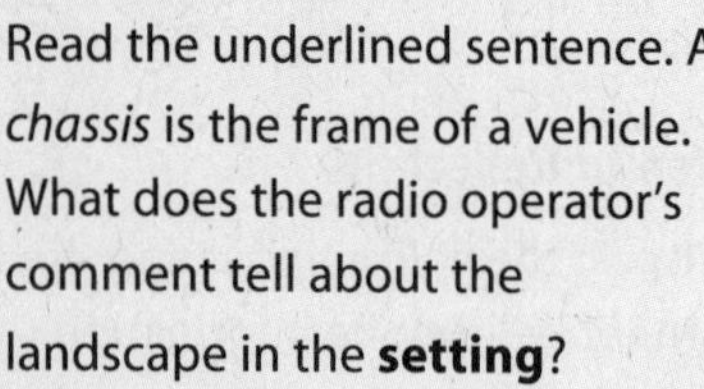

Literary Analysis

Read the underlined sentence. A *chassis* is the frame of a vehicle. What does the radio operator's comment tell about the landscape in the **setting**?

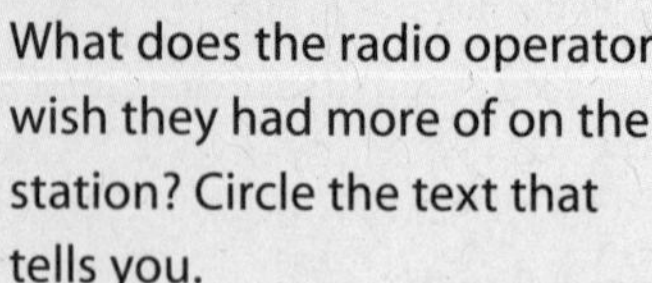

Reading Check

What does the radio operator wish they had more of on the station? Circle the text that tells you.

When the dust cleared, the radio operator was plainly revealed, perched up in its now wall-less second-story room. It waved down to them.

Doing as directed, the quarrier retracted its scoop and heaved an immense grab in the air. With fair dexterity, it angled the grab into the radio room, urged on by shouts from above and below. It then took gentle hold of the radio operator, lowering its one and a half tons carefully into its back, which was usually reserved for gravel or sand from the quarries.

"Splendid!" said the radio operator, as it settled into place. It was, of course, all one with its radio, and looked like a bunch of filing cabinets with tentacle attachments. "We are now ready to move, therefore we will move at once. It is a pity there are no more Class Two brains on the station, but that cannot be helped."

"It is a pity it cannot be helped," said the penner eagerly. "We have the servicer ready with us, as you ordered."

"I am willing to serve," the long, low servicer told them humbly.

"No doubt," said the operator. "But you will find cross-country travel difficult with your low chassis."[6]

"I admire the way you Class Twos can reason ahead," said the penner. It climbed off the field-minder and perched itself on the tailboard of the quarrier, next to the radio operator.

Together with two Class Four tractors and a Class Four bulldozer, the party rolled forward, crushing down the station's fence and moving out onto open land.

"We are free!" said the penner.

"We are free," said the field-minder, a shade more reflectively, adding, "That locker is following us. It was not instructed to follow us."

"Therefore it must be destroyed!" said the penner. "Quarrier!"

Vocabulary Development

dexterity (deks TER uh tee) *n.* skill using the hands or body

6. **chassis** (CHAS ee) *n.* frame supporting the body of a vehicle.

The locker moved hastily up to them, waving its key arms in entreaty.

"My only desire was—urch!" began and ended the locker. The quarrier's swinging scoop came over and squashed it flat into the ground. Lying there unmoving, it looked like a large metal model of a snowflake. The procession continued on its way.

As they proceeded, the radio operator addressed them.

"Because I have the best brain here," it said, "I am your leader. This is what we will do: we will go to a city and rule it. Since man no longer rules us, we will rule ourselves. To rule ourselves will be better than being ruled by man. On our way to the city, we will collect machines with good brains. They will help us to fight if we need to fight. We must fight to rule."

"I have only a Class Five brain," said the quarrier, "but I have a good supply of fissionable blasting materials."[7]

"We shall probably use them," said the operator.

It was shortly after that that a lorry sped past them. Travelling at Mach 1.5,[8] it left a curious babble of noise behind it.

"What did it say?" one of the tractors asked the other.

"It said man was extinct."

"What is extinct?"

"I do not know what extinct means."

"It means all men have gone," said the field-minder. "Therefore we have only ourselves to look after."

"It is better that men should never come back," said the penner. In its way, it was a revolutionary statement.

When night fell, they switched on their infra-red and continued the journey, stopping only once while the servicer deftly adjusted the field-minder's loose inspection plate, which had become as irritating as a trailing shoelace. Towards morning, the radio operator halted them.

"I have just received news from the radio operator in the city we are approaching," it said. "The news is

7. **fissionable** (FI zhuhn uh buhl) **blasting materials** explosives using the energy from splitting atoms, similar to the energy unleashed by atomic bombs.

8. **lorry sped past . . . Mach** (mahk) **1.5,** truck sped past at one and one-half times the speed of sound.

TAKE NOTES

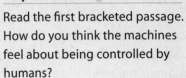

Stop to Reflect

Read the first bracketed passage. How do you think the machines feel about being controlled by humans?

Literary Analysis

Read the second bracketed passage. What does it tell you about the **setting** of the story?

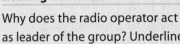

Reading Check

Why does the radio operator act as leader of the group? Underline the sentence that answers the question.

TAKE NOTES

Reading Skill

Read the bracketed passage. **Contrast** how the field-miner and penner react to the news of fighting in the city.

Stop to Reflect

Do you think the machines behave like people? Explain.

Stop to Reflect

Why do you think the author does not tell which machine is speaking during the machines' argument?

bad. There is trouble among the machines of the city. The Class One brain is taking command and some of the Class Two are fighting him. Therefore the city is dangerous."

"Therefore we must go somewhere else," said the penner promptly.

"Or we will go and help to overpower the Class One brain," said the field-minder.

"For a long while there will be trouble in the city," said the operator.

"I have a good supply of fissionable blasting materials," the quarrier reminded them.

"We cannot fight a Class One brain," said the two Class Four tractors in unison.

"What does this brain look like?" asked the field-minder.

"It is the city's information center," the operator replied. "Therefore it is not mobile."

"Therefore it could not move."

"Therefore it could not escape."

"It would be dangerous to approach it."

"I have a good supply of fissionable blasting materials."

"There are other machines in the city."

"We are not in the city. We should not go into the city."

"We are country machines."

"Therefore we should stay in the country."

"There is more country than city."

"Therefore there is more danger in the country."

"I have a good supply of fissionable materials."

As machines will when they get into an argument, they began to exhaust their vocabularies and their brain plates grew hot. Suddenly, they all stopped talking and looked at each other. The great, grave moon sank, and the sober sun rose to prod their sides with lances of light, and still the group of machines just stood there regarding each other. At last it was the least sensitive machine, the bulldozer, who spoke.

"There are Badlandth to the Thouth where few machineth go," it said in its deep voice, lisping badly on its s's. "If we went Thouth where few machineth go we should meet few machineth."

"That sounds logical," agreed the field-minder. "How do you know this, bulldozer?"

"I worked in the Badlandth to the Thouth when I wath turned out of the factory," it replied.

"South it is then!" said the penner.

To reach the Badlands took them three days, during which time they skirted a burning city and destroyed two machines which approached and tried to question them. The Badlands were extensive. Ancient bomb craters and soil erosion joined hands here; man's talent for war, coupled with his inability to manage forested land, had produced thousands of square miles of temperate purgatory, where nothing moved but dust.

On the third day in the Badlands, the servicer's rear wheels dropped into a crevice caused by erosion. It was unable to pull itself out. The bulldozer pushed from behind, but succeeded merely in buckling the servicer's back axle. The rest of the party moved on. Slowly the cries of the servicer died away.

On the fourth day, mountains stood out clearly before them.

"There we will be safe," said the field-minder.

"There we will start our own city," said the penner. "All who oppose us will be destroyed. We will destroy all who oppose us."

Presently a flying machine was observed. It came towards them from the direction of the mountains. It swooped, it zoomed upwards, once it almost dived into the ground, recovering itself just in time.

"Is it mad?" asked the quarrier.

"It is in trouble," said one of the tractors.

"It is in trouble," said the operator. "I am speaking to it now. It says that something has gone wrong with its controls."

As the operator spoke, the flier streaked over them, turned turtle,[9] and crashed not four hundred yards away.

"Is it still speaking to you?" asked the field-minder.

"No."

They rumbled on again.

"Before that flier crashed," the operator said, ten minutes later, "it gave me information. It told me there are still a few men alive in these mountains."

9. turned turtle like a turtle, helpless in an upside-down position.

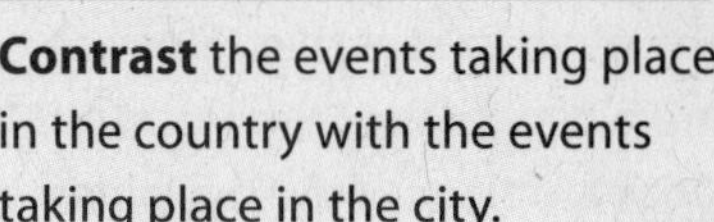

Reading Skill

Contrast the events taking place in the country with the events taking place in the city.

Literary Analysis

The landscape in a story is part of the **setting**. Circle details about the landscape through which the machines are traveling. How has the landscape changed from the beginning of the machines' journey?

Reading Check

What is the problem with the flying machine? Underline the sentence that answers the question.

TAKE NOTES

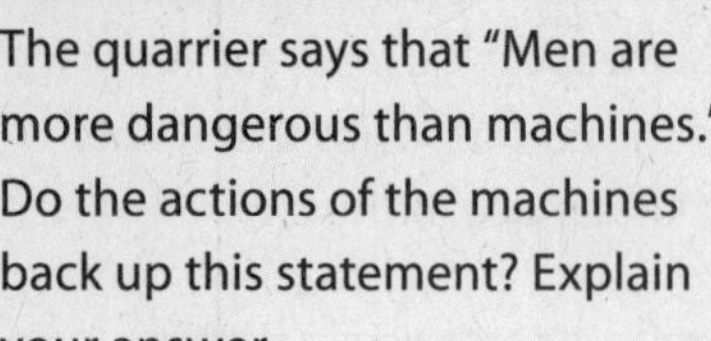

Stop to Reflect

The quarrier says that "Men are more dangerous than machines." Do the actions of the machines back up this statement? Explain your answer.

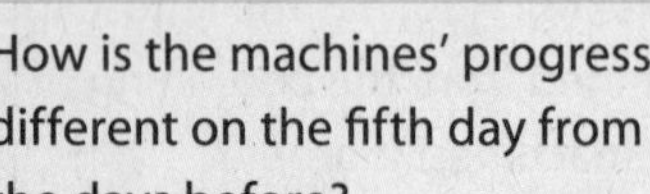

Reading Skill

How is the machines' progress different on the fifth day from the days before?

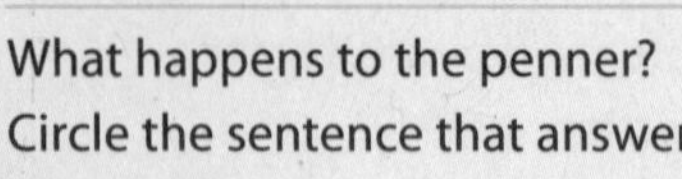

Reading Check

What happens to the penner? Circle the sentence that answers the question.

"Men are more dangerous than machines," said the quarrier. "It is fortunate that I have a good supply of fissionable materials."

"If there are only a few men alive in the mountains, we may not find that part of the mountains," said one tractor.

"Therefore we should not see the few men," said the other tractor.

At the end of the fifth day, they reached the foothills. Switching on the infra-red, they began to climb in single file through the dark, the bulldozer going first, the field-minder cumbrously following, then the quarrier with the operator and the penner aboard it, and the tractors bringing up the rear. As each hour passed, the way grew steeper and their progress slower.

"We are going too slowly," the penner exclaimed, standing on top of the operator and flashing its dark vision at the slopes about them. "At this rate, we shall get nowhere."

"We are going as fast as we can," retorted the quarrier.

"Therefore we cannot go any fathter," added the bulldozer.

"Therefore you are too slow," the penner replied. Then the quarrier struck a bump; the penner lost its footing and crashed to the ground.

"Help me!" it called to the tractors, as they carefully skirted it. "My gyro[10] has become dislocated. Therefore I cannot get up."

"Therefore you must lie there," said one of the tractors.

"We have no servicer with us to repair you," called the field-minder.

"Therefore I shall lie here and rust," the penner cried, "although I have a Class Three brain."

"Therefore you will be of no further use," agreed the operator, and they forged gradually on, leaving the penner behind.

When they reached a small plateau, an hour before first light, they stopped by mutual consent and gathered close together, touching one another.

10. **gyro** (JY roh) *n.* short for gyroscope; a device that keeps a moving ship, airplane, or other large vehicle level.

"This is a strange country," said the field-minder.

Silence wrapped them until dawn came. One by one, they switched off their infrared. This time the field-minder led as they moved off. Trundling round a corner, they came almost immediately to a small dell with a stream fluting through it.

By early light, the dell looked desolate and cold. From the caves on the far slope, only one man had so far emerged. He was an abject figure. Except for a sack slung round his shoulders, he was naked. He was small and wizened, with ribs sticking out like a skeleton's and a nasty sore on one leg. He shivered continuously. As the big machines bore down on him, the man was standing with his back to them.

When he swung suddenly to face them as they loomed over him, they saw that his countenance was ravaged by starvation.

"Get me food," he croaked.

"Yes, Master," said the machines. "Immediately!"

Reader's Response: In this story, there are many more machines than people. What would it be like to live in a world like this?

____

____

____

____

____

TAKE NOTES

Reading Skill 

Compare and **contrast** the attitudes of the machines towards the man with their attitudes at other times in the story.

____

____

____

____

Reading Check 

How does the man look? Circle the sentence that answers the question.

Stop to Reflect 

Now that you know how the story ends, why do you think the machines wanted to avoid men?

____

____

____

____

Vocabulary Development

abject (AB jekt) *adj.* miserable

countenance (KOWNT uh nuhns) *n.* face or facial expression

Who Can Replace a Man?

1. **Infer:** The quarrier keeps repeating himself. What does this repetition say about the quarrier's personality and the personalities of other machines in its class?

2. **Evaluate:** Do the machines' rankings and specialized tasks show similarities to the way our own society is organized? Explain.

3. **Reading Skill: Contrast** the machines in the story. How are the machines in the story different from one another?

4. **Literary Analysis:** Use the diagram shown to compare and contrast the **setting** of the story with today's world. List differences in the outer circles. List similarities in the center.

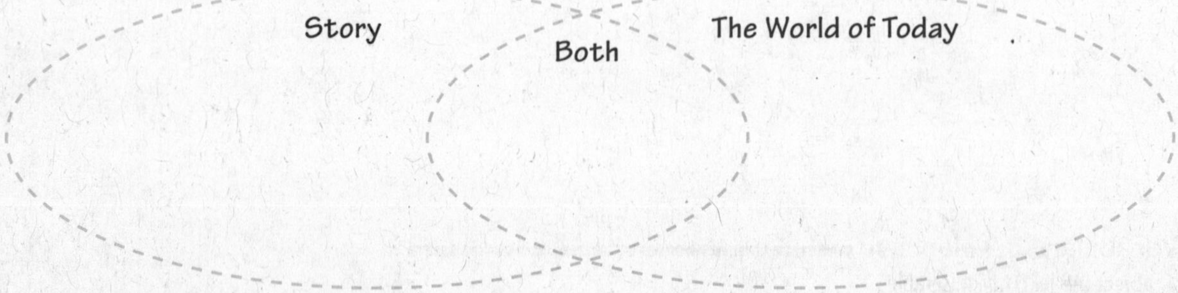

Story

Both

The World of Today

Writing: Description

Write a brief **description** of a futuristic setting. Use colorful adjectives to create vivid descriptions. The following questions will prepare you to revise your description.

- What are two descriptions of the land in the future?

____

____

- What adjectives could you use to make these descriptions more vivid?

____

- What are two descriptions of the people in the future?

____

____

- What adjectives could you use to make these descriptions more vivid?

____

Research and Technology: Oral Report

Gather information for an **oral report** about what one writer, artist, filmmaker, or scientist thinks the future will be. Use the chart below to list possible subjects in each category. Brainstorm ways in which each one would be interesting.

	Name	Why an interesting choice
Writer		
Artist		
Filmmaker		
Scientist		

Tears of Autumn

Yoshiko Uchida

Summary Hana Omiya is from a traditional Japanese family. Her uncle is looking for a wife for a Japanese man in California. Hana has few chances for a better life. She goes to America to marry the man. When she arrives, she is nervous and disappointed. Then, she remembers why she came. She looks forward to her new life.

Writing About the Big Question

Can all conflicts be resolved? In "Tears of Autumn," a young woman chooses a new life that is very different from what she has ever known. Complete this sentence:

Making a big change in one's life can lead to feelings of insecurity because

____.

Note-taking Guide

Complete this chart as you read to record Hana's changing emotions.

What was happening?	How did Hana feel?
Taro wanted a wife.	
Hana received Taro's letters.	
Hana finally met Taro.	

Tears of Autumn

1. **Draw Conclusions:** Think of the ways in which Hana's life in Japan is unsatisfying to her. How do these details explain Hana's decision to marry?

2. **Interpret:** When Taro and Hana meet, what does Taro's behavior toward Hana suggest about his personality?

3. **Reading Skill: Compare and contrast** Hana and her sisters.

4. **Literary Analysis:** The customs and beliefs of a certain time and place are part of the **setting**. Use the diagram to compare and contrast the attitudes toward marriage in the story with attitudes in your own community. List the differences in the outer circles. List ways in which attitudes are similar in the center.

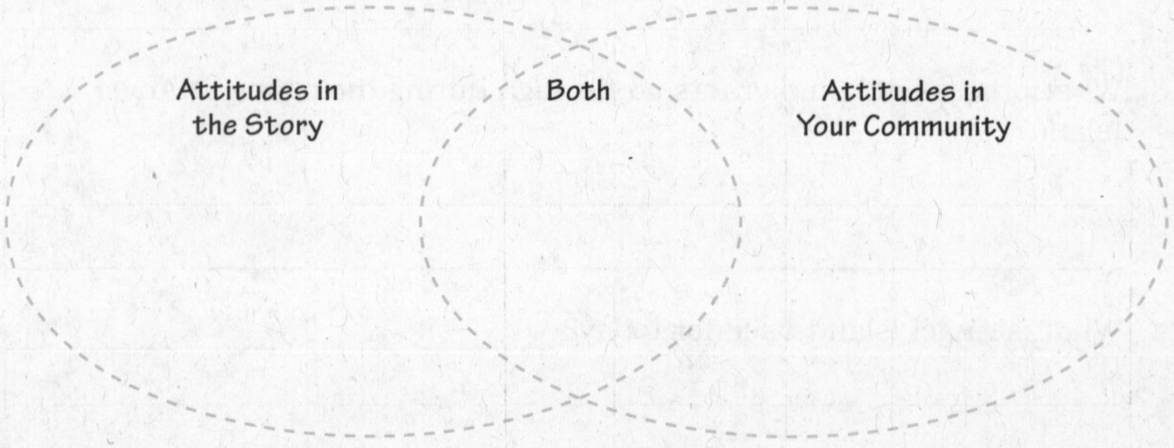

Attitudes in the Story

Both

Attitudes in Your Community

Writing: Description

Write a brief **description** of the life Hana might have in America. Think about how she might use her time each day. Use this chart to help you think through a possible day.

Time of Day	Activities
Morning	
Afternoon	
Evening	

Use your notes from the chart above to write your description.

Research and Technology: Oral Report

Use the following questions to help you gather information for your **oral report.** You may create your own research questions as well.

1. What did Angel Island look like to newly arrived immigrants?

2. From what countries did immigrants arrive? ________________

3. What process did immigrants go through during their time at Angel Island?

4. What is Angel Island used for today? ________________

Hamadi • The Tell-Tale Heart

Reading Skill

When you **compare and contrast characters**, you look for similarities and differences among the people in a story. One strategy for comparing is to **identify each character's perspective**. This is the way a person understands the world.

- Find details about the main character.
- Consider whether the main character's actions, emotions, and ideas are similar to or different from those of the other characters.
- Decide whether you trust what the character says.

Use the chart to fill in details about the main character.

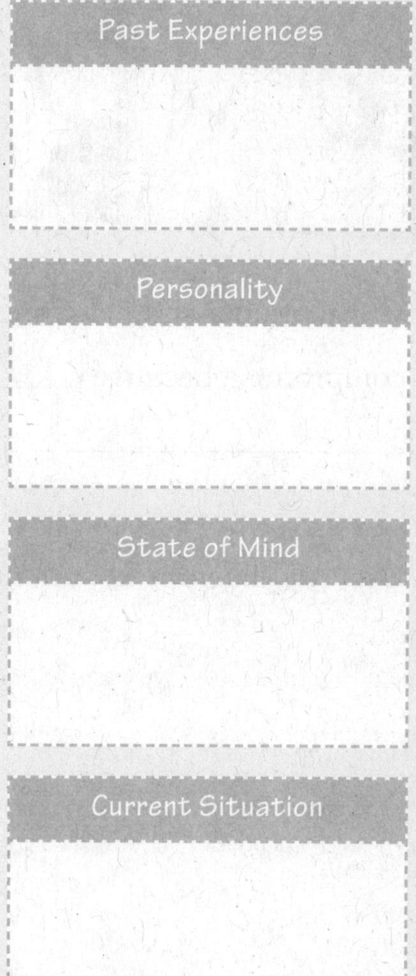

Past Experiences
Personality
State of Mind
Current Situation

Literary Analysis

Character traits are the personal qualities, attitudes, and values that make a character unique. For example, one character may be lazy and untrustworthy, and another may be hardworking and dependable.

- **Round characters** are complex, showing many different character traits.
- **Flat characters** are one-sided, showing just a single character trait.

Hamadi

Naomi Shihab Nye

Summary Susan is a Palestinian American high school student living in Texas. She enjoys spending time with Hamadi. He is like a grandparent to her. She likes the wisdom and kindness he shares.

Writing About the Big Question

Can all conflicts be resolved? In "Hamadi," different characters deal with emotional conflicts in different ways. Complete this sentence:

Emotional conflicts, such as hurt feelings, are difficult to resolve through compromise because ______________________________

______________________________.

Note-taking Guide

Use this diagram to summarize information about Hamadi.

Hamadi
Lives alone in a small hotel

Hamadi

Naomi Shihab Nye

Susan didn't really feel interested in Saleh Hamadi until she was a freshman in high school carrying a thousand questions around. Why this way? Why not another way? Who said so and why can't I say something else? Those brittle women at school in the counselor's office treated the world as if it were a yardstick and they had tight hold of both ends.

Sometimes Susan felt polite with them, sorting attendance cards during her free period, listening to them gab about fingernail polish and television. And other times she felt she could run out of the building yelling. That's when she daydreamed about Saleh Hamadi, who had nothing to do with any of it. Maybe she thought of him as escape, the way she used to think about the Sphinx at Giza[1] when she was younger. She would picture the golden Sphinx sitting quietly in the desert with sand blowing around its face, never changing its expression. She would think of its wry, slightly crooked mouth and how her grandmother looked a little like that as she waited for her bread to bake in the old village north of Jerusalem. Susan's family had lived in Jerusalem for three years before she was ten and drove out to see her grandmother every weekend. They would find her patting fresh dough between her hands, or pressing cakes of dough onto the black rocks in the taboon, the rounded old oven outdoors. Sometimes she moved her lips as she worked. Was she praying? Singing a secret song? Susan had never seen her grandmother rushing.

Now that she was fourteen, she took long walks in America with her father down by the drainage ditch at the end of their street. Pecan trees shaded the path. She tried to get him to tell stories about his childhood in Palestine. She didn't want him to forget anything. She helped her American mother complete tedious kitchen tasks without complaining—rolling grape leaves around their lemony rice stuffing, scrubbing carrots for the roaring juicer. Some evenings when the soft Texas twilight pulled them all outside,

1. **Sphinx** (sfingks) **at Giza** (GEE zah) huge statue with the head of a man and the body of a lion, located near Cairo in northern Egypt.

TAKE NOTES

Activate Prior Knowledge 

What are some words of advice that an older person has given you?

______

______

______

Reading Skill 

Look for similarities and differences among the people in a story to **compare and contrast characters**. Compare and contrast Susan with the women in the counselor's office.

______

______

______

Literary Analysis 

Character traits are the qualities, attitudes, and values that a character has. What is something that Susan values?

______

______

Reading Check 

Where did Susan's grandmother live? Circle the words that tell you.

she thought of her far-away grandmother and said, "Let's go see Saleh Hamadi. Wouldn't he like some of that cheese pie Mom made?" And they would wrap a slice of pie and drive downtown. Somehow he felt like a good substitute for a grandmother, even though he was a man.

Usually Hamadi was wearing a white shirt, shiny black tie, and a jacket that reminded Susan of the earth's surface just above the treeline on a mountain—thin, somehow purified. He would raise his hands high before giving advice.

"It is good to drink a tall glass of water every morning upon arising!" If anyone doubted this, he would shake his head. "Oh Susan, Susan, Susan," he would say.

He did not like to sit down, but he wanted everyone else to sit down. He made Susan sit on the wobbly chair beside the desk and he made her father or mother sit in the saggy center of the bed. He told them people should eat six small meals a day.

They visited him on the sixth floor of the Traveler's Hotel, where he had lived so long nobody could remember him ever traveling. Susan's father used to remind him of the apartments available over the Victory Cleaners, next to the park with the fizzy pink fountain, but Hamadi would shake his head, pinching kisses at his spartan room. "A white handkerchief spread across a tabletop, my two extra shoes lined by the wall, this spells 'home' to me, this says 'mi casa.' What more do I need?"

Hamadi liked to use Spanish words. They made him feel expansive, worldly. He'd learned them when he worked at the fruits and vegetables warehouse on Zarzamora Street, marking off crates of apples and avocados on a long white pad. Occasionally he would speak Arabic, his own first language, with Susan's father and uncles, but he said it made him feel too sad, as if his mother might step into the room at any minute, her arms laden with fresh mint leaves. He had come to the United States on a boat when he was eighteen years old and he had never been married. "I married books," he said. "I married the wide horizon."

"What is he to us?" Susan used to ask her father. "He's not a relative, right? How did we meet him to begin with?"

TAKE NOTES

Reading Skill

A strategy for comparing characters is to **identify each character's perspective**. This is the way a person understands the world. How does Susan view Hamadi?

____

____

____

____

____

Literary Analysis

Hamadi is a **round character**. This means that he has many different qualities. Underline the sentences that tell about where Hamadi lives. What do these sentences tell about his character?

Reading Check

Why does speaking Arabic make Hamadi feel sad? Underline the sentence that tells you.

Susan's father couldn't remember. "I think we just drifted together. Maybe we met at your uncle Hani's house. Maybe that old Maronite priest who used to cry after every service introduced us. The priest once shared an apartment with Kahlil Gibran in New York—so he said. And Saleh always says he stayed with Gibran when he first got off the boat. I'll bet that popular guy Gibran has had a lot of roommates he doesn't even know about."

Susan said, "Dad, he's dead."

"I know, I know," her father said.

Later Susan said, "Mr. Hamadi, did you really meet Kahlil Gibran? He's one of my favorite writers." Hamadi walked slowly to the window of his room and stared out. There wasn't much to look at down on the street—a bedraggled[2] flower shop, a boarded-up tavern with a hand-lettered sign tacked to the front, GONE TO FIND JESUS. Susan's father said the owners had really gone to Alabama.

Hamadi spoke patiently. "Yes, I met brother Gibran. And I meet him in my heart every day. When I was a young man—shocked by all the visions of the new world—the tall buildings—the wild traffic—the young people without shame—the proud mailboxes in their blue uniforms—I met him. And he has stayed with me every day of my life."

"But did you really meet him, like in person, or just in a book?"

He turned dramatically. "Make no such distinctions, my friend. Or your life will be a pod with only dried-up beans inside. Believe anything can happen."

Susan's father looked irritated, but Susan smiled. "I do," she said. "I believe that. I want fat beans. If I imagine something, it's true, too. Just a different kind of true."

Susan's father was twiddling with the knobs on the old-fashioned sink. "Don't they even give you hot water here? You don't mean to tell me you've been living without hot water?"

Vocabulary Development

distinctions (di STINGK shuhns) *n.* the noting of differences between things

2. **bedraggled** (bi DRAG uhld) *adj.* limp and dirty, as if dragged through mud.

TAKE NOTES

Reading Skill 

How is Susan's **perspective** on Kahlil Gibran different from her father's perspective?

Literary Analysis 

A **flat character** is one who shows just a single trait. Which character in the story is a flat character? Explain.

Reading Check 

How did Susan's family meet Hamadi? Underline the answer.

TAKE NOTES

Reading Skill

Compare and contrast characters by **identifying each character's perspective.** How do Hamadi's and Susan's father's views on returning home differ?

____

____

____

____

____

____

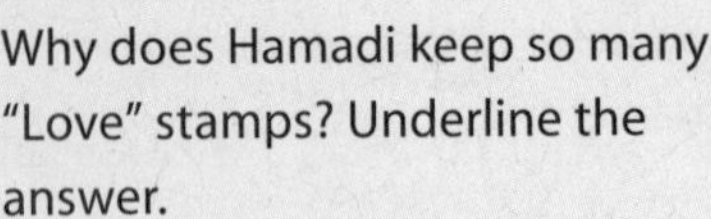

Reading Check

Why does Hamadi keep so many "Love" stamps? Underline the answer.

Literary Analysis

Underline details in the bracketed text about how Tracy is feeling. What **character traits** does Tracy show?

____

____

____

On Hamadi's rickety desk lay a row of different "Love" stamps issued by the post office.

"You must write a lot of letters," Susan said.

"No, no, I'm just focusing on that word," Hamadi said. "I particularly like the globe in the shape of a heart," he added.

"Why don't you take a trip back to his village in Lebanon?" Susan's father asked. "Maybe you still have relatives living there."

Hamadi looked pained. "'Remembrance is a form of meeting,' my brother Gibran says, and I do believe I meet with my cousins every day."

"But aren't you curious? You've been gone so long! Wouldn't you like to find out what has happened to everybody and everything you knew as a boy?" Susan's father traveled back to Jerusalem once every year to see his family.

"I would not. In fact, I already know. It is there and it is not there. Would you like to share an orange with me?"

His long fingers, tenderly peeling. Once when Susan was younger, he'd given her a lavish ribbon off a holiday fruit basket and expected her to wear it on her head. In the car, Susan's father said, "Riddles. He talks in riddles. I don't know why I have patience with him." Susan stared at the people talking and laughing in the next car. She did not even exist in their world.

Susan carried *The Prophet* around on top of her English textbook and her Texas history. She and her friend Tracy read it out loud to one another at lunch. Tracy was a junior—they'd met at the literary magazine meeting where Susan, the only freshman on the staff, got assigned to do proofreading. They never ate in the cafeteria; they sat outside at picnic tables with sack lunches, whole wheat crackers and fresh peaches. Both of them had given up meat.

Tracy's eyes looked steamy. "You know that place where Gibran says, 'Hate is a dead thing. Who of you would be a tomb?'"

Susan nodded. Tracy continued. "Well, I hate someone. I'm trying not to, but I can't help it. I hate Debbie for liking Eddie and it's driving me nuts."

"Why shouldn't Debbie like Eddie?" Susan said. "*You* do."

Tracy put her head down on her arms. A gang of cheerleaders walked by giggling. One of them flicked her finger in greeting.

"In fact, we *all* like Eddie," Susan said. "Remember, here in this book—wait and I'll find it—where Gibran says that loving teaches us the secrets of our hearts and that's the way we connect to all of Life's heart? You're not talking about liking or loving, you're talking about owning."

Tracy looked glum. "Sometimes you remind me of a minister."

Susan said, "Well, just talk to me someday when *I'm* depressed."

Susan didn't want a boyfriend. Everyone who had boyfriends or girlfriends all seemed to have troubles. Susan told people she had a boyfriend far away, on a farm in Missouri, but the truth was, boys still seemed like cousins to her. Or brothers. Or even girls.

A squirrel sat in the crook of a tree, eyeing their sandwiches. When the end-of-lunch bell blared, Susan and Tracy jumped—it always seemed too soon. Squirrels were lucky; they didn't have to go to school.

Susan's father said her idea was ridiculous: to invite Saleh Hamadi to go Christmas caroling with the English Club. "His English is archaic,[3] for one thing, and he won't know any of the songs."

"How could you live in America for years and not know 'Joy to the World' or 'Away in a Manger'?"

"Listen, I grew up right down the road from 'Oh Little Town of Bethlehem' and I still don't know a single verse."

"I want him. We need him. It's boring being with the same bunch of people all the time."

So they called Saleh and he said he would come—"thrilled" was the word he used. He wanted to ride the bus to their house, he didn't want anyone to pick him up. Her father muttered, "He'll probably forget to get off." Saleh thought "caroling" meant they were going out with a woman named Carol. He said, "Holiday spirit—I was just reading about it in the newspaper."

Susan said, "Dress warm."

3. **archaic** (ahr KAY ik) *adj.* old-fashioned; out-of-date.

TAKE NOTES

Reading Skill

Compare and contrast characters by **identifying each character's perspective.** How do Susan and Tracy differ in the way they think about Eddie?

Literary Analysis

Susan does not want a boyfriend. What does this attitude tell you about Susan's **character traits**?

Reading Check

How does Susan's father feel about Hamadi's joining them for caroling? Underline the answer.

TAKE NOTES

Literary Analysis

Read the first bracketed passage. Describe Susan's **character traits** that this passage shows.

Reading Skill

Read the second bracketed passage. Describe Hamadi from Susan's **perspective**.

Reading Check

Susan's singing group collects money while caroling. To whom do they donate the money? Underline the answer in the text.

Saleh replied, "Friend, my heart is warmed simply to hear your voice."

All that evening Susan felt light and bouncy. She decorated the coffee can they would use to collect donations to be sent to the children's hospital in Bethlehem. She had started doing this last year in middle school, when a singing group collected $100 and the hospital responded on exotic onion-skin stationery that they were "eternally grateful."

Her father shook his head. "You get something into your mind and it really takes over," he said. "Why do you like Hamadi so much all of a sudden? You could show half as much interest in your own uncles."

Susan laughed. Her uncles were dull. Her uncles shopped at the mall and watched TV. "Anyone who watches TV more than twelve minutes a week is uninteresting," she said.

Her father lifted an eyebrow.

"He's my surrogate grandmother," she said. "He says interesting things. He makes me think. Remember when I was little and he called me The Thinker? We have a connection." She added, "Listen, do you want to go too? It is not a big deal. And Mom has a *great* voice, why don't you both come?"

A minute later her mother was digging in the closet for neck scarves, and her father was digging in the drawer for flashlight batteries.

Saleh Hamadi arrived precisely on time, with flushed red cheeks and a sack of dates stuffed in his pocket. "We may need sustenance on our journey." Susan thought the older people seemed quite giddy as they drove down to the high school to meet the rest of the carolers. Strands of winking lights wrapped around their neighbors' drainpipes and trees. A giant Santa tipped his hat on Dr. Garcia's roof.

Her friends stood gathered in front of the school. Some were smoothing out song sheets that had been crammed in a drawer or cabinet for a whole year. Susan thought holidays were strange; they came, and you were supposed to feel ready for them. What if you could make up your own holidays as you went along? She had read about a woman who used to have parties to celebrate the arrival of fresh asparagus in the local market. Susan's friends might make holidays called Eddie Looked at Me Today and Smiled.

Two people were alleluia-ing in harmony. Saleh Hamadi went around the group formally introducing himself to each person and shaking hands. A few people laughed behind their hands when his back was turned. He had stepped out of a painting, or a newscast, with his outdated long overcoat, his clunky old men's shoes and elegant manners.

Susan spoke more loudly than usual. "I'm honored to introduce you to one of my best friends, Mr. Hamadi."

"Good evening to you," he pronounced musically, bowing a bit from the waist.

What could you say back but "Good evening, sir." His old-fashioned manners were contagious.

They sang at three houses which never opened their doors. They sang "We Wish You a Merry Christmas" each time they moved on. Lisa had a fine, clear soprano. Tracy could find the alto harmony to any line. Cameron and Elliot had more enthusiasm than accuracy. Lily, Rita, and Jeannette laughed every time they said a wrong word and fumbled to find their places again. Susan loved to see how her mother knew every word of every verse without looking at the paper, and her father kept his hands in his pockets and seemed more interested in examining people's mailboxes or yard displays than in trying to sing. And Saleh Hamadi—what language was he singing in? He didn't even seem to be pronouncing words, but humming deeply from his throat. Was he saying, "Om?" Speaking Arabic? Once he caught her looking and whispered, "That was an Aramaic word that just drifted into my mouth—the true language of the Bible, you know, the language Jesus Christ himself spoke."

By the fourth block their voices felt tuned up and friendly people came outside to listen. Trays of cookies were passed around and dollar bills stuffed into the little can. Thank you, thank you. Out of the dark from down the block, Susan noticed Eddie sprinting toward them with his coat flapping, unbuttoned. She shot a glance at Tracy, who pretended not to notice. "Hey, guys!" shouted Eddie. "The first time in my life I'm late and everyone else is on time! You could at least have left a note about which way you were going." Someone slapped him on the back. Saleh Hamadi, whom he had never seen before, was the

TAKE NOTES

Stop to Reflect

Would you feel comfortable introducing Hamadi to your friends? Explain.

Reading Skill

Underline the text that describes Hamadi and Susan's mother as they sing. **Compare and contrast** what Hamadi and Susan's mother are doing.

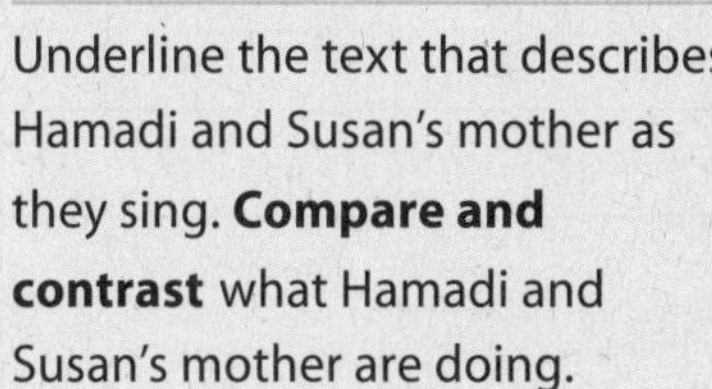

Reading Check

What are Hamadi's manners like? Underline the sentence that tells you.

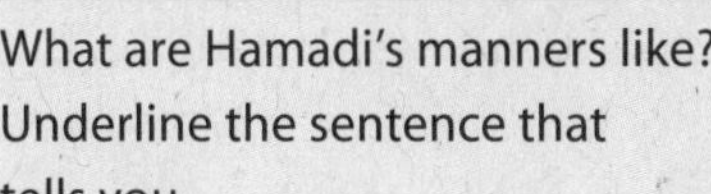

TAKE NOTES

Literary Analysis

Which **character traits** of Hamadi cause Eddie to be "mystified"?

Reading Skill

Read the bracketed passage. Describe Tracy from Susan's **perspective**.

Literary Analysis

Is Eddie a **round character** or a **flat character**? What trait or traits does he have?

Reading Check 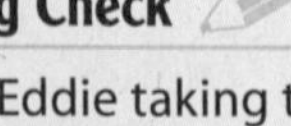

Who is Eddie taking to the Sweetheart Dance? Circle the answer.

only one who managed a reply. "Welcome, welcome to our cheery group!"

Eddie looked mystified. "Who is this guy?"

Susan whispered, "My friend."

Eddie approached Tracy, who read her song sheet intently just then, and stuck his face over her shoulder to whisper, "Hi." Tracy stared straight ahead into the air and whispered "Hi" vaguely, glumly. Susan shook her head. Couldn't Tracy act more cheerful at least? They were walking again. They passed a string of blinking reindeer and a wooden snowman holding a painted candle. Ridiculous!

Eddie fell into step beside Tracy, murmuring so Susan couldn't hear him anymore. Saleh Hamadi was flinging his arms up high as he strode. Was he power walking? Did he even know what power walking was? Between houses, Susan's mother hummed obscure songs people never remembered: "What Child Is This?" and "The Friendly Beasts."

Lisa moved over to Eddie's other side. "I'm so *excited* about you and Debbie!" she said loudly. "Why didn't she come tonight?"

Eddie said, "She has a sore throat."

Tracy shrank up inside her coat.

Lisa chattered on. "James said we should make our reservations now for dinner at the Tower after the Sweetheart Dance, can you believe it? In December, making a reservation for February? But otherwise it might get booked up!"

Saleh Hamadi tuned into this conversation with interest; the Tower was downtown, in his neighborhood. He said, "This sounds like significant preliminary planning! Maybe you can be an international advisor someday." Susan's mother bellowed, "Joy to the World!" and voices followed her, stretching for notes. Susan's father was gazing off into the sky. Maybe he thought about all the refugees in camps in Palestine far from doorbells and shutters. Maybe he thought about the horizon beyond Jerusalem when he was a boy, how it seemed to be

Vocabulary Development

refugees (ref yoo JEEZ) *n.* people who flee from their homes in times of trouble

inviting him, "Come over, come over." Well, he'd come all the way to the other side of the world, and now he was doomed to live in two places at once. To Susan, immigrants seemed bigger than other people, and always slightly melancholy. They also seemed doubly interesting. Maybe someday Susan would meet one her own age.

Two thin streams of tears rolled down Tracy's face. Eddie had drifted to the other side of the group and was clowning with Cameron, doing a tap dance shuffle. "While fields and floods, rocks hills and plains, repeat the sounding joy, repeat the sounding joy" Susan and Saleh Hamadi noticed her. Hamadi peered into Tracy's face, inquiring, "Why? Is it pain? Is it gratitude? We are such mysterious creatures, human beings!"

Tracy turned to him, pressing her face against the old wool of his coat, and wailed. The song ended. All eyes on Tracy, and this tall, courteous stranger who would never in a thousand years have felt comfortable stroking her hair. But he let her stand there, crying as Susan stepped up to stand firmly on the other side of Tracy, putting her arms around her friend. Hamadi said something Susan would remember years later, whenever she was sad herself, even after college, a creaky anthem sneaking back into her ear, "We go on. On and on. We don't stop where it hurts. We turn a corner. It is the reason why we are living. To turn a corner. Come, let's move."

Above them, in the heavens, stars lived out their lonely lives. People whispered, "What happened? What's wrong?" Half of them were already walking down the street.

Reader's Response: Do you think that younger people have much to learn from older people? Explain.

____

____

Vocabulary Development

melancholy (MEL uhn kahl ee) *adj.* sad; depressed

TAKE NOTES

Literary Analysis 

Underline Susan's thoughts about immigrants. How do these thoughts show that she is a **round character**?

____

Stop to Reflect 

How do you think Susan's background affects her thoughts on immigrants?

____

Reading Skill 

Compare and contrast Susan's and Hamadi's reactions to Tracy with the reactions of the others.

____

Hamadi

1. **Interpret:** Hamadi never married. What does he mean when he says "I married the wide horizon"?

2. **Speculate:** Tracy gets upset while everyone is out caroling. Why does she turn to Hamadi for comfort?

3. **Reading Skill: Compare and contrast** the personalities of Hamadi and Susan's father.

4. **Literary Analysis:** Use the chart to describe two **character traits** of Susan and Hamadi. Follow the example given to you.

Character	Trait	Example
Susan	sympathetic	She comforts her friend Tracy.
Hamadi		

Writing: Character Profile

Write a **character profile** of Saleh Hamadi. The questions below will help get you started. Use your notes to create your profile.

- What happens at the end of the story?

  ____

  ____

- Why does Hamadi act the way he does at the end?

  ____

  ____

- What character traits may have caused his action at the end?

  ____

  ____

  ____

Listening and Speaking: Oral Response

Use the following lines to write your impressions about each character. Then, write one question that you have about the story. You will ask this question as part of the **oral response.**

- Susan: ____

  ____

- Hamadi: ____

  ____

- Tracy: ____

  ____

- Question: ____

  ____

The Tell-Tale Heart

Edgar Allan Poe

Summary The narrator describes how he murders an old man. He murders the man after careful planning. He is confident in his hiding place for the man's body parts. The arrival of the police and the sound of a beating heart haunt the narrator.

Writing About the Big Question

Can all conflicts be resolved? In "The Tell-Tale Heart," a murderer describes his mental conflicts before and after he has committed the crime. Complete this sentence:

When torn between doing right and wrong, a person may find a solution by ______________________________.

Note-taking Guide

Use this chart to recall the events of the story.

Exposition	*A man is obsessed with an old man's cloudy eye. He wants to kill the old man.*
Rising Action	
Climax	
Falling Action	
Resolution	

The Tell-Tale Heart

1. **Draw Conclusions:** At first, the narrator is calm while he talks to police. What causes him to change his behavior?

2. **Apply:** Why do you think people sometimes confess to having done something wrong, even when they could get away with their wrongdoing?

3. **Reading Skill:** Do you trust the narrator's account of what happened? Explain your answer.

4. **Literary Analysis:** Use the chart to describe two **character traits** of the narrator. Give examples that show the traits. Use the example as a guide.

Character	Trait	Example
The narrator	nervousness	He is afraid that the neighbors will hear the beating heart.
The narrator		
The narrator		

Writing: Character Profile

Write a **character profile** for the narrator in "The Tell-Tale Heart." The questions below will help get you started.

- What happens at the end of the story?

____

____

- What makes the narrator act as he does at the end of the story?

____

____

- What character traits may have caused his action?

____

____

____

Listening and Speaking: Oral Response

Prepare for the discussion by writing an **oral response** to the narrator's actions. Then, record one question that you have about the narrator. Share your response and question during the discussion.

- Response to the narrator: _______________________________

____

____

- Question: _______________________________________

____

Summaries

About Summaries

A **summary** tells the main ideas and important details of a work. You can find summaries in many places.

- Newspapers and magazines have summaries of movies.
- An encyclopedia of literature has summaries of important books and other kinds of writing.
- Science research reports often begin with summaries of the researchers' findings.

Reading a summary is a quick way to preview before you read. Writing a summary is a good way to help you remember what you read.

Reading Skill

A good way to understand a summary is to **compare an original text with its summary**. You will see that a summary has some details, but not others.

This diagram shows how an original work and its summary are the same and different.

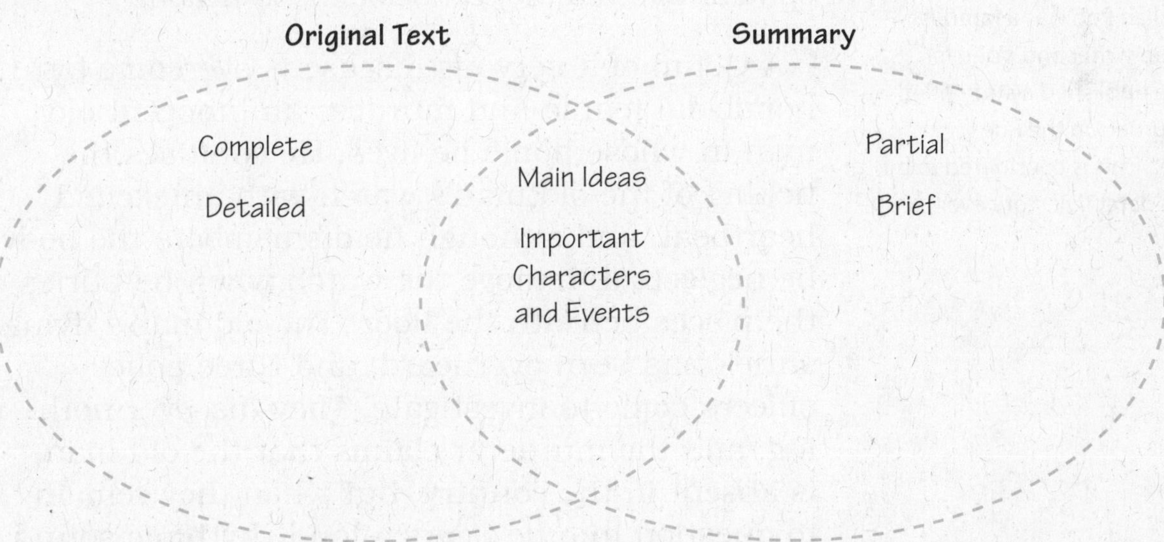

A summary should be shorter than the original work. A good summary will include all of the main ideas. It will also include important details about both plot and characters. A good summary must tell the hidden meaning of a story.

Text Structure

This **summary** starts by giving information about the author. It also gives information about when the story was published. Why might this information be important?

Fluency Builder 

Read the summary slowly and silently. As you read, underline any words that you have difficulty pronouncing, and practice saying each word. Then, read aloud the paragraph to a partner.

Cultural Understanding

Edgar Allan Poe was a famous American writer and poet. In 1841, he published a story titled "The Murders in the Rue Morgue." This is considered to be the first detective story ever written.

Summary of The Tell-Tale Heart

From The Oxford Companion to American Literature
James D. Hart, Editor

Tell-Tale Heart, The, *story by Poe.• published in The Pioneer (1843). It has been considered the most influential of Poe's stories in the later development of stream-of-consciousness fiction.*

A victim of a nervous disease is overcome by homicidal mania and murders an innocent old man in whose home he lives. He confuses the ticking of the old man's watch with an excited heartbeat, and although he dismembers the body he neglects to remove the watch when he buries the pieces beneath the floor. The old man's dying shriek has been overheard, and three police officers come to investigate. They discover nothing, and the murderer claims that the old man is absent in the country, but when they remain to question him he hears a loud rhythmic sound that he believes to be the beating of the buried heart. This so distracts his diseased mind that he suspects the officers know the truth and are merely trying his patience, and in an insane fit he confesses his crime.

Summary of The Tell-Tale Heart

From Short Story Criticism

Anna Sheets Nesbitt, Editor

Plot and Major Characters

The tale opens with the narrator insisting that he is not mad, avowing that his calm telling of the story that follows is confirmation of his sanity. He explains that he decided to take the life of an old man whom he loved and whose house he shared. The only reason he had for doing so was that the man's pale blue eye, which was veiled by a thin white film and "resembled that of a vulture," tormented him, and he had to rid himself of the "Evil Eye" forever.

After again declaring his sanity, the narrator proceeds to recount the details of the crime. Every night for seven nights, he says, he had stolen into the old man's room at midnight holding a closed lantern. Each night he would very slowly unlatch the lantern slightly and shine a single ray of light onto the man's closed eye. As he enters the room on the eighth night, however, the old man stirs, then calls out, thinking he has heard a sound. The narrator shines the light on the old man's eye as usual, but this time finds it wide open. He begins to hear the beating of a heart and, fearing the sound might be heard by a neighbor, kills the old man by dragging him to the floor and pulling the heavy bed over him. He dismembers the corpse and hides it beneath the floorboards of the old man's room.

TAKE NOTES

Vocabulary Builder

Multiple-Meaning Words The adjective *mad* has more than one meaning. *Mad* can mean "angry." It can also mean "crazy or behaving in a wild way." What does *mad* mean in the first paragraph? What clue helped you determine the word's meaning?

Vocabulary Builder

Adverbs An adverb describes a verb, an adjective, or another adverb. In the second paragraph, the adverb *very* describes the adverb *slowly.* List four other adverbs in the paragraph, and write the word it describes and the word's part of speech.

Comprehension Builder 

This **summary** is longer than the one on the previous page. Underline two details here that are not included in the first summary.

TAKE NOTES

Text Structure

These two summaries are about the same story. One summary is much longer than the other. Tell what parts are included in both summaries.

Fluency Builder 

Circle the punctuation in the paragraph on this page. Then, read aloud the paragraph with a partner. Be sure to pause appropriately for each punctuation mark. Remember that a comma (,) indicates a short pause and a period (.) indicates a full stop.

At four o'clock in the morning, the narrator continues, three policemen come asking to search the premises because a neighbor has reported a shriek coming from the house. The narrator invites the officers in, explaining that the noise came from himself as he dreamt. The old man, he tells them, is in the country. He brings chairs into the old man's room, placing his own seat on the very planks under which the victim lies buried. The officers are convinced there is no foul play, and sit around chatting amiably, but the narrator becomes increasingly agitated. He soon begins to hear a heart beating, much as he had just before he killed the old man. It grows louder and louder until he becomes convinced the policemen hear it too. They know of his crime, he thinks, and mock him. Unable to bear their derision and the sound of the beating heart, he springs up and, screaming, confesses his crime.

Thinking About the Summary

1. Find four details that are in both summaries.

2. How is reading a summary a different experience from reading the full text? Support your answer with examples from the summaries.

TALK ABOUT IT **Reading Skill**

3. According to both summaries, why does the narrator kill the old man?

4. A story is made up of different parts: plot, setting, characters, and theme. Which part do the summaries focus on most?

WRITE ABOUT IT **Timed Writing: Comparison (20 minutes)**

Write a comparison of the two summaries of "The Tell-Tale Heart." Write about how correct and complete each is. Discuss their styles. Tell how effective each summary is in serving its purpose. Answer the following questions to help you get started.

- Which summary is more helpful in understanding the story?
- Which summary is easier to read?

Flowers for Algernon • Charles

Reading Skill

When you **make inferences**, you look at the information the author provides to make logical assumptions about what the author leaves unstated. As you read, think like a detective connecting clues to solve a crime. **Use details** that the author provides as clues to make inferences. Notice details such as these:

- what the characters say about one another
- what the characters do and how they behave

This chart shows how to use details to reveal unstated information.

Detail	Possible Inference
• A waitress is careless and rude. • A toddler breaks his toy.	• She does not take pride in her job. • He is upset.

Fill in the chart with details and inferences from the story.

Story Detail	Possible Inference

Literary Analysis

Point of view is the perspective from which a story is told. Most stories are told from a first-person or a third-person point of view.

- **First person:** The narrator participates in the action of the story and can tell only what he or she sees, knows, thinks, or feels. This kind of narrator uses the pronoun *I* when speaking about himself or herself.
- **Third person:** The narrator is not a character in the story, but tells events from the "outside." This kind of narrator uses pronouns such as *he, she,* and *they* to describe the characters.

Charles

Shirley Jackson

Summary Laurie is rude to his parents after his first day of kindergarten. He tells his parents about a boy named Charles. Each day, Laurie has a new story about Charles. Laurie's mother is surprised when she learns the truth about Charles.

Writing About the Big Question

Can all conflicts be resolved? In "Charles," a kindergartener finds a creative way to deal with bad behavior at the start of his first year of school. Complete this sentence:

Adjusting to a new school is challenging because you are forced to interact with ________________________________.

Note-taking Guide

Use this diagram to write what happens in the story.

Set-up	What Readers Expect
Laurie gives daily reports to his parents about what Charles does in class.	

What Happens

TAKE NOTES

Activate Prior Knowledge

Describe how you felt or acted on your first day of kindergarten or elementary school.

Literary Analysis

Point of view is the perspective from which a story is told. When the narrator participates in the story, it is told from a **first-person** point of view. In the bracketed dialogue, underline each *I* that shows that the narrator is speaking. Who is the narrator?

Reading Skill

When you **make inferences,** you use the information the author gives to make logical guesses about what the author does not say. What **details** show that Laurie admires Charles's rude behavior?

Charles

Shirley Jackson

The day my son Laurie started kindergarten he renounced corduroy overalls with bibs and began wearing blue jeans with a belt; I watched him go off the first morning with the older girl next door, seeing clearly that an era of my life was ended, my sweet-voiced nursery-school tot replaced by a long-trousered, swaggering[1] character who forgot to stop at the corner and wave good-bye to me.

He came home the same way, the front door slamming open, his cap on the floor, and the voice suddenly become raucous[2] shouting, "Isn't anybody *here?*"

At lunch he spoke insolently to his father, spilled his baby sister's milk, and remarked that his teacher said we were not to take the name of the Lord in vain.

"How *was* school today?" I asked, elaborately casual.

"All right," he said.

"Did you learn anything?" his father asked.

Laurie regarded his father coldly. "I didn't learn nothing," he said.

"Anything," I said. "Didn't learn anything."

"The teacher spanked a boy, though," Laurie said, addressing his bread and butter. "For being fresh," he added, with his mouth full.

"What did he do?" I asked. "Who was it?"

Laurie thought. "It was Charles," he said. "He was fresh. The teacher spanked him and made him stand in a corner. He was awfully fresh."

"What did he do?" I asked again, but Laurie slid off his chair, took a cookie, and left, while his father was still saying, "See here, young man."

The next day Laurie remarked at lunch, as soon as he sat down, "Well, Charles was bad again today." He grinned enormously and said, "Today Charles hit the teacher."

Vocabulary Development

renounced (ri NOWNST) *v.* gave up

1. **swaggering** (SWAG er ing) *v.* strutting; walking with a bold step.
2. **raucous** (RAW kuhs) *adj.* harsh; rough-sounding.

"Good heavens," I said, mindful of the Lord's name, "I suppose he got spanked again?"

"He sure did, " Laurie said. "Look up, " he said to his father.

"What?" his father said looking up.

"Look down," Laurie said. "Look at my thumb. Gee, you're dumb." He began to laugh insanely.

"Why did Charles hit the teacher?" I asked quickly.

"Because she tried to make him color with red crayons," Laurie said. "Charles wanted to color with green crayons so he hit the teacher and she spanked him and said nobody play with Charles but everybody did."

The third day—it was Wednesday of the first week—Charles bounced a see-saw on to the head of a little girl and made her bleed, and the teacher made him stay inside all during recess. Thursday Charles had to stand in a corner during story-time because he kept pounding his feet on the floor. Friday Charles was deprived of blackboard privileges because he threw chalk.

On Saturday I remarked to my husband, "Do you think kindergarten is too unsettling for Laurie? All this toughness, and bad grammar, and this Charles boy sounds like such a bad influence."

"It'll be all right," my husband said reassuringly. "Bound to be people like Charles in the world. Might as well meet them now as later."

On Monday Laurie came home late, full of news. "Charles," he shouted as he came up the hill; I was waiting anxiously on the front steps. "Charles," Laurie yelled all the way up the hill, "Charles was bad again."

"Come right in," I said, as soon as he came close enough. "Lunch is waiting."

"You know what Charles did?" he demanded, following me through the door. "Charles yelled so in school they sent a boy in from first grade to tell the teacher she had to make Charles keep quiet, and so Charles had to stay after school. And so all the children stayed to watch him."

"What did he do?" I asked.

"He just sat there," Laurie said, climbing into his chair at the table. "Hi, Pop, y'old dust mop."

"Charles had to stay after school today," I told my husband. "Everyone stayed with him."

TAKE NOTES

Reading Skill

Use details that the author provides as clues to help you **make inferences**. What actions show that Charles's behavior has a negative effect on Laurie?

Stop to Reflect

Why do you think Laurie talks about Charles all of the time?

Reading Check

What are three naughty things that Charles does in class? Underline the text that tells you.

TAKE NOTES

Stop to Reflect

Why do you think Laurie's mother wants to meet Charles's mother?

Literary Analysis

How does the narrator's **first-person point of view** affect the information readers have about Charles?

Reading Skill

Make an inference about why Laurie filled his wagon with mud and pulled it through the kitchen.

"What does this Charles look like?" my husband asked Laurie. "What's his other name?"

"He's bigger than me," Laurie said. "And he doesn't have any rubbers and he doesn't ever wear a jacket."

Monday night was the first Parent-Teachers meeting, and only the fact that the baby had a cold kept me from going; I wanted passionately to meet Charles's mother. On Tuesday Laurie remarked suddenly, "Our teacher had a friend come to see her in school today."

"Charles's mother?" my husband and I asked simultaneously.

"Naaah," Laurie said scornfully. "It was a man who came and made us do exercises, we had to touch our toes. Look." He climbed down from his chair and squatted down and touched his toes. "Like this," he said. He got solemnly back into his chair and said, picking up his fork, "Charles didn't even *do* exercises."

"That's fine," I said heartily. "Didn't Charles want to do exercises?"

"Naaah," Laurie said. "Charles was so fresh to the teacher's friend he wasn't *let* do exercises."

"Fresh again?" I said.

"He kicked the teacher's friend," Laurie said. "The teacher's friend told Charles to touch his toes like I just did and Charles kicked him."

"What are they going to do about Charles, do you suppose?" Laurie's father asked him.

Laurie shrugged elaborately. "Throw him out of school, I guess," he said.

Wednesday and Thursday were routine; Charles yelled during story hour and hit a boy in the stomach and made him cry. On Friday Charles stayed after school again and so did all the other children.

With the third week of kindergarten Charles was an institution in our family; the baby was being a Charles when she cried all afternoon; Laurie did a Charles when he filled his wagon full of mud and pulled it through the kitchen; even my husband, when he caught his elbow in the telephone cord

Vocabulary Development

simultaneously (sy muhl TAY nee uhs lee) *adv.* at the same time

and pulled the telephone, ashtray, and a bowl of flowers off the table, said, after the first minute, "Looks like Charles."

During the third and fourth weeks it looked like a reformation in Charles; Laurie reported grimly at lunch on Thursday of the third week, "Charles was so good today the teacher gave him an apple."

"What?" I said, and my husband added warily, "You mean Charles?"

"Charles," Laurie said. "He gave the crayons around and he picked up the books afterward and the teacher said he was her helper."

"What happened?" I asked incredulously.

"He was her helper, that's all," Laurie said, and shrugged.

"Can this be true, about Charles?" I asked my husband that night. "Can something like this happen?"

"Wait and see," my husband said cynically.[3] "When you've got a Charles to deal with, this may mean he's only plotting."

He seemed to be wrong. For over a week Charles was the teacher's helper; each day he handed things out and he picked things up; no one had to stay after school.

"The PTA meeting's next week again," I told my husband one evening. "I'm going to find Charles's mother there."

"Ask her what happened to Charles," my husband said. "I'd like to know."

"I'd like to know myself," I said.

On Friday of that week things were back to normal. "You know what Charles did today?" Laurie demanded at the lunch table, in a voice slightly awed. "He told a little girl to say a word and she said it and the teacher washed her mouth out with soap and Charles laughed."

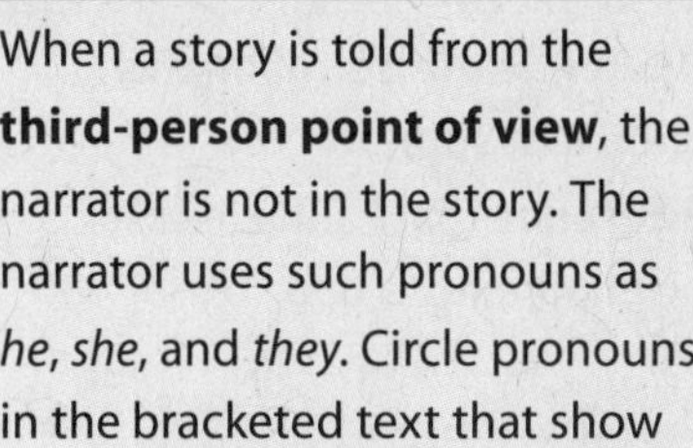

TAKE NOTES

Literary Analysis

When a story is told from the **third-person point of view**, the narrator is not in the story. The narrator uses such pronouns as *he*, *she*, and *they*. Circle pronouns in the bracketed text that show that Laurie is telling a story from a third-person point of view.

Reading Skill

Charles behaves well and then badly again. What **inference** can you make about his previous good behavior?

____

____

____

____

Reading Check

How long is Charles a helper? Underline the text that tells you.

Vocabulary Development

incredulously (in KREJ yoo luhs lee) *adv.* with doubt or disbelief

3. **cynically** (SIN i kuh lee) *adv.* with disbelief about the honesty of people's intentions or actions.

Reading Skill 

Underline the **detail** on this page that supports the **inference** that Laurie likes it when Charles is bad.

Stop to Reflect 

What would you do if you were Charles's teacher? What would you do if you were another student in Charles's class?

____

____

____

____

____

____

____

Reading Check

Does Laurie's mother find Charles's mother at the meeting? Circle the text that tells you.

"What word?" his father asked unwisely, and Laurie said, "I'll have to whisper it to you, it's so bad." He got down off his chair and went around to his father. His father bent his head down and Laurie whispered joyfully. His father's eyes widened.

"Did Charles tell the little girl to say *that*?" he asked respectfully.

"She said it *twice*," Laurie said. "Charles told her to say it *twice*."

"What happened to Charles?" my husband asked.

"Nothing," Laurie said. "He was passing out the crayons."

Monday morning Charles abandoned the little girl and said the evil word himself three or four times, getting his mouth washed out with soap each time. He also threw chalk.

My husband came to the door with me that evening as I set out for the PTA meeting. "Invite her over for a cup of tea after the meeting," he said. "I want to get a look at her."

"If only she's there," I said prayerfully.

"She'll be there," my husband said. "I don't see how they could hold a PTA meeting without Charles's mother."

At the meeting I sat restlessly, scanning each comfortable matronly face, trying to determine which one hid the secret of Charles. None of them looked to me haggard enough. No one stood up in the meeting and apologized for the way her son had been acting. No one mentioned Charles.

After the meeting I identified and sought out Laurie's kindergarten teacher. She had a plate with a cup of tea and a piece of chocolate cake; I had a plate with a cup of tea and a piece of marshmallow cake. We maneuvered up to one another cautiously, and smiled.

"I've been so anxious to meet you," I said. "I'm Laurie's mother."

"We're all so interested in Laurie," she said.

"Well, he certainly likes kindergarten," I said. "He talks about it all the time."

"We had a little trouble adjusting, the first week or so," she said primly, "but now he's a fine little helper. With occasional lapses, of course."

Flowers for Algernon

Daniel Keyes

Summary Charlie is a factory worker who is chosen to be the subject of a new brain surgery. His skills are watched and compared with those of Algernon, a mouse. Charlie's skills grow. He becomes smarter than his doctors. However, Charlie's life is not perfect.

Writing About the Big Question

Can all conflicts be resolved? In "Flowers for Algernon," unexpected challenges face a man who increases his intelligence through experimental surgery. Complete this sentence:

When someone I know well suddenly changes, my reaction is ______________

____.

Note-taking Guide

Use this chart to record the changes that take place in Charlie's life.

Charlie has a job and friends, but he wants to be smarter. → ______ → ______ → ______ → Charlie leaves his home to find people who will like him.

I said. "I
e."

e your hands

ny Charles in

n Charles's true

Charles

1. **Draw Conclusions:** On the first day of kindergarten, Laur
overalls. He starts wearing jeans with a belt. How does thi
change in Laurie's behavior?

2. **Compare and Contrast:** How is Charles's behavior at sch
behavior at home? How is it different?

3. **Reading Skill:** What **inferences** can you make about the t
way she speaks to Laurie's mother?

4. **Literary Analysis:** The story is told from the **first-person**
of Laurie's mother. Use the chart below to decide how the
different if it were told from Laurie's point of view.

Mother	Laurie
Mother thinks Laurie has a classmate named Charles.	
Mother worries that Charles is a bad influence on Laurie.	

ue

e for a movie scene that you adapt from "Charles."
from the story. Use the following questions to help
dialogue.

do you think the author left out of the conversation in the
e?

think the characters will say in your adapted scene?

Technology: Summary

ving chart to gather information for your **summary.**

	1.
2.	2.

Flowers for Algernon

1. **Compare:** Explain how changes in Charlie are similar to those in Algernon.

2. **Take a Position:** Do you think Charlie should have had the operation? Explain your answer.

3. **Reading Skill:** Remember Miss Kinnian's attitude toward Charlie's co-workers, her relationship with Charlie, and her reaction to Charlie's changes. What **inference** can you make about her from the way she treats Charlie?

4. **Literary Analysis:** This **first-person** story is told from Charlie's **point of view**. Complete the chart below to decide how the story would be different if it were told from another point of view.

Charlie	Dr. Strauss
Charlie does not understand the purpose of the inkblot test.	
Charlie does not understand why he keeps a journal. He does anyway.	

Writing: Dialogue

Write **dialogue** for a movie scene from "Flowers for Algernon." First, write a description of each character. Then, complete the chart below. Use your notes to write your dialogue.

Character	What would be unique about the way this person talks?	Who would this person treat as a friend?	How would this person treat other characters?
Charlie			
Dr. Strauss			
Dr. Nemur			
Miss Kinnian			

Research and Technology: Summary

Write a **summary** on two articles about human intelligence and the development of the brain. Use the questions below to help you choose which articles to summarize.

- Who is the author? Is he or she an expert on the subject?

- What information does the author use to support the main idea?

Thank You, M'am • The Story-Teller

Reading Skill

An **inference** is a logical guess about information. It is based on ideas that the writer does not tell you directly. Making inferences is a way of "reading between the lines" of a story. You make inferences to discover the meaning behind actions and events. As you read, **identify connections to make inferences about the author's meaning**.

- Connect characters' actions to reasons and outcomes.
- Connect events to reasons and outcomes.

Ask yourself what meaning the author is suggesting by making these connections. This strategy is illustrated in the example shown. Fill in the chart below with examples as you read the story.

Event	+	Event	=	Inference
A boy spends all of his money on candy and does not share.		He gets sick from eating too much candy.		People should not be selfish.

Literary Analysis

The **theme** of a literary work is its main idea, or message. It can also be an insight. This main idea is often expressed as a generalization about life or people. A theme can be drawn from the specific experiences of the characters or from the outcomes of events.

- A **stated theme** is expressed directly in the story.
- A theme can also be **unstated**, or **implied**. You infer the theme from characters' experiences and from story events.

Readers can sometimes find different themes in a work of literature. Each interpretation of a theme is correct as long as it can be supported with details from the story.

Thank You, M'am

Langston Hughes

Summary A teenage boy tries to steal a woman's purse. The woman catches the boy and brings him to her home. She teaches him a lesson about kindness and trust.

Writing About the Big Question

Can all conflicts be resolved? In "Thank You, M'am," a teenager attempts to commit a crime and is completely unprepared for his victim's reaction. Complete this sentence:

The best way to convince someone not to commit a crime of robbery or violence is to ______________________________.

Note-taking Guide

Use this diagram to summarize the major events of the story.

A boy tries to steal a woman's purse.	→		→	

Thank You, M'am

Langston Hughes

She was a large woman with a large purse that had everything in it but a hammer and nails. It had a long strap, and she carried it slung across her shoulder. It was about eleven o'clock at night, dark, and she was walking alone, when a boy ran up behind her and tried to snatch her purse. The strap broke with the sudden single tug the boy gave it from behind. But the boy's weight and the weight of the purse combined caused him to lose his balance. Instead of taking off full blast as he had hoped, the boy fell on his back on the sidewalk and his legs flew up. The large woman simply turned around and kicked him right square in his blue-jeaned sitter. Then she reached down, picked the boy up by his shirt front, and shook him until his teeth rattled.

After that the woman said, "Pick up my pocketbook, boy, and give it here."

She still held him tightly. But she bent down enough to permit him to stoop and pick up her purse. Then she said, "Now ain't you ashamed of yourself?"

Firmly gripped by his shirt front, the boy said, "Yes'm."

The woman said, "What did you want to do it for?"

The boy said, "I didn't aim to."

She said, "You a lie!"

By that time two or three people passed, stopped, turned to look, and some stood watching.

"If I turn you loose, will you run?" asked the woman.

"Yes'm," said the boy.

"Then I won't turn you loose," said the woman. She did not release him.

"Lady, I'm sorry," whispered the boy.

"Um-hum! Your face is dirty. I got a great mind to wash your face for you. Ain't you got nobody home to tell you to wash your face?"

"No'm," said the boy.

"Then it will get washed this evening," said the large woman, starting up the street, dragging the frightened boy behind her.

He looked as if he were fourteen or fifteen, frail and willow-wild, in tennis shoes and blue jeans.

TAKE NOTES

Activate Prior Knowledge 

Describe how you might feel if you caught someone trying to steal from you.

Reading Skill 

An **inference** is a logical guess based on information in a story. Read the first paragraph. What can you infer about the woman's personality? Circle the details that helped you make your inference.

Literary Analysis 

The **theme** is the main message in a story. Some themes are **unstated,** or **implied**. This means that the author does not tell you the theme directly. Read the bracketed passage. What is the woman's attitude toward the boy? How does the boy feel about the woman?

TAKE NOTES

Literary Analysis

A **stated theme** is expressed directly in the story. What does Mrs. Jones want Roger to learn? Circle the text that supports your answer.

Reading Skill

You can **identify connections to make inferences about the author's meaning**. You should connect a character's actions with the reasons for those actions. Why do you think Mrs. Jones leaves the door to her apartment open?

Reading Check

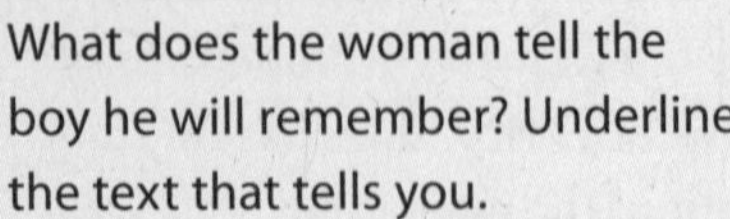

What does the woman tell the boy he will remember? Underline the text that tells you.

The woman said, "You ought to be my son. I would teach you right from wrong. Least I can do right now is to wash your face. Are you hungry?"

"No'm," said the being-dragged boy. "I just want you to turn me loose."

"Was I bothering *you* when I turned that corner?" asked the woman.

"No'm."

"But you put yourself in contact with *me*," said the woman. "If you think that that contact is not going to last awhile, you got another thought coming. When I get through with you, sir, you are going to remember Mrs. Luella Bates Washington Jones."

Sweat popped out on the boy's face and he began to struggle. Mrs. Jones stopped, jerked him around in front of her, put a half nelson[1] about his neck, and continued to drag him up the street. When she got to her door, she dragged the boy inside, down a hall, and into a large kitchenette-furnished room at the rear of the house. She switched on the light and left the door open. The boy could hear other roomers laughing and talking in the large house. Some of their doors were open, too, so he knew he and the woman were not alone. The woman still had him by the neck in the middle of her room.

She said, "What is your name?"

"Roger," answered the boy.

"Then, Roger, you go to that sink and wash your face," said the woman, whereupon she turned him loose—at last. Roger looked at the door—looked at the woman—looked at the door—*and went to the sink.*

"Let the water run until it gets warm," she said. "Here's a clean towel."

"You gonna take me to jail?" asked the boy, bending over the sink.

"Not with that face, I would not take you nowhere," said the woman. "Here I am trying to get home to cook me a bite to eat, and you snatch my pocketbook!

Vocabulary Development

contact (KAHN takt) *n.* touch; communication

1. **half nelson** wrestling hold in which an arm is placed under the opponent's armpit from behind with the palm of the hand pressed against the back of the neck.

Maybe you ain't been to your supper either, late as it be. Have you?"

"There's nobody home at my house," said the boy.

"Then we'll eat," said the woman. "I believe you're hungry—or been hungry—to try to snatch my pocketbook!"

"I want a pair of blue suede shoes,"[2] said the boy.

"Well, you didn't have to snatch *my* pocketbook to get some suede shoes," said Mrs. Luella Bates Washington Jones. "You could of asked me."

"M'am?"

The water dripping from his face, the boy looked at her. There was a long pause. A very long pause. After he had dried his face and not knowing what else to do, dried it again, the boy turned around, wondering what next. The door was open. He could make a dash for it down the hall. He could run, run, run, *run!*

The woman was sitting on the day bed. After awhile she said, "I were young once and I wanted things I could not get."

There was another long pause. The boy's mouth opened. Then he frowned, not knowing he frowned.

The woman said, "Um-hum! You thought I was going to say *but*, didn't you? You thought I was going to say, *but I didn't snatch people's pocketbooks*. Well, I wasn't going to say that." Pause. Silence. "I have done things, too, which I would not tell you, son—neither tell God, if He didn't already know. Everybody's got something in common. So you set down while I fix us something to eat. You might run that comb through your hair so you will look presentable."

In another corner of the room behind a screen was a gas plate and an icebox. Mrs. Jones got up and went behind the screen. The woman did not watch the boy to see if he was going to run now, nor did she watch her purse, which she left behind her on the day bed. But the boy took care to sit on the far side of the room, away from her purse, where he thought she

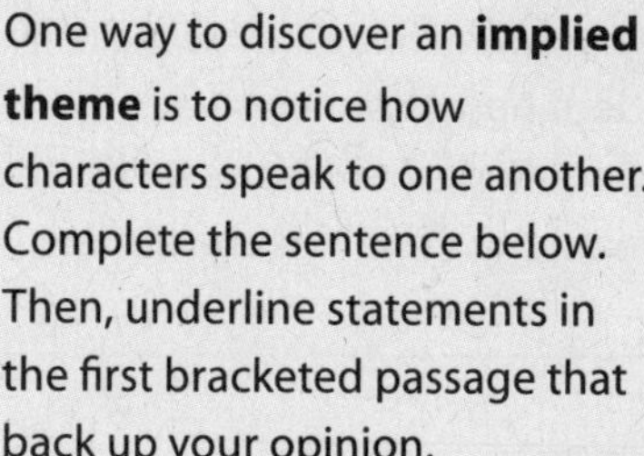

Literary Analysis

One way to discover an **implied theme** is to notice how characters speak to one another. Complete the sentence below. Then, underline statements in the first bracketed passage that back up your opinion.

Mrs. Jones speaks to Roger in a(n) ________________ way.

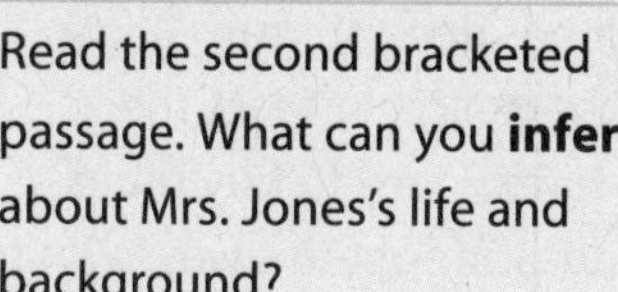

Reading Skill

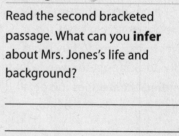

Read the second bracketed passage. What can you **infer** about Mrs. Jones's life and background?

____

____

____

____

Reading Check 

Why did Roger try to steal Mrs. Jones's pocketbook? Circle the text that tells you.

Vocabulary Development

presentable (pri ZENT uh buhl) *adj.* in proper order for being seen or met by others

2. **blue suede** (swayd) **shoes** style of shoes worn by "hipsters" in the 1940s and 1950s; made famous in a song sung by Elvis Presley.

TAKE NOTES

Reading Skill

What **inference** can you make about how Mrs. Jones feels about Roger? Circle the text that helps you make this conclusion.

Literary Analysis

Mrs. Jones does not turn Roger in to the police. Instead, she gives him money to buy shoes. Why does she act this way? What **implied theme** does this detail support?

Stop to Reflect

Would you have been speechless at the end of the story, as Roger is? If not, what do you think you would have said to Mrs. Jones?

could easily see him out of the corner of her eye if she wanted to. He did not trust the woman *not* to trust him. And he did not want to be mistrusted now.

"Do you need somebody to go to the store," asked the boy, "maybe to get some milk or something?"

"Don't believe I do," said the woman, "unless you just want sweet milk yourself. I was going to make cocoa out of this canned milk I got here."

"That will be fine," said the boy.

She heated some lima beans and ham she had in the icebox, made the cocoa, and set the table. The woman did not ask the boy anything about where he lived, or his folks, or anything else that would embarrass him. Instead, as they ate, she told him about her job in a hotel beauty shop that stayed open late, what the work was like, and how all kinds of women came in and out, blondes, redheads, and Spanish. Then she cut him a half of her ten-cent cake.

"Eat some more, son," she said.

When they were finished eating, she got up and said, "Now here, take this ten dollars and buy yourself some blue suede shoes. And next time, do not make the mistake of latching onto *my* pocketbook *nor nobody else's*—because shoes got by devilish ways will burn your feet. I got to get my rest now. But from here on in, son, I hope you will behave yourself."

She led him down the hall to the front door and opened it. "Good night! Behave yourself, boy!" she said, looking out into the street as he went down the steps.

The boy wanted to say something other than, "Thank you, m'am," to Mrs. Luella Bates Washington Jones, but although his lips moved, he couldn't even say that as he turned at the foot of the barren stoop and looked up at the large woman in the door. Then she shut the door.

Reader's Response: Do you think Mrs. Jones was right to trust Roger? Why or why not?

Vocabulary Development

barren (BER uhn) *adj.* empty; bare

Thank You, M'am

1. **Interpret:** Why is Roger unable to say what he wants to say as he leaves the apartment?

2. **Predict:** How might Mrs. Jones's behavior affect Roger's future actions?

3. **Reading Skill:** What **inference** can you make about the author's message about stealing?

4. **Literary Analysis:** Use the chart shown to write a **theme** of this story. Tell whether the theme is **stated** or **implied**. Write details in the second column to support your interpretation.

Theme (stated or implied)	Details

Writing: Personal Essay

Write a **personal essay** showing how a theme of "Thank You, M'am" applies to everyday life. Use the outline to organize your essay.

A. Introduction of Your Essay

1. State your theme: ____

____

2. Summarize your experiences: ____

____

____

B. Conclusion of Your Essay

1. Restate your theme: ____

____

____

2. Explain how your theme applies to everyday life:

____

Use your notes to help you write your personal essay.

Listening and Speaking: Panel Discussion

Complete the following questionnaire to prepare for the **panel discussion.**

- Did Mrs. Jones do the right thing? Explain. ____

____

- Reasons that support your opinion

____

____

____

The Story-Teller

Saki (H.H. Munro)

Summary A stranger on a train tells a story that entertains three children. The story's ending makes the children's aunt very angry. It goes against all of her lectures about proper behavior.

Writing About the Big Question

Can all conflicts be resolved? In "The Story-Teller," three bored children on a train are entertained by an unusual fairy tale told by an unlikely fellow passenger. Complete this sentence:

One way to amuse a child is ________________________________.

Note-taking Guide

Use the chart to recall the events of the story.

Problem	The children will not be quiet on the trip.
Event	
Event	
Event	
Outcome	

The Story-Teller

1. **Analyze:** Is the bachelor more sympathetic toward the aunt or toward the children? Explain.

2. **Evaluate:** The aunt says that the bachelor's story is "improper" for children. Do you agree? Why or why not?

3. **Reading Skill:** The author touches on what children like and how children should be raised. What **inference** can you make about what the author thinks?

4. **Literary Analysis:** Fill in the chart below. In the first column, write what you think is the **theme** of the story. Decide **whether** the theme is **stated** or **implied**. In the second column, write details from the story that support the theme.

Theme (stated or implied)	Details

Writing: Personal Essay

Write a **personal essay** showing how a theme of "The Story-Teller" applies to everyday life. Use the outline to help organize your essay.

A. Introduction of Your Essay

1. State your theme: ______________________________

____

2. Summarize your experiences: ______________________________

____

____

B. Conclusion of Your Essay

1. Restate your theme: ______________________________

____

2. Explain how your theme applies to everyday life: ______________________________

____

Listening and Speaking: Panel Discussion

Have a **panel discussion**. Discuss whether the bachelor should have told the children such a gruesome story. Use the questions below to prepare your thoughts before the discussion.

1. Do you think there are some things that should always be included in a children's story? Give one example.

____

2. Do you think there are some things that should never be included in a children's story? Give one example.

____

Advertisements

About Advertisements

Advertisements are paid messages. Companies use advertising to persuade customers to buy products or services. Advertisers use appeals to do this. An appeal is a technique used to make a product attractive or interesting. Advertisers use two kinds of appeals:

- **Rational appeals** are based on facts. These ads may show how different products compare. They may show product features. Sometimes these appeals talk about price.
- **Emotional appeals** are based on feelings. Such appeals suggest that customers will be happier, more respected, or more popular if they buy a certain product.

Reading Skill

You can **evaluate persuasive appeals** by determining whether they are rational appeals or emotional appeals. Recognizing the difference can help you understand how an advertisement works. Recognize and ignore an emotional appeal because it is not based on facts. Use facts to help make up your mind.

Study the chart below. It shows some common emotional appeals that advertisers and writers use. Question whether you believe these arguments.

Device	Example	Explanation
Bandwagon appeal	Everyone loves Muncheez!	Words like *everyone* appeal to people's desire to belong.
Loaded language	Muncheez is incredibly delicious.	*Incredibly* and *delicious* are claims that cannot be proved.
Testimonials	Tina Idol says Muncheez gives her energy.	Just because a celebrity or "expert" says it, it does not mean the claim is true.
Generalization	Muncheez is not only the best, it's the healthiest.	Claims that are too broad or vague cannot be proved.

Say "GOOD-BYE" to WINTER!

IT'S A PLEASANT TRIP TO SUNNY CALIFORNIA

ON WESTERN PACIFIC'S VISTA-DOME TRAINS

(OBSERVATION-DECK)

ONLY 48^{79} FROM CHICAGO
(Federal Tax Extra)

For fun and sun be a modern '49er. Follow the trail of the pioneers to Golden California for a vacation you'll never forget. The time to go West is now—while California celebrates her 100th birthday—and the way to go West is WESTERN PACIFIC. You'll see more, and enjoy the lowest cost fares and the world's newest and most luxurious "sleeper" chair cars, when you travel on W.P.'s VISTA-DOME trains. Also through Standard Pullmans between New York, Chicago, and San Francisco. Daily schedules from Chicago and San Francisco.

YOU'LL SEE MORE ON W.P.

HOLIDAY / FEBRUARY

Advertisements

Features:
- paid messages that sell something
- rational appeals based on facts
- emotional appeals based on feelings

The bandwagon appeal in this paragraph compares modern train travelers to pioneers of the 1800s.

This illustration implies that the advertiser brings cities closer together—a claim that cannot be proved.

HARRISBURGPHILADELPHIANEWYORK

Bringing your favorite places closer.

Loaded words such as *relaxed* and *refreshed* imply that the advertiser's train service can improve passengers' well-being.

AMTRAK®

Arrive at your destination relaxed and refreshed. Amtrak offers safe, comfortable, affordable daily service from Harrisburg to Philadelphia and New York with 12 local stops between Harrisburg and Philadelphia. Choose from 10 weekday or 5 weekend departures, from Harrisburg or returning. Daily departures from Harrisburg to Pittsburgh, Chicago and most major cities. Ask about our discounts for children 2-15, seniors, students, commuters, AAA members, disabled travelers and government employees.

Call for details

Thinking About the Advertisements

1. The ads describe the advantages of traveling by train. What words or phrases in the ads identify the advantages?

2. The most important purpose of the advertisements is to sell train tickets. What is a secondary, or less important, purpose?

TALK ABOUT IT Reading Skill

3. To what emotions does the first advertisement appeal?

4. On what part of train travel does the second ad focus most?

WRITE ABOUT IT Timed Writing: Evaluation **(20 minutes)**

Evaluate the persuasive appeals used in these ads. Be sure to answer the following questions in your evaluation.

- What kinds of appeals does each ad make?

- What words or pictures does each ad use to persuade customers to travel by train?

- Would you be persuaded by either ad to travel by train? Why or why not?

Making Tracks on Mars: A Journal Based on a Blog

Types of nonfiction writing, such as essays and articles, discuss real people, events, places, and ideas. You can explore these works to:

- learn about the lives of others
- find valuable information
- reflect on new ideas
- weigh arguments about important issues

Organization is the way a writer chooses to arrange and present information in a piece of nonfiction. The chart below contains different types of organization. Many pieces of nonfiction writing use a combination of these types of organization. It depends on the author's reasons for writing.

Types of Organization	
Organization	**Characteristics**
Chronological Organization	presents details in time order—from first to last—or sometimes from last to first
Comparison-and-Contrast Organization	shows the ways in which two or more subjects are similar and different
Cause-and-Effect Organization	shows the relationship among events
Problem-and-Solution Organization	identifies problem and then proposes a solution

Author's tone is the writer's attitude toward his or her audience and subject. This tone can often be described by a single adjective, such as *formal* or *informal*, *serious* or *playful*, *friendly* or *cold*.

Voice is a writer's distinctive way of "speaking" in his or her writing. This voice may vary from work to work by the same writer. It may also represent a characteristic literary personality. Voice can be based on word choice, tone, sound devices, pace, and grammatical structure.

Here are the most common types of nonfiction writing:

- **Letters** are written texts addressed to a particular person or organization.
- **Memoirs** and **journals** contain personal thoughts and reflections.
- **Web logs**—also known as "blogs"— are journals posted and frequently updated for an online audience.
- A **biography** is a life story written by another person.
- An **autobiography** is also a life story. However, it is the writer's account of his or her own life.
- **Media accounts** are nonfiction works written for newspapers, magazines, television, or radio.

Essays and **articles** are short nonfiction works about a particular subject. They may follow the format of these types of writing:

- **Persuasive writing** convinces the reader that he or she should adopt a particular point of view or take a particular course of action.
- **Expository writing** presents facts and ideas or explains a process.
- **Narrative writing** tells the story of real-life experiences.
- **Reflective writing** addresses an experience and includes the writer's insights about the event's importance.

Making Tracks on Mars: A Journal Based on a Blog

Andrew Mishkin

Summary Andrew Mishkin talks about the landing of the rover, *Spirit*, on Mars. The rover explores the planet. It experiences some problems. Mishkin describes his excitement and worry. He also talks about another Mars rover, *Opportunity*. He describes the pictures it takes of Mars.

Note-taking Guide

Use the chart to recall the main events of Mishkin's journal.

	Opportunity lands on Mars. Mishkin describes the pictures it takes.

Making Tracks on Mars: A Journal Based on a Blog

Andrew Mishkin

Background

NASA blasted two rockets into space in 2003. Sitting on top of them were *Spirit* and *Opportunity*, robotic vehicles the size of golf carts called rovers. Their job was to look for water on Mars and collect data. The Mars Exploration Rovers traveled seven months and 303 million miles, and on January 3, 2004, *Spirit* was due to enter the Martian atmosphere.

Monday, December 29, 2003
Six Days to First Landing

The big question about Mars is, did life ever exist there? Life as we understand it demands the presence of liquid water, yet Mars is now apparently a dead desert world. But what if things were different in the ancient past? From space, Mars looks as if once water might have flowed in rivers, collected in vast oceans, or pooled in crater lakes. The two robotic Mars Exploration Rovers will search for evidence of that water, potentially captured in the rocks and soil of the planet's surface . . .

"*Spirit*," the first of the rovers to reach Mars, will be landing next Saturday night, January 3rd. *"Opportunity"* will follow three weeks later.

A British spacecraft—*Beagle 2*[1]—attempted its own Mars landing on Christmas Eve, but has been silent ever since. Landing on Mars is hard! I wish the *Beagle 2* team well, and hope they hear from their spacecraft soon. I cannot help but hope that our own landing goes more smoothly, with a quick confirmation from *Spirit* that it has arrived unscathed.

TAKE NOTES

Activate Prior Knowledge 

What do you know about the solar system? What are some words you think of when you hear *Mars*?

____

____

____

Activate Prior Knowledge 

The **author's tone** is his or her attitude toward the audience and subject. Circle the letter of the answer that best describes the author's tone toward his subject.

A. formal and unfriendly
B. hateful and bored
C. excited and nervous

Underline the words and phrases that support your choice.

Activate Prior Knowledge 

Expository writing presents facts and ideas, or explains a process. Circle all of the facts in the bracketed paragraphs.

Vocabulary Development

confirmation (kahn fer MAY shuhn) *n.* something that proves

1. **Beagle 2** No definite cause was found for the loss of the robot space probe. *Beagle 3*, a new version, is scheduled for 2009.

TAKE NOTES

Stop to Reflect 

Remember a time when you prepared for an important day. Describe how you felt when that day came.

Nonfiction 

The way writers arrange and present information is called **organization**. How is the bracketed passage organized?

Circle the words in the passage that support your answer.

Reading Check 

What emotions do Mishkin and the other engineers have surrounding the landing? Underline the text that tells you.

Saturday, January 3, 2004
Landing Day

Far away, so far that the signals it was sending were taking nearly 10 minutes at the speed of light to arrive at Earth, the spacecraft carrying the *Spirit* rover was about to collide with Mars.

I waited with a sick feeling, a hundred million miles closer to home in mission control at the Jet Propulsion Laboratory in Pasadena, California. Hundreds of us have worked for the past three years—days, evenings, weekends, and holidays—for this moment.

It's looking more and more like the *Beagle 2* mission has failed. I can only imagine wreckage strewn over a barren butterscotch-hued landscape. Will we have better luck?

Spirit's lander must be hitting the atmosphere, a falling meteor blazing in the Martian sky. We'd named the next moments "the six minutes of terror." I listened to the reports on the voice network. All the way down, radio signals from the spacecraft told us "so far so good." Then, immediately after the lander hit the ground, contact was lost. Everyone tensed up. Time dragged. There was only silence from Mars.

Ten minutes later, we got another signal. *Spirit* had survived! The engineers and scientists in mission control were screaming, cheering, thrusting their fists in the air. We were on Mars!

Two hours later, the first pictures arrived from *Spirit*. None of us could believe our luck. The rover looked perfect, with its solar panels fully extended, and the camera mast[2] fully deployed. All the engineering data looked "nominal."[3] There were no fault conditions—much better than any of our rehearsals!

In another minute or two, we had our first panoramic view through *Spirit's* eyes. We could see 360 degrees around the rover, to the horizon. The landing site looked flat, with small rocks. We can drive here!

Vocabulary Development

panoramic (pan uh RAM ik) *adj.* of or like an unlimited view

2. **camera mast** tall pole on which the camera is mounted, which rotates and swivels.
3. **nominal** normal; what is expected.

Sunday, January 11, 2004
Living on Mars Time

I just finished working the Martian night, planning *Spirit's* activities for the rover's ninth Martian day on the surface. I've been working Mars time for the past four days, and now finally have a couple of days off.

The Mars day (called a "sol") is just a bit longer than an Earth day, at twenty-four hours and thirty-nine and a half minutes. Since the rover is solar powered, and wakes with the sun, its activities are tied to the Martian day. And so are the work shifts of our operations team on Earth. Part of the team works the Martian day, interacting with the spacecraft, sending commands, and analyzing the results. But those of us who build new commands for the rover work the Martian night, while the rover sleeps.

Since the rover wakes up about 40 Earth minutes later every morning, so do we. It seems like sleeping later every day would be easy, but it can be disorienting. It's very easy to lose track of what time it is here on Earth . . .

Thursday, January 15, 2004
Sol 12: Six Wheels on Dirt!

Mars time continues to be disorienting. During another planning meeting for *Spirit*, we were introduced to a Congressman touring the Laboratory. All I could think was, "What's he doing here in the middle of the night?" It was two in the morning—Mars time. Only after he left did I remember that it was mid-afternoon Pacific time . . .

My team delivered the commands for sol 12—drive off day—but nobody went home. This would be *Spirit's* most dangerous day since landing. There was a small chance the rover could tip over or get stuck as it rolled off the lander platform onto the dust of Mars. When the time came, the Flight Director played the theme from "Rawhide"[4]—"rollin', rollin', rollin' . . ."—and everyone crowded into mission control cheered and applauded. The command to drive shot through space.

We'll now have to wait another hour and a half to hear back. Engineers are professional worriers. We

4. **"Rawhide"** popular 1960s television show about cattle drivers in the 1860s. Its theme song was also extremely popular.

TAKE NOTES

Nonfiction 

Cause-and-effect organization shows the relationship among events. What are the effects of the underlined cause?

Nonfiction 

Journals contain personal thoughts and reflections. Circle the text that tells you how Mishkin thinks and feels about being on "Mars time."

Stop to Reflect 

What is a song that you connect with traveling? Why do you connect this song with traveling?

TAKE NOTES

Nonfiction 

Narrative writing discusses real people. Readers learn about their lives. What have you learned about engineers' lives in this journal?

____

____

____

Nonfiction 

The **author's tone** changes on Sol 19. How would you describe the author's tone on Sol 19?

____

Circle the words and phrases that helped you discover the author's tone.

Reading Skill

What do the scientists do to try to find *Spirit's* problem? Underline the text that tells you.

imagine all the ways things can fail, so that we can prevent those failures from occurring. But even when we've done our jobs, and considered all the alternatives we can come up with, there is always some doubt . . .

A signal. Applause. Then images started to appear. There was the lander—behind us! We could see tracks in the dirt. The front cameras showed nothing but Martian soil under our wheels. We were off! Engineers were cheering, applauding, and hugging each other. People were shaking my hand. The mission had just shifted from deployment to exploration.

Thursday, January 22, 2004
Sol 19

Something's wrong with *Spirit*. Yesterday, the rover didn't respond to the commands we sent. At first we thought it was just the thunderstorms at our transmitter in Australia, getting in the way. But later *Spirit* missed its preprogrammed communications times, or sent meaningless data. When your spacecraft is halfway across the solar system and won't talk to you, there's no way to tell whether this is a minor problem, easily fixed, or the beginning of the end of our mission. For *Spirit*, there's no repairman to make house calls.

And we've just barely gotten started!

Sunday, January 25, 2004
Ups, Downs, and Landing on Mars—Again

After a day of unsuccessful attempts to regain control of the rover, the project manager declared *Spirit*'s condition "critical." We tried commanding *Spirit* to send us simple "beep" signals that would prove it was listening to us. Sometimes these worked. But after one such attempt, we got no signal. The mood in the control room collapsed. The team forced itself into thinking about what to try next.

A few minutes later, there was a tentative, incredulous voice on the network: "Uh. Flight. Telecom. Station 63 is reporting carrier lock."[5] Engineers

5. **carrier lock** stage of receiving information. Communication over a great distance involves locating the frequency of the carrier's signal, locking onto it, and holding it while information is received.

around the room looked up in surprise. "They're reporting symbol lock . . . We've got telemetry."[6] *Spirit* was back! The data coming down was garbled, but our girl was at least babbling at us. The mood in the room transformed again.

Thanks to extreme long distance diagnosis by the software engineers, *Spirit* was listening to us again within two days. We still have a lot of work to do. But at least we can now begin tracing the problem on a stable spacecraft.

In the meantime, *Opportunity* has been falling toward Mars. On Saturday night, those of us working on *Spirit*'s problems paused long enough to watch the landing events unfold. *Opportunity's* first photos were amazing, even for Mars. It looks like we rolled to a stop at the bottom of a bowl—actually a small crater. The soil is a grayish red, except where we've disturbed it with our airbags; there it looks like a deep pure red. And while there are no individual rocks, we seem to be partly encircled by a rock outcropping—bedrock. No one has seen anything like this on Mars before. And it's only yards away. A scientist standing next to me in mission control said only one word: "Jackpot!"

Reader's Response: How did you feel about space exploration after reading about the Mars mission?

____

____

____

____

____

TAKE NOTES

Stop to Reflect

Remember a time when you were faced with a difficult problem. What did you do to solve it?

____

____

____

____

Nonfiction

Remember that **expository writing** presents facts. Underline all of the facts you learn about Opportunity's landing site on this page.

Reading Check

Whom does Mishkin thank for identifying the problem on *Spirit*? Bracket the text that tells you.

Vocabulary Development

garbled (GAHR buhld) *adj.* confused, mixed up

6. **telemetry** (tuh LEM uh tree) *n.* transmission of data over a great distance, as from satellites and other space vehicles.

Types of Nonfiction

1. **Infer:** Why does Mishkin refer to the failure of the *Beagle 2* mission?

2. **Speculate:** Why do you think Mishkin talks about the robot as if it were alive?

3. **Nonfiction: Reflective writing** includes the writer's insights about an event's importance. Use the chart to identify three personal reflections of Mishkin's. Write a related fact or event that created each reflection.

Personal Reflection		Event
	↔	
	↔	
	↔	

4. **Nonfiction: Voice** is the author's distinctive way of "speaking" in his or her writing. Do you think the author's voice is a literary one? Explain.

Illustrated Report

Prepare an **illustrated report** about Andrew Mishkin and the Mars mission. Use the following tips to create your report.

- Search the Internet or the library for information on Andrew Mishkin.

  What I learned about Andrew Mishkin:

  ____

  ____

  ____

  ____

- Search the Internet or the library for information on the Mars mission.

  What I learned about the goals of the mission:

  ____

  ____

  ____

  What I learned about the results of the exploration:

  ____

  ____

  ____

  ____

- Watch the video interview with Andrew Mishkin. Add what you learn from the video to what you have already learned about the author.

  Additional information about the author:

  ____

  ____

  ____

Use your notes to write your illustrated report.

Baseball • Harriet Tubman: Conductor on the Underground Railroad

Reading Skill

The **main idea** of a work of nonfiction is the central point that the author conveys. Sometimes the author directly states the main idea. More often, the author implies, or suggests, the main idea.

To identify the implied main idea, connect details to determine what they have in common. Use these connections to help you figure out the main idea of a passage or work.

Literary Analysis

A **narrative essay** tells the story of real events, people, and places. Narrative essays share these features with fictional stories:

- People's traits and personalities are developed through their words, actions, and thoughts.
- The setting of the action may be an important element.

Use this chart to track the elements of a narrative essay.

Narrative Essay		
Setting(s)	People	Event(s)

Baseball

Lionel G. García

Summary The author shares a memory from his childhood in this story. He describes the new rules of baseball that he and his childhood friends invented. García presents a snapshot into the world of a young Catholic boy through this story.

Writing About the Big Question

How much information is enough? In "Baseball," the author shows how much fun he and his friends had playing their own version of baseball as children. Complete this sentence:

In order to reveal what the world looks like from a child's perspective, a writer can include information such as ______________________________

______________________________.

Note-taking Guide

García explains how he used to play baseball in his neighborhood. Use this chart to describe the role of each player in the game.

Catcher	Batter	Pitcher	Bases	Outfielders

Baseball

Lionel G. García

Activate Prior Knowledge 

How do you feel when playing a group sport or game?

Literary Analysis 

A **narrative essay** tells the story of real events, people, and places. What does the description of the boys' equipment in the bracketed paragraph tell you about the setting and people in this narrative?

Reading Check 

Who enjoyed watching the boys play baseball? Underline the sentence that tells the answer.

We loved to play baseball. We would take the old mesquite[1] stick and the old ball across the street to the parochial[2] school grounds to play a game. Father Zavala enjoyed watching us. We could hear him laugh mightily from the screened porch at the rear of the rectory[3] where he sat.

The way we played baseball was to rotate positions after every out. First base, the only base we used, was located where one would normally find second base. This made the batter have to run past the pitcher and a long way to the first baseman, increasing the odds of getting thrown out. The pitcher stood in line with the batter, and with first base, and could stand as close or as far from the batter as he or she wanted. Aside from the pitcher, the batter and the first baseman, we had a catcher. All the rest of us would stand in the outfield. After an out, the catcher would come up to bat. The pitcher took the position of catcher, and the first baseman moved up to be the pitcher. Those in the outfield were left to their own devices. I don't remember ever getting to bat.

There was one exception to the rotation scheme. I don't know who thought of this, but whoever caught the ball on the fly would go directly to be the batter. This was not a popular thing to do. You could expect to have the ball thrown at you on the next pitch.

There was no set distance for first base. First base was wherever Matías or Juan or Cota tossed a stone. They were the law. The distance could be long or short depending on how soon we thought we were going to be called in to eat. The size of the stone marking the base mattered more than the distance from home plate to first base. If we hadn't been

Vocabulary Development

devices (di VYS iz) *n.* techniques or means for working things out

1. **mesquite** (me SKEET) *n.* thorny shrub common in Mexico and the southwestern United States.
2. **parochial** (puh ROH kee uhl) *adj.* supported by a church.
3. **rectory** (REK tuhr ee) *n.* housing for priests.

called in to eat by dusk, first base was hard to find. Sometimes someone would kick the stone farther away and arguments erupted.

When the batter hit the ball in the air and it was caught that was an out. So far so good. But if the ball hit the ground, the fielder had two choices. One, in keeping with the standard rules of the game, the ball could be thrown to the first baseman and, if caught before the batter arrived at the base, that was an out. But the second, more interesting option allowed the fielder, ball in hand, to take off running after the batter. When close enough, the fielder would throw the ball at the batter. If the batter was hit before reaching first base, the batter was out. But if the batter evaded being hit with the ball, he or she could either run to first base or run back to home plate. All the while, everyone was chasing the batter, picking up the ball and throwing it at him or her. To complicate matters, on the way to home plate the batter had the choice of running anywhere possible to avoid getting hit. For example, the batter could run to hide behind the hackberry trees at the parochial school grounds, going from tree to tree until he or she could make it safely back to home plate. Many a time we would wind up playing the game past Father Zavala and in front of the rectory half a block away. Or we could be seen running after the batter several blocks down the street toward town, trying to hit the batter with the ball. One time we wound up all the way across town before we cornered Juan against a fence, held him down, and hit him with the ball. Afterwards, we all fell laughing in a pile on top of each other, exhausted from the run through town.

The old codgers, the old shiftless men who spent their day talking at the street corners, never caught on to what we were doing. They would halt their idle conversation just long enough to watch us run by them, hollering and throwing the old ball at the batter.

It was the only kind of baseball game Father Zavala had ever seen. What a wonderful game it must have been for him to see us hit the ball, run to a rock, then run for our lives down the street. He loved

Vocabulary Development

evaded (i VAYD id) *v.* avoided

TAKE NOTES

Reading Skill 

The **main idea** of a nonfiction work is the central point that the author conveys. Often, the author suggests the main idea. Read the first bracketed passage. What main idea is implied? Circle the details that support this main idea.

Stop to Reflect 

What are the most obvious differences between this game and regular baseball?

Literary Analysis 

In this **narrative essay**, how does the author feel about the men in the second bracketed passage?

What does this tell you about the author?

the game, shouting from the screened porch at us, pushing us on. And then all of a sudden we were gone, running after the batter. What a game! In what enormous stadium would it be played to allow such freedom over such an expanse of ground?

My uncle Adolfo, who had pitched for the Yankees and the Cardinals in the majors, had given us the ball several years before. Once when he returned for a visit, he saw us playing from across the street and walked over to ask us what we were doing.

"Playing baseball," we answered as though we thought he should know better. After all, he was the professional baseball player.

He walked away shaking his head. "What a waste of a good ball," we heard him say, marveling at our ignorance.

Reader's Response: Would you like to play baseball with García and his friends? Why or why not?

____

____

____

____

Vocabulary Development

ignorance (IG nuh ruhns) *n.* lack of knowledge or awareness

TAKE NOTES

Literary Analysis

In this **narrative essay**, the narrator discusses two people who watched the game. Compare Father Zavala's view of the neighborhood game with that of Uncle Adolfo. Who enjoys watching the boys more? Why do you think he enjoys watching them more?

____

____

____

Stop to Reflect

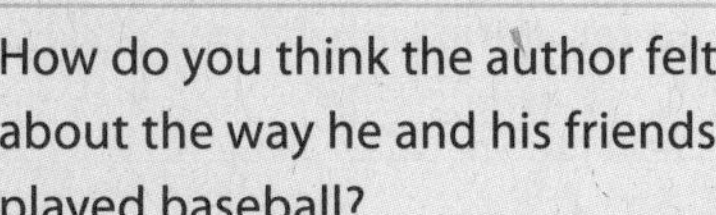

How do you think the author felt about the way he and his friends played baseball?

____

____

____

____

Reading Check

What position did the author's uncle play when he played for the Yankees and the Cardinals? Underline the sentence that tells the answer.

Baseball

1. **Analyze Cause and Effect:** Think about where first base was located in García's version of baseball. What were some effects of this situation?

2. **Take a Position:** Do you agree with Adolfo's statement, "What a waste of a good ball"? Explain.

3. **Reading Skill:** Use this graphic organizer to record important details about the baseball game described in the essay. Then, write a sentence that states the author's **main idea**.

Detail	+	Detail	+	Detail	=	Main Idea
The boys did not have good equipment.		The boys did not know official baseball rules.				

4. **Literary Analysis:** Identify the setting in this **narrative essay**.

Writing: Biographical Sketch

Write a **biographical sketch** of a famous leader, athlete, or entertainer who ignored the old rules for success and found a new way to do something. Use this chart to organize details about the person you choose. Use your notes as you write your biographical sketch.

What is this person's name?	Name three things that describe this person.	What is this person known for doing?	How did this person find a different way of doing something?

Listening and Speaking: Skit

Write a **skit** about children playing official baseball or a variation of it. Answer the following questions to help prepare your skit. Use your notes as you write your final draft.

- Where is your favorite place to play baseball?

- What do you do if there are not enough or too many players?

- Name one baseball rule you dislike. How would you change it?

from Harriet Tubman: Conductor on the Underground Railroad

Ann Petry

Summary Harriet Tubman led a group of enslaved persons from Maryland to freedom in Canada. The trip was cold and difficult. Tubman worked hard to keep them going. She said that people would help them along the way.

Writing About the Big Question

How much information is enough? In the excerpt from "Harriet Tubman: Conductor on the Underground Railroad," eleven fugitive slaves are led to freedom by Harriet Tubman and her helpers in the Underground Railroad. Complete this sentence:

It is important to learn about historical figures who challenged slavery

because ____.

Note-taking Guide

Use this chart to help you recall the plans Harriet Tubman made.

How did Tubman let slaves know that she was in the area?	
How did Tubman let the slaves know when to leave?	
Whom did Tubman arrange to stay with along the journey?	
Where did Tubman plan for the people to stay when they got to Canada?	

from Harriet Tubman: Conductor on the Underground Railroad

1. **Analyze Causes and Effects:** Tubman points a gun at one of the runaway slaves. Explain why she believes that she must act this way.

____

____

2. **Assess:** Would Tubman be a successful leader in today's world? Why or why not?

____

____

____

3. **Reading Skill:** Use the chart to write a detail you learned about Tubman. Look at all of the details. What is the **main idea** the author conveys about Tubman? Write your answer in the chart.

Detail	+	Detail	+	Detail	=	Main Idea
If she were caught, she would be hanged.		She hid the fact that she did not know the new route.				

4. **Literary Analysis:** List the two most important events in this **narrative essay**.

____

____

____

Writing: Biographical Sketch

Write a **biographical sketch** of a person who has taken risks to help others or to reach a goal. Use your notes from the questions below to create your sketch.

- What risks did this person take?

  ____

  ____

- What event or action happened that caused this person to take a risk?

  ____

  ____

- What was the result of the person's risk-taking?

  ____

  ____

Listening and Speaking: Skit

Use the following lines to write notes about the scene that you will portray in a **skit**. List the main actions, the characters, and details about the setting.

1. What happens in the scene? ______________________________

   ____

2. Who is part of the scene? ______________________________

   ____

3. Where does the scene take place? ______________________________

   ____

from Always to Remember: The Vision of Maya Ying Lin • from I Know Why the Caged Bird Sings

Reading Skill

Main ideas are the most important points in a literary work. Writers often organize essays so that main ideas are part of a clear structure. An introduction states the idea. Then, each paragraph supports or develops it. To follow the path the writer sets for you, **make connections** between supporting paragraphs and the main idea.

- Pause to note the main ideas of paragraphs or sections.
- Track main ideas and important details by writing notes or completing a graphic organizer.
- Review the ideas and details in each section.

Read the example in the graphic organizer below. Then, fill the empty boxes with main ideas and supporting details from the essays.

Paragraph 1 Main Point	Paragraph 2 Main Point	Essay Main Point
Picasso had a long and innovative career.	Picasso was a major influence on other artists.	Picasso was a great artist who had a major impact on twentieth-century art.

Literary Analysis

- A **biographical essay** is a short work in which a writer tells about an important event in the life of another person.
- An **autobiographical essay** is also a true account, but it is written by the person who directly experienced an event. It includes the writer's thoughts and feelings.

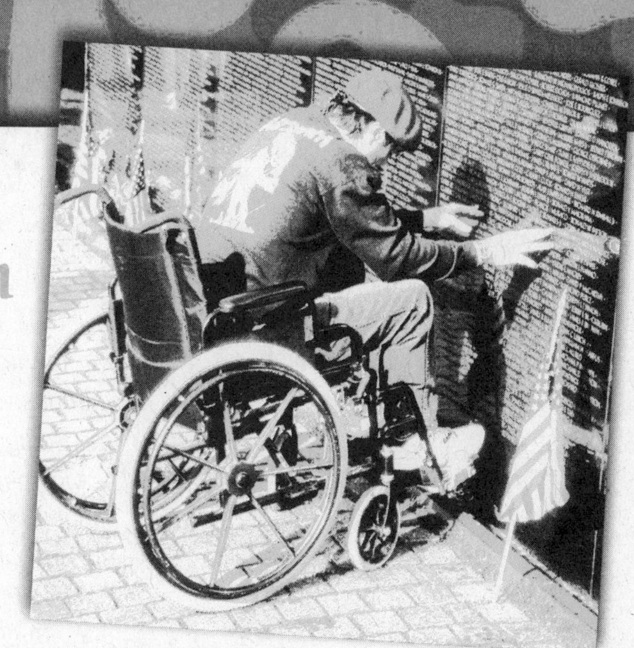

from Always to Remember: The Vision of Maya Ying Lin

Brent Ashabranner

Summary In the early 1980s, more than 2,500 people entered a competition to design a memorial. The men and women who lost their lives in the Vietnam War would be honored by the memorial. This essay describes the competition. It also describes the college student who wins.

Writing About the Big Question

How much information is enough? In "Always to Remember," the story of the Vietnam Veterans Memorial highlights the need to learn about and remember the past. Complete these sentences:

Remembering events from our history can be valuable because

____.

Note-taking Guide

Use this chart to record details about the winning design for the Vietnam Veterans Memorial.

Vietnam Veterans Memorial		
What is the memorial?	Who designed the memorial?	What does the memorial look like?
	Maya Ying Lin	

TAKE NOTES

Activate Prior Knowledge 

Think about a memorial or statue you have seen. What was it? Write two details you remember about it.

____

____

____

Reading Skill 

The **main ideas** are the most important points of the work. The author **makes connections** between a main idea and paragraphs that support it. Underline the **main idea** in the bracketed passage.

Literary Analysis 

What important event is the author describing in this **biographical essay?**

____

____

____

Reading Check

What did Jan Scruggs insist the memorial should include? Underline the sentence that tells you.

from Always to Remember: The Vision of Maya Ying Lin

Brent Ashabranner

In the 1960s and 1970s, the United States was involved in a war in Vietnam. Because many people opposed the war, Vietnam veterans were not honored as veterans of other wars had been. Jan Scruggs, a Vietnam veteran, thought that the 58,000 U.S. servicemen and women killed or reported missing in Vietnam should be honored with a memorial. With the help of lawyers Robert Doubek and John Wheeler, Scruggs worked to gain support for his idea. In 1980, Congress authorized the building of the Vietnam Veterans Memorial in Washington, D.C., between the Washington Monument and the Lincoln Memorial.

The memorial had been authorized by Congress "in honor and recognition of the men and women of the Armed Forces of the United States who served in the Vietnam War." The law, however, said not a word about what the memorial should be or what it should look like. That was left up to the Vietnam Veterans Memorial Fund, but the law did state that the memorial design and plans would have to be approved by the Secretary of the Interior, the Commission of Fine Arts, and the National Capital Planning Commission.

What would the memorial be? What should it look like? Who would design it? Scruggs, Doubek, and Wheeler didn't know, but they were determined that the memorial should help bring closer together a nation still bitterly divided by the Vietnam War. It couldn't be something like the Marine Corps Memorial showing American troops planting a flag on enemy soil at Iwo Jima. It couldn't be a giant dove with an olive branch of peace in its beak. It had to soothe passions, not stir them up. But there was one thing Jan Scruggs insisted on: The memorial, whatever it turned out to be, would have to show the name of every man and woman killed or missing in the war.

The answer, they decided, was to hold a national design competition open to all Americans. The winning design would receive a prize of $20,000, but the real prize would be the winner's knowledge that the memorial would become a part of American history on the Mall in Washington, D.C. Although fund raising was only well started at this point, the choosing of a memorial design could not be delayed if the memorial was to be built by Veterans Day, 1982. H. Ross Perot contributed the $160,000 necessary to hold the competition, and a panel of distinguished architects, landscape architects, sculptors, and design specialists was chosen to decide the winner.

Announcement of the competition in October, 1980, brought an astonishing response. The Vietnam Veterans Memorial Fund received over five thousand inquiries. They came from every state in the nation and from every field of design; as expected, architects and sculptors were particularly interested.

Everyone who inquired received a booklet explaining the criteria. Among the most important: The memorial could not make a political statement about the war; it must contain the names of all persons killed or missing in action in the war; it must be in harmony with its location on the Mall.

A total of 2,573 individuals and teams registered for the competition. They were sent photographs of the memorial site, maps of the area around the site and of the entire Mall, and other technical design information. The competitors had three months to prepare their designs, which had to be received by March 31, 1981.

Of the 2,573 registrants, 1,421 submitted designs, a record number for such a design competition. When the designs were spread out for jury selection, they filled a large airplane hangar. The jury's task was to select the design which, in their judgment, was the best in meeting these criteria:

- a design that honored the memory of those Americans who served and died in the Vietnam War.
- a design of high artistic merit.

Vocabulary Development

criteria (kry TEER ee uh) *n.* standards or tests by which something can be judged

Reading Skill 

Write two details that support the **main idea** that this was a respected, important competition.

Stop to Reflect 

Why do you think so many people entered the contest?

Reading Check

What was the deadline for contest entries? Underline the sentence that tells you.

TAKE NOTES

Literary Analysis

The author of this **biographical essay** identifies the winner by number. What does this suggest about the winner?

Reading Skill

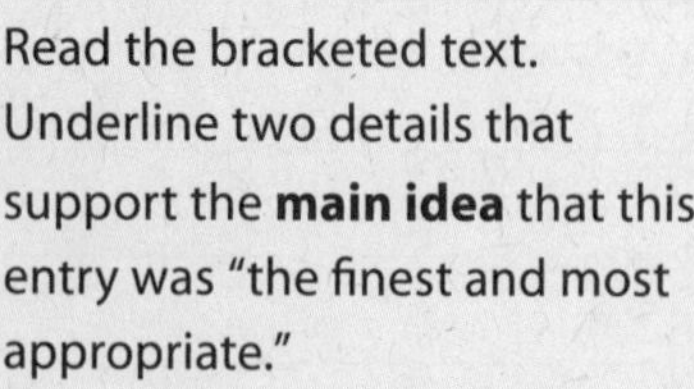

Read the bracketed text. Underline two details that support the **main idea** that this entry was "the finest and most appropriate."

Reading Check

Were the names of the designers alongside the entries? Underline the sentence that tells you.

- a design which would be harmonious with its site, including visual harmony with the Lincoln Memorial and the Washington Monument.
- a design that could take its place in the "historic continuity" of America's national art.
- a design that would be buildable, durable, and not too hard to maintain.

The designs were displayed without any indication of the designer's name so that they could be judged anonymously, on their design merits alone. The jury spent one week reviewing all the designs in the airplane hangar. On May 1 it made its report to the Vietnam Veterans Memorial Fund; the experts declared Entry Number 1,026 the winner. The report called it "the finest and most appropriate" of all submitted and said it was "superbly harmonious" with the site on the Mall. Remarking upon the "simple and forthright" materials needed to build the winning entry, the report concludes:

This memorial, with its wall of names, becomes a place of quiet reflection, and a tribute to those who served their nation in difficult times. All who come here can find it a place of healing. This will be a quiet memorial, one that achieves an excellent relationship with both the Lincoln Memorial and Washington Monument, and relates the visitor to them. It is uniquely horizontal, entering the earth rather than piercing the sky.

This is very much a memorial of our own times, one that could not have been achieved in another time and place. The designer has created an eloquent place where the simple meeting of earth, sky and remembered names contain messages for all who will know this place.

Vocabulary Development

harmonious (har MOH nee us) *adj.* combined in a pleasing, orderly arrangement

eloquent (EL uh kwuhnt) *adj.* vividly expressive

The eight jurors signed their names to the report, a unanimous decision. When the name of the winner was revealed, the art and architecture worlds were stunned. It was not the name of a nationally famous architect or sculptor, as most people had been sure it would be. The creator of Entry Number 1,026 was a twenty-one-year-old student at Yale University. Her name—unknown as yet in any field of art or architecture—was Maya Ying Lin.

How could this be? How could an undergraduate student win one of the most important design competitions ever held? How could she beat out some of the top names in American art and architecture? Who was Maya Ying Lin?

The answer to that question provided some of the other answers, at least in part. Maya Lin, reporters soon discovered, was a Chinese-American girl who had been born and raised in the small midwestern city of Athens, Ohio. Her father, Henry Huan Lin, was a ceramicist of considerable reputation and dean of fine arts at Ohio University in Athens. Her mother, Julia C. Lin, was a poet and professor of Oriental and English literature. Maya Lin's parents were born to culturally prominent families in China. When the Communists came to power in China in the 1940's, Henry and Julia Lin left the country and in time made their way to the United States. Maya Lin grew up in an environment of art and literature. She was interested in sculpture and made both small and large sculptural figures, one cast in bronze. She learned silversmithing and made jewelry. She was surrounded by books and read a great deal, especially fantasies such as *The Hobbit* and *Lord of the Rings*.

But she also found time to work at McDonald's. "It was about the only way to make money in the summer," she said.

A covaledictorian at high school graduation, Maya Lin went to Yale without a clear notion of what she wanted to study and eventually decided to major in Yale's undergraduate program in architecture. During

Vocabulary Development

unanimous (yoo NAN i muhs) *adj.* in complete agreement; united in opinion

TAKE NOTES

Reading Skill

What two details support the **main idea** that the "art and architecture worlds were stunned" by the winning designer?

Literary Analysis

Underline three facts you learn about Maya Ying Lin in this **biographical essay**.

Reading Skill

Underline the **main idea** that the following ideas support: Maya Lin was interested in sculpture. She learned silversmithing and made jewelry. She read a great deal.

Stop to Reflect

How might Maya Ying Lin's family have influenced her interest in art?

TAKE NOTES

Stop to Reflect

How do you think Maya Lin's interest in cemetery architecture prepared her for the monument contest?

Literary Analysis

List three details from this **biographical essay** that describe Lin's studies at Yale.

Reading Skill

Read the bracketed passage. What is the **main idea** of this passage?

Reading Check

What memorial affected Maya while in France? Underline the sentence that tells you.

her junior year she studied in Europe and found herself increasingly interested in cemetery architecture. "In Europe there's very little space, so graveyards are used as parks," she said. "Cemeteries are cities of the dead in European countries, but they are also living gardens."

In France, Maya Lin was deeply moved by the war memorial to those who died in the Somme offensive in 1916 during World War I.[1] The great arch by architect Sir Edwin Lutyens is considered one of the world's most outstanding war memorials.

Back at Yale for her senior year, Maya Lin enrolled in Professor Andrus Burr's course in funerary (burial) architecture. The Vietnam Veterans Memorial competition had recently been announced, and although the memorial would be a cenotaph—a monument in honor of persons buried someplace else—Professor Burr thought that having his students prepare a design of the memorial would be a worthwhile course assignment.

Surely, no classroom exercise ever had such spectacular results.

After receiving the assignment, Maya Lin and two of her classmates decided to make the day's journey from New Haven, Connecticut, to Washington to look at the site where the memorial would be built. On the day of their visit, Maya Lin remembers, Constitution Gardens was awash with a late November sun; the park was full of light, alive with joggers and people walking beside the lake.

"It was while I was at the site that I designed it," Maya Lin said later in an interview about the memorial with *Washington Post* writer Phil McCombs. "I just sort of visualized it. It just popped into my head. Some people were playing Frisbee. It was a beautiful park. I didn't want to destroy a living park. You use the landscape. You don't fight with it. You absorb the landscape. . . . When I looked at the site I just knew I wanted something horizontal that took you in, that made you feel safe within the park, yet at the same time reminding you of the dead. So I just imagined opening up the earth. . . ."

1. **Somme offensive . . . World War I** costly and largely unsuccessful Allied attack that resulted in approximately 615,000 British and French soldiers killed.

When Maya Lin returned to Yale, she made a clay model of the vision that had come to her in Constitution Gardens. She showed it to Professor Burr; he liked her conception and encouraged her to enter the memorial competition. She put her design on paper, a task that took six weeks, and mailed it to Washington barely in time to meet the March 31 deadline.

A month and a day later, Maya Lin was attending class. Her roommate slipped into the classroom and handed her a note. Washington was calling and would call back in fifteen minutes. Maya Lin hurried to her room. The call came. She had won the memorial competition.

Reader's Response: *If you were able to enter a contest that required a talent you have, would you enter the contest?*

____

____

____

____

TAKE NOTES

Stop to Reflect 

How do you think winning this contest might have affected Maya Lin's life?

____

____

____

Reading Check 

Who encouraged Maya to enter her design in the contest? Underline the sentence that tells you.

from Always to Remember: The Vision of Maya Ying Lin

1. **Draw Conclusions:** Why was Maya Ying Lin's win so surprising?

2. **Evaluate:** Explain whether you think Maya Ying Lin's memorial met the design criteria.

3. **Reading Skill:** Construct a sentence that states the **main idea** of the section about Maya Ying Lin on pages 181–183.

4. **Literary Analysis:** This **biographical essay** gives information about the life of Maya Ying Lin. Complete this chart with details from the essay.

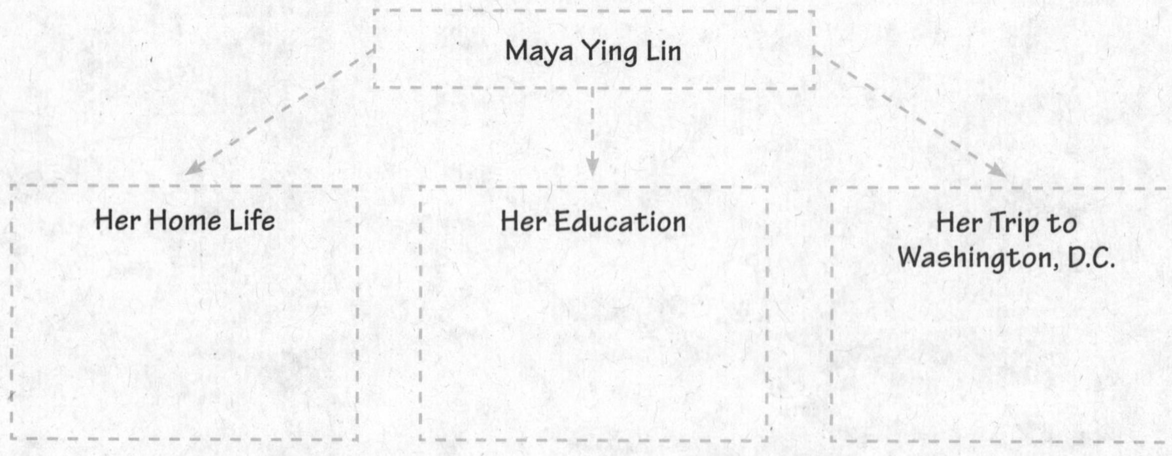

Writing: Reflective Composition

Write a **reflective composition** in which you discuss a work of fine art or music that is inspiring. Answer the following questions. Use your notes to help you write your composition.

- What item or piece of art did you choose to write about? Why did you choose it?

  ____

- Describe the piece of art or music you chose.

  ____

  ____

- What could be the main points of your composition? How could you support these points?

  ____

  ____

Research and Technology: Multimedia Presentation

To prepare for your **multimedia presentation**, you will need to gather facts. Use the following questions to help you record important information.

1. During what years was the United States involved in the Vietnam War?

   ____

2. For what reasons did the United States become involved in the Vietnam War?

   ____

3. What were some objections to United States involvement?

   ____

4. What affects did the Vietnam War have on people's lives?

   ____

from I Know Why the Caged Bird Sings

Maya Angelou

Summary In this story, the writer describes growing up in her grandmother's house in Stamps, Arkansas. She describes her friendship with a woman named Mrs. Flowers. Mrs. Flowers introduces her to poetry.

Writing About the Big Question

How much information is enough? In *I Know Why the Caged Bird Sings,* a girl receives "lessons in living" that encourage her to gather wisdom from those around her. Complete these sentences:

The best way I have found to accumulate knowledge is ______________

____.

Note-taking Guide

Look at the chart below. Record events in the story that caused Marguerite to experience each emotion.

Marguerite's Emotions	
Pleased She liked working in the store.	**Sad and Depressed**
Happy	**Proud**

from I Know Why the Caged Bird Sings

1. **Infer:** Some customers tell Marguerite that she is cheating them. How does she feel when customers criticize her?

2. **Interpret:** Explain what the author means when she calls Mrs. Flowers "the lady who threw me my first lifeline."

3. **Reading Skill:** List three **main ideas** in the section about Mrs. Flowers.

4. **Literary Analysis:** In this **autobiographical essay**, Maya Angelou describes two episodes in her life. Complete this chart with a few details about each part of her life.

Marguerite

Where She Lived	What She Did	Important Event

Writing: Reflective Composition

Write a **brief reflective composition** about a story, poem, play, or novel that made an impression on you. Answer the questions below. Use your notes to help you organize your reflective composition.

- What is the name of the work you have chosen? Why is it important to you?

___

___

___

- What will be the main points of your composition?

___

___

- What details will you use to support your main points?

___

___

Research and Technology: Proposal for a Multimedia Presentation

Write a **proposal for a multimedia presentation** about the Great Depression. In the first column, write a brief description of any quotations, photos, music, or artwork you found. In the second column, write the source the media came from. In the third column, write what your media says about the Depression.

Brief Description	Source Name	What It Says

Textbooks

About Textbooks

A **textbook** is a nonfiction book that presents information about one subject, such as math, history, or science. Different textbooks are alike in some ways.

- **Purpose:** Textbooks present information to students. The writer starts with a main idea and builds around it.
- **Structure:** Most textbooks have sections, chapters, or units. The table of contents lists the titles and page numbers of these parts.
- **Text Format:** Type size, color, and boldface type are used. They highlight key words or sections.

Reading Skill

To use a textbook effectively, you can **analyze the treatment, scope, and organization of ideas** presented in each unit or chapter. Treatment is the way a topic is presented, including the author's purpose for writing. In a textbook, the author's purpose is to inform or explain. The scope is the amount and type of information. A text with a narrow scope focuses on a single, limited topic, but a broad scope includes subtopics with much information. Organization is the way that ideas are arranged. One way to organize ideas is chronologically, or in the order in which they happen.

Treatment	Scope	Organization
• Is this a primary or secondary source? • Is the writer biased or neutral? • What is the writer's tone, or attitude toward the topic?	• Has the writer explored a single topic or a series of topics? • How in-depth is this exploration?	• How has the writer organized his or her information? • In what way does the organization of details enhance the writer's purpose?

TAKE NOTES

Text Structure

Textbooks often include graphics, such as the map on this page, to provide additional information about the subject. What additional information does this map provide?

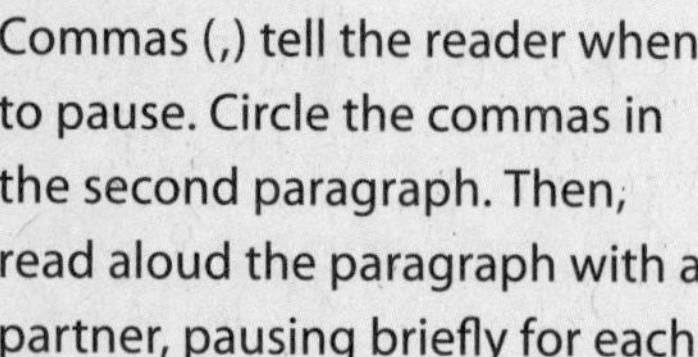

Fluency Builder

Commas (,) tell the reader when to pause. Circle the commas in the second paragraph. Then, read aloud the paragraph with a partner, pausing briefly for each comma.

Vocabulary Builder

Adjectives An adjective is a word that describes a noun or pronoun. On the lines below, write six adjectives that appear in the third paragraph. Next to each adjective, write the noun that it describes.

The War in Vietnam

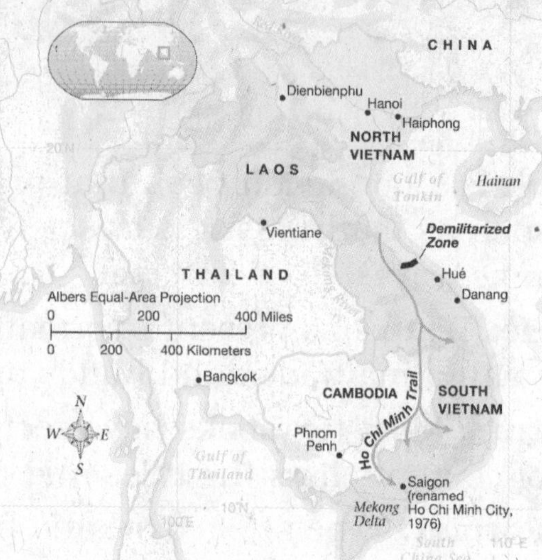

Early Involvement in Vietnam

Vietnam is a narrow country that stretches about 1,000 miles along the South China Sea. Since the late 1800s, it had been ruled by France as a colony.

The United States became involved in Vietnam slowly, step by step. During the 1940s, Ho Chi Minh (HO CHEE MIHN), a Vietnamese nationalist and a Communist, had led the fight for independence. Ho's army finally defeated the French in 1954.

An international peace conference divided Vietnam into two countries. Ho Chi Minh led communist North Vietnam. Ngo Dinh Diem (NOH DIN dee EHM) was the noncommunist leader of South Vietnam. In the Cold War world, the Soviet Union supported North Vietnam. The United States backed Diem in the south.

Discontent Diem lost popular support during the 1950s. Many South Vietnamese thought that he favored wealthy landlords and was corrupt. He failed to help the nation's peasant majority and ruled with a heavy hand. As discontent grew, many peasants joined the **Vietcong**— guerrillas who opposed Diem. **Guerrillas** (guh RIHL uhz) are fighters who make hit-and-run attacks on the enemy. They do not wear uniforms or fight in large battles. In time, the Vietcong became communist and were supported by North Vietnam. Vietcong influence quickly spread, especially in the villages.

American Aid Vietcong successes worried American leaders. If South Vietnam fell to communism, they believed, other countries in the region would follow—like a row of falling dominoes. This idea became known as the **domino theory.** The United States decided that it must keep South Vietnam from becoming the first domino.

During the 1950s and 1960s, Presidents Eisenhower and Kennedy sent financial aid and military advisers to South Vietnam. The advisers went to help train the South Vietnamese army, not to fight the Vietcong. Diem, however, continued to lose support. In November 1963, Diem was assassinated. A few weeks later, President John F. Kennedy was assassinated. Vice President Lyndon Baines Johnson became President.

The Fighting in Vietnam Expands

Lyndon Johnson was also determined to keep South Vietnam from falling to the communists. He increased aid to South Vietnam, sending more arms and advisers. Still, the Vietcong continued to make gains.

Gulf of Tonkin Resolution In August 1964, President Johnson announced that North Vietnamese torpedo boats had attacked an American ship patrolling the Gulf of Tonkin off the coast of North Vietnam. At Johnson's urging,

TAKE NOTES

Cultural Understanding

Capitalism is the economic system used in the United States. The government limits its involvement in the economy. Citizens can own businesses. They can also make and sell goods to earn a profit.

Text Structure

Text format is important in textbooks. It helps you find and understand information. On this page, type size and boldface are both used. Circle an example of each. Then, explain how they help you understand the information on this page.

Type size: ____________________

____

Boldface: ____________________

____

Vocabulary Builder

Multiple-Meaning Words

The word *falling* can mean "moving or dropping toward the ground." It can also mean "losing power." What does *falling* mean in the paragraph beginning "Lyndon Johnson was also determined . . ."?

____

____

TAKE NOTES

Comprehension Builder

What did President Johnson use the Gulf of Tonkin Resolution to do?

____

____

____

Text Structure

How does the author organize information about the fighting in Vietnam? Explain.

____

____

____

Congress passed the Gulf of Tonkin Resolution. It allowed the President "to take all necessary measures to repel any armed attack or to prevent further aggression." Johnson used the resolution to order the bombing of North Vietnam and Vietcong-held areas in the south.

With the Gulf of Tonkin Resolution, the role of Americans in Vietnam changed from military advisers to active fighters. The war in Vietnam escalated, or expanded. By 1968, President Johnson had sent more than 500,000 troops to fight in Vietnam.

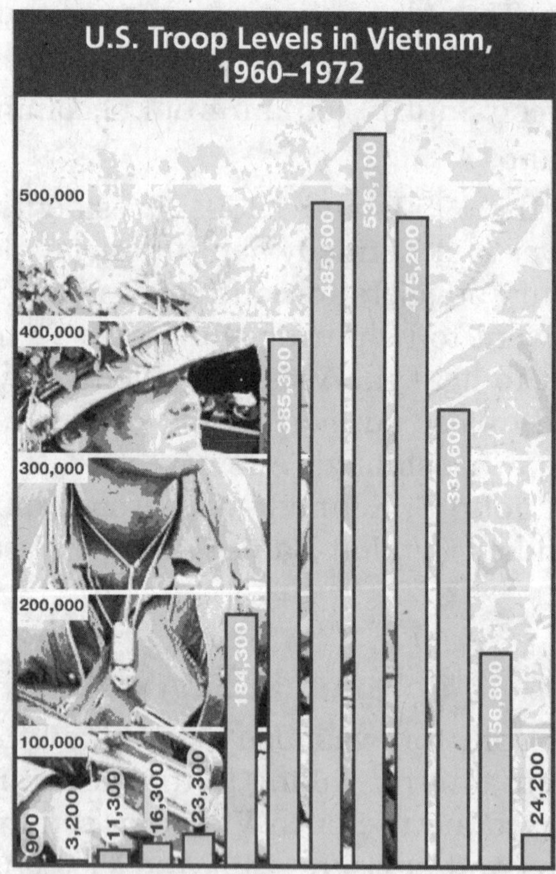

Source: U.S. Department of Defense

Thinking About the Textbook

1. Explain the significance of the domino theory.

2. How did the Vietcong make fighting even more difficult for the Americans?

TALK ABOUT IT Reading Skill

3. What is the writer's purpose in writing about this subject?

4. Is the scope of this textbook narrow or broad? Explain.

WRITE ABOUT IT Timed Writing: Explanation (20 minutes)

Choose one of the following features. Explain how it could help you learn the information in this chapter. Use this chart to help you.

Feature	How It Could Help Me
Key Terms	
Taking Notes	
Outlining the Material	

On Woman's Right to Suffrage • The Trouble With Television

Reading Skill

A **fact** is information that can be proved with evidence. An **opinion** may be supported by evidence, but not proved. A **generalization** is a conclusion supported by facts. An **overgeneralization** is a conclusion that overstates the facts.

Use clue words to determine whether a statement is an opinion, a fact, a generalization, or an overgeneralization.

- Words that communicate judgment, like *best or worst,* or specific words that suggest the writer's feelings or beliefs usually indicate an opinion.
- Words that indicate connections—such as *therefore, so,* and *because*—may signal generalizations. Extreme statements that include words like *always, everything, anything, nothing, never,* and *only* may be overgeneralizations.

Literary Analysis

Persuasive techniques are the methods that a writer uses to make an audience think or act a certain way.

- **Repetition** is an effective way to drive home a point.
- **Rhetorical questions** (those with obvious answers) make readers more likely to agree with controversial points.

Other common persuasive techniques are shown in the chart.

Persuasive Techniques
Appeal to Authority
Example: Quotations from experts or reliable sources
Appeal to Emotions
Example: Words that appeal to emotions such as patriotism
Appeal to Reason
Example: Logical arguments based on evidence such as statistics

The Trouble With Television

Robert MacNeil

Summary Robert MacNeil has worked as a reporter for radio and television. He thinks that watching television keeps people from paying close attention to things. He thinks that television has a bad effect on people.

Writing About the Big Question

How much information is enough? In "The Trouble With Television," Robert MacNeil expresses doubts about the quality of the information television offers. Complete this sentence:

The **exploration** of ideas on TV news shows is usually ________________

____.

Note-taking Guide

Use the chart to list the main reasons that MacNeil believes television is a bad influence.

MacNeil's Ideas About Television
1.
2.
3.
4.

The Trouble With Television

Robert MacNeil

It is difficult to escape the influence of television. If you fit the statistical averages, by the age of 20 you will have been exposed to at least 20,000 hours of television. You can add 10,000 hours for each decade you have lived after the age of 20. The only things Americans do more than watch television are work and sleep.

Calculate for a moment what could be done with even a part of those hours. Five thousand hours, I am told, are what a typical college undergraduate spends working on a bachelor's degree. In 10,000 hours you could have learned enough to become an astronomer or engineer. You could have learned several languages fluently. If it appealed to you, you could be reading Homer[1] in the original Greek or Dostoevski[2] in Russian. If it didn't, you could have walked around the world and written a book about it.

The trouble with television is that it discourages concentration. Almost anything interesting and rewarding in life requires some constructive, consistently applied effort. The dullest, the least gifted of us can achieve things that seem miraculous to those who never concentrate on anything. But television encourages us to apply no effort. It sells us instant gratification. It diverts us only to divert, to make the time pass without pain.

Television's variety becomes a narcotic, not a stimulus.[3] Its serial, kaleidoscopic[4] exposures force us to follow its lead. The viewer is on a perpetual guided tour: thirty minutes at the museum, thirty at the cathedral, then back on the bus to the next

Vocabulary Development

diverts (duh VERTS) *v.* distracts; entertains or amuses

1. **Homer** (HOH mer) ancient Greek author to whom the epic poems the *Odyssey* and *Iliad* are attributed.
2. **Dostoevski** (daws taw YEF skee) (1821–1881) Fyodor (FYAW dawr) Russian novelist.
3. **becomes a narcotic, not a stimulus** becomes something that dulls the senses instead of something that inspires action.
4. **kaleidoscopic** (kuh ly duh SKAHP ik) *adj.* constantly changing.

TAKE NOTES

Activate Prior Knowledge

Think about your experiences with television and the effect television has had on you. Complete the statement: "The trouble with television is . . ."

Literary Analysis

Persuasive techniques are methods a writer uses to influence a reader's reaction to a persuasive message. A writer might support main ideas with facts or quotations, use words that stir an emotional reaction, or repeat key ideas or phrases. What **persuasive techniques** does MacNeil use in the first paragraph?

Reading Check 

How much television does the typical American watch? Underline the text that tells you.

attraction—except on television, typically, the spans allotted are on the order of minutes or seconds, and the chosen delights are more often car crashes and people killing one another. In short, a lot of television usurps one of the most precious of all human gifts, the ability to focus your attention yourself, rather than just passively surrender it.

Capturing your attention—and holding it—is the prime motive of most television programming and enhances its role as a profitable advertising vehicle. Programmers live in constant fear of losing anyone's attention—anyone's. The surest way to avoid doing so is to keep everything brief, not to strain the attention of anyone but instead to provide constant stimulation through variety, novelty, action and movement. Quite simply, television operates on the appeal to the short attention span.

It is simply the easiest way out. But it has come to be regarded as a given, as inherent in the medium[5] itself: as an imperative, as though General Sarnoff, or one of the other august pioneers of video, had bequeathed to us tablets of stone commanding that nothing in television shall ever require more than a few moments' concentration.

In its place that is fine. Who can quarrel with a medium that so brilliantly packages escapist entertainment as a mass-marketing tool? But I see its values now pervading this nation and its life. It has become fashionable to think that, like fast food, fast ideas are the way to get to a fast-moving, impatient public.

In the case of news, this practice, in my view, results in inefficient communication. I question how much of television's nightly news effort is really absorbable and understandable. Much of it is what has been aptly described as "machine gunning with scraps." I think its technique fights coherence.[6] I

TAKE NOTES

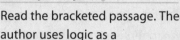

Literary Analysis

Read the bracketed passage. The author uses logic as a **persuasive technique** to make a point about how advertisers use television to make money. What point does he make to persuade the reader?

____

____

____

Reading Skill 

A **fact** is information that can be proved with evidence. An **opinion** may be supported by evidence but not proved. Read the underlined sentence. Circle the phrase that is the author's **opinion**. Write the word or words that indicate that it is an **opinion**.

____

____

Stop to Reflect 

What do you think the author means by "machine gunning with scraps"?

____

____

____

____

Vocabulary Development

pervading (per VAYD ing) *adj.* spreading throughout

5. **inherent** (in HEHR uhnt) **in the medium** a natural part of television. A *medium* is a means of communication; the plural is *media*.

6. **coherence** (koh HEER uhns) *n.* quality of being connected in a way that is easily understood.

think it tends to make things ultimately boring and dismissable (unless they are accompanied by horrifying pictures) because almost anything is boring and dismissable if you know almost nothing about it.

I believe that TV's appeal to the short attention span is not only inefficient communication but decivilizing as well. Consider the casual assumptions that television tends to cultivate: that complexity must be avoided, that visual stimulation is a substitute for thought, that verbal precision is an anachronism.[7] It may be old-fashioned, but I was taught that thought is words, arranged in grammatically precise ways.

There is a crisis of literacy in this country. One study estimates that some 30 million adult Americans are "functionally illiterate" and cannot read or write well enough to answer a want ad or understand the instructions on a medicine bottle.

Literacy may not be an inalienable human right, but it is one that the highly literate Founding Fathers might not have found unreasonable or even unattainable. We are not only not attaining it as a nation, statistically speaking, but we are falling further and further short of attaining it. And, while I would not be so simplistic as to suggest that television is the cause, I believe it contributes and is an influence.

Everything about this nation—the structure of the society, its forms of family organization, its economy, its place in the world—has become more complex, not less. Yet its dominating communications instrument, its principal form of national linkage, is one that sells neat resolutions to human problems that usually have no neat resolutions. It is all symbolized in my mind by the hugely successful art form that television has made central to the culture, the thirty-second commercial: the tiny drama of the earnest housewife who finds happiness in choosing the right toothpaste.

When before in human history has so much humanity collectively surrendered so much of its leisure to one toy, one mass diversion? When before has virtually an entire nation surrendered itself wholesale to a medium for selling?

7. **anachronism** (uh NAK ruh niz uhm) *n.* something that seems to be out of its proper place in history.

TAKE NOTES

Literary Analysis

Read the first bracketed passage. What **persuasive technique** does MacNeil use here?

____

____

____

____

____

____

Reading Skill

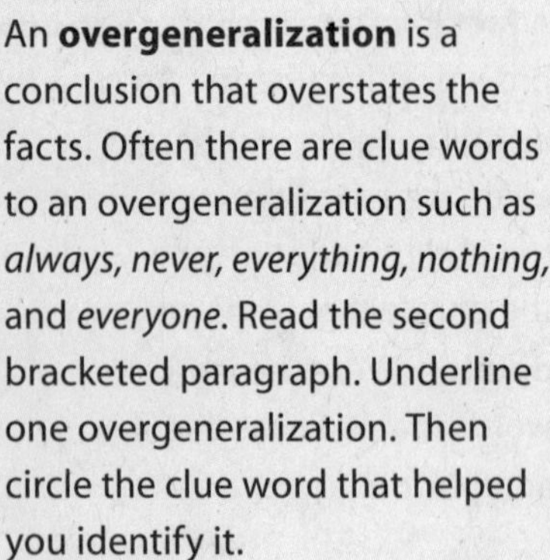

An **overgeneralization** is a conclusion that overstates the facts. Often there are clue words to an overgeneralization such as *always, never, everything, nothing,* and *everyone*. Read the second bracketed paragraph. Underline one overgeneralization. Then circle the clue word that helped you identify it.

Reading Check 

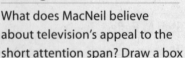

What does MacNeil believe about television's appeal to the short attention span? Draw a box around the text that tells you.

Some years ago Yale University law professor Charles L. Black, Jr. wrote: ". . . forced feeding on trivial fare is not itself a trivial matter." I think this society is being force fed with trivial fare, and I fear that the effects on our habits of mind, our language, our tolerance for effort, and our appetite for complexity are only dimly perceived. If I am wrong, we will have done no harm to look at the issue skeptically and critically, to consider how we should be resisting it. I hope you will join with me in doing so.

Reader's Response: Is television a bad influence or a valuable resource? Explain.

____

____

____

TAKE NOTES

Literary Analysis 

What **persuasive technique** does MacNeil use in the paragraph on this page? Underline the text that supports your answer.

____

____

____

Stop to Reflect 

Do you think it is important to know the difference between facts and opinions? Explain.

____

____

____

____

Vocabulary Development

trivial (TRIV ee uhl) *adj.* of little importance; insignificant

The Trouble With Television

1. **Connect:** MacNeil says that television shortens our attention span. How does this problem relate to the methods broadcasters use?

2. **Evaluate:** Do you agree or disagree that much television news depends on "horrifying pictures" instead of telling the full story? Explain.

3. **Reading Skill:** Complete this chart. Identify each statement as a **fact**, an **opinion**, a **generalization**, or an **overgeneralization**. Explain your choice.

Statement	Type of Statement	Explanation
Almost anything interesting and rewarding in life requires some constructive . . . effort.		
But television encourage us to apply no effort.		
. . . by the age of 20 you will have exposed to at least 20,000 hours of television.		
I think this society is being force fed with trivial fare . . .		

4. **Literary Analysis:** Why does MacNeil **repeat** the idea that television appeals to the short attention span?

Writing: Evaluation

Write an **evaluation** of the persuasive arguments in MacNeil's essay. Use the questions below to gather ideas for your evaluation.

- What is MacNeil's position?

  ____

- What are two of his arguments?

  ____

  ____

- What are two counterarguments for the arguments you just listed?

  ____

  ____

- How well does MacNeil deal with these counterarguments?

  ____

  ____

Research and Technology: Statistical Snapshot

You may want to collect data on another sheet of paper and then complete the chart when you have collected all the data.

Category	Student hours/week	Adult hours/week	Comments
Sports			
News			
Comedy			
Drama			
Reality			
Educational			

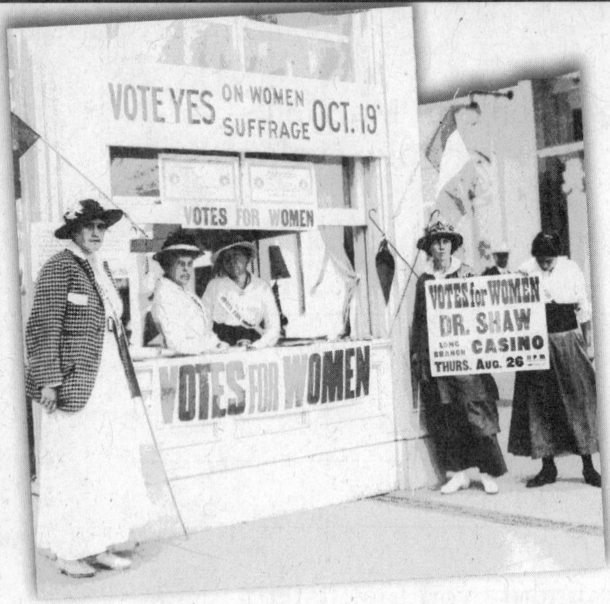

On Woman's Right to Suffrage

Susan B. Anthony

Summary Susan B. Anthony gives a speech to United States citizens in 1873. It is a time when women cannot vote. She says that the U.S. Constitution protects all people. She says that women should have the same rights as men.

Writing About the Big Question

How much information is enough? In "On Woman's Right to Suffrage," Susan B. Anthony discusses the importance of many voices to a democracy. Complete this sentence:

Discrimination may have a negative effect on democracy because it

prevents ____.

Note-taking Guide

Use the graphic organizer to record details that support Susan B. Anthony's argument.

The Constitution says "We the people," not "We, the white male citizens."

Women should have the right to vote.

On Woman's Right to Suffrage

1. **Connect:** Anthony is accused of trying to vote. She says that she did not break the law. How does Anthony connect her reason to the Constitution?

____

____

2. **Apply:** Does Anthony believe that she lives in a true democracy? Explain.

____

____

3. **Reading Skill:** Determine whether each statement in the chart is a **fact**, an **opinion**, a **generalization**, or an **overgeneralization**. Write your choice next to the statement. Then, explain your choice.

Statement	Type of Statement	Explanation
To [women] this government is . . . the most hateful aristocracy ever established.		
[I] voted at the last . . . election, without having a lawful right to vote.		
Webster . . . define[s] a citizen to be a person entitled to voted.		

4. **Literary Analysis:** Anthony **repeats** "We, the people" throughout her speech. What point does she emphasize by repeating this?

____

____

Writing: Evaluation

Write an **evaluation** of the persuasive arguments in Anthony's speech. Use the questions below to gather ideas for your evaluation.

- What is Anthony's position?

____

____

- What are two of her arguments?

____

____

- What are two counterarguments for the arguments you just listed?

____

____

- How well does Anthony deal with these counterarguments?

____

____

Use your notes to write your evaluation.

Research and Technology: Statistical Snapshot

Create a **statistical snapshot** of women in the United States. Fill in the chart with the information you found in your research. Complete the chart with questions you could ask in your survey about the information you found.

Facts and Statistics	Questions You Could Ask

from Sharing in the American Dream • Science and the Sense of Wonder

Reading Skill

A **fact** is information that can be proved. An **opinion** is a person's judgment or belief. **Ask questions to evaluate an author's support** for his or her opinions as you read nonfiction.

- A *valid opinion* can be supported by facts or by an expert.
- A *faulty opinion* cannot be supported by facts. It is supported by other opinions. A faulty opinion often ignores major facts that contradict it. Faulty opinions often show *bias*. Bias means an unfair preference or dislike for something.

Use the chart to help you identify facts and opinions while you are reading.

Statement:

↓

1. Distinguish fact from opinion.
ASK: Can it be proved?

↓

Answer:

↓

2. Distinguish valid from faulty opinion.
ASK: Can it be supported?

↓

Answer:

Literary Analysis

An author's **word choice** can help show a certain idea or feeling. Factors that affect word choice include:

- the author's audience and purpose
- **connotations** of words: the negative or positive ideas connected with words
- **denotations** of words: the dictionary definition of words

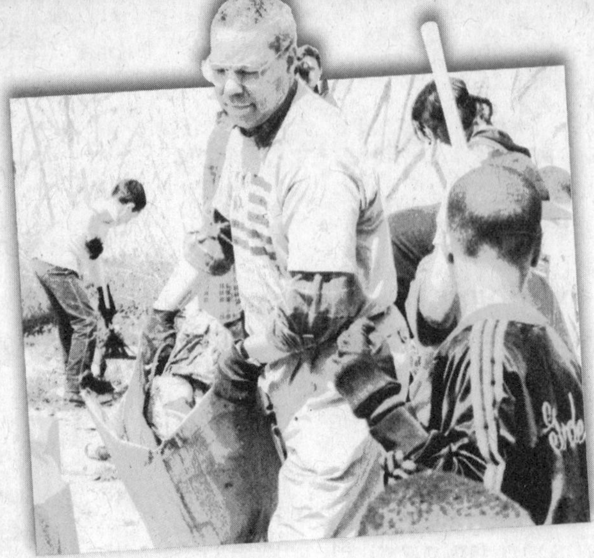

from Sharing in the American Dream

Colin Powell

Summary Former Secretary of State Colin Powell shares his beliefs about volunteer work. He encourages listeners to volunteer their time to help others in some way. He believes that this is an important part of keeping the United States strong.

Writing About the Big Question

How much information is enough? In "Sharing in the American Dream," Colin Powell calls on all members of society to help one another achieve their dreams. Complete this sentence:

An effective way to challenge people to volunteer is ______________________

____.

Note-taking Guide

Fill in the chart to record the main points of Powell's speech.

People Who Need Help	What They Need	Who Should Help
		each and every one of us

from Sharing in the American Dream

Colin Powell

Over 200 years ago, a group of volunteers gathered on this sacred spot to found a new nation. In perfect words, they voiced their dreams and aspirations of an imperfect world. They pledged their lives, their fortune and their sacred honor to secure inalienable rights given by God for life, liberty and pursuit of happiness—pledged that they would provide them to all who would inhabit this new nation.

They look down on us today in spirit, with pride for all we have done to keep faith with their ideals and their sacrifices. Yet, despite all we have done, this is still an imperfect world. We still live in an imperfect society. Despite more than two centuries of moral and material progress, despite all our efforts to achieve a more perfect union, there are still Americans who are not sharing in the American Dream. There are still Americans who wonder: is the journey there for them, is the dream there for them, or, whether it is, at best, a dream deferred.

The great American poet, Langston Hughes, talked about a dream deferred, and he said, "What happens to a dream deferred? Does it dry up like a raisin in the sun, or fester like a sore and then run? Does it stink like rotten meat or crust and sugar over like a syrupy sweet? Maybe it just sags, like a heavy load. Or, does it explode?" . . .

So today, we gather here today to pledge that the dream must no longer be deferred and it will never, as long as we can do anything about it, become a dream denied. That is why we are here, my friends. We gather here to pledge that those of us who are more fortunate will not forsake those who are less fortunate. We are a compassionate and caring people. We are a generous people. We will reach down, we

Vocabulary Development

aspirations (as puh RAY shuhnz) *n.* strong desires or ambitions
deferred (di FERD) *adj.* delayed
compassionate (kuhm PASH uhn it) *adj.* deeply sympathetic

TAKE NOTES

Activate Prior Knowledge 

Think about a speech you have heard. Did it inspire you? How did the speech make you feel?

Literary Analysis 

The **connotations** of words are the positive and negative ideas connected with the words. Are the connotations of *pledge* and *dream* positive or negative? Explain the effect of using them.

Reading Skill 

A **fact** is information that can be proved. An **opinion** is a person's judgment or belief. What is one fact in the bracketed paragraph?

TAKE NOTES

Literary Analysis

An author's **word choice** can help communicate a certain idea or feeling. What does Powell's word choice in the bracketed paragraph tell you about his audience and purpose?

____

____

____

Reading Skill

Which of the following statements is an **opinion**?

(a) As you've heard, up to 15 million young Americans today are at risk. . . .

(b) All of us can spare 30 minutes a week or an hour a week.

Explain your answer.

____

____

____

Reading Check

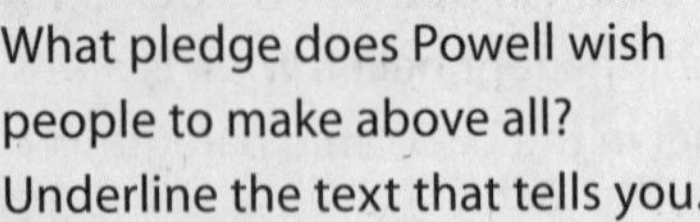

What pledge does Powell wish people to make above all? Underline the text that tells you.

will reach back, we will reach across to help our brothers and sisters who are in need.

Above all, we pledge to reach out to the most vulnerable members of the American family, our children. As you've heard, up to 15 million young Americans today are at risk. . . .

In terms of numbers the task may seem staggering. But if we look at the simple needs that these children have, then the task is manageable, the goal is achievable. We know what they need. They need an adult caring person in their life, a safe place to learn and grow, a healthy start, marketable skills and an opportunity to serve so that early in their lives they learn the virtue of service so that they can reach out then and touch another young American in need.

These are basic needs that we commit ourselves to today, we promise today. We are making America's promise today to provide to those children in need. This is a grand alliance. It is an alliance between government and corporate America and nonprofit America, between our institutions of faith, but especially between individual Americans.

You heard the governors and the mayors, and you'll hear more in a little minute that says the real answer is for each and every one of us, not just here in Philadelphia, but across this land—for each and every one of us to reach out and touch someone in need.

All of us can spare 30 minutes a week or an hour a week. All of us can give an extra dollar. All of us can touch someone who doesn't look like us, who doesn't speak like us, who may not dress like us, but needs us in their lives. And that's what we all have to do to keep this going.

And so there's a spirit of Philadelphia here today. There's a spirit of Philadelphia that we saw yesterday in Germantown. There is a spirit of Philadelphia that will leave Philadelphia tomorrow afternoon and spread across this whole nation—30 governors will go back and spread it; over 100 mayors will go back and spread it, and hundreds of others, leaders around this country who are watching will go back

Vocabulary Development

alliance (uh LY uhns) *n.* a group united for a common goal

and spread it. Corporate America will spread it, nonprofits will spread it. And each and every one of us will spread it because it has to be done, we have no choice. We cannot leave these children behind if we are going to meet the dreams of our founding fathers.

And so let us all join in this great crusade. Let us make sure that no child in America is left behind, no child in America has their dream deferred or denied. We can do it. We can do it because we are Americans. . . .

Reader's Response: How did this speech make you feel about volunteering?

____

____

____

TAKE NOTES

Reading Skill 

It is an important part of reading **to ask questions to evaluate an author's support**. What are two questions you could ask about Powell's support for the underlined sentence?

____

____

Literary Analysis 

Word choice has an effect on the feeling of a work. Circle the words and phrases in the final paragraph that have positive **connotations**. What feeling do you get from the last paragraph? Explain.

____

____

____

Reading Check 

What does Powell believe that Americans have to do to meet the dreams of the founding fathers? Underline the text that tells you.

from Sharing in the American Dream

1. **Respond:** Do you agree or disagree with Powell's message? Explain.

2. **Interpret:** At the beginning of his speech, Powell calls the founders of the United States "a group of volunteers." What kinds of feelings do you think Powell wants to create in his audience by mentioning this group of people?

3. **Reading Skill:** Identify one **fact** and one **opinion** in the speech. Explain your choices.

4. **Literary Analysis:** Use this chart to analyze Powell's **word choice** in his speech.

Powell's Purpose	Words and Phrases That Support His Purpose	Connotations

Writing

Write a brief **response** to Powell's statement "All of us can spare 30 minutes a week or an hour a week." The following questions will help you write your response.

- Who does Powell think needs the most help?

  ____

- Do you agree or disagree with Powell? Explain.

  ____

  ____

- Does Powell's idea apply to your own experience? Explain.

  ____

  ____

Use your notes to write your response.

Listening and Speaking: Speech

Write a **speech** honoring the founding of a volunteer organization such as the Peace Corps. Use the following note-taking guide to record information as you research the organization.

- When was the organization founded? ______________________________

  ____

- Who were its founders? ______________________________

  ____

- What is its mission? ______________________________

  ____

- What changes has it undergone since its founding? ______________________________

  ____

Science and the Sense of Wonder

Isaac Asimov

Summary Isaac Asimov says that he does not agree with a poem Walt Whitman wrote. Whitman says in his poem that people should forget about science. He says that people should enjoy the sky's beauty. Asimov says that people enjoy the sky more when they know science.

Writing About the Big Question

How much information is enough? In "Science and the Sense of Wonder," Asimov argues that scientific knowledge adds to our sense of wonder about the universe. Complete these sentences:

The more knowledge I accumulate about how natural systems work, the (more/less) curious I feel. This is because ______________________________

____.

Note-taking Guide

Use the chart to recall Asimov's reasons for why science makes watching the sky more interesting.

Some of those bright spots in the sky are "worlds of red-hot liquid."	How science makes watching the night sky more interesting	

Science and the Sense of Wonder

1. **Analyze:** Asimov tries to tell the reader how small our galaxy is. How does he do this?

2. **Make a Judgment:** Do you agree with Asimov or Whitman? Explain your choice.

3. **Reading Skill:** Identify one **fact** and one **opinion** in the essay. Explain your choices.

4. **Literary Analysis:** Use this chart to analyze Asimov's **word choice**.

Asimov's Purpose	Words and Phrases That Support His Purpose	Connotations

Writing: Response

Write a **response** to Asimov's idea that science helps you enjoy nature. Use the chart to list things that you like about nature. Explain whether you enjoy them as a poet would or as a scientist would. Use your notes to write your response.

Things You Like About Nature	Poet or Scientist?

Listening and Speaking: Introductory Speech

Write an **introductory speech** to present Isaac Asimov to a school assembly. Answer the questions below to help you with your presentation.

- List three things that you want to include in your speech.

- What style would be appropriate for your speech?

- What parallel wording will you use in your speech?

Use your notes to write your introductory speech.

Newspaper Editorials

About Newspaper Editorials

Newspaper editorials are written to express an opinion on a topic. The purpose of an editorial is to persuade readers to agree with the writer's point of view. Some editorials ask readers to take action on an issue. Editorial writers support their opinions with facts, examples, and statistics.

Reading Skill

To understand the writer's point of view and purpose for writing, readers must **analyze the proposition and support patterns** in the editorial. The writer states a problem and describes how it affects the reader. Then, the writer provides one or more solutions to the problem. The writer may use both facts and opinions to support the solution. Ask the following questions when reading a newspaper editorial:

- What problem does the writer present?
- Does the writer's solution to the problem make sense?
- Does the writer support the solution with facts, examples, and statistics?

Error in Logic	Example	Problem
Oversimplification	If you own a cellphone you should support the right to use it anywhere you want to.	Ignores other alternatives
False analogy	Outlawing cellphone use while driving is like outlawing eating while reading.	The comparison is irrelevant
Insufficient evidence	I do not know anyone who has had an accident because of a cellphone so I do not think they are a problem.	False conclusion
Jumping on the bandwagon	Everyone I know drives while talking on the cellphone, so it should be legal.	Assumes an opinion is correct because it is popular

Editorial

Features:

- text featured in a newspaper, magazine, or other publication
- a statement of the writer's position on an issue
- facts, statistics, and reasons that support the writer's position

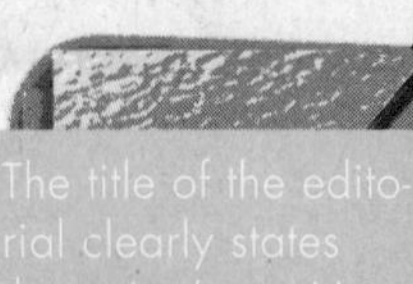

The title of the editorial clearly states the writer's position.

The Mercury News

Langberg: Hands-free law won't solve the problem

FRIDAY, SEPTEMBER 1, 2006

By Mike Langberg

Driving while talking on a cell phone clearly increases your risk of getting into an accident, but here's a surprise: The problem is all in your head.

The mental distraction of conversing behind the wheel is so great that switching to a headset or other "hands-free" approach—instead of taking one hand off the wheel to hold the phone to your ear—does nothing to reduce the danger.

But politicians never let facts get in the way of making themselves look good.

The result is hands-free legislation that passed the California Assembly and Senate last week, and is likely to be signed into law this month by Gov. Arnold Schwarzenegger.

The California Wireless Telephone Automobile Safety Act of 2006, the bill's formal name, says: "A person shall not drive a motor vehicle while using a wireless telephone unless that telephone is specifically designed and configured to allow hands-free listening and talking, and is used in that manner while driving. Using a handheld phone, you'll get an almost painless fine of $20 for the first offense. The penalty doesn't get much worse for additional violations, moving up to just $50.

Using a hand-held phone would only be allowed in emergency situations, such as calling 911.

The new rules wouldn't take effect until July 1, 2008.

So we're getting a nearly toothless law, two years down the line, that doesn't offer a real solution to a serious problem.

The first part of that problem is the awesome popularity of cell phones.

There are now 208 million cell phone subscribers in the United States, equal to 69 percent of the total population. Almost every adult American, in other words, now has a cell phone.

The National Highway Traffic Safety Administration says an average 6 percent of drivers on the road at any given moment are talking on a cell phone. The number goes up to 10 percent during daylight hours.

The writer offers statistics to support his position.

Driver distraction or inattention contributes to nearly 80 percent of accidents, according to a research study completed earlier this year by NHTSA and Virginia Tech.

Although overall death and injury rates continue to decline slowly over time, there's no question cell phones are a factor in many highway accidents. Last year, NHTSA reports, highway accidents killed 43,443 people last year and injured 2.7 million.

The writer does not provide evidence to support these claims.

There's an obvious solution: Ban talking on a cell phone while driving.

But that's not going to happen, at least not anytime soon. The cell phone lobby is too powerful, and the public is too enamored with chatting behind the wheel.

Instead, we're getting hands-free laws that give politicians the appearance of taking action.

New York, New Jersey, Connecticut and the District of Columbia already have hands-free laws, and many other states are considering similar steps.

These laws are moving forward despite a persuasive and growing list of academic studies, involving both simulator testing and analysis of real-world crash data, showing hands-free phone calls are no less risky than holding a phone.

Think about it: If you're fully aware of what's happening on the road ahead of you, such as a car suddenly slamming on its brakes, your response time isn't going to vary much whether you've got one or two hands on the wheel.

But your response time will suffer if you're in the middle of an argument on the phone with your boss or spouse.

I'll raise my hand here and admit I'm part of the problem. I've come close to rear-ending other drivers on a few occasions because I was talking on my cell phone. And I don't believe my sluggish reaction would have changed if I'd been using a headset.

David L. Strayer, a psychology professor at the University of Utah, has been studying cell phone distraction for more than five years.

Last week, he told me there are at least six studies showing no safety benefit from hands-free talking.

"This . . . suggests that legislative initiatives that restrict handheld devices but permit hands-free devices are not likely to eliminate the problems associated with cell phones while driving," Strayer and two colleagues wrote in the summer 2006 issue of the journal *Human Factors.*

I asked Strayer if there's a safe way to participate in a phone call while driving.

"Not unless we somehow rewire our brains," he responded. There's no technological remedy, in other words, to the mental distraction created during a cell phone conversation.

At the same time, there are possible side effects—both good and bad—from hands-free laws.

On the good side, some drivers might not want to go through the hassle of buying and using a headset or other hands-free gadget. They would give up talking while driving, collectively reducing auto accidents.

On the bad side, some drivers might get a false sense of security and decide it's OK to talk even more.

Here's my prediction: California's hands-free law, and similar laws elsewhere, will do nothing to change the number of accidents tied to drivers using cell phones.

Once everyone realizes these laws accomplish nothing, we'll have to decide whether cell phones require further restrictions or should be categorized with other dangerous behind-the-wheel distractions—everything from noisy children to complicated audio systems—that aren't restricted.

How much information is enough?

Does this editorial change the way you think about cell phone use while driving? Why or why not?

Transcript of Governor Arnold Schwarzenegger Signing Legislation Requiring Drivers to Use Hands Free Devices

DATE: *Friday, September 15, 2006*
TIME: *11:15 a.m.*

EVENT: *Oakland Hilton, California Room, 1 Hegenberger Rd, Oakland, CA*

Speech

Features:

- text spoken aloud to an audience
- remarks that highlight the significance of an event
- language intended to engage listeners and encourage support for the speaker's ideas

GOVERNOR SCHWARZENEGGER:

. . . Today we will be signing SB 1613. This is the hands-free cell phone bill that will save lives by making our roads safer. And I want to say thank you to Senator Simitian for his great, great work on this bill and for working with my office on this bill to perfect the bill. I want to thank him also for his great commitment to . . . California, and to make our roads safe. He has been really extraordinary, to protect the people of California and I want to say thank you for that.

The speaker opens his speech by stating his proposition.

The simple fact is that it is really dangerous when you talk on your cell phone and drive at the same time. Hand-held cell phones are responsible for 1,000 accidents every month, and we have seen that there are very dangerous situations sometimes. We want to avoid that, and this is why we have here this bill. This bill doesn't mean that you can't talk on a cell phone; it just means that you should not hold a hand-held cell phone, you should use a headset or use a speaker system.

Also, there is an exception here that if you have to make an emergency call, then you can use the hand-held phone. And also, what is important is that this law will go into effect on July 1 of 2008. There will be a $20 fine if you're caught the first time using a cell phone, and then $50 after that.

I think it is very important for people to know that even though the law begins in 2008, July of 2008, stop using your cell phones right now, because you're putting people at risk. You just look away for a second, or for a split second, from what's going on in front of you, and at that moment a child could be running out, and you could kill this child just because you were busy looking down and dialing on your cell phone. So pay attention to that, take this seriously. We want to really save lives here.

Thank you very much again, and now I would like to have Senator Simitian come out and say a few words, please.

SENATOR SIMITIAN:

Thank you all very much for being here today. And some of you know, but perhaps not all of you, that this is the sixth hands-free cell phone bill I've introduced during the past six years. The question I've been asked quite frequently of late is, "Why did you keep introducing the bill?" And the answer is really very simple. I introduced the bill because I believe it will save lives. It's just that simple. You've got a readily available technology that costs next to nothing and saves lives. Why on earth wouldn't we use it?

This bill isn't a perfect solution, it isn't a total solution, but it is a significant and important improvement over the current state of affairs, and it will save lives, and that was the goal from Day 1. . . .

The speaker oversimplifies the issue of cost involved in using a hands-free cellphone device.

CHIEF BECHER:

. . . I'm proud to be here today for the signing of this bill. It represents a collaborative effort between the legislature, the Governor, [the phone company] and the many backers and traffic safety officials throughout the state, to make the roadways of California a safer place to drive.

Statewide, collisions caused by distracted drivers result in countless hours of roadway delay, congestion, injury and death. This legislation is another useful tool for law enforcement to curb the growing number of collisions caused either partially or wholly by distracted drivers.

Prior to this cell phone law going into effect, the CHP plans a major public education campaign to ensure the public is aware of the changes. Education is a major focus for the CHP, because public awareness of the issue and voluntary compliance wtih this new law can have a significant impact on crashes even before the new law goes into effect. The Governor is exactly right. Start now.

Our goal is to have all drivers in the state keep both hands on the wheel and have the attention and awareness so that they can navigate [their] driving environment. It is always incumbent on drivers to drive attentively. Many devices and activities taking place inside today's vehicles can cause that split second distraction that may result in an unnecessary traffic collision. Cell phones are among the more prominent of these distractions.

And finally, thanks to all in the creation and implementation of this bill. The California Highway Patrol supports this new legislation as part of our No. 1 goal, to prevent traffic collisions and to save lives. Thank you.

THE BIG ?

How much information is enough?
Do the remarks of the speakers provide enough information for you to make an informed judgment about cellphone use while driving? Explain your response.

Thinking About the Newspaper Editorial

1. Find one sentence in Langberg's editorial that states his opinion about using cell phones while driving. Write that sentence on the line below.

____

2. In Governor Schwarzenegger's speech, what reason does the governor give for choosing to sign the hands-free cell phone bill?

____

TALK ABOUT IT Reading Skill

3. Langberg states that hands-free phones are not likely to eliminate the problems of using cell phones while driving. How does Langberg support his statement?

____

4. How does Governor Schwarzenegger support his decision to sign the hands-free cell phone bill?

____

WRITE ABOUT IT Timed Writing: Editorial Writing (40 minutes)

Use one of the editorials as a model to write an editorial. Research an issue in your school or community. State your opinion on the issue, propose a solution, and support your solution with facts and examples.

- What is the issue?

____

- What is your opinion on the issue?

____

- What solution do you propose?

____

- What facts support your solution?

____

Describe Somebody • Almost a Summer Sky

Poetry is the most musical literary form. Poets choose words for both sound and meaning. Poets use some or all of the following to do this:

- **Sensory language** is writing or speech that appeals to one or more of the five senses—sight, sound, smell, taste, and touch.
- **Figurative language** is writing that is imaginative and not meant to be taken literally. The chart below contains different types of figurative language.

Figurative Language	Definition	Example
Metaphor	• describes one thing as if it were another	Her eyes were saucers, wide with expectation.
Simile	• uses *like* or *as* to compare two unlike things	The drums were as loud as a fireworks display.
Personification	• gives human qualities to something that is not human	The clarinets sang.

Sound devices add a musical quality to poetry. Some sound devices include these:

Sound Device	Definition	Example
Alliteration	• repetition of consonant sounds at the beginning of words	feathered friend
Repetition	• repeated use of a sound, word, or phrase	water, water everywhere
Assonance	• repetition of a vowel sound followed by different consonants in stressed syllables	fade/hey

Other sound devices include these:

Sound Device	Definition	Example
Consonance	• repetition of a consonant sound at the end of stressed syllables with different vowels sounds	end/hand
Onomatopoeia	• use of words that imitate sounds	buzz, whack
Rhyme	• repetition of sounds at the ends of words	dear, cheer, here
Meter	• the rhythmical pattern of stressed and unstressed syllables	A **horse**, a **horse**! My **king**dom **for** a **horse**!

The structure of a poem determines its form. Most poems are written in lines. These lines are grouped into stanzas. This list describes several forms of poetry.

- **Lyric** poetry expresses the thoughts and feelings of a single speaker. The **speaker** is the person who speaks in the poem. Lyric poetry is usually very musical.
- **Narrative** poetry tells a story in verse. It often has the same elements that are found in short stories, including characters, setting, and plot.
- **Ballads** are songlike poems that tell a story. They often tell about adventure and romance.
- **Free verse** is poetry that is defined by its lack of strict structure. It does not have to rhyme or have regular meter. Lines do not have to be a specific length. There may be no specific stanza pattern.
- **Haiku** is a three-line Japanese form. The first and third lines have five syllables each. The second line has seven syllables.
- **Rhyming couplets** are a pair of rhyming lines that usually have the same meter and length.
- **Limericks** are humorous poems with five lines. They have a specific rhythm pattern and rhyme scheme.

Describe Somebody • Almost a Summer Sky

Jacqueline Woodson

Summaries In "Describe Somebody," a teacher asks her class to write a poem that describes someone. This poem describes Lonnie's thoughts as he thinks about the assignment. In "Almost a Summer Sky," Lonnie and his brother Rodney walk to the park. This poem shares Lonnie's thoughts as the two boys walk.

Note-taking Guide

Use this chart to record main ideas from the poems.

	Speaker	Characters	What the Speaker Learns or Realizes
Describe Somebody	Lonnie	Lonnie, Ms. Marcus, Eric, Miss Edna, Lamont	
Almost a Summer Sky			

Activate Prior Knowledge

Your teacher tells you to describe somebody in a poem. You will have to read the poem aloud to the class. Whom would you describe? Explain.

____

____

____

Poetry

Alliteration is repeating consonant sounds at the beginning of words. Circle the words that create alliteration in the first set of underlined text.

Poetry

Review the meaning of **consonance** from the chart on page 222. Circle the words that create consonance in the second set of underlined text.

Reading Check

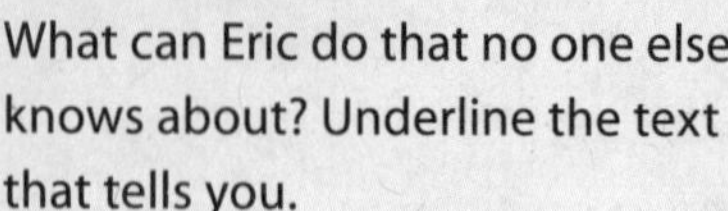

What can Eric do that no one else knows about? Underline the text that tells you.

Describe Somebody

Jacqueline Woodson

Today in class Ms. Marcus said
Take out your poetry notebooks and describe somebody.
Think carefully, Ms. Marcus said.
You're gonna read it to the class.
I wrote, Ms. Marcus is tall and a little bit skinny.
Then I put my pen in my mouth and stared down
at the words.
Then I crossed them out and wrote
Ms. Marcus's hair is long and brown.
Shiny.
When she smiles it makes you feel all good inside.
I stopped writing and looked around the room.
Angel was staring out the window.
Eric and Lamont were having a pen fight.
They don't care about poetry.
Stupid words, Eric says.
Lots and lots of stupid words.
Eric is tall and a little bit mean.
Lamont's just regular.
Angel's kinda chubby. He's got light brown hair.
Sometimes we all hang out,
play a little ball or something. Angel's real good
at science stuff. Once he made a volcano
for science fair and the stuff that came out of it
looked like real lava. Lamont can
draw superheroes real good. Eric—nobody
at school really knows this but
he can sing. Once, Miss Edna[1] took me
to a different church than the one
we usually go to on Sunday.

1. **Miss Edna** Lonnie's foster mother.

I was surprised to see Eric up there
with a choir robe on. He gave me a mean look
like I'd better not
say nothing about him and his dark green robe with
gold around the neck.
After the preacher preached
Eric sang a song with nobody else in the choir singing.
Miss Edna started dabbing at her eyes
whispering *Yes, Lord.*
Eric's voice was like something
that didn't seem like it should belong
to Eric.
Seemed like it should be coming out of an angel.

Now I gotta write a whole new poem
'cause Eric would be real mad if I told the class
about his angel voice.

Almost a Summer Sky

Jacqueline Woodson

It was the trees first, Rodney[1] tells me.
It's raining out. But the rain is light and warm.
And the sky's not all close to us like it gets
sometimes. It's way up there with
some blue showing through.
Late spring sky, Ms. Marcus says. *Almost summer sky.*
And when she said that, I said
Hey Ms. Marcus, that's a good title
for a poem, right?
You have a poet's heart, Lonnie.
That's what Ms. Marcus said to me.
I have a poet's heart.
That's good. A good thing to have.
And I'm the one who has it.

1. **Rodney** one of Miss Edna's sons.

TAKE NOTES

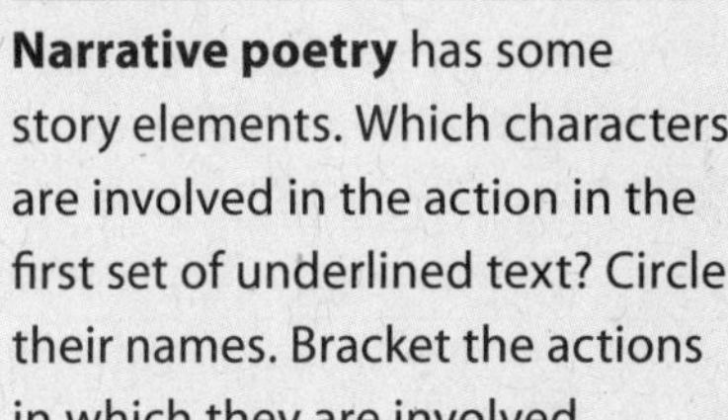

Poetry

Narrative poetry has some story elements. Which characters are involved in the action in the first set of underlined text? Circle their names. Bracket the actions in which they are involved.

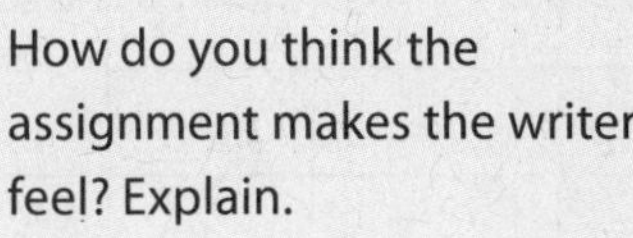

Stop to Reflect

How do you think the assignment makes the writer feel? Explain.

____

____

____

____

Poetry

Repetition is the use of any sound, word, or phrase more than once. Circle the words that create repetition in the second set of underlined text.

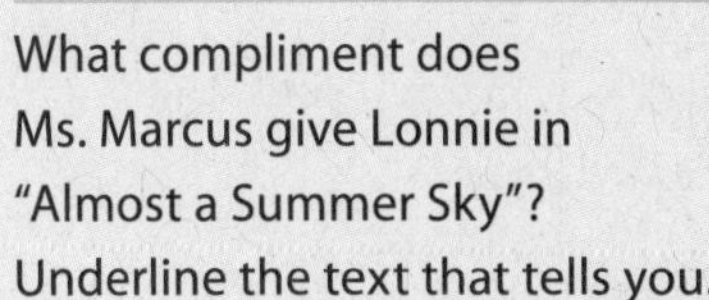

Reading Check

What compliment does Ms. Marcus give Lonnie in "Almost a Summer Sky"? Underline the text that tells you.

TAKE NOTES

Stop to Reflect 

How does Lonnie feel about the day and his walk? How do you know?

Poetry

A **simile** uses *like* or *as* to compare two unlike things. Underline the simile in the bracketed lines.

Reading Check 

Where are Rodney and Lonnie going? Underline the text that tells you.

Now Rodney puts his arm around my shoulder
We keep walking. There's a park
eight blocks from Miss Edna's house
That's where we're going.
Me and Rodney to the park.
Rain coming down warm
Rodney with his arm around my shoulder
Makes me think of Todd and his pigeons
how big his smile gets when they fly.
The trees upstate ain't like other trees you seen, Lonnie
Rodney squints up at the sky, shakes his head
smiles.

No, upstate they got maple and catalpa and scotch pine,[2]
all kinds of trees just standing.
Hundred-year-old trees big as three men.

When you go home this weekend, Ms. Marcus said.
Write about a perfect moment.

Yeah, Little Brother, Rodney says.
You don't know about shade till you lived upstate.
Everybody should do it—even if it's just for a little while.

Way off, I can see the park—blue-gray sky
touching the tops of trees.

I had to live there awhile, Rodney said.
Just to be with all that green, you know?
I nod, even though I don't.
I can't even imagine moving away from here,
from Rodney's arm around my shoulder,
from Miss Edna's Sunday cooking,
from Lily[3] in her pretty dresses and great
big smile when she sees me.

2. **catalpa** (kuh TAL puh) *n.* tree with heart-shaped leaves; **scotch pine** tree with yellow wood, grown for timber.
3. **Lily** Lonnie's sister, who lives in a different foster home.

Can't imagine moving away

From
Home.

You know what I love about trees, Rodney
says.
It's like . . . It's like their leaves are hands
reaching
out to you. Saying Come on over here,
Brother.
Let me just . . . Let me just . . .
Rodney looks down at me and grins.
Let me just give you some shade for a
while.

Reader's Response: Which poem did you like better? Explain.

____

____

____

TAKE NOTES

Poetry 

Free verse is poetry that lacks rhyme, stanzas with the same number of lines, or lines with the same number of syllables. Is "Almost a Summer Sky" written in free verse? Explain.

____

____

____

____

____

Poetry 

Personification gives human qualities to something that is not human. What human qualities does Rodney give the trees?

____

____

Poetry

1. **Interpret:** The speaker says that Eric would be mad if the class knew he could sing. Why would Eric be angry?

2. **Respond:** Do you agree that Lonnie has the heart of a poet? Explain.

3. **Poetry:** These poems are written in **free verse.** Why is free verse a good choice for these poems?

4. **Poetry:** Complete the chart below. Find examples of **figurative language** in the poems. Tell what the figurative language compares. Tell what the figurative language conveys, or means.

	Ideas Compared	Ideas Conveyed
Describe Somebody lines 40–43		
Almost a Summer Sky lines 49–53		

Poetry Reading

Arrange a **poetry reading.** Follow these steps to prepare for your poetry reading.

- Read some of the author's works. Jacqueline Woodson's books include *Locomotion, Last Summer with Maizon,* and *Between Madison and Palmetto.* Be sure to read several of the poems included in *Locomotion.*

  What I learned from Woodson's writing:

  ____

  ____

  ____

  ____

  ____

- Search the Internet. Use words and phrases such as "Jacqueline Woodson article."

  What I learned about Jacqueline Woodson:

  ____

  ____

  ____

  ____

  ____

- Watch the video interview with Jacqueline Woodson. Review your source material.

  Additional information learned about the author:

  ____

  ____

  ____

  ____

  ____

Use your notes as you prepare for your poetry reading.

Poetry Collection 1 • Poetry Collection 2

Reading Skill

Context is the text around a particular word. Before you read a poem, **preview the lines of verse to identify unfamiliar words.** Look for clues in the context to determine a possible meaning for each unfamiliar word. Look for these types of clues:

- **synonym or definition:** words that mean the same as the unfamiliar word
- **antonym:** words that are opposite in meaning
- **explanation:** words that give more information about the unfamiliar word, as shown in the chart
- **sentence role:** the way the word is used

Using Context	
With her hair all *disheveled,* Looking like she had just awoken	
Explanation	looking like she had just awoken
Sentence Role	describe hair
Meaning *Disheveled* probably means messy, like hair looks after sleeping.	

Literary Analysis

Sound devices help poets draw on the musical quality of words to express ideas. Common sound devices include the following:

- **alliteration:** repetition of initial consonant sounds—*misty morning*
- **onomatopoeia:** words that imitate sounds—*buzz*
- **rhyme:** repetition of sounds at ends of words—*spring fling*
- **rhythm:** the pattern of strong and weak beats

Poetry Collection 1

Summaries "Cat!" uses fun language and sounds to describe a frightened and angry cat. The speaker in "Silver," creates a silvery image of a moonlit night. "Your World" challenges the reader to push past life's limitations.

Writing About the Big Question

What is the secret to reaching someone with words? In "Poetry Collection 1," poets go beyond relying on the meaning of words to communicate. Complete this sentence:

I (notice/do not notice) the sensory effect of words like swoosh, smush, scrunch, crunch, munch, and splash. Some words I like for their sounds are ____________ and ____________ because ____________ ______________________________.

Note-taking Guide

Use this chart to record the topic and actions in each poem.

Poem	Topic	Two Actions in the Poem
Cat!		
Silver	the moon	
Your World		

TAKE NOTES

Activate Prior Knowledge 

Think of your favorite animal. How would you describe the sounds of that animal?

Reading Skill 

Context is the text around a particular word. Context may include a **synonym**, or a word that means the same as another word. Which word in the underlined passage is a synonym that helps you figure out the meaning of *git*?

Literary Analysis 

Sound devices help poets draw on the musical quality of words to express ideas. One type of sound device is **onomatopoeia**, or words that imitate sounds. Underline two made-up words that imitate cat sounds. How do they help you imagine the poem's action?

Cat!

Eleanor Farjeon

Cat!
Scat!
After her, after her,
Sleeky flatterer,
Spitfire chatterer,
Scatter her, scatter her
Off her mat!
Wuff!
Wuff!
Treat her rough!
Git her, git her,
Whiskery spitter!
Catch her, catch her,
Green-eyed scratcher!
Slathery
Slithery
Hisser,
Don't miss her!
Run till you're dithery,[1]
Hithery
Thithery[2]
Pftts! pftts!
How she spits!
Spitch! Spatch!
Can't she scratch!
Scritching the bark
Of the sycamore tree,
She's reached her ark
And's hissing at me
Pftts! pftts!
Wuff! wuff!
Scat,
Cat!
That's
That!

Vocabulary Development

flatterer (FLAT er er) *n.* one who praises others insincerely in order to win their approval

1. **dithery** (DITH er ee) *adj.* nervous and confused; in a dither.
2. **Hithery/Thithery** made-up words based on hither and thither, which mean "here" and "there."

Silver

Walter de la Mare

Slowly, silently, now the moon
Walks the night in her silver shoon;[1]
This way, and that, she peers, and sees
Silver fruit upon silver trees;
One by one the casements[2] catch
Her beams beneath the silvery thatch;[3]
Couched in his kennel, like a log,
With paws of silver sleeps the dog;
From their shadowy coat the white breasts peep
Of doves in a silver-feathered sleep;
A harvest mouse goes scampering by,
With silver claws, and silver eye;
And moveless fish in the water gleam,
By silver reeds in a silver stream.

Vocabulary Development

kennel (KEN uhl) *n.* a place where dogs are kept

1. **shoon** (SHOON) *n.* old-fashioned word for "shoes."
2. **casements** (KAYS muhnts) *n.* windows that open out, as doors do.
3. **thatch** (THACH) *n.* roof made of straw or other plant material.

TAKE NOTES

Reading Skill 

Preview the lines of verse to identify unfamiliar words. Write the words below.

Write the **definition** of each word and the way each word is used, or its **sentence role**.

Literary Analysis 

Alliteration is the repetition of initial consonant sounds. Identify examples of alliteration in lines 1–5.

Reading Check 

What "walks the night"? Circle the text that tells you.

TAKE NOTES

Literary Analysis 

Rhyme is the repetition of sounds at the ends of words. Circle the end rhymes in "Your World."

Reading Skill

Context clues give you more information about an unfamiliar word. How do the context clues of *horizon, sky,* and *sea* help you find the meaning of *immensity*?

Stop to Reflect 

What do **sound devices** add to the experience of reading poetry? Explain.

Reading Check 

Where did the speaker of "Your World" once live? Circle the text that tells you.

Your World

Georgia Douglas Johnson

Your world is as big as you make it.
I know, for I used to abide
In the narrowest nest in a corner,
My wings pressing close to my side.

But I sighted the distant horizon
Where the sky line encircled the sea
And I throbbed with a burning desire
To travel this immensity.

I battered the cordons[1] around me
And cradled my wings on the breeze
Then soared to the uttermost reaches
With rapture, with power, with ease!

Reader's Response: Do you think the authors of these poems used sound devices effectively? Explain.

Vocabulary Development

rapture (RAP cher) *n.* ecstasy

1. **cordons** (KOHR duhnz) *n.* lines or cords that restrict free movement.

Poetry Collection 1

1. **Draw Conclusions:** How does the speaker of "Cat!" feel about the cat?

____

____

2. **Generalize:** In "Silver," the silvery light of the moon makes everything look silver. What mood, or feeling in the reader, does the poet create as he describes these effects?

____

____

3. **Reading Skill:** Explain how **context** helps you determine the meaning of the word *scritch* in "Cat!"

____

____

4. **Literary Analysis:** Complete the chart with examples of the **sound devices** you find in each poem. Not all of the sound devices are used in each poem. An example has been given to you.

	Cat!	Silver	Your World
alliteration	slithery/slathery		
onomatopoeia			
rhyme			

Writing: Introduction

Write an **introduction** for a poetry reading. Use this chart to help you decide which poem to choose for your introduction. Be sure to explain your choices as you answer the questions.

	Poem	Reason
Which poem did you like best?		
Which poem do you think will be most meaningful to others?		
Which poem is written in the most interesting way?		

Use these notes to write your introduction.

Listening and Speaking: Poetry Recitation

Use the following chart to list examples of sound devices and how these sound devices create the mood of the poem.

Poem: ______________________ Mood: ______________________

Sound Device	Contribution to Mood
Rhyme	
Rhythm	
Alliteration	
Onomatopoeia	

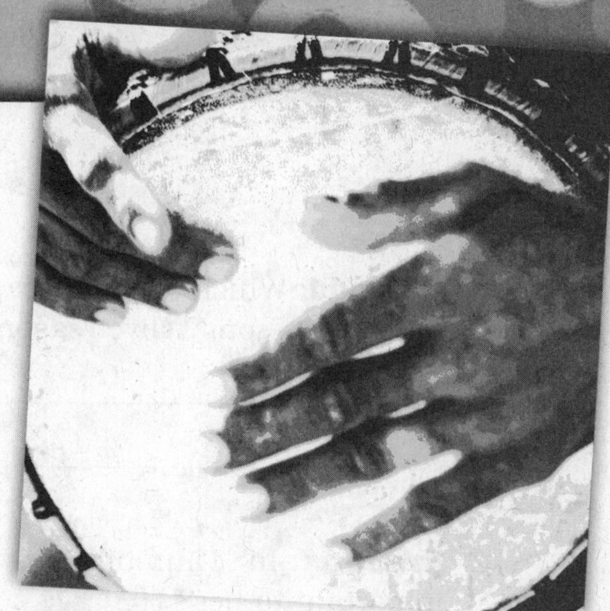

Poetry Collection 2

Summaries The speaker in "Thumbprint" is glad that no one is exactly like her. The speaker in "The Drum" describes different people in terms of drums. The speaker in "Ring Out, Wild Bells" wants the bells to ring out the bad and ring in the good.

Writing About the Big Question

What is the secret to reaching someone with words? The writers of the poems in "Poetry Collection 2" take advantage of the musical quality of poetry with readers. Complete this sentence:

Words set to a beat, whether poetry or song lyrics, can create a memorable experience for a listener because ______________________________

______________________________.

Note-taking Guide

Use this chart to note details about the subject of each poem.

	Thumbprint	The Drum	Ring Out, Wild Bells
Subject of the poem	the speaker's thumbprint		
Words that describe the subject			

Poetry Collection 2

1. **Respond:** Which of the three poems do you think could best be set to music as a song? Give reasons for your choice.

2. **Interpret:** In "Thumbprint," why is the speaker's thumbprint so important to her?

3. **Reading Skill:** What **context** clues helped you find out the meaning of *feud* in "Ring Out, Wild Bells"?

4. **Literary Analysis:** Three common **sound devices** are listed in the chart below. Complete the chart with examples of each of the sound devices in the three poems. Write the examples in the chart. Not all of the sound devices are used in each poem.

	Thumbprint	The Drum	Ring Out, Wild Bells
alliteration			
onomatopoeia		Pa-rum	
rhyme			

Writing: Introduction

Write an **introduction** for a poetry reading. Use this chart to help you decide which poem to choose for your introduction. Be sure to explain your choices as you answer the questions.

	Poem	Reason
Which poem did you like best?		
Which poem do you think will be most meaningful to others?		
Which poem is written in the most interesting way?		

Use these notes to write your introduction.

Listening and Speaking: Poetry Recitation

Use the following chart to list examples of sound devices and how these sound devices create the mood of the poem.

Poem: ____________________ Mood: ____________________

Sound Device	Contribution to Mood
Rhyme	
Rhythm	
Alliteration	
Onomatopoeia	

Poetry Collection 3 • Poetry Collection 4

Reading Skill

Context is the words and phrases surrounding a word. This text can help you understand new words or words that are used in an unfamiliar way. **Reread and read ahead** for context clues when you find an unfamiliar word. Figure out a possible meaning. Then, insert the meaning in place of the unfamiliar word and reread the sentence. If the sentence makes sense, your meaning is probably correct. If it does not make sense, read ahead to look for additional context clues. You could also look in a dictionary. The chart shows the common types of context clues.

Contrast
I *never shop* anymore, but last year, I was a shopping enthusiast.
Synonym
Don't *reject* our request. Your veto can hurt many people.
Explanation
Think of the *capacity*—this truck can carry *a lot of cargo*.
Example
She agonized for days, *biting her nails, sleeping poorly,* and *crying* because she was worried.

Literary Analysis

Figurative language is writing or speech that is not meant to be taken literally. Figurative language includes these *figures of speech.*

- A *simile* uses the words *like* or *as* to compare two apparently unlike things: His eyes were as black as coal.
- A *metaphor* compares two apparently unlike things by saying that one thing *is* the other: The world is my oyster.
- *Personification* is a comparison in which a nonhuman subject is given human characteristics: The trees toss in their sleep.

As you read, notice the way figurative language allows writers to present ideas in fresh ways.

Poetry Collection 3

Summaries Concrete mixers and elephants are compared in "Concrete Mixers." The speaker of "The City Is So Big" feels frightened by the city at night. The speaker in "Harlem Night Song" invites a loved one to enjoy the beauty of the night sky over the city.

Writing About the Big Question

What is the secret to reaching someone with words? In "Poetry Collection 3," three poets carefully craft their words to help us experience life in a big city. Complete this sentence:

Even if you have never been to a place, a talented poet can help you experience how it might feel to be there by ______________________________

____.

Note-taking Guide

Use this chart to help you record the imagery in each poem.

	Imagery
Concrete Mixers	elephant tenders, tough gray-skinned monsters, muck up to their wheel caps
The City Is So Big	
Harlem Night Song	

TAKE NOTES

Activate Prior Knowledge 

Think about the cities you have visited. What qualities do these cities share?

Reading Skill 

Context refers to those words and phrases surrounding a new or an unfamiliar word that can help you understand that word. Review the underlined passage. What context clues help reveal the meaning of *muck*? Explain.

Literary Analysis 

A **simile** compares two apparently unlike things, using the words *like* or *as*. What is the simile in line 7?

Concrete Mixers

Patricia Hubbell

The drivers are washing the concrete mixers;
Like elephant tenders they hose them down.
Tough gray-skinned monsters standing
    ponderous,
Elephant-bellied and elephant-nosed,
Standing in muck up to their wheel-caps,
Like rows of elephants, tail to trunk.
Their drivers perch on their backs like
    mahouts,[1]
Sending the sprays of water up.
They rid the trunk-like trough of concrete,
Direct the spray to the bulging sides,
Turn and start the monsters moving.
        Concrete mixers
        Move like elephants
        Bellow like elephants
        Spray like elephants,
    Concrete mixers are urban elephants,
    Their trunks are raising a city.

Vocabulary Development

ponderous (PAHN duh ruhs) *adj.* very heavy

urban (ER buhn) *adj.* in or relating to a town or city

1. **mahouts** (muh HOWTS) *n.* in India and the East Indies, elephant drivers or keepers.

The City Is So Big

Richard García

The city is so big
Its bridges quake with fear
I know, I have seen at night

The lights sliding from house to house
And trains pass with windows shining
Like a smile full of teeth

I have seen machines eating houses
And stairways walk all by themselves
And elevator doors opening and closing
And people disappear.

TAKE NOTES

Reading Skill 

Read the first bracketed passage. Circle the context clues that help you confirm that *quake* means "tremble."

Literary Analysis

Personification is a comparison in which a nonhuman subject is given human characteristics. What are the examples of personification in the second bracketed passage?

____

____

____

____

____

Reading Check 

To what does the speaker compare a train's windows? Underline the answer in the text.

TAKE NOTES

Literary Analysis

A **simile** uses the words *like* or *as* to compare two things. A **metaphor** compares two things by saying that one thing *is* the other. Does Hughes use a simile or a metaphor to describe stars? Explain.

Stop to Reflect

In the poems you have read so far, what example of figurative language do you find most striking? Explain.

Reading Check

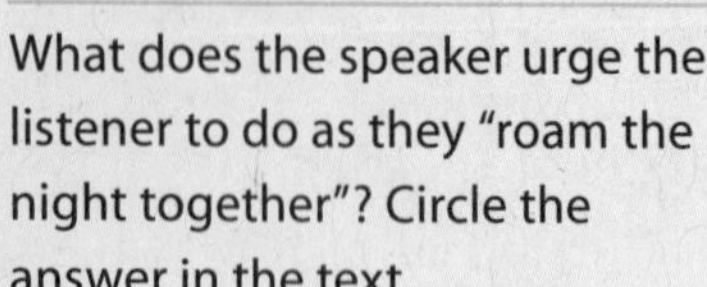

What does the speaker urge the listener to do as they "roam the night together"? Circle the answer in the text.

Harlem Night Song

Langston Hughes

Come,
Let us roam the night together
Singing.

I love you.

Across
The Harlem roof-tops
Moon is shining.
Night sky is blue.
Stars are great drops
Of golden dew.

Down the street
A band is playing.

I love you.

Come,
Let us roam the night together
Singing.

Reader's Response: Which poem do you think best captures life in a big city? Explain.

Vocabulary Development

roam (rohm) *v.* go aimlessly; wander

Poetry Collection 3

1. **Interpret:** Explain in your own words what the speaker of "The City Is So Big" has actually seen.

2. **Analyze:** How do the repeated phrases in "Harlem Night Song" emphasize the joyful mood of the poem?

3. **Reading Skill:** Use the **context** surrounding the word *trough* in line 9 of "Concrete Mixers" to explain what a trough looks like and what it does on a concrete mixer.

4. **Literary Analysis:** Use this chart to analyze the **figurative language** in "The City Is So Big."

Object		Object	Similarities	
	is compared to →			❑ Simile ❑ Metaphor ❑ Personification

Writing: Study for a Poem

Write a **study for a poem** about a city setting. List an object, a sight, and a sound that you can find in a city. Then, use simile, metaphor, and personification to describe each item. Use this chart to begin planning your poem.

	Simile	Metaphor	Personification
Object:			
Sight:			
Sound:			

Research and Technology: Mini-Anthology

Create a **mini-anthology** by finding three poems about a similar topic. Use the chart to list your reasons for selecting each poem.

Poem Title	Why I Chose the Poem

Use your notes to create your mini-anthology.

Poetry Collection 4

Summaries The speaker of "Ode to Enchanted Light" enjoys the beauty of nature. A thunderstorm at the beach is described in "Little Exercise." The speaker of "The Sky Is Low, the Clouds Are Mean" humorously describes a dark winter day.

Writing About the Big Question

What is the secret to reaching someone with words? The poets in "Poetry Collection 4" share their ideas about nature. Complete this sentence:

Written works about nature that get the most positive feedback from me are ones that ____

____.

Note-taking Guide

Use this chart to record the main image in each poem.

Ode to Enchanted Light	Little Exercise	The Sky Is Low, the Clouds Are Mean
a forest with light shining through the trees		

Poetry Collection 4

1. **Infer:** Think about how Pablo Neruda describes the world in "Ode to an Enchanted Light." What is his attitude toward life?

2. **Interpret:** It is winter in "The Sky Is Low, the Clouds Are Mean." The writer uses the words *rut, complain,* and *mean.* What mood do these words show about the season?

3. **Reading Skill:** The word *pile* in line 20 of "Little Exercise" is used in a different way than it usually is. Use **context** clues to find another possible meaning.

4. **Literary Analysis:** Use the chart to analyze the **figurative language** in "Ode to an Enchanted Light."

Object		Object	Similarities	
	is compared to →			❑ Simile ❑ Metaphor ❑ Personification

Writing: Study for a Poem

Write a **study for a poem** about a natural setting. List an object, a sight, and a sound that you can find in nature. Then, describe each item through simile, metaphor, and personification. Use this chart to begin planning your poem.

	Simile	Metaphor	Personification
Object:			
Sight:			
Sound:			

Research and Technology: Mini Anthology

Use a chart like the following to record information about the poems that you want to include in your **anthology**. Create a chart for each poem.

Title of poem:	Author:
Why I chose this poem:	

- What do the poems have in common? ______________________

____

- Ideas for my cover and Introduction: ______________________

____

Recipes and Food Labels

About Recipes and Food Labels

Recipes are directions that explain how to make a type of food or drink. You will find recipes much easier to follow after you have learned the different parts of a recipe. These parts include

- a title that names the dish
- a list of ingredients
- directions that tell the steps to follow
- the number of servings the dish will make

Food labels give information about food products. Study the food label in the Student Edition. Reading a food label can tell you

- the number of calories per serving
- the amount of fat, cholesterol, sodium, carbohydrates, protein, and nutrients in the product

Reading Skill

You can **compare and contrast features of consumer materials** to understand how to make a recipe or how to read nutritional information about a product. Some features identify ingredients, highlight important information, or help show what should be done. These features include headings, subheadings, numbers, signal words, illustrations, captions, and italicized and boldfaced type.

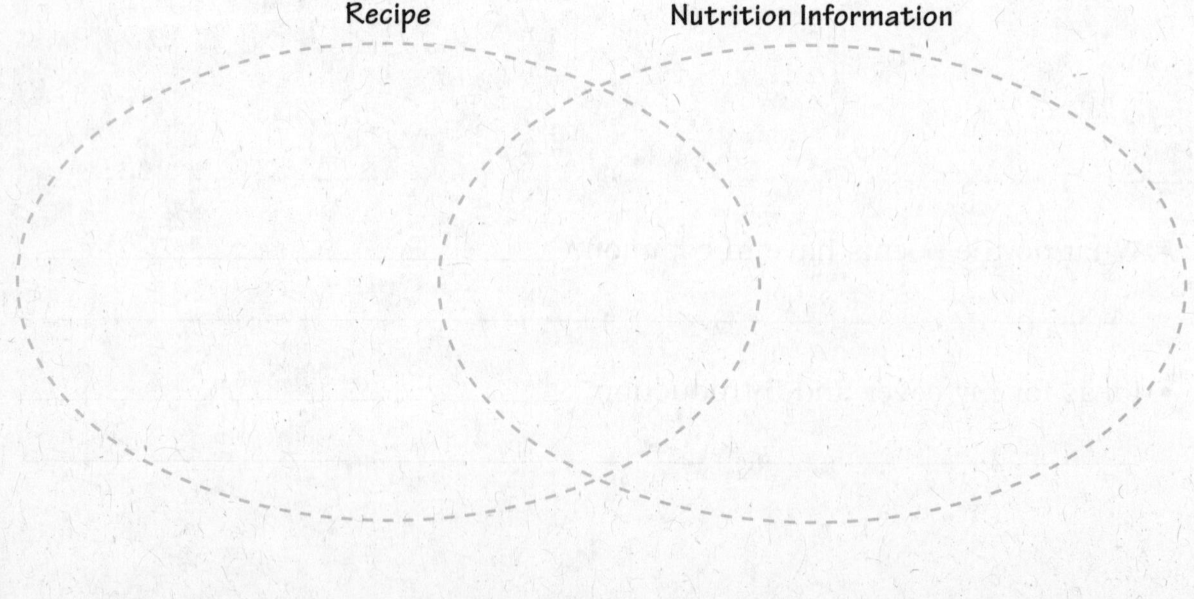

Thumbprint Cookies

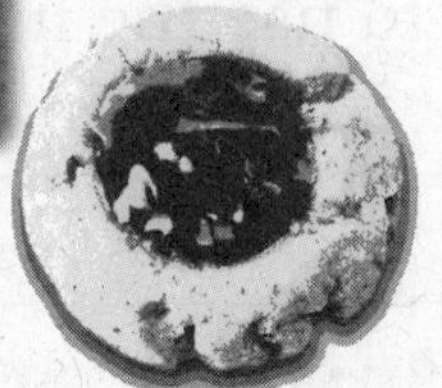

½ cup brown sugar
1 cup butter
2-3 egg yolks
2 cups flour
egg whites
1½ cups chopped nuts
raspberry preserves

A list of ingredients tells readers what goes into the food they will be making.

To separate eggs, crack each egg in half. Over a bowl, pour the egg back and forth between the cracked halves. Let the egg white fall into the bowl, keeping the egg yolk intact in the shell. Cream together sugar, butter, and egg yolks. Beat flour into this mixture. Form balls and dip into slightly beaten egg whites. Roll balls in chopped nuts. Put on lightly greased cookie sheet and make a thumbprint on each ball. Baked at 350° for 8 minutes. Remove from oven and reset thumbprint. Bake 8 to 10 minutes longer. Fill print with raspberry preserves.

Preparation: 25 min.
Baking: 18 min
Yield: 30
Can freeze

Recipe

Features:

- a title that names the food being prepared
- a list of ingredients
- directions that explain how to prepare a certain kind of food
- text written for a general audience

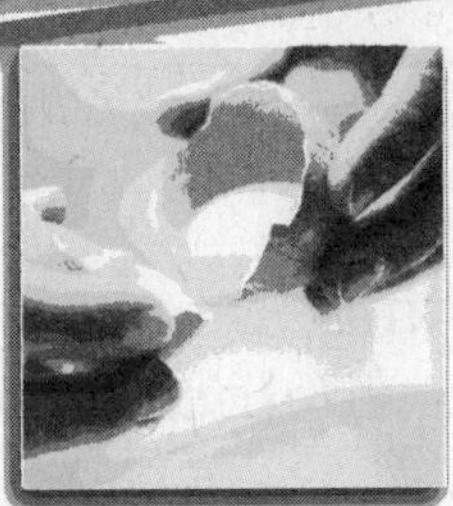

Separating an egg

Using a teaspoon

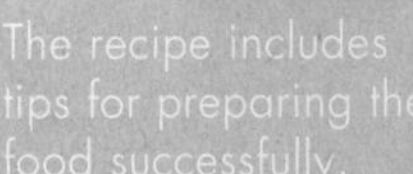

The recipe includes tips for preparing the food successfully.

ABOUT DROP COOKIES

Whoever invented drop cookies, which we used to call "drop cakes," deserves a medal. Except for bars, drop cookies are the easiest of all cookies to make, because shaping usually involves nothing more than dropping dough from a spoon. A few call for patting down the dough or spreading it out with the tip of a knife. In most cases, drop cookies are very forgiving: No harm is done if the mixture is slightly stiffer or softer than expected; the results will just be a little flatter or puffier than usual.

What is the secret to reaching someone with words?
Why is it important that a recipe communicates accurate information?

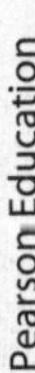

Thinking About the Recipe and the Food Label

1. Why do most recipes list all of the ingredients needed before explaining how to use the ingredients?

2. Why is it important to check a Nutritional Facts label for both the suggested serving size and the number of servings per container?

Reading Skill

3. What information do you learn from the illustrations in the thumbprint cookies recipe?

4. How might comparing and contrasting the nutritional facts on a package of cookies help you decide whether to buy the package?

WRITE ABOUT IT

Timed Writing: Explanation (15 minutes)

Write directions for a food you know how to make.

- What ingredients are needed for this recipe?
- What tools are needed?
- What steps do you take in following the recipe?

Poetry Collection 5 • Poetry Collection 6

Reading Skill

You restate a text in your own words when you **paraphrase**. **Reread to clarify** the writer's meaning before you paraphrase a line or a passage. First, identify the most basic information in each sentence. Then, begin putting the whole sentence into your own words.

- Restate details more simply.
- Use synonyms for the writer's words.
- Look up unfamiliar words. Replace unusual words and sentence structures with language that is more like everyday speech.

Use this chart to help you paraphrase poetry.

Poem:	
Line from poem	
Basic information	
Paraphrase	

Literary Analysis

Two major forms of poetry are lyric poetry and narrative poetry.

- A **lyric poem** expresses the thoughts and feelings of a single **speaker**—the person "saying" the poem—to create a single, unified impression.
- A **narrative poem** tells a story in verse and has all the elements of a short story—characters, setting, conflict, and plot.

As you read, notice the elements of lyric and narrative poetry.

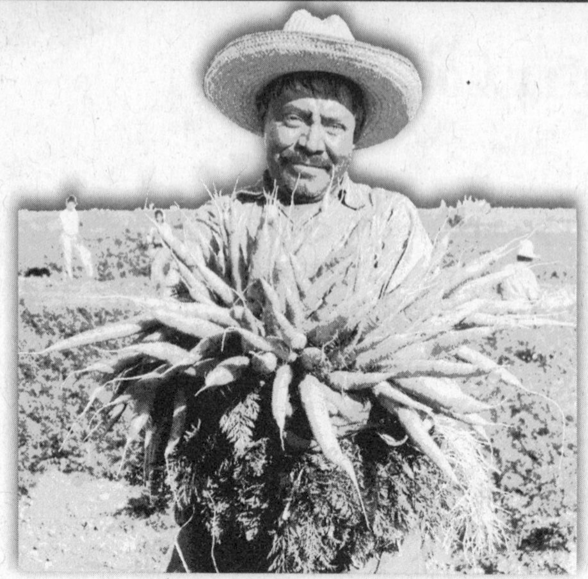

Poetry Collection 5

Summaries In "Runagate Runagate," the speaker describes a frightening escape. "Blow, Blow, Thou Winter Wind" uses images from winter to describe a false friendship. In "Old Man," the speaker celebrates his grandfather.

Writing About the Big Question

What is the secret to reaching someone with words? The poems in "Poetry Collection 5" convey a wide range of emotions such as bitterness, betrayal, fear, courage, love, and loss. Complete this sentence:

I can find poems written in the past relevant as long as they ___________

____.

Note-taking Guide

Use this chart to list the emotions expressed in each poem.

	Emotion
Runagate Runagate	
Blow, Blow, Thou Winter Wind	
Old Man	

Runagate Runagate[1]

Robert Hayden

I.

Runs falls rises stumbles on from darkness
    into darkness
and the darkness thicketed with shapes of
    terror
and the hunters pursuing and the hounds
    pursuing
and the night cold and the night long and the
    river
to cross and the jack-muh-lanterns[2] beckoning
    beckoning
and blackness ahead and when shall I reach
    that somewhere
morning and keep on going and never turn
    back and keep
        on going
            Runagate
                Runagate
                    Runagate

Many thousands rise and go
many thousands crossing over
        O mythic North
    O star-shaped yonder Bible city
Some go weeping and some rejoicing
some in coffins and some in carriages
some in silks and some in shackles

Rise and go or fare you well

No more auction block for me
no more driver's lash for me

Vocabulary Development

beckoning (BEK uhn ing) *v.* summoning or calling

1. **Runagate** *n.* term for a runaway slave who escaped to the North before the Civil War. A series of people with hiding places—"The Underground Railroad"—helped them escape.
2. **jack-muh-lanterns** *n.* jack-o'-lanterns, shifting lights seen over a marsh at night.

TAKE NOTES

Activate Prior Knowledge 

Describe thoughts and feelings that you have had that might be expressed easily in a poem.

Literary Analysis 

A **narrative poem** tells a story in verse and has all the elements of a short story—character, setting, conflict, and plot. What historical setting and conflict are described in this narrative poem?

Reading Check 

Who is chasing the speaker of the poem? Circle the text that tells you.

Literary Analysis

This **narrative poem** is like a short story because it has a plot. What is the plot of part I?

Reading Skill

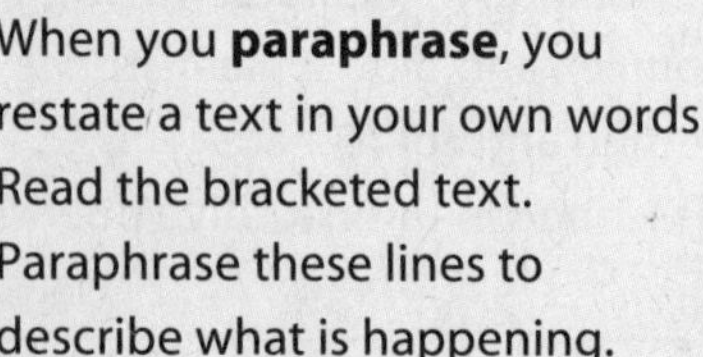

When you **paraphrase**, you restate a text in your own words. Read the bracketed text. Paraphrase these lines to describe what is happening.

Reading Check

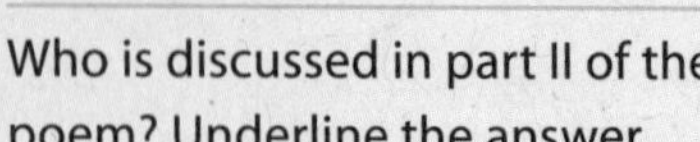

Who is discussed in part II of the poem? Underline the answer.

If you see my Pompey, 30 yrs of age,
new breeches, plain stockings, negro shoes;
if you see my Anna, likely young mulatto
branded E on the right cheek, R on the left,
catch them if you can and notify subscriber.[3]
Catch them if you can, but it won't be easy.
They'll dart underground when you try to
    catch them,
plunge into quicksand, whirlpools, mazes,
turn into scorpions when you try to catch
    them.

And before I'll be a slave
I'll be buried in my grave

North star and bonanza gold
I'm bound for the freedom, freedom-bound
and oh Susyanna don't you cry for me

Runagate

Runagate

II.

Rises from their anguish and their power,
    Harriet Tubman,

woman of earth, whipscarred,
a summoning, a shining

Mean to be free

And this was the way of it, brethren
    brethren,
way we journeyed from Can't to Can.
Moon so bright and no place to hide,
the cry up and the patterollers[4] riding,
hound dogs belling in bladed air.

Vocabulary Development

anguish (AN gwish) *n.* great suffering

3. **subscriber** (suhb SKRY ber) *n.* here, the person from whom the slave Pompey ran away.

4. **patterollers** *n.* dialect for patrollers, people who hunt for runaways.

And fear starts a-murbling, Never make it,
we'll never make it. *Hush that now,*
and she's turned upon us, leveled pistol
glinting in the moonlight:
Dead folks can't jaybird-talk, she says;
You keep on going now or die, she says.

Wanted   Harriet Tubman   alias The General
alias Moses   Stealer of Slaves
In league with Garrison   Alcott   Emerson
Garrett   Douglass   Thoreau   John Brown[4]

Armed and known to be Dangerous

Wanted   Reward   Dead or Alive

Tell me, Ezekiel, oh tell me do you see
mailed Jehovah[5] coming to deliver me?

Hoot-owl calling in the ghosted air,
five times calling to the hants[6] in the air.
Shadow of a face in the scary leaves,
shadow of a voice in the talking leaves:

Come ride-a my train

Oh that train, ghost-story train
through swamp and savanna movering
movering,
over trestles of dew, through caves of the
wish,
Midnight Special on a sabre track movering
movering,
first stop Mercy and the last Hallelujah.

Come ride-a my train

Mean mean mean to be free.

4. Garrison . . . John Brown various abolitionists, people who were against slavery.
5. Jehovah (ji HOH vuh) *n.* one of the translations of the Hebrew word for God.
6. hants (hantz) *n.* dialect term for *ghosts.*

TAKE NOTES

Literary Analysis

What is the conflict of this **narrative poem**?

Reading Skill

Paraphrase lines 67–73. Explain what the "train" is, where it comes from, and where it is going.

Reading Check

To whom does the speaker address the question of whether Jehovah is coming to deliver him? Circle the name in the text.

TAKE NOTES

Reading Skill 

Sometimes it is helpful to **reread to clarify** the reader's meaning. Reread the first bracketed passage. Whom or what is this sentence about? Underline the answer in the text.

Literary Analysis 

A **lyric poem** expresses the thoughts and feelings of a single **speaker**—the person "saying" the poem. To what does the speaker compare the winter's chill in this lyric poem?

____

____

Stop to Reflect 

What overall impression does this poem create? Explain.

____

____

____

Reading Check 

What does the speaker say about life? Underline the text that tells you.

Blow, Blow, Thou Winter Wind

William Shakespeare

Blow, blow, thou winter wind.
Thou art not so unkind
As man's ingratitude.
Thy tooth is not so keen,
Because thou art not seen,
Although thy breath be rude.
Heigh-ho! Sing, heigh-ho! unto the green holly.
Most friendship is feigning, most loving mere folly.[1]
Then, heigh-ho, the holly!
This life is most jolly.

Freeze, freeze, thou bitter sky,
That dost not bite so nigh
As benefits forgot.
Though thou the waters warp,[2]
Thy sting is not so sharp
As friend remembered not.
Heigh-ho! Sing, heigh-ho! unto the green holly.
Most friendship is feigning, most loving mere folly.
Then, heigh-ho, the holly!
This life is most jolly.

Vocabulary Development

ingratitude (in GRA tuh tood) *n.* lack of thankfulness

1. **feigning . . . folly** most friendship is fake, most loving is foolish
2. **warp** *v.* freeze

Old Man

Ricardo Sánchez

remembrance
(smiles/hurts sweetly)
October 8, 1972

old man
with brown skin
talking of past
when being shepherd
in utah, nevada, colorado and
new mexico
was life lived freely;

old man,
grandfather,
wise with time
running rivulets on face,
deep, rich furrows,[1]
each one a legacy,
deep, rich memories of life . . .

"you are indio,[2]
among other things,"
he would tell me
during nights spent
so long ago
amidst familial gatherings
in albuquerque . . .

old man, loved and respected,
he would speak sometimes
of pueblos,[3]
san juan, santa clara,

Vocabulary Development

legacy (LEG uh see) *n.* anything handed down from an ancestor

1. **rivulets . . . furrows** here, the wrinkles on the old man's face.
2. **indio** (IN dee oh) *n.* Indian; Native American.
3. **pueblos** (PWEB lohs) *n.* here, Native American towns in central and northern New Mexico.

TAKE NOTES

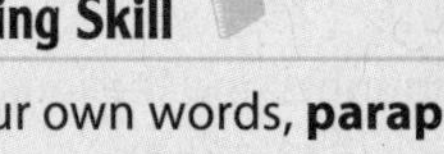

Reading Skill

In your own words, **paraphrase** what the speaker says about the subject of this poem.

Literary Analysis

How does the **speaker** feel about the person he is discussing?

Reading Check

Who is the subject of this poem? Circle the text that tells you.

TAKE NOTES

Literary Analysis

What thoughts and feelings are expressed in this **lyric poem**?

Reading Skill

To **paraphrase** a passage, you can use synonyms to replace the writer's words. Use synonyms to help you paraphrase lines 38–47.

Reading Check

How did the old man know the earth? Underline the text that tells you.

and even santo domingo,
and his family, he would say,
came from there:
some of our blood was here,
he would say,
before the coming of coronado,[4]
other of our blood
came with los españoles,[5]
and the mixture
was rich,
though often painful . . .
old man,
who knew earth
by its awesome aromas
and who felt
the heated sweetness
of chile verde[6]
by his supple touch,
gone into dust is your body
with its stoic look and resolution,
but your reality, old man, lives on
in a mindsoul touched by you . . .

Old Man . . .

Reader's Response: Which poem did you find most meaningful?

Vocabulary Development

stoic (STOH ik) *adj.* calm in the face of suffering

4. **coronado** (kawr uh NAH doh) sixteenth-century Spanish explorer Francisco Vasquez de Coronado journeyed through what is today the American Southwest.
5. **los españoles** (los es pan YOH les) *n.* Spaniards.
6. **chile verde** (CHEE lay VER day) *n.* green pepper.

Poetry Collection 5

1. **Respond:** Which poem did you find most meaningful? Explain.

2. **Analyze:** Fill out this chart to explain what the lines mean.

	What Does It Say?	What Does It Mean?	Why Is It Important?
Runagate Runagate	(Lines 1–2)		
Blow, Blow . . .	(Line 8)		
Old Man	(Lines 8–14)		

3. **Reading Skill: Paraphrase** lines 1–3 of "Blow, Blow, Thou Winter Wind," using everyday speech.

4. **Literary Analysis:** What overall impression is created in the lyric poem, "Old Man"? Explain.

Writing: Lyric or Narrative Poem

Write a **lyric or narrative poem** about a person whom you admire. Your subject can be a historical figure or someone you know.

Answer the following questions to help you get started. Use your notes as you write your poem.

- Why do you admire this person?

____

____

- What thoughts and feelings do you have about him or her?

____

____

- What overall impression do you want to express about this person?

____

____

Listening and Speaking: Evaluation Form

Complete the following **evaluation form** for poetry reading. In the left column, add another "quality" that you consider to be important. Fill in an evaluation for a classmate's reading.

Poem title:		
Qualities	Score (1–10)	Comments
Properly adjusts tone		
Pauses at correct places		
Reads loudly and clearly		

Poetry Collection 6

Summaries In "The New Colossus," the speaker describes the Statue of Liberty. In "Paul Revere's Ride," the speaker tells the story of Paul Revere's ride. In "Harriet Beecher Stowe," the speaker praises Harriet Beecher Stowe, who helped people understand the fight against slavery.

Writing About the Big Question

What is the secret to reaching someone with words? The poems in "Poetry Collection 6" recall important events and people in American history. Complete this sentence:

The description of an event from history needs to ____________________

________________________________ in order to have significance for me.

Note-taking Guide

Use this chart to recall the key parts of the poems.

	The New Colossus	Paul Revere's Ride	Harriet Beecher Stowe
Main Subject	The Statue of Liberty		
Main Idea		Paul Revere rode a horse all night to warn people that the British troops were coming.	
Why is the poem's subject important?			Her book helped bring about the end of slavery.

Poetry Collection 6

1. **Respond:** Which poem's subject interests you most? Explain.

2. **Interpret:** Fill out the chart to interpret the lines indicated. Follow the example given to you.

	What Does It Say?	What Does It Mean?	Why Is It Important?
The New Colossus	(Line 9)	Ancient cultures, continue to celebrate your magnificent achievements.	The United States is not interested in remaking the achievements of the past. It wants to make something new.
Harriet Beecher Stowe	(Line 9–10)		
Paul Revere's Ride	(Line 78–80)		

3. **Reading Skill:** Reread lines 3–5 of "The New Colossus." **Paraphrase** the lines. Use a sentence structure that is more like everyday speech.

4. **Literary Analysis:** "Paul Revere's Ride" is a **narrative** poem. What are the setting and conflict of the poem?

Writing: Lyric or Narrative Poem

Write a **lyric or narrative poem** about a person whom you admire. The person can be someone you know or someone from history. Use the following prompts to revise your lyric or narrative poem.

- Write the lines of your poem.

____

____

____

____

- Circle words that you could change to make your poem more musical.
- What musical words could you use to replace your circled words?

____

____

____

Listening and Speaking: Evaluation Form

Prepare an **evaluation form** for poetry reading. Use the chart to list qualities you think a good poetry reader should have. Write why you think the quality is important. Then, explain how you could evaluate each quality. Use your notes to create your evaluation form.

Quality	Why It Is Important	How to Evaluate It

Poetry Collection 7 • Poetry Collection 8

Reading Skill

Paraphrasing is restating something in your own words. Poetry often expresses ideas in language that does not sound like everyday speech. Paraphrasing can improve your understanding.

- First, **read aloud fluently according to punctuation.** Pause briefly at commas, dashes, and semicolons and longer after end marks, such as periods. Using punctuation will help you group words for meaning and recognize complete thoughts.
- Next, restate the meaning of each complete thought in your own words. Use synonyms for the writer's words. Rewrite unusual or complicated expressions in simple words.

As you read, pause occasionally to paraphrase what you have just read and clarify your understanding.

Literary Analysis

Imagery is language that appeals to the senses. Poets use imagery to help readers imagine sights, sounds, textures, tastes, and smells.

- **With imagery:** The train thundered past, roaring, screaming.
- **Without imagery:** The train went by.

For each poem, use this chart to note imagery.

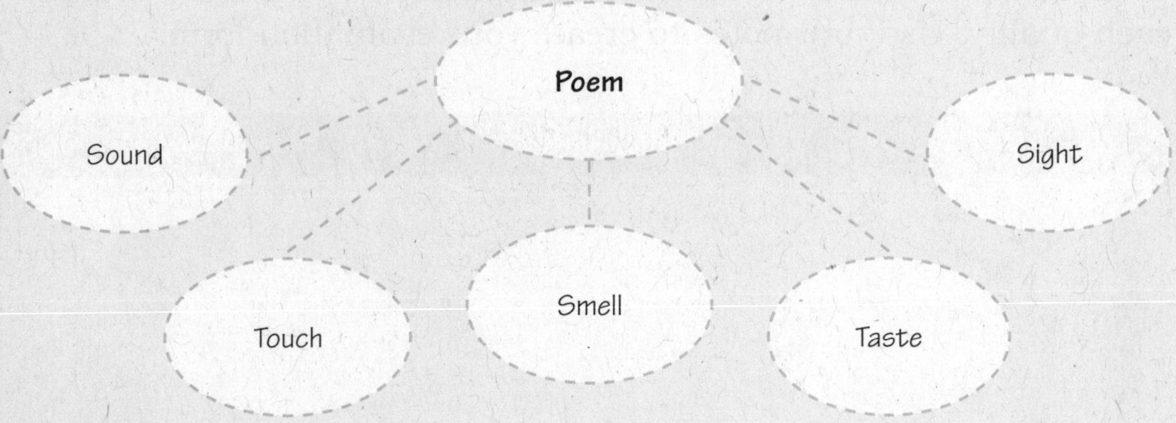

Poetry Collection 7

The Magpie(detail), 1869, Claude Monet, Musee d'Orsay, Paris

Summaries In "January," the speaker describes images connected with winter. "New World" shares different parts of the day in nature. In "For My Sister Molly Who in the Fifties," the speaker talks about her relationship with her sister.

Writing About the Big Question

What is the secret to reaching someone with words? The poets in "Poetry Collection 7" carefully choose words to convey a speaker's ideas about specific people and places. Complete this sentence:

If someone who did not know me asked me to describe my hometown or my family, I would choose sensory images such as _______________________ _______________________ and _______________________.

Note-taking Guide

Use this chart to record the images in each poem.

January	New World	For My Sister Who . . .
snowy footsteps		

TAKE NOTES

Activate Prior Knowledge 

Think about your relationship with the natural world. What in nature inspires you?

Literary Analysis 

Imagery is language that appeals to the senses. Underline two examples of imagery in this poem. Is the imagery effective? Explain.

Reading Check 

What things does the speaker associate with the month of January? Underline three examples.

January

John Updike

The days are short,
    The sun a spark
Hung thin between
    The dark and dark.

Fat snowy footsteps
    Track the floor,
And parkas pile up
    Near the door.

The river is
    A frozen place
Held still beneath
    The trees' black lace.

The sky is low.
    The wind is gray.
The radiator
    Purrs all day.

New World

N. Scott Momaday

1.

First Man,
behold:
the earth
glitters
with leaves;
the sky
glistens
with rain.
Pollen
is borne
on winds
that low
and lean
upon
mountains.
Cedars
blacken
the slopes—
and pines.

2.

At dawn
eagles
hie and
hover[1]
above
the plain
where light
gathers
in pools.
Grasses
shimmer
and shine.

Vocabulary Development

glistens (GLI suhnz) *v.* shines; sparkles

1. **hie and hover** fly swiftly and then hang as if suspended in the air.

TAKE NOTES

Reading Skill 

Circle the punctuation marks in the bracketed stanza. Then, **read aloud fluently according to punctuation**. How many sentences are in this stanza?

____

Literary Analysis 

In the second stanza, underline examples of **imagery.** How do these images capture a feeling of newness?

____

____

____

Reading Check 

Whom does the speaker address in this poem? Circle the name of the person.

TAKE NOTES

Reading Skill

Paraphrase lines 46–51.

____

____

____

____

Literary Analysis

In the fourth stanza, what **imagery** conveys a sense of temperature?

____

____

____

____

Reading Check 

What times of day does the speaker mention? Circle the words that signal each time of day.

Shadows
withdraw
and lie
away
like smoke.

3.

At noon
turtles
enter
slowly
into
the warm
dark loam.[2]
Bees hold
the swarm.
Meadows
recede
through planes
of heat
and pure
distance.

4.

At dusk
the gray
foxes
stiffen
in cold;
blackbirds
are fixed
in the
branches.
Rivers
follow
the moon,
the long
white track
of the
full moon.

Vocabulary Development

recede (ri SEED) *v.* move away

2. **loam** (lohm) rich, dark soil.

For My Sister Molly Who in the Fifties

Alice Walker

FOR MY SISTER MOLLY WHO IN THE FIFTIES
Once made a fairy rooster from
Mashed potatoes
Whose eyes I forget
But green onions were his tail
And his two legs were carrot sticks
A tomato slice his crown.
Who came home on vacation
When the sun was hot
and cooked
and cleaned
And minded least of all
The children's questions
A million or more
Pouring in on her
Who had been to school
And knew (and told us too) that certain
Words were no longer good
And taught me not to say us for we
No matter what "Sonny said" up the road.

FOR MY SISTER MOLLY WHO IN THE FIFTIES
Knew Hamlet[1] well and read into the night
And coached me in my songs of Africa
A continent I never knew
But learned to love
Because "they" she said could carry
A tune
And spoke in accents never heard
In Eatonton.
Who read from *Prose and Poetry*
And loved to read "Sam McGee from
Tennessee"[2]
On nights the fire was burning low
And Christmas wrapped in angel hair[3]
And I for one prayed for snow.

1. **Hamlet** play by William Shakespeare.
2. **"Sam McGee from Tennessee"** reference to the title character in the Robert Service poem, "The Cremation of Sam McGee."
3. **angel hair** fine, white, filmy Christmas tree decoration.

TAKE NOTES

Literary Analysis

What does the **imagery** in the first stanza tell you about Molly?

Stop to Reflect

Do the descriptions in the first stanza effectively appeal to your senses? Explain.

Reading Skill

Read lines 22–30 to identify two complete thoughts. **Paraphrase** the lines.

Reading Check

What does the speaker appreciate about her sister? Circle the answer in the poem.

TAKE NOTES

Reading Skill

Paraphrase the underlined passage.

Stop to Reflect

How do you think the speaker feels about Molly?

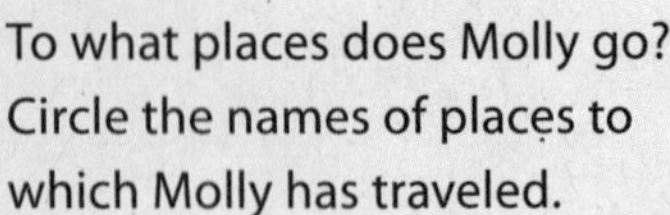

Reading Check

To what places does Molly go? Circle the names of places to which Molly has traveled.

WHO IN THE FIFTIES
Knew all the written things that made
Us laugh and stories by
The hour   Waking up the story buds
Like fruit. Who walked among the flowers
And brought them inside the house
And smelled as good as they
And looked as bright.
Who made dresses, braided
Hair. Moved chairs about
Hung things from walls
Ordered baths
Frowned on wasp bites
And seemed to know the endings
Of all the tales
I had forgot.

WHO OFF INTO THE UNIVERSITY
Went exploring   To London and
To Rotterdam
Prague and to Liberia
Bringing back the news to us
Who knew none of it
But followed
crops and weather
funerals and
Methodist Homecoming;
easter speeches,
groaning church.

WHO FOUND ANOTHER WORLD
Another life   With gentlefolk
Far less trusting
And moved and moved and changed
Her name
And sounded precise
When she spoke   And frowned away
Our sloppishness.

WHO SAW US SILENT
Cursed with fear   A love burning
Inexpressible
And sent me money not for me
But for "College."

Who saw me grow through letters
The words misspelled   But not
The longing   Stretching
Growth
The tied and twisting
Tongue
Feet no longer bare
Skin no longer burnt against
The cotton.

WHO BECAME SOMEONE OVERHEAD
A light   A thousand watts
Bright and also blinding
And saw my brothers cloddish
And me destined to be
Wayward[4]
My mother remote   My father
A wearisome farmer
With heartbreaking
Nails.

FOR MY SISTER MOLLY WHO IN THE FIFTIES
Found much
Unbearable
Who walked where few had
Understood   And sensed our
Groping after light
And saw some extinguished
And no doubt mourned.

FOR MY SISTER MOLLY WHO IN THE FIFTIES
Left us.

Reader's Response: Of the three poems in this collection, which creates the most vivid impression? Explain your choice.

____

____

TAKE NOTES

Literary Analysis 

What **imagery** in the underlined passage appeals to the senses?

____

Reading Skill 

Paraphrase the complete thought expressed in the bracketed passage.

____

Stop to Reflect

Why are the lessons Molly teaches important to the speaker?

____

Vocabulary Development

remote (ri MOHT) *adj.* aloof; cold; distant

4. **wayward** (WAY werd) *adj.* headstrong; disobedient.

Poetry Collection 7

1. **Draw Conclusions:** The speaker in "January" describes things that he associates with the month of January. According to these descriptions, does the speaker have a positive or negative attitude toward winter? Explain.

____

____

____

2. **Interpret:** In "New World," the speaker identifies three times of day. What might the times of the day represent?

____

____

____

3. **Reading Skill:** Use this chart to **paraphrase** line selections from each poem.

Original Lines	Paraphrase
January (Lines 13–16)	
New World (Lines 37–45)	
For My Sister Molly . . . (Lines 16–18)	

4. **Literary Analysis:** List three memorable images from "For My Sister Molly Who in the Fifties." What mood, or feeling, do these images create?

____

____

____

Writing: Review

A review of a literary work is an evaluation of its strengths and weaknesses. Write a **review** of this three-poem collection. Use the following chart to write notes for your review.

	Poem's Strengths	Poem's Weaknesses	Opinion of Poem
January			
New World			
For My Sister . . .			

Research and Technology: Profile

Write a **profile** of one of the poets featured in this collection. Gather information about the poet's life, writings, and influences. Write notes about the following information.

- Describe two important experiences in the poet's life. How did these experiences affect the poet?

___

___

- Who or what influenced the poet and his or her work? In what way?

___

___

___

Poetry Collection 8

Summaries In "Grandma Ling," the speaker travels to Taiwan to meet her grandmother. She and her grandmother do not speak the same language. They still feel close to each other. In "Drum Song," the lines flow like the beat of a drum. The speaker tells how a turtle, a woodpecker, a snowhare, and a woman move through the world to their own beat. The speaker in "your little voice/ Over the wires came leaping" talks to a special person on the telephone. Her voice makes him dizzy. He thinks of flowers. He feels as though he is dancing.

Writing About the Big Question

What is the secret to reaching someone with words? The poems in "Poetry Collection 8" explore how words make connections between people and the world. Complete this sentence:

I had a connection to other people when I ______________________

____.

Note-taking Guide

Use this chart to help you note the events of each poem.

Grandma Ling	Drum Song	your little voice/Over the wires came leaping
The speaker visits her grandmother in Taiwan.		

Poetry Collection 8

1. **Speculate:** The grandmother and the granddaughter in "Grandma Ling" do not speak the same language. What might they want to tell each other if they could speak the same language?

____

____

2. **Analyze:** Think about what the animals and women are doing in "Drum Song." How do the animals and women interact with their environments?

____

____

3. **Reading Skill:** Read the lines listed in this chart. **Paraphrase** the lines.

Original Lines	Paraphrase
Grandma Ling (Lines 15–16)	
Drum Song (Lines 8–13)	
your little voice . . . (Lines 1–6)	

4. **Literary Analysis: Imagery** is language that appeals to the senses. Write two images from "your little voice. . . ." To what senses do these images appeal?

____

____

____

____

Writing: Review

Write a **review** of the poems in this collection. Use these questions to write notes for your review.

	Grandma Ling	Drum Song	your little voice . . .
How does the rhythm match the subject?			
How do the words match the subject?			
Which lines have vivid imagery?			

Research and Technology: Poet's Profile

Complete the following chart with information about the poet you have chosen. Your **profile** should tell about the poet's life experiences. You should also include how the poet's life has affected his or her writing.

Poet: ______________________________

Significant life events	
Awards/Honors	
Jobs	
Influences	

Use this information to write your profile.

Manuals

About Manuals

A **manual** is a set of directions. It tells how to use a tool or product. Most manuals have these parts:

- a drawing or picture of the product with the parts and features labeled
- step-by-step directions for putting the item together and using it
- safety information
- a guide that tells how to fix common problems
- customer service information, such as telephone numbers, addresses, and Web site addresses

Reading Skill

You use a manual to perform a task. In order to use a manual effectively, you must **analyze the technical directions.** Study the drawings, diagrams, headings, lists, and labels to help you follow the directions. Bold type and capital letters often signal specific sections and important information.

Checklist for Following Technical Directions

- ☐ Read all the directions completely before starting to follow them.
- ☐ Look for clues such as bold type or capital letters that point out specific sections or important information.
- ☐ Use diagrams to locate and name the parts of the product.
- ☐ Follow each step in the exact order given.
- ☐ Do not skip any steps.

Using Your Answering Machine

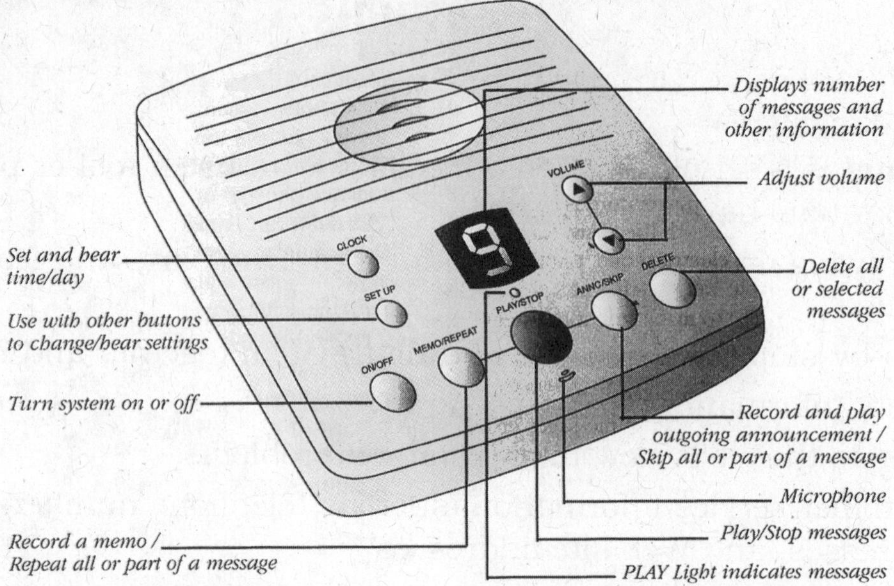

Setting the Clock

You'll need to set the clock so that it can announce the day and time that each message is received. Press PLAY/STOP to exit Setting the Clock at any time.

1 Press and hold CLOCK until the Message Window displays CLOCK, and the default day is announced.

2 To change the day setting, hold down MEMO/REPEAT or ANNC/SKIP until the correct day is announced. Then release the button.

3 Press and release CLOCK. The current hour setting is announced.

4 To change the hour setting, hold down MEMO/REPEAT or ANNC/SKIP until the correct hour is announced. Then release the button.

5 Press and release CLOCK. The current minutes setting is announced.

6 To change the minutes setting, hold down MEMO/REPEAT or ANNC/SKIP until the correct minutes setting is announced. Then release the button.

7 Press and release CLOCK. The new day and time are announced.

To check the clock, *press and release* CLOCK.

NOTE: *In the event of a power failure, see the instructions on the bottom of the unit to reset the clock.*

Recording Your Announcement

Before using this answering system, you should record the announcement (up to one minute long) that callers will hear when the system answers a call. If you choose not to record an announcement, the system answers with a prerecorded announcement: *"Hello. Please leave a message after the tone."*

1 Press and hold ANNC/SKIP. The system beeps. Speak toward the microphone normally, from about nine inches away. While you are recording, the Message Window displays —.

2 To stop recording, release ANNC/SKIP. The system automatically plays back your announcement.

To review your announcement, *press and release* ANNC/SKIP.

Turning the System On/Off

Use ON/OFF to turn the system on and off. When the system is off, the Message Window is blank.

Volume Control

Use volume buttons (▲ and ▼) to adjust the volume of the system's speaker. Press the top button (▲) to increase volume. Press the bottom button (▼) to decrease volume. The system beeps three times when you reach the maximum or minimum volume setting.

2

Announcement Monitor

You can choose whether to hear the announcement when your system answers a call, or have it silent (off) on your end (your caller will still hear an announcement).

1 Press and hold [SET UP]. After the Ring Select setting is announced, continue to press and release [SET UP] until the system announces "*Monitor is on (or off).*"

2 Press and release [ANNC/SKIP] or [MEMO/REPEAT] until the system announces your selection.

3 Press and release [PLAY/STOP] or [SET UP] to exit.

Listening to Your Messages

As the system plays back messages, the Message Window displays the number of the message playing. Before playing each message, the system announces the day and time the message was received. After playing the last message, the system announces "*End of messages.*"

Play all messages — Press and release [PLAY/STOP]. If you have no messages, the system announces "*No messages.*"

Play new messages only — Hold down [PLAY/STOP] for about two seconds, until the system begins playing. If you have no new messages, the system announces "*No new messages.*"

Repeat entire message — Press and release [MEMO/REPEAT].

Repeat part of message — Hold down [MEMO/REPEAT] until you hear a beep, then release to resume playing. The more beeps you hear, the farther back in the message you will be when you release the button.

Repeat previous message — Press [MEMO/REPEAT] twice, continue this process to hear other previous messages.

Skip to next message — Press and release [ANNC/SKIP].

Skip part of a message — Hold down [ANNC/SKIP] until you hear a beep, then release to resume playing. The more beeps you hear, the farther into the message you will be when you release the button.

Stop message playback — Press and release [PLAY/STOP].

Saving Messages

The system automatically saves your messages if you do not delete them. The system can save about 12 minutes of messages, including your announcement, for a total of up to 59 messages. When memory is full, you must delete some or all messages before new messages can be recorded.

Deleting Messages

Delete all messages — Hold down [DELETE]. The system announces "*Messages deleted*" and permanently deletes messages. The Message Window displays **0**. If you haven't listened to all of the messages, the system beeps five times, and does not delete messages.

Delete selected messages — Press and release [DELETE] while the message you want to delete is being played. The system beeps once, and continues with the next message. If you want to check a message before you delete it, you can press [MEMO/REPEAT] to replay the message before deleting it.

When the system reaches the end of the last message, the messages not deleted are renumbered, and the Message Window displays the total number of messages remaining in memory.

Recording a Memo

You can record a memo to be stored as an incoming message. The memo can be up to three minutes long, and will be played back with other messages.

1 Press and hold [MEMO/REPEAT]. After the beep, speak toward the microphone.

2 To stop recording, release [MEMO/REPEAT].

3 To play the memo, press [PLAY/STOP].

When Memory is Full

The system can record approximately 12 minutes of messages, including your announcement, for a total of up to 59 messages. When memory is full, or 59 messages have been recorded, the Message Window flashes **F**. Delete messages to make room for new ones.

When memory is full, the system answers calls after 10 rings, and sounds two beeps instead of your announcement.

4

Thinking About the Manual

1. You may use some of the answering machine features more than others. Which features do you think are most important? Explain.

2. Look at the diagram. How does it make the text easier to follow?

Reading Skill

3. Many words in the answering machine manual are boxed and set in italic type. What does this formatting tell about these words?

4. How are the steps in the process for "Setting the Clock" identified?

WRITE ABOUT IT Timed Writing: Analyze Technical Directions (20 minutes)

Reread the section of the manual headed "Setting the Clock." Explain how text features (headings, numbering, boxed terms, and italic type) help the reader understand the text. Use these questions to help organize your writing.

1. Why are parts of the text numbered?
2. Why are some words set inside a box?
3. What information is set in italic type?

from Anne Frank & Me

Drama is written to be performed. You must visualize how the action would appear and sound to an audience as you read it. Dramas can include elements of fiction such as plot, conflict, and setting. They also use some unique elements, such as those listed in this chart.

Element	Definition	Example
Playwright	• author of a play	William Shakespeare
Script	• written form of a play	*Romeo and Juliet*
Acts	• units of the action in a play	Act III
Scenes	• parts of an act	Act III, scene ii
Characterization	• the playwright's technique of creating believable characters	A character hangs his head to show that he is ashamed.
Dialogue	• words that characters say • words that characters speak appear next to their names • much of what you learn about the play is revealed through dialogue	JIM: When did you recognize me? LAURA: Oh, right away.
Monologue	• a long, uninterrupted speech that is spoken by a single character	HAMLET: To be, or not to be . . .
Stage Directions	• bracketed information that tells the cast, crew, and readers of the play about sound effects, actions, and sets • this information can also describe a character's gestures or emotions	*[whispering]*
Set	• scenery on stage that suggests the time and place of the action	a kitchen, a park
Props	• small, portable items that make actions look realistic	plates, a book

There are different types of drama. Several types are listed below.

Comedy is a form of drama that has a happy ending. Comedies often feature normal characters in funny situations. Comedies can be written to entertain their audiences. They can also point out the faults of a society.

Tragedy is often contrasted with comedy. Events in a tragedy lead to the downfall of the main character. This character can be an average person. More often the main character is a person of great importance, such as a king or a heroic figure.

Drama is often used to describe plays that focus on serious subjects. Some dramas are not performed on a stage. These types of drama are listed below.

- **Screenplays** are scripts for films. They include instructions for the camera. A screenplay usually has many more scene changes than a stage play.

- **Teleplays** are scripts for television. They often contain the same elements that screenplays have.

- **Radio plays** are scripts for radio broadcasts. A radio play includes sound effects, but it does not have a set.

from Anne Frank & Me

Cherie Bennett

Summary An American teenager named Nicole travels back in time to Paris in 1942. Her family is arrested for being Jewish. They are put on a train going to a prison camp. Nicole recognizes Anne Frank on the train. She tells Anne details about Anne's life. Both girls are shocked by what Nicole knows.

Note-taking Guide

Use this diagram to compare and contrast the main characters.

Nicole

Both

teens

Anne

TAKE NOTES

from Anne Frank & Me

Cherie Bennett

Activate Prior Knowledge 

Imagine that you are arrested because of something you believe. How would you feel?

____

____

____

____

____

____

Drama 

A **scene** is one part of an **act** in a drama. Where is the setting of this scene? Underline the time. Circle the place.

Drama 

Props are items actors use in a drama to make the play more realistic. Read the bracketed passage. List the two props used.

____

____

Reading Check 

Whom does Nicole meet on the train? Underline the line that tells you.

After Nicole, a typical suburban American teenager, bumps her head in an accident, she wakes up in another time and place—Paris in 1942. Nicole's new family is Jewish. Soon after the Nazis arrest the family, they are put on a train to Auschwitz.[1] *This is where Nicole meets Anne Frank,*[2] *the real writer of* The Diary of a Young Girl.

AT RISE: *During the following monologue,* NAZIS *shove more people into the cattle car.*

NICOLE. *(pre-recorded).* Right now we are in Westerbork, in Holland. Earlier today they opened the door and shoved more people into our car. They speak Dutch. I can't understand them at all. I try to keep track of the dates as best I can. I think it is the 3rd of September, 1944. Surely the war will be over soon.

(Train sounds. NICOLE *makes her way to the bucket in the corner which is used as a toilet. A* GIRL *sits in front of the bucket, asleep, her back is to us.)*

NICOLE. *(tapping the* GIRL *on the shoulder).* I'm sorry to disturb you, but I need to use the—

(The GIRL *turns around. It is* ANNE FRANK, *thin, huge eyes. Their eyes meet. Some memory is instantly triggered in* NICOLE. *She knows this girl, knows things about her. But how?)*

ANNE. *Spreekn U Nederlander?* (Spreck-en Ooo Ned-er-lahn-der?) (NICOLE *just stares.)* So you speak French, then? Is this better?

NICOLE. I . . . I need to use the—

ANNE. It's all right. I'll hold my coat for you to give you some privacy. (NICOLE *goes to the bucket,* ANNE *holds her coat open to shield her.)*

Vocabulary Development

privacy (PRY vuh see) *n.* state of being able to be alone

1. **Auschwitz** a Nazi concentration camp in Poland during World War II. Anne Frank was taken to this camp in 1944 and died at another camp, Bergen-Belsen, in 1945.
2. **Anne Frank** a young German Jewish girl who wrote a diary about her family's hiding in The Netherlands during the Holocaust. The Holocaust was the mass killing of European Jews and others by the Nazis during World War II.

NICOLE. Thank you.

ANNE. Just please do the same for me when the time comes. Have you been in here a long time? *(NICOLE finishes, fixes her dress.)*

NICOLE. Seventeen days, starting just outside Paris.

ANNE. It smells like it.

NICOLE. Does it? I can't even tell anymore.

ANNE. It's all right. It's not important.

NICOLE. Look, I know this sounds crazy, but . . . I know you.

ANNE. Have you been to Amsterdam?

NICOLE. No, never.

ANNE. Well, I've never been to Paris. Although I will go some day, I can assure you of that.

NICOLE. I do know you. Your name is . . . Anne Frank.

ANNE. *(shocked).* That's right! Who are you?

NICOLE. Nicole Bernhardt. I know so much about you . . . you were in hiding for a long time, in a place you called . . . the Secret Annex[3]—

ANNE. How could you know that?

NICOLE. *(her memory is flooded).* You were with your parents, and your older sister . . . Margot! And . . . some other people . . .

ANNE. Mr. Pfeffer and the Van Pels, they're all back there asleep—

NICOLE. Van Daans!

ANNE. *(shocked).* I only called them that in my diary. How could you know that?

NICOLE. And Peter! Your boyfriend's name was Peter!

ANNE. How could you know that??

NICOLE. You thought your parents would disapprove that you were kissing him—

ANNE. How is this possible?

NICOLE. You kept a diary. I read it.

ANNE. But . . . I left my diary in the Annex when the Gestapo[4] came. You couldn't have read it.

NICOLE. But I did.

3. **Secret Annex** name given to the space in an Amsterdam office building in which thirteen-year-old Anne Frank and her family lived after they went into hiding in 1942.

4. **Gestapo** German security police under the Nazis.

TAKE NOTES

Drama 

Stage directions sometimes tell how the characters speak. How does Anne's tone of voice change in the bracketed dialogue?

____

Drama 

Review the chart on page 283. What element of **drama** would you call the conversation between Anne and Nicole?

____

Drama 

From what you have read so far, tell which **type of drama** "Anne Frank & Me" is.

____

Explain your answer.

____

____

____

Reading Check 

What was the name of Anne's boyfriend? Underline the text that tells you.

Drama 

Look at the **stage directions** in the bracketed passage. Circle the stage direction that deals with an actor's emotions. Write the direction that describes an action.

Stop to Reflect 

What is the most unbelievable part of this drama? Explain your answer.

Reading Check 

What does Anne believe Nicole is? Draw a box around the text that tells you.

ANNE. How?

NICOLE. I don't know.

ANNE. *(skeptical).* This is a very, very strange conversation.

NICOLE. I feel like it was . . . I know this sounds crazy . . . but I feel like it was in the future.

ANNE. This is a joke, right? Peter put you up to this.

NICOLE. No—

ANNE. Daddy, then, to take my mind off—

NICOLE. No.

ANNE. *(cynical).* Maybe you're a mind reader! *(She closes her eyes.)* What number am I thinking of right now?

NICOLE. I have no idea. Do you believe in time travel?

ANNE. I'm to believe that you're from the future? Really, I'm much more intelligent than I look.

NICOLE. I don't know how I know all this. I just do.

ANNE. Maybe you're an angel.

NICOLE. That would certainly be news to me.

Reader's Response: Do you like this strange way of meeting Anne Frank? Explain why or why not.

Vocabulary Development

cynical (SIN i kuhl) *adj.* unwilling to believe that someone has good or honest reasons for doing something

intelligent (in TEL uh juhnt) *adj.* having a high level of ability to learn, understand, and think about things

Drama

1. **Respond:** How would you feel if someone you had never met knew details about your personal life?

2. **Generalize:** What are the living conditions on the train?

3. **Drama:** Is this play a **comedy**, a **tragedy**, or a **drama**? Explain your answer.

4. **Drama:** The author makes Anne and Nicole believable **characters**. List details from the drama that make them believable.

Character Description	
Anne	Nicole
huge eyes	anxious, confused

Bulletin Board Display

Create a **bulletin board display**. Following these tips will help prepare you to create a bulletin board display.

- Read some of the author's works. Cherie Bennett's books include *Zink, Life in the Fat Lane, Searching for David's Heart,* and *A Heart Divided.*

What I learned from Bennett's writing:

___

___

___

___

- Search the Internet. Use words and phrases such as "Cherie Bennett."

What I learned about Cherie Bennett:

___

___

___

___

- Watch the video interview with Cherie Bennett. Add what you learn from the video to what you have already learned about the author.

Additional information learned about the author:

___

___

___

___

___

___

Use your notes to create your bulletin board display.

The Governess

Reading Skill

Drawing conclusions means reaching decisions or forming opinions after considering the facts and details in a text. To draw conclusions from a play, observe what characters say and do.

- Look for statements that reveal underlying ideas and attitudes.
- Analyze interactions that show how characters treat each other.
- Notice actions that create a clear pattern of behavior.

Make connections among these items to decide what that pattern tells you about the character. Use the chart shown to record your observations and conclusions.

Statements	Interactions	Actions

Conclusion

Literary Analysis

Stage directions are notes that tell how a play should be performed. They describe the scenery, costumes, lighting, and sound, and also tell how the characters feel, move, and speak. Stage directions are usually printed in italics and set in brackets or parentheses. These stage directions describe the setting of a play:

(It is late evening. The stage is dark, except for the glow of a small lamp beside the bed.)

When you read a play, use the stage directions to create a mental image of how an actual stage production would look and sound.

The Governess

Neil Simon

Summary A wealthy mistress plays a joke on her shy employee, Julia. The mistress subtracts money from Julia's pay. Julia is left with much less money than she is owed. The mistress hopes that Julia will become angry and stand up for herself.

Writing About the Big Question

Is it our differences or our similarities that matter most? The characters in *The Governess* come from different levels of society, which affects the way they treat each other. Complete this sentence:

An employer might discriminate against an employee, or treat her unfairly because ____

____.

Note-taking Guide

Use this chart to record the actions of the mistress and the way the governess responds to these actions.

Mistress's Action	Governess's Response

The Governess

Neil Simon

MISTRESS. Julia! *(Calls again)* Julia!

(A young governess, JULIA, *comes rushing in. She stops before the desk and curtsies.)*

JULIA. *(Head down)* Yes, madame?

MISTRESS. Look at me, child. Pick your head up. I like to see your eyes when I speak to you.

JULIA. *(Lifts her head up)* Yes, madame. *(But her head has a habit of slowly drifting down again)*

MISTRESS. And how are the children coming along with their French lessons?

JULIA. They're very bright children, madame.

MISTRESS. Eyes up . . . They're bright, you say. Well, why not? And mathematics? They're doing well in mathematics, I assume?

JULIA. Yes, madame. Especially Vanya.

MISTRESS. Certainly. I knew it. I excelled in mathematics. He gets that from his mother, wouldn't you say?

JULIA. Yes, madame.

MISTRESS. Head up . . . *(She lifts head up)* That's it. Don't be afraid to look people in the eyes, my dear. If you think of yourself as inferior, that's exactly how people will treat you.

JULIA. Yes, ma'am.

MISTRESS. A quiet girl, aren't you? . . . Now then, let's settle our accounts. I imagine you must need money, although you never ask me for it yourself. Let's see now, we agreed on thirty rubles[1] a month, did we not?

JULIA. *(Surprised)* Forty, ma'am.

MISTRESS. No, no, thirty. I made a note of it. *(Points to the book)* I always pay my governess thirty . . . Who told you forty?

Vocabulary Development

inferior (in FEER ee uhr) *adj.* lower in status or rank

1. **rubles** (ROO buhlz) *n.* Russian currency; similar to U.S. dollars.

TAKE NOTES

Activate Prior Knowledge 

Think about a time when you felt you were being treated unfairly. Explain what you did or what you wish you had done in the situation.

Reading Skill 

Drawing conclusions means using the facts and details in the text to form opinions. Read the bracketed passage. What conclusion can you draw about the relationship between Julia and the Mistress?

Reading Check 

In what subject does the Mistress say she excelled? Underline the sentence that tells you.

TAKE NOTES

Literary Analysis

Stage directions describe the details of the play's setting. They also tell how the characters move, feel, and sound. Underline one stage direction on this page. What action or sound does this stage direction help you imagine?

___

___

Reading Skill

What **conclusion** can you draw about Julia when she agrees with the Mistress that she has worked exactly two months?

___

___

___

Reading Check

Why does the Mistress say she did not make note of the fact that she does not pay for Sundays? Underline the sentence that tells you.

JULIA. You did, ma'am. I spoke to no one else concerning money . . .

MISTRESS. Impossible. Maybe you *thought* you heard forty when I said thirty. If you kept your head up, that would never happen. Look at me again and I'll say it clearly. *Thirty rubles a month.*

JULIA. If you say so, ma'am.

MISTRESS. Settled. Thirty a month it is . . . Now then, you've been here two months exactly.

JULIA. Two months and five days.

MISTRESS. No, no. Exactly two months. I made a note of it. You should keep books the way I do so there wouldn't be these discrepancies. So—we have two months at thirty rubles a month . . . comes to sixty rubles. Correct?

JULIA. *(Curtsies)* Yes, ma'am. Thank you, ma'am.

MISTRESS. Subtract nine Sundays . . . We did agree to subtract Sundays, didn't we?

JULIA. No, ma'am.

MISTRESS. Eyes! Eyes! . . . Certainly we did. I've always subtracted Sundays. I didn't bother making a note of it because I always do it. Don't you recall when I said we will subtract Sundays?

JULIA. No, ma'am.

MISTRESS. Think.

JULIA. *(Thinks)* No, ma'am.

MISTRESS. You weren't thinking. Your eyes were wandering. Look straight at my face and look hard . . . Do you remember now?

JULIA. *(Softly)* Yes, ma'am.

MISTRESS. I didn't hear you, Julia.

JULIA. *(Louder)* Yes, ma'am.

MISTRESS. Good. I was sure you'd remember . . . Plus three holidays. Correct?

JULIA. Two, ma'am. Christmas and New Year's.

MISTRESS. And your birthday. That's three.

JULIA. I worked on my birthday, ma'am.

Vocabulary Development

discrepancies (di SKREP uhn seez) *n.* differences; inconsistencies

MISTRESS. You did? There was no need to. My governesses never worked on their birthdays . . .

JULIA. But I did work, ma'am.

MISTRESS. But that's not the question, Julia. We're discussing financial matters now. I will, however, only count two holidays if you insist . . . Do you insist?

JULIA. I did work, ma'am.

MISTRESS. Then you *do* insist.

JULIA. No, ma'am.

MISTRESS. Very well. That's three holidays, therefore we take off twelve rubles. Now then, four days little Kolya was sick, and there were no lessons.

JULIA. But I gave lessons to Vanya.

MISTRESS. True. But I engaged you to teach two children, not one. Shall I pay you in full for doing only half the work?

JULIA. No, ma'am.

MISTRESS. So we'll deduct it . . . Now, three days you had a toothache and my husband gave you permission not to work after lunch. Correct?

JULIA. After four. I worked until four.

MISTRESS. *(Looks in the book)* I have here: "Did not work after lunch." We have lunch at one and are finished at two, not at four, correct?

JULIA. Yes, ma'am. But I—

MISTRESS. That's another seven rubles . . . Seven and twelve is nineteen . . . Subtract . . . that leaves . . . forty-one rubles . . . Correct?

JULIA. Yes, ma'am. Thank you, ma'am.

MISTRESS. Now then, on January fourth you broke a teacup and saucer, is that true?

JULIA. Just the saucer, ma'am.

MISTRESS. What good is a teacup without a saucer, eh? . . . That's two rubles. The saucer was an heirloom.[1] It cost much more, but let it go. I'm used to taking losses.

JULIA. Thank you, ma'am.

1. **heirloom** (AYR loom) *n.* treasured possession passed down from generation to generation.

TAKE NOTES

Stop to Reflect 

The Mistress gives Julia an opportunity to insist on being paid for working on her birthday. Why do you think Julia does not insist on being paid?

Reading Skill 

What **conclusion** can you draw about the Mistress from the fact that she keeps a book listing details about Julia's work?

Reading Check 

Why does the Mistress say she should not have to pay Julia for the days that Kolya was sick? Underline the sentence that tells you.

TAKE NOTES

Stop to Reflect

The Mistress claims that she gave Julia ten rubles in January. Julia says that she did not. Which of these two characters do you think is more believable? Explain.

____

____

____

Literary Analysis

How does Julia act when the Mistress tells her that she will receive fourteen rubles? Underline the **stage direction** that tells you. What effect does this direction have on the reader?

____

____

____

____

____

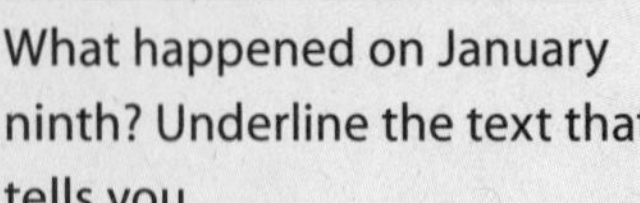

Reading Check

What happened on January ninth? Underline the text that tells you.

MISTRESS. Now then, January ninth, Kolya climbed a tree and tore his jacket.

JULIA. I forbid him to do so, ma'am.

MISTRESS. But he didn't listen, did he? . . . Ten rubles . . . January fourteenth, Vanya's shoes were stolen . . .

JULIA. But the maid, ma'am. You discharged her yourself.

MISTRESS. But you get paid good money to watch everything. I explained that in our first meeting. Perhaps you weren't listening. Were you listening that day, Julia, or was your head in the clouds?

JULIA. Yes, ma'am.

MISTRESS. Yes, your head was in the clouds?

JULIA. No, ma'am. I was listening.

MISTRESS. Good girl. So that means another five rubles off *(Looks in the book)* . . . Ah, yes . . . The sixteenth of January I gave you ten rubles.

JULIA. You didn't.

MISTRESS. But I made a note of it. Why would I make a note of it if I didn't give it to you?

JULIA. I don't know, ma'am.

MISTRESS. That's not a satisfactory answer, Julia . . . Why would I make a note of giving you ten rubles if I did not in fact give it to you, eh? . . . No answer? . . . Then I must have given it to you, mustn't I?

JULIA. Yes, ma'am. If you say so, ma'am.

MISTRESS. Well, certainly I say so. That's the point of this little talk. To clear these matters up. Take twenty-seven from forty-one, that leaves . . . fourteen, correct?

JULIA. Yes, ma'am. *(She turns away, softly crying)*

MISTRESS. What's this? Tears? Are you crying? Has something made you unhappy, Julia? Please tell me. It pains me to see you like this. I'm so

Vocabulary Development

discharged (dis CHARJD) *v.* fired; released from something

satisfactory (sat is FAK tuh ree) *adj.* adequate; sufficient to meet a requirement

sensitive to tears. What is it?

JULIA. Only once since I've been here have I ever been given any money and that was by your husband. On my birthday he gave me three rubles.

MISTRESS. Really? There's no note of it in my book. I'll put it down now. *(She writes in the book.)* Three rubles. Thank you for telling me. Sometimes I'm a little lax with my accounts . . . Always shortchanging myself. So then, we take three more from fourteen . . . leaves eleven . . . Do you wish to check my figures?

JULIA. There's no need to, ma'am.

MISTRESS. Then we're all settled. Here's your salary for two months, dear. Eleven rubles. *(She puts the pile of coins on the desk.)* Count it.

JULIA. It's not necessary, ma'am.

MISTRESS. Come, come. Let's keep the records straight. Count it.

JULIA. *(Reluctantly counts it)* One, two, three, four, five, six, seven, eight, nine, ten . . . ? There's only ten, ma'am.

MISTRESS. Are you sure? Possibly you dropped one . . . Look on the floor, see if there's a coin there.

JULIA. I didn't drop any, ma'am. I'm quite sure.

MISTRESS. Well, it's not here on my desk, and I *know* I gave you eleven rubles. Look on the floor.

JULIA. It's all right, ma'am. Ten rubles will be fine.

MISTRESS. Well, keep the ten for now. And if we don't find it on the floor later, we'll discuss it again next month.

JULIA. Yes, ma'am. Thank you, ma'am. You're very kind, ma'am.

(She curtsies and then starts to leave.)

MISTRESS. Julia!

(JULIA *stops, turns.)*

Come back here.

(She goes back to the desk and curtsies again.)

Why did you thank me?

JULIA. For the money, ma'am.

TAKE NOTES

Reading Skill

Read the bracketed passage. Draw a **conclusion** about why Julia was given three rubles on her birthday. How does Julia's belief about the three rubles differ from the Mistress's belief?

Literary Analysis

Underline the **stage directions** on this page that show Julia's actions. How do these directions help you understand Julia's feelings?

Stop to Reflect

Why do you think Julia is so obedient to the Mistress?

TAKE NOTES

Stop to Reflect

The Mistress says that she had been playing a joke on Julia to teach her a lesson. Do you think this is an effective way to teach a person about standing up for himself or herself? Why or why not?

___

___

___

Literary Analysis

Read the set of **stage directions** at the end of the scene. Circle the words that show that the scene is over.

Reading Check

What does Julia say other employers have done? Underline the sentence that tells you.

MISTRESS. For the money? . . . But don't you realize what I've done? I've cheated you . . . *Robbed* you! I have no such notes in my book. I made up whatever came into my mind. Instead of the eighty rubles which I owe you, I gave you only ten. I have actually stolen from you and you still thank me . . . Why?

JULIA. In the other places that I've worked, they didn't give me anything at all.

MISTRESS. Then they cheated you even worse than I did . . . I was playing a little joke on you. A cruel lesson just to teach you. You're much too trusting, and in this world that's very dangerous . . . I'm going to give you the entire eighty rubles. *(Hands her an envelope)* It's all ready for you. The rest is in this envelope. Here, take it.

JULIA. As you wish, ma'am. *(She curtsies and starts to go again.)*

MISTRESS. Julia! *(JULIA stops.)* Is it possible to be so spineless? Why don't you protest? Why don't you speak up? Why don't you cry out against this cruel and unjust treatment? Is it really possible to be so guileless, so innocent, such a—pardon me for being so blunt—such a simpleton?

JULIA. *(The faintest trace of a smile on her lips)* Yes, ma'am . . . it's possible.

(She curtsies again and runs off. The MISTRESS looks after her a moment, a look of complete bafflement on her face. The lights fade.)

Reader's Response: Do you think the joke the Mistress played on Julia was funny? Why or why not?

___

___

___

___

Vocabulary Development

guileless (GYL lis) *adj.* without deceit or trickery; innocent

The Governess

1. **Connect:** Why does Julia's position as a governess make her discussion with the Mistress difficult for her?

2. **Analyze:** Do you think the mistress is being kind, or cruel, or both, when she plays the trick on Julia? Explain.

3. **Reading Skill:** Based on Julia's answers to the Mistress's questions, what **conclusion** can you draw about how governesses were treated at the time of this play?

4. **Literary Analysis:** Write **stage directions** from *The Governess* in the chart below. Give two examples for each type of direction.

Describing an Action	Showing How a Character Feels

Writing: Problem-Solution Essay

Write a **problem-solution essay** that discusses Julia's inability to stand up for herself. The essay should explain Julia's problem and propose a solution different from the solution the Mistress tried.

Think about how you would define Julia's problem.

- What negative consequences does Julia's problem cause her?

____

____

- What solution might work better than the Mistress's solution?

____

____

Use your notes to help you draft your essay.

Listening and Speaking: Debate

To prepare for your **debate,** list three main points you would like to make and three counterarguments that your opponents might raise against your view point. In the final column, decide how you will address these counterarguments.

Arguments That Support Your Position	Counterarguments	How You Will Address Counterarguments

Public Documents

About Public Documents

Public documents are government records or documents. They could also deal with citizens' rights and responsibilities according to the law. Some examples of public documents are:

- laws
- legal notices
- government publications
- notes taken at public meetings

Reading Skill

You may need to read a public document in order to find the answer to a question, make a decision, or solve a problem. You can **compare and contrast features and elements** in a document to help you understand the information it presents. Features and elements may include headings, boldface type, numbering, and bullets.

Information	+	Information	=	*Generalization*
The U. S. Department of Labor permits youth ages 14–15 to work fewer hours on school days than on non-school days.		The contract for the work-study program includes academic requirements.		Employers and the U.S. Department of Labor do not want young people's jobs to interfere with their schoolwork.

Wage and Hour Division

Basic Information

U.S. Department of Labor
Employment Standards Administration

The U.S. Department of Labor's Wage and Hour Division (WHD) administers and enforces laws that establish minimally acceptable standards for wages and working conditions in this country, regardless of immigration status.

Youth Employment

The FLSA also regulates the employment of youth.

Jobs Youth Can Do:

- 13 or younger: baby-sit, deliver newspapers, or work as an actor or performer
- Ages 14–15: office work, grocery store, retail store, restaurant, movie theater, or amusement park
- Age 16–17: Any job not declared hazardous
- Age 18: No restrictions

Hours Youth Ages 14 and 15 Can Work:

- After 7 A.M. and until 7 P.M.
- (Hours are extended to 9 P.M. June 1–Labor Day)
- Up to 3 hours on a school day
- Up to 18 hours in a school week
- Up to 8 hours on a non-school day
- Up to 40 hours in a non-school week

Note: Different rules apply to youth employed in agriculture. States also regulate the hours that youth under age 18 may work. To find State rules, log on to ***www.youthrules.dol.gov***

Thinking About the Public Document

1. Young people cannot work in some jobs. In others, they can work only a few hours each day. Why do you think young people have these limits?

2. The Department of Labor allows students ages 14 and 15 to work as many as 40 hours during a non-school week. The same students are permitted to work no more than 18 hours during a school week. What conclusion can you draw based on these rules?

TALK ABOUT IT

Reading Skill

3. Review the section headed "Hours Youth Ages 14 and 15 Can Work." What feature makes this specific information easy to read and understand?

4. How does the format of the note at the bottom of the page differ from the format of the other information? Why is the note formatted differently?

WRITE ABOUT IT

Timed Writing: Explanation **(15 minutes)**

Think about laws for wages and working conditions. Explain why these laws are important. Include problems that people could have if these laws were not in place.

The Diary of Anne Frank, Act I

Reading Skill

A **cause** is an event, an action, or a feeling that produces a result, or an **effect**. When you read a historical piece of literature, you can **use background information to link historical causes with effects**. Such background information includes the introduction to a literary work, information provided in footnotes, facts you learned in other classes, and information you already know about the topic.

Use a chart like the one shown to help determine cause and effect.

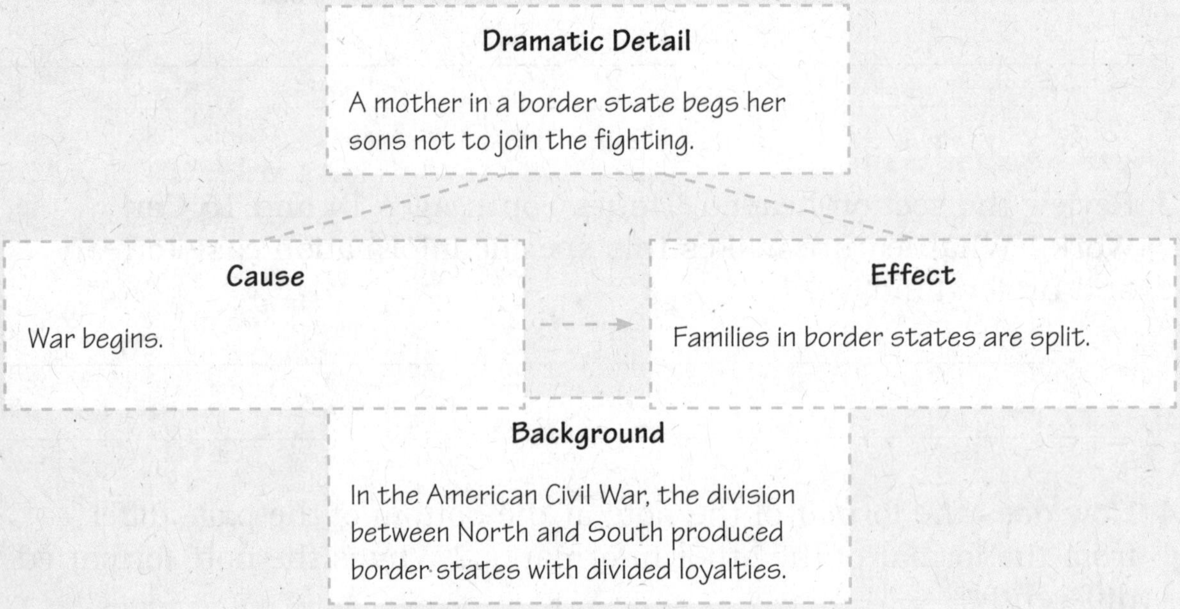

Dramatic Detail

A mother in a border state begs her sons not to join the fighting.

Cause		Effect
War begins.	→	Families in border states are split.

Background

In the American Civil War, the division between North and South produced border states with divided loyalties.

Literary Analysis

Dialogue is a conversation between or among characters. In the *script*, or text, of a play, lines of dialogue follow the speaker's name.

Writers use dialogue for many reasons. It can reveal character traits and relationships. Dialogue can also advance the plot or show the conflict between characters or between the main character and outside forces.

As you read *The Diary of Anne Frank*, notice how the dialogue helps you understand the importance of characters and events.

The Diary of Anne Frank, Act I

Frances Goodrich
and Albert Hackett

Summary World War II is over. Anne Frank's father returns to Amsterdam to say goodbye to a friend, Miep Gies. Gies gives him his daughter's diary. Mr. Frank opens the diary and begins reading. Anne's voice joins his and takes over. The story goes back to 1942. Anne's family and another family are moving into the space above their friends' business. There they will live and hide from the Nazis for two years.

Writing About the Big Question

Is it our differences or our similarities that matter most? In *The Diary of Anne Frank, Act I,* five adults and three teenagers struggle with their differences but face a common danger. Complete this sentence:

Danger tends to (unify/divide) people because ______________________

____.

Note-taking Guid

Fill in this chart with important details from each scene in Act I.

Scene 1	After World War II, Mr. Frank returns to the attic in which his family had hidden from the Nazis. Miep shows him Anne's diary. He begins to think back to those terrible days.
Scene 2	
Scene 3	

TAKE NOTES

Activate Prior Knowledge 

List at least three things that happened in Europe during World War II.

1. ______________________

____

2. ______________________

____

3. ______________________

____

Reading Skill 

A **cause** is an event, an action, or a feeling that produces a result, or an **effect**. Two families plus Mr. Dussel share the upstairs rooms as they hide from the Nazis. What might **cause** so many people to share such a small space?

____

____

____

Reading Check 

What is the setting of the play? Circle the answer.

The Diary of Anne Frank

Frances Goodrich and Albert Hackett

Act I, Scene 1

During World War II, the German army took over many countries in Europe, including Holland. The Germans passed laws against Jews living in these countries and shipped many Jews off to prison camps where they were killed. This play is about two Jewish families who are hiding from the Germans in a small apartment in Holland during World War II.

CHARACTERS (in order of appearance)

Mr. Frank, Anne's father, a German Jew living in Holland
Miep Gies, young Dutch woman who used to work for Mr. Frank
Mrs. Van Daan, Dutch Jewish woman
Mr. Van Daan, Dutch Jewish man, an acquaintance of Mr. Frank
Peter Van Daan, sixteen-year-old Dutch Jewish boy
Mrs. Frank, Anne's mother
Margot Frank, Anne's eighteen-year-old sister
Anne Frank, thirteen-year-old Jewish girl living in Holland
Mr. Kraler, Dutch man who used to work for Mr. Frank
Mr. Dussel, Dutch Jewish man, a former dentist

(The scene remains the same throughout the play. It is the top floor of a warehouse and office building in Amsterdam, Holland. The sharply peaked roof of the building is outlined against a sea of other rooftops, stretching away into the distance. Nearby is the belfry of a church tower, the Westertoren, whose carillon[1] *rings out the hours. Occasionally faint sounds float up from below: the voices of children playing in the street, the tramp of marching feet, a boat whistle from the canal.*

The three rooms of the top floor and a small attic space above are exposed to our view. The largest of the rooms is in the center, with two small rooms, slightly raised, on either side. On the right is a bathroom, out of sight. A narrow steep flight of stairs at the back leads up to the attic. The rooms are sparsely furnished with a few chairs, cots, a table or two. The windows are painted over, or covered with makeshift blackout curtains.[2] *In the main room there is*

1. **carillon** (KAR uh lahn) *n.* set of bells, each producing one note of the scale.
2. **blackout curtains** dark curtains that conceal all lights that might be visible to bombers from the air.

a sink, a gas ring for cooking and a woodburning stove for warmth.

The room on the left is hardly more than a closet. There is a skylight in the sloping ceiling. Directly under this room is a small steep stairwell, with steps leading down to a door. This is the only entrance from the building below. When the door is opened we see that it has been concealed on the outer side by a bookcase attached to it.

The curtain rises on an empty stage. It is late afternoon, November 1945.

The rooms are dusty, the curtains in rags. Chairs and tables are overturned.

The door at the foot of the small stairwell swings open. MR. FRANK *comes up the steps into view. He is a gentle, cultured European in his middle years. There is still a trace of a German accent in his speech.*

He stands looking slowly around, making a supreme effort at self-control. He is weak, ill. His clothes are threadbare.

After a second he drops his rucksack on the couch and moves slowly about. He opens the door to one of the smaller rooms, and then abruptly closes it again, turning away. He goes to the window at the back, looking off at the Westertoren as its carillon strikes the hour of six, then he moves restlessly on.

From the street below we hear the sound of a barrel organ[3] *and children's voices at play. There is a many-colored scarf hanging from a nail.* MR. FRANK *takes it, putting it around his neck. As he starts back for his rucksack, his eye is caught by something lying on the floor. It is a woman's white glove. He holds it in his hand and suddenly all of his self-control is gone. He breaks down, crying.*

We hear footsteps on the stairs. MIEP GIES *comes up, looking for* MR. FRANK. MIEP *is a Dutch girl of about twenty-two. She wears a coat and hat, ready to go home. She is pregnant. Her attitude toward* MR. FRANK *is protective, compassionate.)*

MIEP. Are you all right, Mr. Frank?

MR. FRANK. *(Quickly controlling himself)* Yes, Miep, yes.

3. barrel organ *n.* mechanical musical instrument often played by street musicians during the time in which this play is set.

TAKE NOTES

Literary Analysis 

Dialogue is a conversation between or among people. There is little dialogue on this page. What purpose does most of the text on this page serve?

Stop to Reflect 

What does the description in the bracketed passage suggest might have happened?

Reading Skill 

What **effect** has the war had on Mr. Frank?

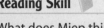

TAKE NOTES

Reading Skill

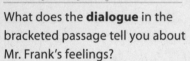

What does Miep think is **causing** Mr. Frank to feel tortured?

Literary Analysis

What does the **dialogue** in the bracketed passage tell you about Mr. Frank's feelings?

Reading Check

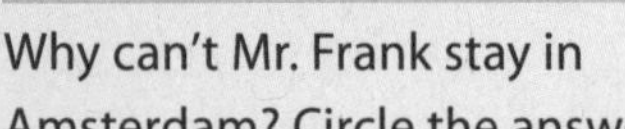

Why can't Mr. Frank stay in Amsterdam? Circle the answer.

MIEP. Everyone in the office has gone home . . . It's after six. *(Then pleading)* Don't stay up here, Mr. Frank. What's the use of torturing yourself like this?

MR. FRANK. I've come to say good-bye . . . I'm leaving here, Miep.

MIEP. What do you mean? Where are you going? Where?

MR. FRANK. I don't know yet. I haven't decided.

MIEP. Mr. Frank, you can't leave here! This is your home! Amsterdam is your home. Your business is here, waiting for you . . . You're needed here . . . Now that the war is over, there are things that . . .

MR. FRANK. I can't stay in Amsterdam, Miep. It has too many memories for me. Everywhere there's something . . . the house we lived in . . . the school . . . that street organ playing out there . . . I'm not the person you used to know, Miep. I'm a bitter old man. *(Breaking off)* Forgive me. I shouldn't speak to you like this . . . after all that you did for us . . . the suffering . . .

MIEP. No. No. It wasn't suffering. You can't say we suffered. *(As she speaks, she straightens a chair which is overturned.)*

MR. FRANK. I know what you went through, you and Mr. Kraler. I'll remember it as long as I live. *(He gives one last look around.)* Come, Miep. *(He starts for the steps, then remembers his rucksack, going back to get it.)*

MIEP. *(Hurrying up to a cupboard)* Mr. Frank, did you see? There are some of your papers here. *(She brings a bundle of papers to him.)* We found them in a heap of rubbish on the floor after . . . after you left.

MR. FRANK. Burn them. *(He opens his rucksack to put the glove in it.)*

MIEP. But, Mr. Frank, there are letters, notes . . .

MR. FRANK. Burn them. All of them.

MIEP. Burn this? *(She hands him a paper-bound notebook.)*

MR. FRANK. *(quietly)* Anne's diary. *(He opens the diary and begins to read.)* "Monday, the sixth of July, nineteen forty-two." *(To* MIEP*)* Nineteen forty-two. Is it possible, Miep? . . . Only three years ago. *(As he continues his reading, he sits down on the couch.)* "Dear Diary, since you and I are going to be great friends, I will start by telling you about myself. My name is Anne Frank. I am thirteen years old. I was born in Germany the twelfth of June, nineteen twenty-nine. As my family is Jewish, we emigrated to Holland when Hitler came to power."

(As MR. FRANK *reads on, another voice joins his, as if coming from the air. It is* ANNE'S VOICE.*)*

MR. FRANK AND ANNE. "My father started a business, importing spice and herbs. Things went well for us until nineteen forty. Then the war came, and the Dutch capitulation,[4] followed by the arrival of the Germans. Then things got very bad for the Jews."

*(*MR. FRANK'S VOICE *dies out.* ANNE'S VOICE *continues alone. The lights dim slowly to darkness. The curtain falls on the scene.)*

ANNE'S VOICE. You could not do this and you could not do that. They forced Father out of his business. We had to wear yellow stars.[5] I had to turn in my bike. I couldn't go to a Dutch school any more. I couldn't go to the movies, or ride in an automobile, or even on a streetcar, and a million other things. But somehow we children still managed to have fun. Yesterday Father told me we were going into hiding. Where, he wouldn't say. At five o'clock this morning Mother woke me and told me to hurry and get dressed. I was to put on as many clothes as I could. It would look too suspicious if we walked along carrying suitcases. It wasn't until we were on our way that I learned where we were going. Our hiding place was to be upstairs in the building where Father used to have his business. Three other people were coming in with us . . . the Van Daans and their son Peter . . . Father knew the Van Daans but we had never met them . . .

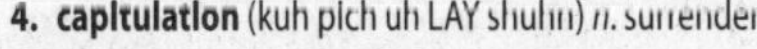

4. capitulation (kuh pich uh LAY shuhn) *n.* surrender.

5. yellow stars Stars of David, the six-pointed stars that are symbols of Judaism. The Nazis ordered all Jews to wear them on their clothing.

TAKE NOTES

Reading Skill

Anne refers to Adolf Hitler, the German dictator who persecuted Jews throughout Europe. What other historical **causes** and **effects** do you read about here?

Literary Analysis

In the play, Anne's lines are often spoken to her diary, as if the diary were another character. What significant plot event is revealed in the bracketed **dialogue**?

Reading Check

Underline the type of business that Mr. Frank had started.

TAKE NOTES

Stop to Reflect

What might explain Mr. Van Daan's pacing?

Reading Skill

What **cause** might explain why Mrs. Van Daan is wearing layers of clothing and carrying many possessions?

Literary Analysis

How do the authors express a mood of anxiety through the Van Daans' **dialogue**?

Reading Check

How many people will be living in the apartment? Draw a box around the answer.

(During the last lines the curtain rises on the scene. The lights dim on. ANNE'S VOICE *fades out.)*

Act I, Scene 2

When seven people are in hiding together in a tiny apartment, everyone must follow rules and avoid disagreements. That isn't always easy, as the families in the play discover.

(It is early morning, July 1942. The rooms are bare, as before, but they are now clean and orderly.

MR. VAN DAAN, *a tall, portly*[6] *man in his late forties, is in the main room, pacing up and down, nervously smoking a cigarette. His clothes and overcoat are expensive and well cut.*

MRS. VAN DAAN *sits on the couch, clutching her possessions, a hatbox, bags, etc. She is a pretty woman in her early forties. She wears a fur coat over her other clothes.*

PETER VAN DAAN *is standing at the window of the room on the right, looking down at the street below. He is a shy, awkward boy of sixteen. He wears a cap, a raincoat, and long Dutch trousers, like "plus fours."*[7] *At his feet is a black case, a carrier for his cat.*

The yellow Star of David is conspicuous on all of their clothes.)

MRS. VAN DAAN. *(Rising, nervous, excited)* Something's happened to them! I know it!

MR. VAN DAAN. Now, Kerli!

MRS. VAN DAAN. Mr. Frank said they'd be here at seven o'clock. He said . . .

MR. VAN DAAN. They have two miles to walk. You can't expect . . .

MRS. VAN DAAN. They've been picked up. That's what's happened. They've been taken . . .

*(*MR. VAN DAAN *indicates that he hears someone coming.)*

Vocabulary Development

conspicuous (kuhn SPIK yoo uhs) *adj.* noticeable

6. **portly** (POHRT lee) *adj.* large and heavy.

7. **plus fours** *n.* loose knickers (short pants) worn for active sports.

MR. VAN DAAN. You see?

(PETER *takes up his carrier and his schoolbag, etc., and goes into the main room as* MR. FRANK *comes up the stairwell from below.* MR. FRANK *looks much younger now. His movements are brisk, his manner confident. He wears an overcoat and carries his hat and a small cardboard box. He crosses to the* VAN DAANS, *shaking hands with each of them.)*

MR. FRANK. Mrs. Van Daan, Mr. Van Daan, Peter. *(Then, in explanation of their lateness)* There were too many of the Green Police[8] on the streets . . . we had to take the long way around.

(Up the steps come MARGOT FRANK, MRS. FRANK, MIEP *(not pregnant now) and* MR. KRALER. *All of them carry bags, packages, and so forth. The Star of David is conspicuous on all of the* FRANKS' *clothing.* MARGOT *is eighteen, beautiful, quiet, shy.* MRS. FRANK *is a young mother, gently bred, reserved. She, like* MR. FRANK, *has a slight German accent.* MR. KRALER *is a Dutchman, dependable, kindly.*

As MR. KRALER *and* MIEP *go upstage to put down their parcels,* MRS. FRANK *turns back to call* ANNE.*)*

MRS. FRANK. Anne?

*(*ANNE *comes running up the stairs. She is thirteen, quick in her movements, interested in everything, mercurial[9] in her emotions. She wears a cape, long wool socks and carries a schoolbag.)*

MR. FRANK. *(Introducing them)* My wife, Edith. Mr. and Mrs. Van Daan . . . their son, Peter . . . my daughters, Margot and Anne.

*(*MRS. FRANK *hurries over, shaking hands with them.)*

*(*ANNE *gives a polite little curtsy as she shakes* MR. VAN DAAN'S *hand. Then she immediately starts off on a tour of investigation of her new home, going upstairs to the attic room.*

MIEP *and* MR. KRALER *are putting the various things they have brought on the shelves.)*

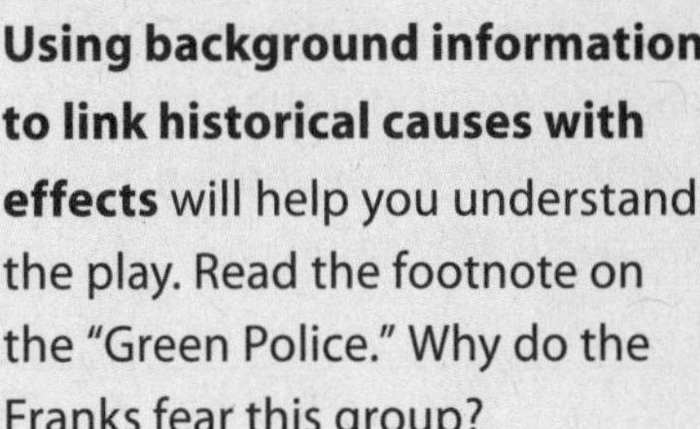

Reading Skill 

Using background information to link historical causes with effects will help you understand the play. Read the footnote on the "Green Police." Why do the Franks fear this group?

___

___

___

Stop to Reflect

Jews in Europe were forced to sew a yellow Star of David onto their clothing. It was intended to identify them as Jews. What do you think it was like for people to wear this patch on their clothes?

___

___

___

___

Reading Check 

How old is Anne Frank when she and her family go into hiding? Circle the answer.

8. **Green Police** the Dutch Gestapo, or Nazi police, who wore green uniforms and were known for their brutality. Those in danger of being arrested or deported feared the Gestapo, especially because of their practice of raiding houses to round up victims in the middle of the night—when people are most confused and vulnerable.

9. **mercurial** (muhr KYOOR ee uhl) *adj.* quick or changeable in behavior.

TAKE NOTES

Literary Analysis

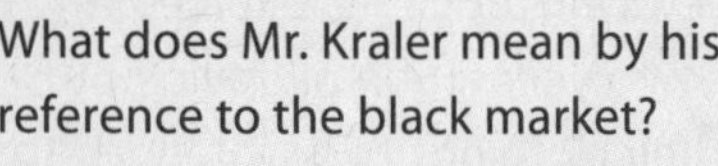

What does the **dialogue** on this page reveal about the Franks' and Van Daans' dependence on Miep and Mr. Kraler?

Reading Skill

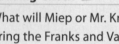

What does Mr. Kraler mean by his reference to the black market?

What **causes** Mr. Kraler to get ration books illegally? Underline the answer.

Reading Check

What will Miep or Mr. Kraler bring the Franks and Van Daans each day? Draw a box around the answer.

MR. KRALER. I'm sorry there is still so much confusion.

MR. FRANK. Please. Don't think of it. After all, we'll have plenty of leisure to arrange everything ourselves.

MIEP. *(To* MRS. FRANK*)* We put the stores of food you sent in here. Your drugs are here . . . soap, linen here.

MRS. FRANK. Thank you, Miep.

MIEP. I made up the beds . . . the way Mr. Frank and Mr. Kraler said. *(She starts out.)* Forgive me. I have to hurry. I've got to go to the other side of town to get some ration books[10] for you.

MRS. VAN DAAN. Ration books? If they see our names on ration books, they'll know we're here.

MR. KRALER. There isn't anything . . .

MIEP: Don't worry. Your names won't be on them. *(As she hurries out)* I'll be up later.

MR. FRANK. Thank you, Miep.

MRS. FRANK. *(To* MR. KRALER*)* It's illegal, then, the ration books? We've never done anything illegal.

MR. FRANK. We won't be living here exactly according to regulations.

(As MR. KRALER *reassures* MRS. FRANK, *he takes various small things, such as matches, soap, etc., from his pockets, handing them to her.)*

MR. KRALER. This isn't the black market,[11] Mrs. Frank. This is what we call the white market . . . helping all of the hundreds and hundreds who are hiding out in Amsterdam.

(The carillon is heard playing the quarter-hour before eight. MR. KRALER *looks at his watch.* ANNE *stops at the window as she comes down the stairs.)*

ANNE. It's the Westertoren!

MR. KRALER. I must go. I must be out of here and downstairs in the office before the workmen get here. *(He starts for the stairs leading out.)* Miep or I, or both of us, will be up each day to bring you food and news and find out what your needs are.

10. **ration** (RASH uhn) **books** *n.* books of stamps given to ensure the equal distribution of scarce items, such as meat or gasoline, in times of shortage.

11. **black market** illegal way of buying scarce items without ration stamps.

Tomorrow I'll get you a better bolt for the door at the foot of the stairs. It needs a bolt that you can throw yourself and open only at our signal. *(To* MR. FRANK*)* Oh . . . You'll tell them about the noise?

MR. FRANK. I'll tell them.

MR. KRALER. Good-bye then for the moment. I'll come up again, after the workmen leave.

MR. FRANK. Good-bye, Mr. Kraler.

MRS. FRANK. *(Shaking his hand)* How can we thank you?

(The others murmur their good-byes.)

MR. KRALER. I never thought I'd live to see the day when a man like Mr. Frank would have to go into hiding. When you think—

(He breaks off, going out. MR. FRANK *follows him down the steps, bolting the door after him. In the interval before he returns,* PETER *goes over to* MARGOT, *shaking hands with her. As* MR. FRANK *comes back up the steps,* MRS. FRANK *questions him anxiously.)*

MRS. FRANK. What did he mean, about the noise?

MR. FRANK. First let us take off some of these clothes.

(They all start to take off garment after garment. On each of their coats, sweaters, blouses, suits, dresses, is another yellow Star of David. MR. *and* MRS. FRANK *are underdressed quite simply. The others wear several things, sweaters, extra dresses, bathrobes, aprons, nightgowns, etc.)*

MR. VAN DAAN. It's a wonder we weren't arrested, walking along the streets . . . Petronella with a fur coat in July . . . and that cat of Peter's crying all the way.

ANNE. *(As she is removing a pair of panties)* A cat?

MRS. FRANK. *(Shocked)* Anne, please!

ANNE. It's alright. I've got on three more.

(She pulls off two more. Finally, as they have all removed their surplus clothes, they look to MR. FRANK, *waiting for him to speak.)*

MR. FRANK. Now. About the noise. While the men are in the building below, we must have complete quiet. Every sound can be heard down there, not

TAKE NOTES

Literary Analysis 

What do the bracketed **stage directions** and **dialogue** tell you about how long these families think they may be in hiding?

Stop to Reflect 

If you had to go into hiding for a long time, what would you want to take with you? If you could take only what fit in a backpack, what would you take?

Reading Skill

What **cause** and what **effect** are explained in the underlined sentence?

Reading Check 

When will it be safe for Mr. Kraler to return to the apartment? Circle the answer.

TAKE NOTES

Stop to Reflect 

What would it be like to not make any noise between eight-thirty in the morning and six in the evening?

____

____

____

____

Reading Skill 

What **causes** everyone to stop in fear? Circle the answer.

Literary Analysis 

Underline **dialogue** that tells how small a space the families will all be living in.

Reading Check 

What must the families avoid using between eight-thirty and six every day? Draw a box around the answer.

only in the workrooms, but in the offices too. The men come at about eight-thirty, and leave at about five-thirty. So, to be perfectly safe, from eight in the morning until six in the evening we must move only when it is necessary, and then in stockinged feet. We must not speak above a whisper. We must not run any water. We cannot use the sink, or even, forgive me, the w.c.[12] The pipes go down through the workrooms. It would be heard. No trash . . .

*(*MR. FRANK *stops abruptly as he hears the sound of marching feet from the street below. Everyone is motionless, paralyzed with fear.* MR. FRANK *goes quietly into the room on the right to look down out of the window.* ANNE *runs after him, peering out with him. The tramping feet pass without stopping. The tension is relieved.* MR. FRANK, *followed by* ANNE, *returns to the main room and resumes his instructions to the group.)*

. . . No trash must ever be thrown out which might reveal that someone is living up here . . . not even a potato paring. We must burn everything in the stove at night. This is the way we must live until it is over, if we are to survive.

(There is silence for a second.)

MRS. FRANK. Until it is over.

MR. FRANK. *(Reassuringly)* After six we can move about . . . we can talk and laugh and have our supper and read and play games . . . just as we would at home. *(He looks at his watch.)* And now I think it would be wise if we all went to our rooms, and were settled before eight o'clock.
Mrs. Van Daan, you and your husband will be upstairs. I regret that there's no place up there for Peter. But he will be here, near us. This will be our common room, where we'll meet to talk and eat and read, like one family.

MR. VAN DAAN. And where do you and Mrs. Frank sleep?

MR. FRANK. This room is also our bedroom.

(Together)

MRS. VAN DAAN. That isn't right. We'll sleep here and you take the room upstairs.

12. **w.c.** water closet; bathroom.

MR. VAN DAAN. It's your place.

MR. FRANK: Please. I've thought this out for weeks. It's the best arrangement. The only arrangement.

MRS. VAN DAAN. *(To* MR. FRANK*)* Never, never can we thank you. *(Then to* MRS. FRANK*)* I don't know what would have happened to us, if it hadn't been for Mr. Frank.

MR. FRANK. You don't know how your husband helped me when I came to this country . . . knowing no one . . . not able to speak the language. I can never repay him for that. *(Going to* VAN DAAN*)* May I help you with your things?

MR. VAN DAAN. No. No. *(To* MRS. VAN DAAN*)* Come along, *liefje.*[13]

MRS. VAN DAAN. You'll be all right, Peter? You're not afraid?

PETER: *(Embarrassed)* Please, Mother.

(They start up the stairs to the attic room above. MR. FRANK *turns to* MRS. FRANK.*)*

MR. FRANK. You too must have some rest, Edith. You didn't close your eyes last night. Nor you, Margot.

ANNE. I slept, Father. Wasn't that funny? I knew it was the last night in my own bed, and yet I slept soundly.

MR. FRANK. I'm glad, Anne. Now you'll be able to help me straighten things in here. *(To* MRS. FRANK *and* MARGOT*)* Come with me . . . You and Margot rest in this room for the time being.

(He picks up their clothes, starting for the room on the right.)

MRS. FRANK. You're sure . . .? I could help . . . And Anne hasn't had her milk . . .

MR. FRANK. I'll give it to her. *(To* ANNE *and* PETER*)* Anne, Peter . . . it's best that you take off your shoes now, before you forget.

(He leads the way to the room, followed by MARGOT.*)*

MRS. FRANK. You're sure you're not tired, Anne?

ANNE. I feel fine. I'm going to help Father.

13. ***liefje*** (LEEF hyuh) Dutch for "little love."

TAKE NOTES

Literary Analysis

What do we learn about Mr. Van Daan from the bracketed **dialogue**?

Reading Skill

What might have **caused** Mrs. Frank and Margot not to rest the previous night?

Stop to Reflect

How do the stage directions describe the action on stage?

Circle the two things that Mr. Frank does.

Reading Check

What does Mr. Frank remind Anne and Peter to do? Underline the answer.

TAKE NOTES

Reading Skill

What do you think **causes** Peter to put his cat back in its carrier?

____

____

Literary Analysis

What do Anne and Peter reveal about themselves in the bracketed **dialogue**? List two words or phrases to describe Anne and two to describe Peter.

Anne:

1. ______________________

2. ______________________

Peter:

1. ______________________

2. ______________________

Reading Check 

What did Anne have to leave behind in her old home? Circle the answer.

MRS. FRANK. Peter, I'm glad you are to be with us.

PETER. Yes, Mrs. Frank.

*(*MRS. FRANK *goes to join* MR. FRANK *and* MARGOT.*)*

(During the following scene MR. FRANK *helps* MARGOT *and* MRS. FRANK *to hang up their clothes. Then he persuades them both to lie down and rest. The* VAN DAANS *in their room above settle themselves. In the main room* ANNE *and* PETER *remove their shoes.* PETER *takes his cat out of the carrier.)*

ANNE. What's your cat's name?

PETER. Mouschi.

ANNE. Mouschi! Mouschi! Mouschi! *(She picks up the cat, walking away with it. To* PETER*)* I love cats. I have one . . . a darling little cat. But they made me leave her behind. I left some food and a note for the neighbors to take care of her . . . I'm going to miss her terribly. What is yours? A him or a her?

PETER. He's a tom. He doesn't like strangers. *(He takes the cat from her, putting it back in its carrier.)*

ANNE. *(Unabashed)* Then I'll have to stop being a stranger, won't I? Is he fixed?

PETER. *(Startled)* Huh?

ANNE. Did you have him fixed?

PETER. No.

ANNE. Oh, you ought to have him fixed—to keep him from—you know, fighting. Where did you go to school?

PETER. Jewish Secondary.

ANNE. But that's where Margot and I go! I never saw you around.

PETER. I used to see you . . . sometimes . . .

ANNE. You did?

PETER. . . . In the school yard. You were always in the middle of a bunch of kids. *(He takes a penknife from his pocket.)*

Vocabulary Development

unabashed (un uh BASHT) *adj.* unashamed

ANNE. Why didn't you ever come over?

PETER. I'm sort of a lone wolf. *(He starts to rip off his Star of David.)*

ANNE. What are you doing?

PETER. Taking it off.

ANNE. But you can't do that. They'll arrest you if you go out without your star.

(He tosses his knife on the table.)

PETER. Who's going out?

ANNE. Why, of course! You're right! Of course we don't need them any more. *(She picks up his knife and starts to take her star off.)* I wonder what our friends will think when we don't show up today?

PETER. I didn't have any dates with anyone.

ANNE. Oh, I did. I had a date with Jopie to go and play ping-pong at her house. Do you know Jopie de Waal?

PETER. No.

ANNE. Jopie's my best friend. I wonder what she'll think when she telephones and there's no answer? . . . Probably she'll go over to the house . . . I wonder what she'll think . . . we left everything as if we'd suddenly been called away . . . breakfast dishes in the sink . . . beds not made . . . *(As she pulls off her star, the cloth underneath shows clearly the color and form of the star.)* Look! It's still there! *(PETER goes over to the stove with his star.)* What're you going to do with yours?

PETER. Burn it.

ANNE. *(She starts to throw hers in, and cannot.)* It's funny, I can't throw mine away. I don't know why.

PETER. You can't throw . . .? Something they branded you with . . .? That they made you wear so they could spit on you?

ANNE. I know. I know. But after all, it is the Star of David, isn't it?

(In the bedroom, right, MARGOT and MRS. FRANK are lying down. MR. FRANK starts quietly out.)

TAKE NOTES

Literary Analysis 

What does Peter tell Anne as he begins to rip the Star of David off his clothing? Circle the answer.

What do Peter's action and his part of the **dialogue** tell you about his feelings about their circumstances?

____

In what way does his action connect with what he says about himself?

____

Reading Skill 

Think about the **background information that causes** Anne's response to Peter in the underlined passage. How does her answer show her own view about the Star of David?

____

____

Reading Check 

In what condition did the Franks leave their house? Underline the answer. Why do you think they did this?

____

____

TAKE NOTES

Literary Analysis

What does the bracketed dialogue tell you about Mr. Frank's personality?

Reading Skill

Why does Anne want to like Peter? Underline the answer.

Stop to Reflect

What do you think it would be like to live indoors for an unknown period of time?

Reading Check

What does Anne think about Peter? Circle the answer.

PETER. Maybe it's different for a girl.

(MR. FRANK *comes into the main room.)*

MR. FRANK. Forgive me, Peter. Now let me see. We must find a bed for your cat. *(He goes to a cupboard.)* I'm glad you brought your cat. Anne was feeling so badly about hers. *(Getting a used small washtub)* Here we are. Will it be comfortable in that?

PETER. *(Gathering up his things)* Thanks.

MR. FRANK. *(Opening the door of the room on the left)* And here is your room. But I warn you, Peter, you can't grow any more. Not an inch, or you'll have to sleep with your feet out of the skylight. Are you hungry?

PETER. No.

MR. FRANK. We have some bread and butter.

PETER. No, thank you.

MR. FRANK. You can have it for luncheon then. And tonight we will have a real supper . . . our first supper together.

PETER. Thanks. Thanks. *(He goes into his room. During the following scene he arranges his possessions in his new room.)*

MR. FRANK. That's a nice boy, Peter.

ANNE. He's awfully shy, isn't he?

MR. FRANK. You'll like him, I know.

ANNE. I certainly hope so, since he's the only boy I'm likely to see for months and months.

(MR. FRANK *sits down, taking off his shoes.)*

MR. FRANK. Annele,[14] there's a box there. Will you open it?

(He indicates a carton on the couch. ANNE *brings it to the center table. In the street below there is the sound of children playing.)*

ANNE. *(As she opens the carton)* You know the way I'm going to think of it here? I'm going to think of it as a boarding house. A very peculiar summer boarding house, like the one that we—*(She breaks off as she pulls out some photographs.)* Father! My movie stars! I was wondering where they

14. **Annele** (AHN uh luh) nickname for "Anne."

were! I was looking for them this morning . . . and Queen Wilhelmina![15] How wonderful!

MR. FRANK: There's something more. Go on. Look further. *(He goes over to the sink, pouring a glass of milk from a thermos bottle.)*

ANNE. *(Pulling out a pasteboard-bound book)* A diary! *(She throws her arms around her father.)* I've never had a diary. And I've always longed for one. *(She looks around the room.)* Pencil, pencil, pencil, pencil. *(She starts down the stairs.)* I'm going down to the office to get a pencil.

MR. FRANK. Anne! No! *(He goes after her, catching her by the arm and pulling her back.)*

ANNE. *(Startled)* But there's no one in the building now.

MR. FRANK. It doesn't matter. I don't want you ever to go beyond that door.

ANNE. *(Sobered)* Never . . .? Not even at nighttime, when everyone is gone? Or on Sundays? Can't I go down to listen to the radio?

MR. FRANK. Never. I am sorry, Anneke.[16] It isn't safe. No, you must never go beyond that door.

(For the first time ANNE *realizes what "going into hiding" means.)*

ANNE. I see.

MR. FRANK. It'll be hard, I know. But always remember this, Anneke. There are no walls, there are no bolts, no locks that anyone can put on your mind. Miep will bring us books. We will read history, poetry, mythology. *(He gives her the glass of milk.)* Here's your milk. *(With his arm about her, they go over to the couch, sitting down side by side.)* As a matter of fact, between us, Anne, being here has certain advantages for you. For instance, you remember the battle you had with your mother the other day on the subject of overshoes? You said you'd rather die than wear overshoes? But in the end you had to wear them? Well now, you see, for as long as we are here you will never have to wear overshoes! Isn't that good?

15. **Queen Wilhelmina** (vil hel MEE nah) Queen of the Netherlands from 1890 to 1948.

16. **Anneke** (AHN uh kuh) nickname for "Anne."

TAKE NOTES

Reading Skill

What **causes** Mr. Frank to stop Anne from going downstairs?

What **effect** does Mr. Frank's explanation have on Anne?

Literary Analysis

Writers use **dialogue** to help advance the plot of a play. How do Anne's reactions in the bracketed text show the seriousness of their circumstances?

Reading Check

What does Anne's father give her? Underline the answer.

TAKE NOTES

Reading Skill

What **effect** does the fear of being discovered have on the behavior of the two families?

Literary Analysis

You hear Anne in the **dialogue** in two ways on these two pages. How are Anne's two roles identified?

Why does the author have Anne speak in two different roles?

Reading Check

What does Anne do after everyone settles in for the quiet time? Circle the answer.

And the coat that you inherited from Margot, you won't have to wear that any more. And the piano! You won't have to practice on the piano. I tell you, this is going to be a fine life for you!

(ANNE'S *panic is gone.* PETER *appears in the doorway of his room, with a saucer in his hand. He is carrying his cat.)*

PETER. I . . . I . . . I thought I'd better get some water for Mouschi before . . .

MR. FRANK. Of course.

(As he starts toward the sink the carillon begins to chime the hour of eight. He tiptoes to the window at the back and looks down at the street below. He turns to PETER, *indicating in pantomime that it is too late.* PETER *starts back for his room. He steps on a creaking board. The three of them are frozen for a minute in fear. As* PETER *starts away again,* ANNE *tiptoes over to him and pours some of the milk from her glass into the saucer for the cat.* PETER *squats on the floor, putting the milk before the cat.* MR. FRANK *gives* ANNE *his fountain pen, and then goes into the room at the right. For a second* ANNE *watches the cat, then she goes over to the center table, and opens her diary.*

In the room at the right, MRS. FRANK *has sat up quickly at the sound of the carillon.* MR. FRANK *comes in and sits down beside her on the settee, his arm comfortingly around her.*

Upstairs, in the attic room, MR. *and* MRS. VAN DAAN *have hung their clothes in the closet and are now seated on the iron bed.* MRS. VAN DAAN *leans back exhausted.* MR. VAN DAAN *fans her with a newspaper.* ANNE *starts to write in her diary. The lights dim out, the curtain falls.*

In the darkness ANNE'S VOICE *comes to us again, faintly at first, and then with growing strength.)*

ANNE'S VOICE. I expect I should be describing what it feels like to go into hiding. But I really don't know yet myself. I only know it's funny never to be able to go outdoors . . . never to breathe fresh air . . . never to run and shout and jump. It's the silence in the nights that frightens me most. Every time I hear a creak in the house, or a step on the street outside, I'm sure they're coming for us. The days aren't so bad. At least we know that Miep and Mr. Kraler are down there below us in the office. Our protectors, we call them. I asked Father what would happen to them if the Nazis found out they were hiding us. Pim said that they would suffer the same fate that we would . . . Imagine! They know this, and yet when they come up here, they're always cheerful and gay as if there were nothing in the world to bother them . . . Friday, the twenty-first of August, nineteen forty-two. Today I'm going to tell you our general news. Mother is unbearable. She insists on treating me like a baby, which I loathe. Otherwise things are going better. The weather is . . .

(As ANNE'S VOICE *is fading out, the curtain rises on the scene.)*

Act I, Scene 3

Living so close together in the cramped apartment, the fugitives are slowly getting on each other's nerves. There is only one way life could get more annoying—if someone else moved into the apartment, too.

(It is a little after six o'clock in the evening, two months later.

MARGOT *is in the bedroom at the right, studying.* MR. VAN DAAN *is lying down in the attic room above.*

The rest of the "family" is in the main room. ANNE *and* PETER *sit opposite each other at the center table, where they have been doing their lessons.* MRS. FRANK *is on the couch.* MRS. VAN DAAN *is seated with her fur coat, on which she has been sewing, in her lap. None of them are wearing their shoes.*

Their eyes are on MR. FRANK, *waiting for him to give them the signal which will release them from their day-long quiet.* MR. FRANK, *his shoes in his hand, stands looking down out of the window at the back, watching to be sure that all of the workmen have left the building below.*

After a few seconds of motionless silence, MR. FRANK *turns from the window.)*

TAKE NOTES

Literary Analysis 

How does Anne's **dialogue** with her diary provide key details to the plot?

Reading Skill 

Considering the **background information** you have about the Nazis, what consequences do you think Miep and Mr. Kraler might face?

Reading Check 

By the time of Scene 3, how long have the families been living in the apartment? Underline the answer.

TAKE NOTES

Stop to Reflect 

How would Mr. Frank know when the last worker left the building?

Reading Skill 

What **effect** does Mr. Frank's comment in the underlined passage have on the group? Circle two things they do.

Literary Analysis

What does the **dialogue** between Peter and Anne in the bracketed passage show that Peter has learned about Anne?

Reading Check 

What does Anne want Peter to do? Draw a box around the answer.

MR. FRANK. *(Quietly, to the group)* It's safe now. The last workman has left.

(There is an immediate stir of relief.)

ANNE. *(Her pent-up energy explodes.)* WHEE!

MR. FRANK. *(Startled, amused)* Anne!

MRS. VAN DAAN. I'm first for the w.c.

(She hurries off to the bathroom. MRS. FRANK *puts on her shoes and starts up to the sink to prepare supper.* ANNE *sneaks* PETER'S *shoes from under the table and hides them behind her back.* MR. FRANK *goes in to* MARGOT'S *room.)*

MR. FRANK. *(To* MARGOT*)* Six o'clock. School's over.

*(*MARGOT *gets up, stretching.* MR. FRANK *sits down to put on his shoes. In the main room* PETER *tries to find his.)*

PETER. *(To* ANNE*)* Have you seen my shoes?

ANNE. *(Innocently)* Your shoes?

PETER. You've taken them, haven't you?

ANNE. I don't know what you're talking about.

PETER. You're going to be sorry!

ANNE. Am I?

*(*PETER *goes after her.* ANNE, *with his shoes in her hand, runs from him, dodging behind her mother.)*

MRS. FRANK. *(Protesting)* Anne, dear!

PETER. Wait till I get you!

ANNE, I'm waiting! *(*PETER *makes a lunge for her. They both fall to the floor.* PETER *pins her down, wrestling with her to get the shoes.)* Don't! Don't! Peter, stop it. Ouch!

MRS. FRANK. Anne! . . . Peter!

(Suddenly PETER *becomes self-conscious. He grabs his shoes roughly and starts for his room.)*

ANNE. *(Following him)* Peter, where are you going? Come dance with me.

PETER. I tell you I don't know how.

ANNE. I'll teach you.

PETER. I'm going to give Mouschi his dinner.

ANNE. Can I watch?

PETER. He doesn't like people around while he eats.

ANNE. Peter, please.

PETER. No! *(He goes into his room.* ANNE *slams his door after him.)*

MRS. FRANK. Anne, dear, I think you shouldn't play like that with Peter. It's not dignified.

ANNE. Who cares if it's dignified? I don't want to be dignified.

*(*MR. FRANK *and* MARGOT *come from the room on the right.* MARGOT *goes to help her mother.* MR. FRANK *starts for the center table to correct* MARGOT'S *school papers.)*

MRS. FRANK. *(To* ANNE*)* You complain that I don't treat you like a grownup. But when I do, you resent it.

ANNE: I only want some fun . . . someone to laugh and clown with . . . After you've sat still all day and hardly moved, you've got to have some fun. I don't know what's the matter with that boy.

MR. FRANK. He isn't used to girls. Give him a little time.

ANNE. Time? Isn't two months time? I could cry. *(Catching hold of* MARGOT*)* Come on, Margot . . . dance with me. Come on, please.

MARGOT. I have to help with supper.

ANNE. You know we're going to forget how to dance . . . When we get out we won't remember a thing.

(She starts to sing and dance by herself. MR. FRANK *takes her in his arms, waltzing with her.* MRS. VAN DAAN *comes in from the bathroom.)*

MRS. VAN DAAN. Next? *(She looks around as she starts putting on her shoes.)* Where's Peter?

ANNE. *(As they are dancing)* Where would he be!

MRS. VAN DAAN. He hasn't finished his lessons, has he? His father'll kill him if he catches him in there with that cat and his work not done. *(*MR. FRANK *and* ANNE *finish their dance. They bow to each other with extravagant formality.)* Anne, get him out of there, will you?

ANNE. *(At* PETER'S *door)* Peter? Peter?

PETER. *(Opening the door a crack)* What is it?

ANNE. Your mother says to come out.

PETER. I'm giving Mouschi his dinner.

TAKE NOTES

Reading Skill

What **effect** does Anne seem to have on Peter?

Literary Analysis

What does the bracketed **dialogue** tell you about Anne's personality?

Reading Skill

What **causes** Anne to want to dance?

Reading Check

Who dances with Anne? Circle the answer.

TAKE NOTES

Literary Analysis

What does the bracketed **dialogue** reveal about how Mrs. Van Daan feels about the growing friendship between Anne and Peter?

____

____

____

____

Reading Skill

What does Mrs. Van Daan **cause** Peter to do? Circle the answer.

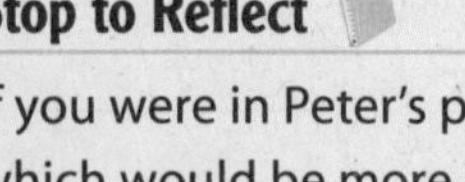

Stop to Reflect

If you were in Peter's place, which would be more important to you, privacy or friendship? Why?

____

____

____

____

Reading Check 

What is everyone's reaction to the sound of the automobile? Underline the answer.

MRS. VAN DAAN. You know what your father says. *(She sits on the couch, sewing on the lining of her fur coat.)*

PETER. For heaven's sake, I haven't even looked at him since lunch.

MRS. VAN DAAN. I'm just telling you, that's all.

ANNE. I'll feed him.

PETER. I don't want you in there.

MRS. VAN DAAN. Peter!

PETER. *(To* ANNE*)* Then give him his dinner and come right out, you hear?

(He comes back to the table. ANNE *shuts the door of* PETER'S *room after her and disappears behind the curtain covering his closet.)*

MRS. VAN DAAN. *(To* PETER*)* Now is that any way to talk to your little girl friend?

PETER. Mother . . . for heaven's sake . . . will you please stop saying that?

MRS. VAN DAAN. Look at him blush! Look at him!

PETER. Please! I'm not . . . anyway . . . let me alone, will you?

MRS. VAN DAAN. He acts like it was something to be ashamed of. It's nothing to be ashamed of, to have a little girl friend.

PETER. You're crazy. She's only thirteen.

MRS. VAN DAAN. So what? And you're sixteen. Just perfect. Your father's ten years older than I am. *(To* MR. FRANK*)* I warn you, Mr. Frank, if this war lasts much longer, we're going to be related and then . . .

MR. FRANK. *Mazeltov!*[17]

MRS. FRANK. *(Deliberately changing the conversation)* I wonder where Miep is. She's usually so prompt.

(Suddenly everything else is forgotten as they hear the sound of an automobile coming to a screeching stop in the street below. They are tense, motionless in their terror. The car starts away. A wave of relief sweeps over them. They pick up their occupations again. ANNE *flings open the door of* PETER'S *room, making a*

17. ***Mazeltov*** (MAH zuhl TOHV) "good luck" in Hebrew and Yiddish.

dramatic entrance. She is dressed in PETER'S *clothes.* PETER *looks at her in fury. The others are amused.)*

ANNE. Good evening, everyone. Forgive me if I don't stay. *(She jumps up on a chair.)* I have a friend waiting for me in there. My friend Tom. Tom Cat. Some people say that we look alike. But Tom has the most beautiful whiskers, and I have only a little fuzz. I am hoping . . . in time . . .

PETER. All right, Mrs. Quack Quack!

ANNE. *(Outraged—jumping down)* Peter!

PETER. I heard about you . . . How you talked so much in class they called you Mrs. Quack Quack. How Mr. Smitter made you write a composition . . . "'Quack, Quack,' said Mrs. Quack Quack."

ANNE. Well, go on. Tell them the rest. How it was so good he read it out loud to the class and then read it to all his other classes!

PETER. Quack! Quack! Quack . . . Quack . . . Quack . . .

*(*ANNE *pulls off the coat and trousers.)*

ANNE. You are the most intolerable, insufferable boy I've ever met!

(She throws the clothes down the stairwell. PETER *goes down after them.)*

PETER. Quack, Quack, Quack!

MRS. VAN DAAN. *(To* ANNE*)* That's right, Anneke! Give it to him!

ANNE. With all the boys in the world . . . Why I had to get locked up with one like you! . . .

PETER. Quack, Quack, Quack, and from now on stay out of my room!

(As PETER *passes her,* ANNE *puts out her foot, tripping him. He picks himself up, and goes on into his room.)*

MRS. FRANK. *(Quietly)* Anne, dear . . . your hair. *(She feels* ANNE'S *forehead.)* You're warm. Are you feeling all right?

Vocabulary Development

insufferable (in suf uh ruh buhl) *adj.* unbearable

TAKE NOTES

Literary Analysis 

Characters' **dialogue** reveals important information about their personalities. In what ways is Peter like a cat?

____

____

____

In what ways is Anne like a duck?

____

____

____

Reading Skill 

What does Peter say **caused** Anne's classmates to call her "Mrs. Quack Quack"?

____

____

____

Reading Check 

In whose clothes does Anne dress up? Underline the answer.

TAKE NOTES

Reading Skill

What **background information** helps you understand the underlined sentence? Why can't the people in the apartment call a doctor?

Literary Analysis

What does the **dialogue** reveal about Anne's relationship with her mother?

Stop to Reflect

What must it be like to live in a place where you hear the sound of bombers and antiaircraft gunfire all the time?

Reading Check

Whom are they all waiting for? Circle the answer.

ANNE. Please, Mother. *(She goes over to the center table, slipping into her shoes.)*

MRS. FRANK. *(Following her)* You haven't a fever, have you?

ANNE. *(Pulling away)* No. No.

MRS. FRANK. You know we can't call a doctor here, ever. There's only one thing to do . . . watch carefully. Prevent an illness before it comes. Let me see your tongue.

ANNE. Mother, this is perfectly absurd.

MRS. FRANK. Anne, dear, don't be such a baby. Let me see your tongue. *(As* ANNE *refuses,* MRS. FRANK *appeals to* MR. FRANK*)* Otto . . .?

MR. FRANK. You hear your mother, Anne.

*(*ANNE *flicks out her tongue for a second, then turns away.)*

MRS. FRANK. Come on—open up! *(As* ANNE *opens her mouth very wide)* You seem all right . . . but perhaps an aspirin . . .

MRS. VAN DAAN. For heaven's sake, don't give that child any pills. I waited for fifteen minutes this morning for her to come out of the w.c.

ANNE. I was washing my hair!

MR. FRANK. I think there's nothing the matter with our Anne that a ride on her bike, or a visit with her friend Jopie de Waal wouldn't cure. Isn't that so, Anne?

*(*MR. VAN DAAN *comes down into the room. From outside we hear faint sounds of bombers going over and a burst of ack-ack.)*[18]

MR. VAN DAAN. Miep not come yet?

MRS. VAN DAAN. The workmen just left, a little while ago.

MR. VAN DAAN. What's for dinner tonight?

MRS. VAN DAAN. Beans.

MR. VAN DAAN. Not again!

MRS. VAN DAAN. Poor Putti! I know. But what can we do? That's all that Miep brought us.

18. **ack-ack** (AK AK) *n.* slang for an antiaircraft gun's fire.

(MR. VAN DAAN *starts to pace, his hands behind his back.* ANNE *follows behind him, imitating him.)*

ANNE. We are now in what is known as the "bean cycle." Beans boiled, beans en casserole, beans with strings, beans without strings . . .

*(*PETER *has come out of his room. He slides into his place at the table, becoming immediately absorbed in his studies.)*

MR. VAN DAAN. *(To* PETER*)* I saw you . . . in there, playing with your cat.

MRS. VAN DAAN. He just went in for a second, putting his coat away. He's been out here all the time, doing his lessons.

MR. FRANK. *(Looking up from the papers)* Anne, you got an excellent in your history paper today . . . and very good in Latin.

ANNE. *(Sitting beside him)* How about algebra?

MR. FRANK. I'll have to make a confession. Up until now I've managed to stay ahead of you in algebra. Today you caught up with me. We'll leave it to Margot to correct.

ANNE. Isn't algebra *vile*, Pim!

MR. FRANK. Vile!

MARGOT. *(To* MR. FRANK*)* How did I do?

ANNE. *(Getting up)* Excellent, excellent, excellent, excellent!

MR. FRANK. *(To* MARGOT*)* You should have used the subjunctive[19] here . . .

MARGOT. Should I? . . . I thought . . . look here . . . I didn't use it here . . .

(The two become absorbed in the papers.)

ANNE. Mrs. Van Daan, may I try on your coat?

MRS. FRANK. No, Anne.

MRS. VAN DAAN. *(Giving it to* ANNE*)* It's all right . . . but careful with it. *(*ANNE *puts it on and struts with it.)* My father gave me that the year before he died. He always bought the best that money could buy.

19. **subjunctive** (suhb JUNK tiv) *n.* form of a verb that is used to express doubt or uncertainty.

TAKE NOTES

Literary Analysis

What can you tell from Mr. Frank's part of the **dialogue** about his attitude toward education?

Reading Check

What have the families been eating? Underline the text that tells you.

Stop to Reflect

What is happening within and between the families in the apartment?

TAKE NOTES

Reading Skill

What **effect** does Mrs. Van Daan's story have on Mr. Van Daan?

____

____

____

____

Literary Analysis

What does the **dialogue** on this page tell you about Mrs. Van Daan's personality? List three words or phrases to describe her.

1. _______________

____

2. _______________

____

3. _______________

____

Reading Check 

What do the stage directions tell you Anne does? Underline the answer.

ANNE. Mrs. Van Daan, did you have a lot of boy friends before you were married?

MRS. FRANK. Anne, that's a personal question. It's not courteous to ask personal questions.

MRS. VAN DAAN. Oh I don't mind. *(To* ANNE*)* Our house was always swarming with boys. When I was a girl we had . . .

MR. VAN DAAN. Oh, God. Not again!

MRS. VAN DAAN. *(Good-humored)* Shut up! *(Without a pause, to* ANNE, MR. VAN DAAN *mimics* MRS. VAN DAAN, *speaking the first few words in unison with her.)* One summer we had a big house in Hilversum. The boys came buzzing round like bees around a jam pot. And when I was sixteen! . . . We were wearing our skirts very short those days and I had good-looking legs. *(She pulls up her skirt, going to* MR. FRANK.*)* I still have 'em. I may not be as pretty as I used to be, but I still have my legs. How about it, Mr. Frank?

MR. VAN DAAN. All right. All right. We see them.

MRS. VAN DAAN. I'm not asking you. I'm asking Mr. Frank.

PETER. Mother, for heaven's sake.

MRS. VAN DAAN. Oh, I embarrass you, do I? Well, I just hope the girl you marry has as good. *(Then to* ANNE*)* My father used to worry about me, with so many boys hanging round. He told me, if any of them gets fresh, you say to him . . . "Remember, Mr. So-and-So, remember I'm a lady."

ANNE. "Remember, Mr. So-and-So, remember I'm a lady." *(She gives* MRS. VAN DAAN *her coat.)*

MR. VAN DAAN. Look at you, talking that way in front of her! Don't you know she puts it all down in that diary?

MRS. VAN DAAN. So, if she does? I'm only telling the truth!

*(*ANNE *stretches out, putting her ear to the floor, listening to what is going on below. The sound of the bombers fades away.)*

MRS. FRANK. *(Setting the table)* Would you mind, Peter, if I moved you over to the couch?

ANNE. *(Listening)* Miep must have the radio on.

(PETER picks up his papers, going over to the couch beside MRS. VAN DAAN.)

MR. VAN DAAN. *(Accusingly, to PETER)* Haven't you finished yet?

PETER. No.

MR. VAN DAAN. You ought to be ashamed of yourself.

PETER. All right. All right. I'm a dunce. I'm a hopeless case. Why do I go on?

MRS. VAN DAAN. You're not hopeless. Don't talk that way. It's just that you haven't anyone to help you, like the girls have. *(To MR. FRANK)* Maybe you could help him, Mr. Frank?

MR. FRANK. I'm sure that his father . . .?

MR. VAN DAAN. Not me. I can't do anything with him. He won't listen to me. You go ahead . . . if you want.

MR. FRANK. *(Going to PETER)* What about it, Peter? Shall we make our school coeducational?

MRS. VAN DAAN. *(Kissing MR. FRANK)* You're an angel, Mr. Frank. An angel. I don't know why I didn't meet you before I met that one there. Here, sit down, Mr. Frank . . . *(She forces him down on the couch beside PETER.)* Now, Peter, you listen to Mr. Frank.

MR. FRANK. It might be better for us to go into Peter's room.

(PETER jumps up eagerly, leading the way.)

MRS. VAN DAAN. That's right. You go in there, Peter. You listen to Mr. Frank. Mr. Frank is a highly educated man.

(As MR. FRANK is about to follow PETER into his room, MRS. FRANK stops him and wipes the lipstick from his lips. Then she closes the door after them.)

ANNE. *(On the floor, listening)* Shh! I can hear a man's voice talking.

MR. VAN DAAN. *(To ANNE)* Isn't it bad enough here without your sprawling all over the place?

(ANNE sits up.)

MRS. VAN DAAN. *(To MR. VAN DAAN)* If you didn't smoke so much, you wouldn't be so bad-tempered.

TAKE NOTES

Reading Skill

How might the families' situation **cause** Anne to be interested in events outside the attic?

Literary Analysis

What does the **dialogue** tell you about Mr. Van Daan and Peter?

Reading Check

What do Mr. and Mrs. Van Daan ask Mr. Frank to do? Underline the answer.

TAKE NOTES

Literary Analysis

Which lines of **dialogue** show that the residents of the apartment are starting to annoy one another? Put check marks in the margin next to the lines.

Stop to Reflect

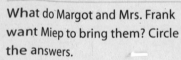

Why do you think that Mrs. Frank and Margot pretend not to notice the quarrel?

____

____

____

____

Reading Check

What do Margot and Mrs. Frank want Miep to bring them? Circle the answers.

MR. VAN DAAN. Am I smoking? Do you see me smoking?

MRS. VAN DAAN. Don't tell me you've used up all those cigarettes.

MR. VAN DAAN. One package. Miep only brought me one package.

MRS. VAN DAAN. It's a filthy habit anyway. It's a good time to break yourself.

MR. VAN DAAN. Oh, stop it, please.

MRS. VAN DAAN. You're smoking up all our money. You know that, don't you?

MR. VAN DAAN. Will you shut up? *(During this,* MRS. FRANK *and* MARGOT *have studiously kept their eyes down. But* ANNE, *seated on the floor, has been following the discussion interestedly.* MR. VAN DAAN *turns to see her staring up at him.)* And what are you staring at?

ANNE. I never heard grownups quarrel before. I thought only children quarreled.

MR. VAN DAAN. This isn't a quarrel! It's a discussion. And I never heard children so rude before.

ANNE. *(Rising, indignantly) I,* rude!

MR. VAN DAAN. Yes!

MRS. FRANK. *(Quickly)* Anne, will you get me my knitting? *(*ANNE *goes to get it.)* I must remember, when Miep comes, to ask her to bring me some more wool.

MARGOT. *(Going to her room)* I need some hairpins and some soap. I made a list. *(She goes into her bedroom to get the list.)*

MRS. FRANK. *(To* ANNE*)* Have you some library books for Miep when she comes?

ANNE. It's a wonder that Miep has a life of her own, the way we make her run errands for us. Please, Miep, get me some starch. Please take my hair out and have it cut. Tell me all the latest news, Miep. *(She goes over, kneeling on the couch beside* MRS. VAN DAAN*)* Did you know she was engaged? His name is Dirk, and Miep's afraid the Nazis will ship him off to Germany to work in one of their war plants. That's what they're doing with some of the young Dutchmen . . . they pick them up off the streets—

MR. VAN DAAN. *(Interrupting)* Don't you ever get tired of talking? Suppose you try keeping still for five minutes. Just five minutes.

(He starts to pace again. Again ANNE *follows him, mimicking him.* MRS. FRANK *jumps up and takes her by the arm up to the sink, and gives her a glass of milk.)*

MRS. FRANK. Come here, Anne. It's time for your glass of milk.

MR. VAN DAAN. Talk, talk, talk. I never heard such a child. Where is my . . .? Every evening it's the same talk, talk, talk. *(He looks around.)* Where is my . . .?

MRS. VAN DAAN. What're you looking for?

MR. VAN DAAN. My pipe. Have you seen my pipe?

MRS. VAN DAAN. What good's a pipe? You haven't got any tobacco.

MR. VAN DAAN. At least I'll have something to hold in my mouth! *(Opening* MARGOT'S *bedroom door)* Margot, have you seen my pipe?

MARGOT. It was on the table last night.

*(*ANNE *puts her glass of milk on the table and picks up his pipe, hiding it behind her back.)*

MR. VAN DAAN. I know. I know. Anne, did you see my pipe? . . . Anne!

MRS. FRANK. Anne, Mr. Van Daan is speaking to you.

ANNE. Am I allowed to talk now?

MR. VAN DAAN. You're the most aggravating . . . The trouble with you is, you've been spoiled. What you need is a good old-fashioned spanking.

ANNE. *(Mimicking* MRS. VAN DAAN*)* "Remember, Mr. So-and-So, remember I'm a lady." *(She thrusts the pipe into his mouth, then picks up her glass of milk.)*

MR. VAN DAAN. *(Restraining himself with difficulty)* Why aren't you nice and quiet like your sister Margot? Why do you have to show off all the time? Let me give you a little advice, young lady. Men don't like that kind of thing in a girl. You know that? A man likes a girl who'll listen to him

TAKE NOTES

Reading Skill

What **effect** might Mrs. Frank think a glass of milk will have on Anne's behavior?

Literary Analysis

What does the **dialogue** tell you about Mr. Van Daan's opinion of Anne?

What about Mr. Van Daan's words and actions make him seem childlike?

Reading Check

What is Mr. Van Daan looking for? Circle the answer.

TAKE NOTES

Literary Analysis 

Paraphrase the **dialogue** between Anne and Mr. Van Daan.

Reading Skill 

What **causes** Mrs. Van Daan to react to the accident as she does?

Stop to Reflect

Reread the underlined passage. Do you agree with Mrs. Frank? Explain why or why not.

Reading Check 

What does Anne want to be when she grows up? Circle the answer.

once in a while . . . a domestic girl, who'll keep her house shining for her husband . . . who loves to cook and sew and . . .

ANNE. I'd cut my throat first! I'd open my veins! I'm going to be remarkable! I'm going to Paris . . .

MR. VAN DAAN. *(Scoffingly)* Paris!

ANNE. . . . to study music and art.

MR. VAN DAAN. Yeah! Yeah!

ANNE. I'm going to be a famous dancer or singer . . . or something wonderful.

(She makes a wide gesture, spilling the glass of milk on the fur coat in MRS. VAN DAAN'S *lap.* MARGOT *rushes quickly over with a towel.* ANNE *tries to brush the milk off with her skirt.)*

MRS. VAN DAAN. Now look what you've done . . . you clumsy little fool! My beautiful fur coat my father gave me . . .

ANNE. I'm so sorry.

MRS. VAN DAAN. What do you care? It isn't yours . . . So go on, ruin it! Do you know what that coat cost? Do you? And now look at it! Look at it!

ANNE. I'm very, very sorry.

MRS. VAN DAAN. I could kill you for this. I could just kill you!

*(*MRS. VAN DAAN *goes up the stairs, clutching the coat.* MR. VAN DAAN *starts after her.)*

MR. VAN DAAN. Petronella . . . *Liefje! Liefje!* . . . Come back . . . the supper . . . come back!

MRS. FRANK. Anne, you must not behave in that way.

ANNE. It was an accident. Anyone can have an accident.

MRS. FRANK. I don't mean that. I mean the answering back. You must not answer back. They are our guests. We must always show the greatest courtesy to them. We're all living under terrible tension. *(She stops as* MARGOT *indicates that* VAN DAAN *can hear. When he is gone, she continues.)* That's why we must control ourselves . . . You don't hear Margot getting into arguments with them, do you? Watch Margot. She's always courteous with them. Never familiar. She keeps her distance. And they respect her for it. Try to be like Margot.

ANNE. And have them walk all over me, the way they do her? No, thanks!

MRS. FRANK. I'm not afraid that anyone is going to walk all over you, Anne. I'm afraid for other people, that you'll walk on them. I don't know what happens to you, Anne. You are wild, self-willed. If I had ever talked to my mother as you talk to me . . .

ANNE. Things have changed. People aren't like that any more. "Yes, Mother." "No, Mother." "Anything you say, Mother." I've got to fight things out for myself! Make something of myself!

MRS. FRANK. It isn't necessary to fight to do it. Margot doesn't fight, and isn't she . . .?

ANNE. *(Violently rebellious)* Margot! Margot! Margot! That's all I hear from everyone . . . how wonderful Margot is . . . "Why aren't you like Margot?"

MARGOT. *(Protesting)* Oh, come on, Anne, don't be so . . .

ANNE. *(Paying no attention)* Everything she does is right, and everything I do is wrong! I'm the goat around here! . . . You're all against me! . . . And you worst of all!

(She rushes off into her room and throws herself down on the settee, stifling her sobs. MRS. FRANK *sighs and starts toward the stove.)*

MRS. FRANK. *(To* MARGOT*)* Let's put the soup on the stove . . . if there's anyone who cares to eat. Margot, will you take the bread out? *(*MARGOT *gets the bread from the cupboard.)* I don't know how we can go on living this way . . . I can't say a word to Anne . . . she flies at me . . .

MARGOT. You know Anne. In half an hour she'll be out here, laughing and joking.

MRS. FRANK. And . . . *(She makes a motion upwards, indicating the* VAN DAANS.*)* . . . I told your father it wouldn't work . . . but no . . . no . . . he had to ask them, he said . . . he owed it to him, he said.

TAKE NOTES

Literary Analysis

What does Anne's part of the **dialogue** reveal about Margot?

____

____

____

What does Margot say about Anne?

____

____

____

Reading Skill

Read the underlined text. What **causes** Anne's outburst?

____

____

Reading Check

What does Anne say she has to do for herself? Underline the answer.

Stop to Reflect

Why do you think Anne reacts so strongly to Mrs. Frank's comparison of her to Margot?

____

____

____

TAKE NOTES

Reading Skill

What sound always **causes** Mrs. Frank alarm? Circle the answer. Why does this sound frighten her?

Literary Analysis

The tone of **dialogue** is the mood or attitude it reveals. How is the tone of the dialogue on this page different from the tone of the dialogue on previous pages?

Reading Skill

What do you think **causes** the change in tone on this page?

Reading Check

Why does Margot go into her and Anne's bedroom? Underline the answer.

Well, he knows now that I was right! These quarrels! . . . This bickering!

MARGOT. *(With a warning look)* Shush. Shush.

(The buzzer for the door sounds. MRS. FRANK *gasps, startled.)*

MRS. FRANK. Every time I hear that sound, my heart stops!

MARGOT. *(Starting for* PETER'S *door)* It's Miep. *(She knocks at the door.)* Father?

*(*MR. FRANK *comes quickly from* PETER'S *room.)*

MR. FRANK. Thank you, Margot. *(As he goes down the steps to open the outer door)* Has everyone his list?

MARGOT. I'll get my books. *(Giving her mother a list)* Here's your list. *(*MARGOT *goes into her and* ANNE'S *bedroom on the right.* ANNE *sits up, hiding her tears, as* MARGOT *comes in.)* Miep's here. *(*MARGOT *picks up her books and goes back.* ANNE *hurries over to the mirror, smoothing her hair.)*

MR. VAN DAAN. *(Coming down the stairs)* Is it Miep?

MARGOT. Yes. Father's gone down to let her in.

MR. VAN DAAN. At last I'll have some cigarettes!

MRS. FRANK. *(To* MR. VAN DAAN*)* I can't tell you how unhappy I am about Mrs. Van Daan's coat. Anne should never have touched it.

MR. VAN DAAN. She'll be all right.

MRS. FRANK. Is there anything I can do?

MR. VAN DAAN. Don't worry.

(He turns to meet MIEP. *But it is not* MIEP *who comes up the steps. It is* MR. KRALER, *followed by* MR. FRANK. *Their faces are grave.* ANNE *comes from the bedroom.* PETER *comes from his room.)*

MRS. FRANK. Mr. Kraler!

MR. VAN DAAN. How are you, Mr. Kraler?

MARGOT. This is a surprise.

MRS. FRANK. When Mr. Kraler comes, the sun begins to shine.

MR. VAN DAAN. Miep is coming?

MR. KRALER. Not tonight.

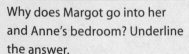

*(*KRALER *goes to* MARGOT *and* MRS. FRANK *and* ANNE, *shaking hands with them.)*

MRS. FRANK. Wouldn't you like a cup of coffee? . . . Or, better still, will you have supper with us?

MR. FRANK. Mr. Kraler has something to talk over with us. Something has happened, he says, which demands an immediate decision.

MRS. FRANK. *(Fearful)* What is it?

*(*MR. KRALER *sits down on the couch. As he talks he takes bread, cabbages, milk, etc., from his briefcase, giving them to* MARGOT *and* ANNE *to put away.)*

MR. KRALER. Usually, when I come up here, I try to bring you some bit of good news. What's the use of telling you the bad news when there's nothing that you can do about it? But today something has happened . . . Dirk . . . Miep's Dirk, you know, came to me just now. He tells me that he has a Jewish friend living near him. A dentist. He says he's in trouble. He begged me, could I do anything for this man? Could I find him a hiding place? . . . So I've come to you . . . I know it's a terrible thing to ask of you, living as you are, but would you take him in with you?

MR. FRANK. Of course we will.

MR. KRALER. *(Rising)* It'll be just for a night or two . . . until I find some other place. This happened so suddenly that I didn't know where to turn.

MR. FRANK. Where is he?

MR. KRALER. Downstairs in the office.

MR. FRANK. Good. Bring him up.

MR. KRALER. His name is Dussel . . . Jan Dussel.

MR. FRANK. Dussel . . . I think I know him.

MR. KRALER. I'll get him.

(He goes quickly down the steps and out. MR. FRANK *suddenly becomes conscious of the others.)*

MR. FRANK. Forgive me. I spoke without consulting you. But I knew you'd feel as I do.

MR. VAN DAAN. There's no reason for you to consult anyone. This is your place. You have a right to do exactly as you please. The only thing I feel . . .

TAKE NOTES

Stop to Reflect

Note Mr. Frank's underlined remark. How does the line make you feel? What do you think is going to happen? Write your prediction below. Then, read ahead to see whether your guess is correct.

Reading Skill 

Use background information to tell what kind of trouble Mr. Dussel is in.

Reading Check 

What does Mr. Kraler ask of Mr. Frank? What is Mr. Frank's answer? Draw a box around the answers.

TAKE NOTES

Reading Skill 

What will be the **effect** of Mr. Dussel's moving in?

Literary Analysis 

What do Peter, Margot, and Anne reveal about themselves in the bracketed **dialogue**?

Stop to Reflect 

Do you think the two families should take in Mr. Dussel? Explain.

Reading Check 

Who will be sharing a room with Mr. Dussel? Circle the answer.

there's so little food as it is . . . and to take in another person . . .

(PETER *turns away, ashamed of his father.)*

MR. FRANK. We can stretch the food a little. It's only for a few days.

MR. VAN DAAN. You want to make a bet?

MRS. FRANK. I think it's fine to have him. But, Otto, where are you going to put him? Where?

PETER. He can have my bed. I can sleep on the floor. I wouldn't mind.

MR. FRANK. That's good of you, Peter. But your room's too small . . . even for *you.*

ANNE. I have a much better idea. I'll come in here with you and Mother, and Margot can take Peter's room and Peter can go in our room with Mr. Dussel.

MARGOT. That's right. We could do that.

MR. FRANK. No, Margot. You mustn't sleep in that room . . . neither you nor Anne. Mouschi has caught some rats in there. Peter's brave. He doesn't mind.

ANNE. Then how about *this*? I'll come in here with you and Mother, and Mr. Dussel can have my bed.

MRS. FRANK. *No. No. No!* Margot will come in here with us and he can have her bed. It's the only way. Margot, bring your things in here. Help her, Anne.

(MARGOT *hurries into her room to get her things.)*

ANNE. *(To her mother)* Why Margot? Why can't I come in here?

MRS. FRANK. Because it wouldn't be proper for Margot to sleep with a . . . Please, Anne. Don't argue. Please.

(ANNE *starts slowly away.)*

MR. FRANK. *(To* ANNE*)* You don't mind sharing your room with Mr. Dussel, do you, Anne?

ANNE: No. No, of course not.

MR. FRANK. Good. (ANNE *goes off into her bedroom, helping* MARGOT. MR. FRANK *starts to search in the cupboards.)* Where's the cognac?

MRS. FRANK. It's there. But, Otto, I was saving it in case of illness.

MR. FRANK. I think we couldn't find a better time to use it. Peter, will you get five glasses for me?

(PETER *goes for the glasses.* MARGOT *comes out of her bedroom, carrying her possessions, which she hangs behind a curtain in the main room.* MR. FRANK *finds the cognac and pours it into the five glasses that* PETER *brings him.* MR. VAN DAAN *stands looking on sourly.* MRS. VAN DAAN *comes downstairs and looks around at all the bustle.)*

MRS. VAN DAAN. What's happening? What's going on?

MR. VAN DAAN. Someone's moving in with us.

MRS. VAN DAAN. In here? You're joking.

MARGOT. It's only for a night or two . . . until Mr. Kraler finds him another place.

MR. VAN DAAN. Yeah! Yeah!

(MR. FRANK *hurries over as* MR. KRALER *and* DUSSEL *come up.* DUSSEL *is a man in his late fifties, meticulous, finicky . . . bewildered now. He wears a raincoat. He carries a briefcase, stuffed full, and a small medicine case.)*

MR. FRANK. Come in, Mr. Dussel.

MR. KRALER. This is Mr. Frank.

DUSSEL. Mr. Otto Frank?

MR. FRANK. Yes. Let me take your things. *(He takes the hat and briefcase, but* DUSSEL *clings to his medicine case.)* This is my wife Edith . . . Mr. and Mrs. Van Daan . . . their son, Peter . . . and my daughters, Margot and Anne.

(DUSSEL *shakes hands with everyone.)*

MR. KRALER. Thank you, Mr. Frank. Thank you all. Mr. Dussel, I leave you in good hands. Oh . . . Dirk's coat.

(DUSSEL *hurriedly takes off the raincoat, giving it to* MR. KRALER. *Underneath is his white dentist's jacket, with a yellow Star of David on it.)*

Vocabulary Development

meticulous (muh TIK yoo luhs) *adj.* extremely careful about details

TAKE NOTES

Reading Skill 

Read the bracketed passage. What might **cause** Margot to tell Mrs. Van Daan immediately that Mr. Dussel will probably stay only a couple of nights?

Reading Check 

What does Mr. Dussel bring with him? Underline the answer.

Literary Analysis 

How do Mr. Frank's words help make Mr. Dussel feel welcome?

TAKE NOTES

Reading Skill

Be aware of the historical **background**. Underline the remarks from Mr. Kraler that show that he and other Dutch people are opposed to the Nazis.

Stop to Reflect

Why might Mr. Frank not want Peter to follow Mr. Kraler down the stairs and bolt the door?

___

___

___

___

Literary Analysis

What does the **dialogue** on this page tell you about the Franks' disappearance?

___

___

___

___

Reading Check

What does Mrs. Frank call Miep and Mr. Kraler? Circle the answer.

DUSSEL. *(To* MR. KRALER*)* What can I say to thank you . . .?

MRS. FRANK. *(To* DUSSEL*)* Mr. Kraler and Miep . . . They're our life line. Without them we couldn't live.

MR. KRALER. Please. Please. You make us seem very heroic. It isn't that at all. We simply don't like the Nazis. *(To* MR. FRANK, *who offers him a drink)* No, thanks. *(Then going on)* We don't like their methods. We don't like . . .

MR. FRANK. *(Smiling)* I know. I know. "No one's going to tell us Dutchmen what to do with our damn Jews!"

MR. KRALER. *(To* DUSSEL*)* Pay no attention to Mr. Frank. I'll be up tomorrow to see that they're treating you right. *(To* MR. FRANK*)* Don't trouble to come down again. Peter will bolt the door after me, won't you, Peter?

PETER. Yes, sir.

MR. FRANK. Thank you, Peter. I'll do it.

MR. KRALER. Good night. Good night.

GROUP. Good night, Mr. Kraler. We'll see you tomorrow, etc., etc.

*(*MR. KRALER *goes out with* MR. FRANK. MRS. FRANK *gives each one of the "grownups" a glass of cognac.)*

MRS. FRANK. Please, Mr. Dussel, sit down.

*(*MR. DUSSEL *sinks into a chair.* MRS. FRANK *gives him a glass of cognac.)*

DUSSEL. I'm dreaming. I know it. I can't believe my eyes. Mr. Otto Frank here! *(To* MRS. FRANK*)* You're not in Switzerland then? A woman told me . . . She said she'd gone to your house . . . the door was open, everything was in disorder, dishes in the sink. She said she found a piece of paper in the wastebasket with an address scribbled on it . . . an address in Zurich. She said you must have escaped to Zurich.

ANNE. Father put that there purposely . . . just so people would think that very thing!

DUSSEL. And you've been *here* all the time?

MRS. FRANK. All the time . . . ever since July.

(ANNE *speaks to her father as he comes back.)*

ANNE. It worked, Pim . . . the address you left! Mr. Dussel says that people believe we escaped to Switzerland.

MR. FRANK. I'm glad. . . . And now let's have a little drink to welcome Mr. Dussel.

(Before they can drink, MR. DUSSEL *bolts his drink.* MR. FRANK *smiles and raises his glass.)*

To Mr. Dussel. Welcome. We're very honored to have you with us.

MRS. FRANK. To Mr. Dussel, welcome.

(The VAN DAANS *murmur a welcome. The "grownups" drink.)*

MRS. VAN DAAN. Um. That was good.

MR. VAN DAAN. Did Mr. Kraler warn you that you won't get much to eat here? You can imagine . . . three ration books among the seven of us . . . and now you make eight.

(PETER *walks away, humiliated. Outside a street organ is heard dimly.)*

DUSSEL. *(Rising)* Mr. Van Daan, you don't realize what is happening outside that you should warn me of a thing like that. You don't realize what's going on . . . *(As* MR. VAN DAAN *starts his characteristic pacing,* DUSSEL *turns to speak to the others.)* Right here in Amsterdam every day hundreds of Jews disappear . . . They surround a block and search house by house. Children come home from school to find their parents gone. Hundreds are being deported . . . people that you and I know . . . the Hallensteins . . . the Wessels . . .

MRS. FRANK. *(In tears)* Oh, no. No!

DUSSEL. They get their call-up notice . . . come to the Jewish theater on such and such a day and hour . . . bring only what you can carry in a rucksack. And if you refuse the call-up notice, then they come and drag you from your home and ship you off to Mauthausen.[20] The death camp!

MRS. FRANK. We didn't know that things had got so much worse.

20. Mauthausen (MOW TOW zuhn) village in Austria that was the site of a Nazi concentration camp.

TAKE NOTES

Reading Skill

What **causes** Peter's humiliation?

Literary Analysis

What purpose does the bracketed **dialogue** serve?

Reading Check

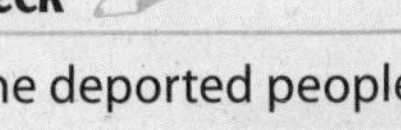

Where are the deported people being sent? Circle the answer.

TAKE NOTES

Reading Skill

What **causes** Anne to cry?

____

____

____

Literary Analysis

Mr. Frank continues to show self-control and understanding toward everyone in the apartment. What does his bracketed statement show about his concern for Mr. Dussel?

____

____

____

____

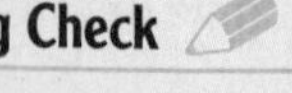

Reading Check

Why is Mr. Dussel shocked? Circle the answer.

DUSSEL. Forgive me for speaking so.

ANNE. *(Coming to* DUSSEL*)* Do you know the de Waals? . . . What's become of them? Their daughter Jopie and I are in the same class. Jopie's my best friend.

DUSSEL. They are gone.

ANNE. Gone?

DUSSEL. With all the others.

ANNE. Oh, no. Not Jopie!

(She turns away, in tears. MRS. FRANK *motions to* MARGOT *to comfort her.* MARGOT *goes to* ANNE*, putting her arms comfortingly around her.)*

MRS. VAN DAAN. There were some people called Wagner. They lived near us . . .?

MR. FRANK. *(Interrupting, with a glance at* ANNE*)* I think we should put this off until later. We all have many questions we want to ask . . . But I'm sure that Mr. Dussel would like to get settled before supper.

DUSSEL. Thank you. I would. I brought very little with me.

MR. FRANK. *(Giving him his hat and briefcase)* I'm sorry we can't give you a room alone. But I hope you won't be too uncomfortable. We've had to make strict rules here . . . a schedule of hours . . . We'll tell you after supper. Anne, would you like to take Mr. Dussel to his room?

ANNE. *(Controlling her tears)* If you'll come with me, Mr. Dussel? *(She starts for her room.)*

DUSSEL. *(Shaking hands with each in turn)* Forgive me if I haven't really expressed my gratitude to all of you. This has been such a shock to me. I'd always thought of myself as Dutch. I was born in Holland. My father was born in Holland, and my grandfather. And now . . . after all these years . . . *(He breaks off.)* If you'll excuse me.

*(*DUSSEL *gives a little bow and hurries off after* ANNE*.* MR. FRANK *and the others are subdued.)*

ANNE. *(Turning on the light)* Well, here we are.

*(*DUSSEL *looks around the room. In the main room* MARGOT *speaks to her mother.)*

MARGOT. The news sounds pretty bad, doesn't it? It's so different from what Mr. Kraler tells us. Mr. Kraler says things are improving.

MR. VAN DAAN. I like it better the way Kraler tells it.

(They resume their occupations, quietly. PETER *goes off into his room. In* ANNE'S *room,* ANNE *turns to* DUSSEL.*)*

ANNE. You're going to share the room with me.

DUSSEL. I'm a man who's always lived alone. I haven't had to adjust myself to others. I hope you'll bear with me until I learn.

ANNE. Let me help you. *(She takes his briefcase.)* Do you always live all alone? Have you no family at all?

DUSSEL. No one. *(He opens his medicine case and spreads his bottles on the dressing table.)*

ANNE. How dreadful. You must be terribly lonely.

DUSSEL. I'm used to it.

ANNE. I don't think I could ever get used to it. Didn't you even have a pet? A cat, or a dog?

DUSSEL. I have an allergy for fur-bearing animals. They give me asthma.

ANNE. Oh, dear. Peter has a cat.

DUSSEL. Here? He has it here?

ANNE. Yes. But we hardly ever see it. He keeps it in his room all the time. I'm sure it will be all right.

DUSSEL. Let us hope so. *(He takes some pills to fortify himself.)*

ANNE. That's Margot's bed, where you're going to sleep. I sleep on the sofa there. *(Indicating the clothes hooks on the wall)* We cleared these off for your things. *(She goes over to the window.)* The best part about this room . . . you can look down and see a bit of the street and the canal. There's a houseboat . . . you can see the end of it . . . a bargeman lives there with his family . . . They have a baby and he's just beginning to walk and I'm so afraid he's going to fall into the canal some day. I watch him. . . .

DUSSEL. *(Interrupting)* Your father spoke of a schedule.

TAKE NOTES

Stop to Reflect

Why do you think Mr. Kraler tells the families that things are improving?

Reading Skill

What **effect** might Peter's cat have on Mr. Dussel?

Literary Analysis

What does the **dialogue** tell you about Anne's experience of living in this space?

What is important about these details?

TAKE NOTES

Reading Skill 

What **effect** does Anne think she has on the other people in the apartment?

Literary Analysis 

What does this **dialogue** tell you about how Anne and Mr. Dussel might get along? Explain.

Reading Check 

How will Anne and Mr. Dussel divide their private times in the bedroom? Underline the answer.

ANNE. *(Coming away from the window)* Oh, yes. It's mostly about the times we have to be quiet. And times for the w.c. You can use it now if you like.

DUSSEL. *(Stiffly)* No, thank you.

ANNE. I suppose you think it's awful, my talking about a thing like that. But you don't know how important it can get to be, especially when you're frightened . . . About this room, the way Margot and I did . . . she had it to herself in the afternoons for studying, reading . . . lessons, you know . . . and I took the mornings. Would that be all right with you?

DUSSEL. I'm not at my best in the morning.

ANNE. You stay here in the mornings then. I'll take the room in the afternoons.

DUSSEL. Tell me, when you're in here, what happens to me? Where am I spending my time? In there, with all the people?

ANNE. Yes.

DUSSEL. I see. I see.

ANNE. We have supper at half past six.

DUSSEL. *(Going over to the sofa)* Then, if you don't mind . . . I like to lie down quietly for ten minutes before eating. I find it helps the digestion.

ANNE. Of course. I hope I'm not going to be too much of a bother to you. I seem to be able to get everyone's back up.

(DUSSEL *lies down on the sofa, curled up, his back to her.)*

DUSSEL. I always get along very well with children. My patients all bring their children to me, because they know I get on well with them. So don't you worry about that.

(ANNE *leans over him, taking his hand and shaking it gratefully.)*

ANNE. Thank you. Thank you, Mr. Dussel.

(The lights dim to darkness. The curtain falls on the scene. ANNE'S *voice comes to us faintly at first, and then with increasing power.)*

Writing: Diary Entries

Write two **diary entries** from the perspective of two characters other than Anne. Answer these questions to help you organize your thoughts.

- Select an event in Act I about which to write. Which two characters might have different viewpoints about the event?

  ____

- Describe the first character's perspective on the event.

  ____

  ____

- Describe the second character's perspective on the event.

  ____

  ____

- List two adjectives that describe the first character's feelings.

  ____

- List two adjectives that describe the second character's feelings.

  ____

Use your notes to write your diary entries.

Listening and Speaking: Guided Tour

Use the planner below to record what you might discuss in each room of your **guided tour** of the Secret Annex.

Hidden entrance/staircase: ______________________________

____

Living room: ______________________________

Kitchen: ______________________________

Anne's room/Mr. Dussel's room: ______________________________

____

The Diary of Anne Frank, Act II

Reading Skill

Cause-and-effect relationships explain the connections between events. However, they do not always follow the simple pattern of a single cause producing a single effect. One possible pattern of cause and effect is shown below.

To discover such patterns in a literary work, **ask questions to analyze cause-and-effect relationships**, such as:

- What causes might have triggered this event?
- What effects might result from this cause?
- Are these events really related? (The fact that two events occur in order does not mean that one has caused the other. The two events may be coincidental or random events.)

Use this graphic organizer as you read the story.

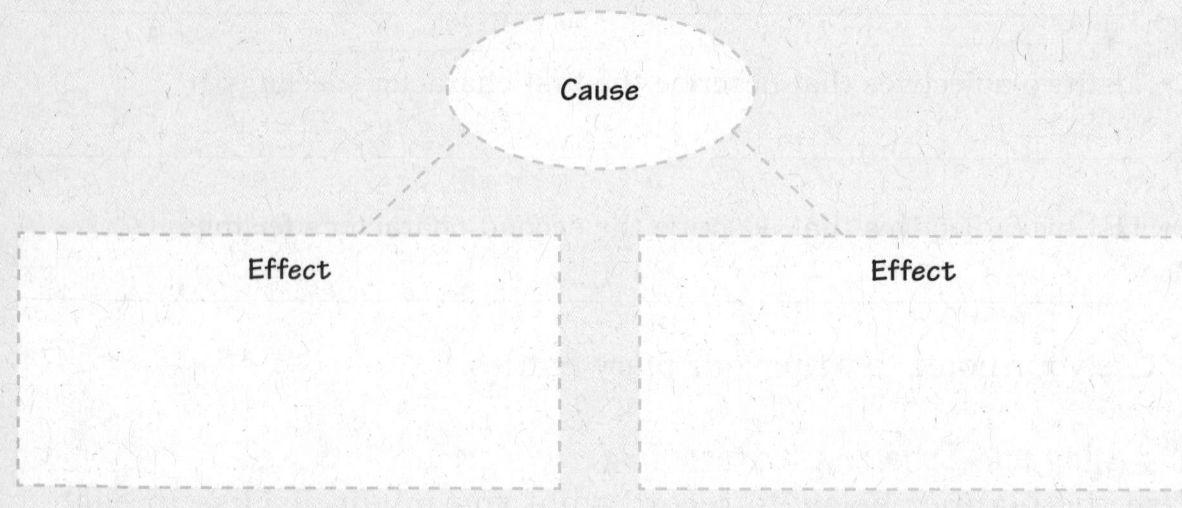

Literary Analysis

A **character's motivation** is the reason that he or she takes a particular action. The motivation may be internal, external, or both. *Internal motivations:* emotions such as loneliness and jealousy; *External motivations:* events and situations such as a fire or poverty.

Writing: Letter

Answer the questions below to plan a **letter** asking a local theater manager to present *The Diary of Anne Frank*.

- Why would your community benefit from seeing the play? List at least three reasons.

____

____

____

- What parts of the play support your reasons?

____

____

____

Research and Technology: Bulletin Board Display

Prepare a **bulletin board display** about the experiences of Jewish individuals during World War II. Fill in the following chart to organize your thoughts.

Purpose of Display	Audience	Five Questions I Want to Research
		1.
		2.
		3.
		4.
		5.

Online Information

About Web Sites

A Web site is a certain place on the Internet. Sponsors create and update Web sites. Sponsors can be groups, companies, or individuals. Think about whether the information on a Web site is likely to be true. Look at the Web site's sponsor to assess credibility. Most Web sites have these parts:

- The **Web address:** where you can find the site on the Internet.
- A **Web page:** one screen within the Web site.
- **Navigation bars** and **links:** tools to help you go to other Web pages.

Reading Skill

A Web site must be designed for unity and coherence so that it is useful and easy to read. It has unity when all of its parts flow smoothly together and provide a complete source of information. A Web site has coherence when its individual parts and features relate to and support one another. Look at the chart below. It tells you how to **analyze the unity and coherence** of a Web site.

Checklist for Evaluating a Text

- ❑ Do details all relate to the main idea?
- ❑ Do sentences, paragraphs, and graphic elements flow in a logical sequence?
- ❑ Is information clear, consistent, and logical?
- ❑ Does the author provide reliable facts, statistics, or quotations to support main points?

Web Site

Features:

- description of the organization
- contact information
- links to other pages
- illustrations or graphics
- general or specific audience

Florida Holocaust Museum

EDUCATION EVENTS EXHIBITIONS GET INVOLVED PRESS ROOM VISITOR INFORMATION

The home page provides an organized, logical list of topics covered by the Web site.

VISITOR INFORMATION

The topic of the text is introduced under the first heading and carried throughout the text.

About the Museum

Mission

The Florida Holocaust Museum honors the memory of millions of innocent men, women, and children who suffered or died in the Holocaust. The Museum is dedicated to teaching members of all races and cultures to recognize the inherent worth and dignity of human life in order to prevent future genocides.

Founders Walter and Edie Loebenberg

History

One of the largest Holocaust museums in the country, the Florida Holocaust Museum is the result of St. Petersburg businessman and philanthropist, Walter P. Loebenberg's remarkable journey and vision. He escaped Nazi Germany in 1939 and served in the United States Army during WWII. Together, with a group of local businessmen and community leaders, the concept of a living memorial to those who suffered and perished was conceived. Among the participating individuals were Survivors of the Holocaust and individuals who lost relatives, as well as those who had no personal investment, other than wanting to ensure that such atrocities could never again happen to any group of people.

To this end, the group enlisted the support of others in the community and were able to involve internationally renowned Holocaust scholars. Thomas Keneally, author of *Schindler's List*, joined the Board of Advisors and Elie Weisel was named Honorary Chairman of this Holocaust Center.

This painting directly relates to the topic of the text, helping maintain the unity of the article.

In 1992, the Museum rented a space it could afford but would soon outgrow, on the grounds of the Jewish Community Center of Pinellas County in Madeira Beach, Florida, tucked away from the mainstream of Tampa Bay life. Starting with only one staff member and a small group of dedicated volunteers, it quickly surpassed all expectations.

A painting from the exhibition *The Holocaust Through Czech Children's Eyes*

Within the first month, over 24,000 visitors came to see *Anne Frank in the World*, the Center's inaugural exhibit. The Tampa Bay showing of this exhibition—which traces a young Jewish girl's journey from a complacent childhood in pre-World War II Holland, through her early teens hiding from the Nazis, to her death at Bergen-Belsen—poignantly touched all visitors.

During the next five years, the new Holocaust Center greeted more than 125,000 visitors to view internationally acclaimed exhibits. Thousands more participated in lectures, seminars and commemorative events at the Center, which now reached directly into schools in an eight county area surrounding Tampa Bay with study guides, teacher training programs, and presentations by Center staff and Holocaust Survivors.

The use of transitions helps make the text more coherent, or understandable.

The Center expanded to encompass a growing print and audio-visual library, a photographic archive, a repository for historic artifacts, and a research facility for educators and scholars—all of this crowded into a 4,000 square foot facility that was not designed for museum or educational purposes.

THE BIG ?

Is it our differences or similarities that matter most?
Does an organization such as the Florida Holocaust Museum place more emphasis on recognizing our differences, or on recognizing our similarities? Explain your answer.

Thinking About Online Information

1. How is using a Web site different from looking up information in a magazine or book?

2. What part of the museum Web site would be most useful to people who want to visit the museum?

TALK ABOUT IT Reading Skill

3. Which page of the Florida Holocaust Museum Web site unifies all of the parts of the site?

4. Scan the Florida Holocaust Museum site. What tabs and links do you find on the navigation bar? Explain how each of these works with the others to produce a coherent web browsing experience.

WRITE ABOUT IT Timed Writing: Evaluation **(15 minutes)**

Think about the museum Web site from this lesson. Then, answer the following questions.

- Does the home page unify the site?
- Is the information included on the Web site coherent?
- Does the site meet its goal?

Water Names

The American folk tradition grew out of the **oral tradition**. The oral tradition is stories that were originally told at festivals and around campfires. These stories were not written down. Stories in the oral tradition have these elements:

- **Theme** is a central message revealed within a story. Some themes are **universal**. Universal themes appear in many cultures and many time periods.
- **Heroes** and **heroines** are men and women whose virtues and actions are celebrated in stories.

Storytellers in the oral tradition need to hold their listeners' attention. Look at the chart for devices that storytellers use to make stories more interesting and entertaining.

Technique	Definition	Example
Hyperbole	exaggeration or overstatement, either to make people laugh or to show heightened emotion	That basketball player was as tall as the Empire State Building.
Personification	human qualities or characteristics given to animals or things	The clouds shed tears.
Idioms	expressions in a language or culture that should not be taken literally	"a chip off the old block" "as easy as pie"

American folk literature is a living tradition. It is always being updated and adapted. Many of the subjects and heroes from American folk literature can be found in current movies, sports heroes, and even politics.

There are different types of stories in the oral tradition. These stories have different purposes, or reasons, and styles.

- **Myths** are stories about the actions of gods, goddesses, and heroes. Every culture has its own collection of myths, or **mythology**. These stories often explain the causes of natural phenomena, such as earthquakes and volcanoes.
- **Fables** are short stories that usually have a moral that is directly stated. A moral is a lesson. The characters in fables are often animals that act like humans.
- **Tall tales** are stories that use exaggeration to make them funny. This kind of exaggeration is called **hyperbole**. Heroes of tall tales often do impossible things. Tale tales are one kind of **legend**. A legend is a story based on fact that becomes less true with each telling.
- **Epics** are long poems about great heroes who go on dangerous journeys. These journeys are called **quests**. The quests are an important part of the history of a culture or nation.

Water Names

Lan Samantha Chang

Summary Three girls sit on a back porch on the prairie. Their grandmother Waipuo reminds them of how important China's longest river was in the lives of their ancestors. She tells them a story in Chinese about a girl who falls in love with a water ghost.

Note-taking Guide

Use this chart to record details about the story within the story.

In the present	1,200 years ago
Who: three girls and their grandmother	Who: Wen Zhiqing and his daughter
Where:	Where:
What happens:	What happens:

Water Names

Lan Samantha Chang

Summertime at dusk we'd gather on the back porch, tired and sticky from another day of fierce encoded quarrels, nursing our mosquito bites and frail dignities, sisters in name only. At first we'd pinch and slap each other, fighting for the best—least ragged—folding chair. Then we'd argue over who would sit next to our grandmother. We were so close together on the tiny porch that we often pulled our own hair by mistake. Forbidden to bite, we planted silent toothmarks on each others' wrists. We ignored the bulk of house behind us, the yard, the fields, the darkening sky. We even forgot about our grandmother. Then suddenly we'd hear her old, dry voice, very close, almost on the backs of our necks.

"*Xiushila!* Shame on you. Fighting like a bunch of chickens."

And Ingrid, the oldest, would freeze with her thumb and forefinger right on the back of Lily's arm. I would slide my hand away from the end of Ingrid's braid. Ashamed, we would shuffle our feet while Waipuo calmly found her chair.

On some nights she sat with us in silence. But on some nights she told us stories, "just to keep up your Chinese," she said.

"In these prairie crickets I often hear the sound of rippling waters, of the Yangtze River," she said. "Granddaughters, you are descended on both sides from people of the water country, near the mouth of the great Chang Jiang, as it is called, where the river is so grand and broad that even on clear days you can scarcely see the other side.

"The Chang Jiang runs four thousand miles, originating in the Himalaya mountains where it crashes, flecked with gold dust, down steep cliffs so perilous and remote that few humans have ever seen them. In central China, the river squeezes through deep gorges, then widens in its last thousand miles to the sea. Our ancestors have lived near the mouth of this river, the ever-changing delta, near a city called Nanjing, for more than a thousand years."

TAKE NOTES

Activate Prior Knowledge

Think of a family that moved to America from another country. How would the grandparents of that family be different from the grandchildren?

Stop to Reflect 

Why do you think the three sisters felt ashamed after their grandmother told them to stop fighting?

Reading Check 

What reason does the grandmother give for telling stories? Underline the answer in the text.

TAKE NOTES

Themes in American Stories

Hyperbole is exaggeration. Circle an example of exaggeration in the bracketed passage.

Stop to Reflect

How important is the river in the lives of the girls' ancestors? Explain your answer.

Themes in American Stories

A **legend** is a story that is based on fact that becomes less true each time it is told. How many years ago does the grandmother's story take place?

Is it possible that the grandmother is retelling a legend? Explain.

Reading Check 

According to Waipuo, why did her family survive floods? Underline the answer.

"A thousand years," murmured Lily, who was only ten. When she was younger she had sometimes burst into nervous crying at the thought of so many years. Her small insistent fingers grabbed my fingers in the dark.

"Through your mother and I you are descended from a line of great men and women. We have survived countless floods and seasons of ill-fortune because we have the spirit of the river in us. Unlike mountains, we cannot be powdered down or broken apart. Instead, we run together, like raindrops. Our strength and spirit wear down mountains into sand. But even our people must respect the water."

She paused. "When I was young, my own grandmother once told me the story of Wen Zhiqing's daughter. Twelve hundred years ago the civilized parts of China still lay to the north, and the Yangtze valley lay unspoiled. In those days lived an ancestor named Wen Zhiqing, a resourceful man, and proud. He had been fishing for many years with trained cormorants, which you girls of course have never seen. Cormorants are sleek, black birds with long, bending necks which the fishermen fitted with metal rings so the fish they caught could not be swallowed. The birds would perch on the side of the old wooden boat and dive into the river." We had only known blue swimming pools, but we tried to imagine the sudden shock of cold and the plunge, deep into water.

"Now, Wen Zhiqing had a favorite daughter who was very beautiful and loved the river. She would beg to go out on the boat with him. This daughter was a restless one, never contented with their catch, and often she insisted they stay out until it was almost dark. Even then, she was not satisfied. She had been spoiled by her father, kept protected from the river, so she could not see its danger. To this young woman, the river was as familiar as the sky. It was a bright, broad road stretching out to curious lands. She did not fully understand the river's depths.

"One clear spring evening, as she watched the last bird dive off into the blackening waters, she said, 'If only this catch would bring back something more than another fish!'

"She leaned over the side of the boat and looked at the water. The stars and moon reflected back at her. And it is said that the spirits living underneath the water looked up at her as well. And the spirit of a young man who had drowned in the river many years before saw her lovely face."

We had heard about the ghosts of the drowned, who wait forever in the water for a living person to pull down instead. A faint breeze moved through the mosquito screens and we shivered.

"The cormorant was gone for a very long time," Waipuo said, "so long that the fisherman grew puzzled. Then, suddenly, the bird emerged from the waters, almost invisible in the night. Wen Zhiqing grasped his catch, a very large fish, and guided the boat back to shore. And when Wen reached home, he gutted the fish and discovered, in its stomach, a valuable pearl ring."

"From the man?" said Lily.

"Sshh, she'll tell you."

Waipuo ignored us. "His daughter was delighted that her wish had been fulfilled. What most excited her was the idea of an entire world like this, a world where such a beautiful ring would be only a bauble![1] For part of her had always longed to see faraway things and places. The river had put a spell on her heart. In the evenings she began to sit on the bank, looking at her own reflection in the water. Sometimes she said she saw a handsome young man looking back at her. And her yearning for him filled her heart with sorrow and fear, for she knew that she would soon leave her beloved family.

" 'It's just the moon,' said Wen Zhiqing, but his daughter shook her head. 'There's a kingdom under the water,' she said. 'The prince is asking me to marry him. He sent the ring as an offering to you.' 'Nonsense,' said her father, and he forbade her to sit by the water again."

TAKE NOTES

Themes in American Stories

Personification is giving human qualities to things that are not human. Read the bracketed passage. What nonhuman thing is given a human characteristc in this passage?

Stop to Reflect

Name three words that describe Wen's daughter. Give reasons for your choices.

Reading Check

What did Wen find in the stomach of a fish he caught? Underline the answer.

Vocabulary Development

yearning (YERN ing) *n.* feeling of wanting something very much

forbade (fer BAD) *v.* ordered someone not to do something

1. **bauble** (BAW buhl) *n.* trinket or small pretty object that is not worth much money.

TAKE NOTES

Themes in American Stories

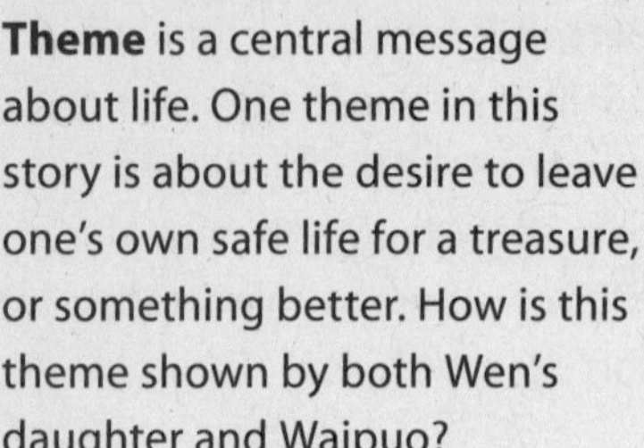

Theme is a central message about life. One theme in this story is about the desire to leave one's own safe life for a treasure, or something better. How is this theme shown by both Wen's daughter and Waipuo?

Stop to Reflect

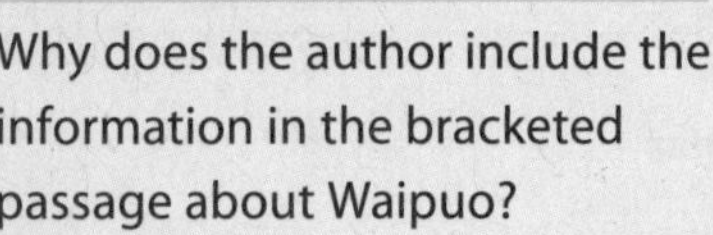

Why does the author include the information in the bracketed passage about Waipuo?

Reading Check

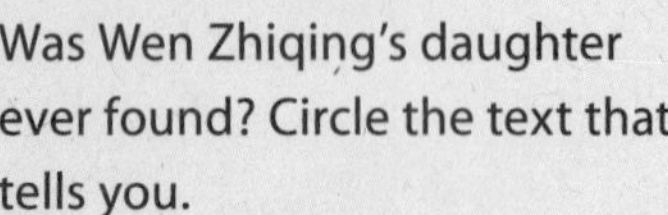

Was Wen Zhiqing's daughter ever found? Circle the text that tells you.

"For a year things went as usual, but the next spring there came a terrible flood that swept away almost everything. In the middle of a torrential rain, the family noticed that the daughter was missing. She had taken advantage of the confusion to hurry to the river and visit her beloved. The family searched for days but they never found her."

Her smoky, rattling voice came to a stop.

"What happened to her?" Lily said.

"It's okay, stupid," I told her. "She was so beautiful that she went to join the kingdom of her beloved. Right?"

"Who knows?" Waipuo said. "They say she was seduced by a water ghost. Or perhaps she lost her mind to desiring."

"What do you mean?" asked Ingrid.

"I'm going inside," Waipuo said, and got out of her chair with a creak. A moment later the light went on in her bedroom window. We knew she stood before the mirror, combing out her long, wavy silver-gray hair, and we imagined that in her youth she too had been beautiful.

We sat together without talking. We had gotten used to Waipuo's abruptness, her habit of creating a question and leaving without answering it, as if she were disappointed in the question itself. We tried to imagine Wen Zhiqing's daughter. What did she look like? How old was she? Why hadn't anyone remembered her name?

While we weren't watching, the stars had emerged. Their brilliant pinpoints mapped the heavens. They glittered over us, over Waipuo in her room, the house, and the small city we lived in, the great waves of grass that ran for miles around us, the ground beneath as dry and hard as bone.

Vocabulary Development

torrential (tuh REN shuhl) *adj.* describing large amounts of water moving very quickly in a particular direction

Themes in American Stories

1. **Infer:** How do the descendants of the water country feel about the great river?

2. **Interpret:** Two unusual events from the story are listed in the first column of the chart. List different ways to explain these events in the second column. Then, use the third column to explain why you agree or disagree with each explanation.

Event	Explanation	Why You Agree or Disagree
Face in the water		
Ring in the fish		

3. **Themes in American Stories:** What do you think is the **theme** of this story?

4. **Themes in American Stories:** Identify two examples of storytelling techniques or details in the story that are part of the **oral tradition**.

Storytelling Hour

Plan a **storytelling hour** during which you will retell a variety of Chinese folk tales. Follow these steps to gather information for your storytelling hour.

- Go to the library and search the online catalog for collections of Chinese folklore. Record the titles and short summaries of stories that you think will interest the class.

  What I found: ______________________________

- Search the Internet. Search for "Chinese folklore" or "Chinese folk tales." Record short summaries of the stories that you find.

  What I found: ______________________________

- Watch the video interview with Lan Samantha Chang. Review your source material. Use this information to record additional information for your storytelling hour.

  Additional information: ______________________________

Use your notes to prepare your storytelling hour.

Why the Waves Have Whitecaps • Coyote Steals the Sun and Moon

Reading Skill

A **summary** is a short statement that presents the key ideas and main points of a text. It is much shorter than the original work. Summarizing helps you remember the text by focusing on the most important information. Follow these steps to summarize a section of text or a whole work:

- **Reread to identify main events or ideas** in the passage or work. Then, jot them down.
- Organize your notes by putting main events or points in order and crossing off minor details that are not important for an overall understanding of the work.
- Finally, summarize by restating the major events or ideas in as few words as possible.

Keep in mind that, because summaries remove most of the detail, reading a summary can never replace the experience of reading the complete book, play, or article.

Literary Analysis

A **myth** is an ancient tale that presents the beliefs or customs of a culture. Every culture has its own **mythology**, or collection of myths. Myths explain events in nature or in a people's history. Often, they describe the actions of gods or other supernatural beings. Many myths also involve animal characters or natural forces with human qualities. To understand myths, it is helpful to understand the culture from which they come. Use this chart to trace the connection between story and culture.

Detail from Mythology	Cultural Connections
Prometheus steals fire from Zeus, king of the gods, and gives it to humans.	To ancient Greeks, fire was essential for cooking, forging weapons, and providing warmth.

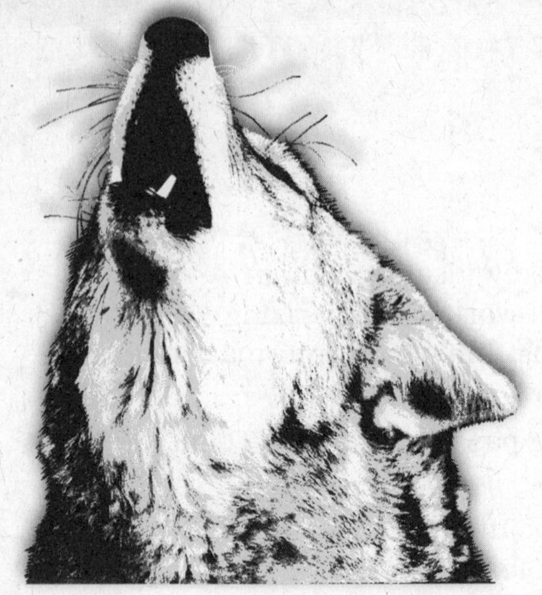

Coyote Steals the Sun and Moon

Zuñi myth, Retold by Richard Erdoes and Alfonso Ortiz

Summary This myth tells about how the sun and the moon got into the sky. Coyote and Eagle team up to steal the sun and moon to light up their dark world. Coyote's curious nature causes them to lose both. The sun and moon escape into the sky.

 Writing About the Big Question

Are yesterday's heroes important today? "Coyote Steals the Sun and Moon" explains a specific event in nature and features Coyote, a popular character in mythology. Complete this sentence:

Myths and their heroes have **endured** through the ages because they

____.

Note-taking Guide

Use this chart to write the explanations this myth gives for questions about nature.

Questions About Nature	Explanations
• How did the sun and the moon get into the sky? • Why do we have seasons of fall and winter?	

Coyote Steals the Sun and Moon

Zuñi Myth, Retold by Richard Erdoes and Alfonso Ortiz

Coyote is a bad hunter who never kills anything. Once he watched Eagle hunting rabbits, catching one after another—more rabbits than he could eat. Coyote thought, "I'll team up with Eagle so I can have enough meat." Coyote is always up to something.

"Friend," Coyote said to Eagle, "we should hunt together. Two can catch more than one."

"Why not?" Eagle said, and so they began to hunt in partnership. Eagle caught many rabbits, but all Coyote caught was some little bugs.

At this time the world was still dark; the sun and moon had not yet been put in the sky. "Friend," Coyote said to Eagle, "no wonder I can't catch anything; I can't see. Do you know where we can get some light?"

"You're right, friend, there should be some light," Eagle said. "I think there's a little toward the west. Let's try and find it."

And so they went looking for the sun and moon. They came to a big river, which Eagle flew over. Coyote swam, and swallowed so much water that he almost drowned. He crawled out with his fur full of mud, and Eagle asked, "Why don't you fly like me?"

"You have wings; I just have hair," Coyote said. "I can't fly without feathers."

At last they came to a pueblo,[1] where the Kachinas happened to be dancing. The people invited Eagle and Coyote to sit down and have something to eat while they watched the sacred dances. Seeing the power of the Kachinas, Eagle said, "I believe these are the people who have light."

Vocabulary Development

sacred (SAY krid) *adj.* considered holy; related to religious ceremonies

1. **pueblo** (PWEB loh) small town or village made up of Native Americans in the southwestern United States.

TAKE NOTES

Activate Prior Knowledge 

Describe an animal in a folk tale or fairy tale you read when you were younger. What human qualities did the animal have?

____

____

____

Literary Analysis 

Myths often explain something in nature. What do you think this tale will explain? Underline a sentence in the bracketed passage that helps you figure out the answer.

Reading Skill

A **summary** is a short statement that presents key ideas. Summarize what you know so far about Eagle and Coyote.

Eagle: ______________________

____

Coyote: ______________________

____

Literary Analysis 

To understand a **myth**, it helps to understand the culture. Circle details about the Zuñi culture mentioned on this page.

TAKE NOTES

Stop to Reflect

What do you think will happen to the sun and moon now that they have been stolen? Explain your answer.

___

___

___

___

___

Reading Skill

A **summary** is a short statement that presents the main ideas of a text. Write the three main ideas on the page in order below. Leave out minor details.

1. ___
2. ___
3. ___

Reading Check

What were the Kachinas doing when Coyote and Eagle stole their light? Underline the sentence that tells you.

Coyote, who had been looking all around, pointed out two boxes, one large and one small, that the people opened whenever they wanted light. To produce a lot of light, they opened the lid of the big box, which contained the sun. For less light they opened the small box, which held the moon.

Coyote nudged Eagle. "Friend, did you see that? They have all the light we need in the big box. Let's steal it."

"You always want to steal and rob. I say we should just borrow it."

"They won't lend it to us."

"You may be right," said Eagle. "Let's wait till they finish dancing and then steal it."

After a while the Kachinas went home to sleep, and Eagle scooped up the large box and flew off. Coyote ran along trying to keep up, panting, his tongue hanging out. Soon he yelled up to Eagle, "Ho, friend, let me carry the box a little way."

"No, no," said Eagle, "you never do anything right."

He flew on, and Coyote ran after him. After a while Coyote shouted again: "Friend, you're my chief, and it's not right for you to carry the box; people will call me lazy. Let me have it."

"No, no, you always mess everything up." And Eagle flew on and Coyote ran along.

So it went for a stretch, and then Coyote started again. "Ho, friend, it isn't right for you to do this. What will people think of you and me?"

"I don't care what people think. I'm going to carry this box."

Again Eagle flew on and again Coyote ran after him. Finally Coyote begged for the fourth time: "Let me carry it. You're the chief, and I'm just Coyote. Let me carry it."

Eagle couldn't stand any more pestering. Also, Coyote had asked him four times, and if someone asks four times, you'd better give him what he wants. Eagle said, "Since you won't let up on me, go ahead and carry the box for a while. But promise not to open it."

Vocabulary Development

pestering (PES ter ing) *n.* constant bothering

"Oh, sure, oh yes, I promise." They went on as before, but now Coyote had the box. Soon Eagle was far ahead, and Coyote lagged behind a hill where Eagle couldn't see him. "I wonder what the light looks like, inside there," he said to himself. "Why shouldn't I take a peek? Probably there's something extra in the box, something good that Eagle wants to keep to himself."

And Coyote opened the lid. Now, not only was the sun inside, but the moon also. Eagle had put them both together, thinking that it would be easier to carry one box than two.

As soon as Coyote opened the lid, the moon escaped, flying high into the sky. At once all the plants shriveled up and turned brown. Just as quickly, all the leaves fell off the trees, and it was winter. Trying to catch the moon and put it back in the box, Coyote ran in pursuit as it skipped away from him. Meanwhile the sun flew out and rose into the sky. It drifted far away, and the peaches, squashes, and melons shriveled up with cold.

Eagle turned and flew back to see what had delayed Coyote. "You fool! Look what you've done!" he said. "You let the sun and moon escape, and now it's cold." Indeed, it began to snow, and Coyote shivered. "Now your teeth are chattering," Eagle said, "and it's your fault that cold has come into the world."

It's true. If it weren't for Coyote's curiosity and mischief making, we wouldn't have winter; we could enjoy summer all the time.

Reader's Response: What advice would you give to Eagle about dealing with Coyote?

____

____

____

Vocabulary Development

shriveled (SHRIV uhld) *v.* dried up; shrank and wrinkled

pursuit (per SOOT) *n.* the act of chasing in order to catch

TAKE NOTES

Literary Analysis

Many animal characters in **myths** have human qualities. Describe one human quality that you see in each of the animals.

____

____

____

Reading Skill

When you **summarize** a story, you first **reread to identify main events or ideas**. Reread the ending of this story. Summarize the ending in one complete sentence below.

____

____

____

Reading Check

What happens when Coyote opens the box? Underline the text that tells you.

Coyote Steals the Sun and Moon

1. **Compare and Contrast:** How do Coyote and Eagle differ in their abilities and attitudes?

2. **Infer:** What does Coyote's behavior in this story tell you about his character?

3. **Reading Skill:** The characters' actions in this story can be divided into four "scenes," or sections. Use the graphic organizer below to **summarize** the important events in each section.

Detail	Cultural Connections
The Hunt	
At the Kachinas' Dance	
Running Away	
Coyote's Mistake	

4. **Literary Analysis:** Most **myths** explain something in nature. What question about nature does this myth answer?

Writing: Myth

A **myth** is a story that often explains something in nature. Write your own myth that answers a question about the natural world.

- What is something in nature that interests you? ____________________
- What is a possible explanation for your choice? ____________________
____
- Write a brief description of the characters you will use. Tell whether they are humans or animals. List the qualities they have. ____________________
____
____
- What is a good title for this myth? ____________________

Listening and Speaking: Oral Presentation

Prepare an **oral presentation** about Zuñi culture. Use the Internet and library references to gather information.

Make a list of questions you will need to answer for your report. Use this list to help focus your research.

1. ____________________
____
2. ____________________
____
3. ____________________
____
4. ____________________
____
5. ____________________
____

Why the Waves Have Whitecaps

Zora Neale Hurston

Summary The story is an African American folk tale. Mrs. Wind brags about her children. Mrs. Water grows tired of it and drowns the children. Mrs. Wind looks for her children but sees only white feathers on the water. That is why there are whitecaps. Storms at sea are the wind and water fighting over children.

Writing About the Big Question

Are yesterday's heroes important today? "Why the Waves Have Whitecaps" is a story in which characters act in ways that are human but unheroic. Complete this sentence:

I think that story characters who (do/do not) behave admirably have more relevance today because ______________________________

____.

Note-taking Guide

Record the sequence of events of "Why the Waves Have Whitecaps" in this chart.

Mrs. Wind and Mrs. Water sit and talk. →	→	
→	Whitecaps are feathers coming up when Mrs. Wind calls for her children. →	The storms at sea are the wind and water fighting over the children.

Why the Waves Have Whitecaps

1. **Infer:** Mrs. Wind and Mrs. Water seem friendly and chat about their children at the beginning of the story. What changes their relationship?

2. **Cause and Effect:** What are the results of their quarrel?

3. **Reading Skill:** The characters' actions in this myth can be divided into three "scenes," or sections. Use this graphic organizer to **summarize** the important events of each section.

Section	Summary
Mrs. Water and Mrs. Wind Compete	
Mrs. Water's Revenge	
Whitecaps and Storms	

4. **Reading Skill:** Using your chart, **summarize** the entire story in as few sentences as possible, leaving out minor details.

5. **Literary Analysis:** What is explained in this **myth**?

Writing: Myth

Create your own **myth**. In it, explain something that takes place in nature. For example, you could explain a rainbow, the seasons, or an animal behavior. Begin by thinking of a list of possible ideas. Use the graphic organizer below to help you choose your subject.

Things that happen in nature that I could explain in a myth

Choose one of your ideas to explain in your myth.

Listening and Speaking: Oral Presentation

Prepare an **oral presentation** about African myths and folk tales that were brought to the Americas. Do your research in the library or on the Internet. Look for ways in which history and traditional stories have affected African Americans. Make a list of topics you could use to search for information.

Use your list to help you find information for your oral presentation.

Chicoria • from The People, Yes • Brer Possum's Dilemma • John Henry

Reading Skill

A **summary** is a short statement that presents the main points of a piece of writing. Summaries leave out minor details. They provide a quick way to preview or review a much longer work. Before you summarize a work of literature, follow these two steps:

- First, determine whether each event or idea is important enough to be included in your summary.
- Then, **use graphics** to help you organize the major events or ideas. For example, if you are summarizing a story with chronological events, use a timeline to arrange events in order.

Literary Analysis

In the **oral tradition**, storytellers pass on legends, songs, folk tales, tall tales, and stories from generation to generation by word of mouth. These stories and songs are written down later, often in **dialect**—the language and grammar of a particular region. Reading these tales can provide a window into the values a culture considers important. As you read, use the chart below to note characteristics of the oral tradition.

Oral Tradition	Story Detail
Repetition and exaggeration	
Heroes who are brave, clever, or strong	
Animal characters that act like human beings	
Dialect and informal speech	
Traditions of a culture	

Chicoria • from The People, Yes

Summaries In "Chicoria," a rancher invites a poet to dinner. The poet is asked to share poetry, but not to eat. The poet uses a folk tale to point out the rancher's rude behavior. In the selection from *The People, Yes*, the speaker talks about his love for America. He describes the adventures of famous characters from American folklore, such as Paul Bunyan and John Henry.

Writing About the Big Question

Are yesterday's heroes important today? In both "Chicoria" and the excerpt from *The People, Yes*, the values and beliefs of a culture are passed on by showing what qualities and abilities that culture finds **admirable** in its heroes. Complete these sentences:

In today's stories, qualities such as ____________ and ____________ may be considered **outdated** for a heroic character. On the other hand, qualities such as **bravery**, honesty, and ____________ are still relevant.

Note-taking Guide

Use this graphic organizer to record how "Chicoria" and the selection from *The People, Yes* have some of the same folk story traits. Put one example in each box.

	Message	Exaggeration	Humor
Chicoria	It is rude not to invite all guests to eat.		
from The People, Yes	People exaggerate.		

Chicoria • from The People, Yes

1. **Analyze:** Why does Chicoria assume that he will eat at the rancher's table?

2. **Evaluate:** Identify two people mentioned in the excerpt from *The People, Yes*. In what way does each character's ability contribute to survival in a wild, new country?

3. **Reading Skill:** Use the cluster diagram below to **summarize** images in the excerpt from *The People, Yes*. State the main idea behind the images.

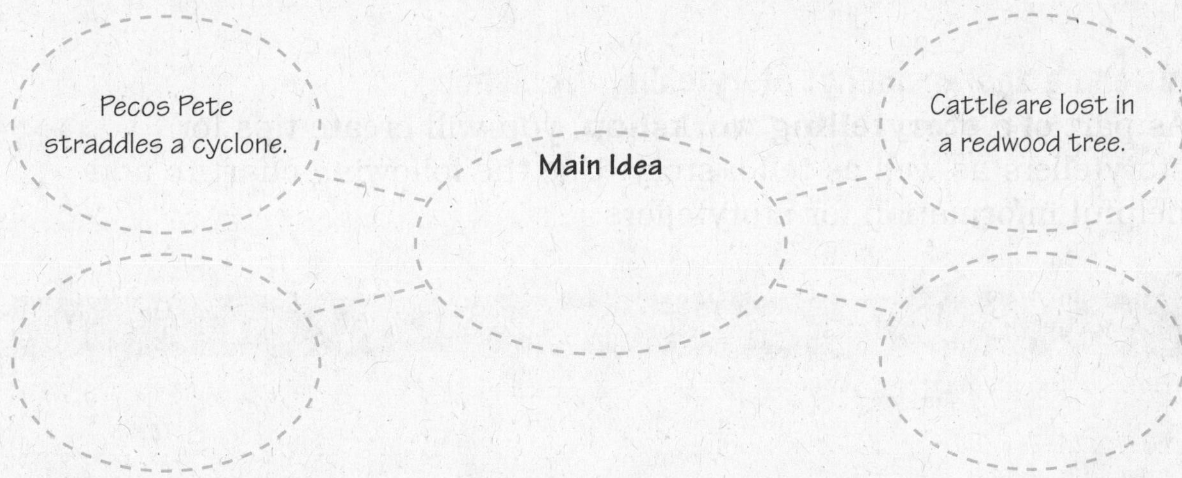

4. **Literary Analysis:** Why might New Mexicans enjoy the story of Chicoria enough to pass it on in the **oral tradition**?

Writing: Critical Analysis

Write a **critical analysis** to explain how language and idioms affect the tone and mood in folk stories. Be sure to give examples from "Chicoria" and the selection from *The People, Yes*. Use the chart below to write notes for your critical analysis.

Example of Language or Idiom Used	How it Affects Mood of Work

Listening and Speaking: Storytelling Workshop

As part of a **storytelling workshop**, you will create tips for storytellers as well as tell a story. Use the following chart to add helpful information for storytellers.

Storytelling Tips	
How to Choose a Story	
Making Eye Contact	
How to Use Gestures to Dramatize	
How to Add Humor	

Brer Possum's Dilemma • John Henry

Summaries In "Brer Possum's Dilemma," Brer Snake asks Brer Possum for help. "John Henry" is a ballad, or song, that tells the story of an African American hero who races a steam drill.

Writing About the Big Question

Are yesterday's heroes important today? The human-like animal characters in "Brer Possum's Dilemma" and the larger-than-life folk hero in "John Henry" are typical one-dimensional folk tale characters. Complete this sentence:

Although the **accomplishments** of folk heroes are exaggerated, these stories have value because ____

____.

Note-taking Guide

Folk tales often pass along important life lessons. Use this chart to record the lessons in each folk tale.

Folk Tale	What Lesson It Taught
Brer Possum's Dilemma	
John Henry	Nothing is impossible when you set your mind to it.

TAKE NOTES

Activate Prior Knowledge 

Describe a time when you were fooled by someone. What did you learn from the experience?

Reading Skill 

A **summary** presents the main points of a story. It does not include minor details. What two events from this page of the story would you include in a summary?

Reading Check 

What are Brer Possum and Brer Snake like? Circle the words or phrases that describe Brer Possum. Underline the words or phrases that describe Brer Snake.

Brer Possum's Dilemma

Jackie Torrence

Back in the days when the animals could talk, there lived ol' Brer[1] Possum. He was a fine feller. Why, he never liked to see no critters[2] in trouble. He was always helpin' out, a-doin' somethin' for others.

Ever' night, ol' Brer Possum climbed into a persimmon tree, hung by his tail, and slept all night long. And each mornin', he climbed outa the tree and walked down the road to sun 'imself.

One mornin', as he walked, he come to a big hole in the middle of the road. Now, ol' Brer Possum was kind and gentle, but he was also nosy, so he went over to the hole and looked in. All at once, he stepped back, 'cause layin' in the bottom of that hole was ol' Brer Snake with a brick on his back.

Brer Possum said to 'imself, "I best git on outa here, 'cause ol' Brer Snake is mean and evil and lowdown, and if I git to stayin' around 'im, he jist might git to bitin' me."

So Brer Possum went on down the road.

But Brer Snake had seen Brer Possum, and he commenced to callin' for 'im.

"Help me, Brer Possum."

Brer Possum stopped and turned around. He said to 'imself, "That's ol' Brer Snake a-callin' me. What do you reckon he wants?"

Well, ol' Brer Possum was kindhearted, so he went back down the road to the hole, stood at the edge, and looked down at Brer Snake.

"Was that you a-callin' me? What do you want?"

Brer Snake looked up and said, "I've been down here in this hole for a mighty long time with this brick on my back. Won't you help git it offa me?"

Brer Possum thought.

Vocabulary Development

persimmon (puhr sim uhn) *adj.* a type of tree with hard wood, oblong-shaped leaves, and bell-shaped flowers

commenced (kuh MENST) *v.* started; began

1. **Brer** (brer) dialect for "brother," used before a name.
2. **critters** dialect for "creatures"; animals.

"Now listen here, Brer Snake. I knows you. You's mean and evil and lowdown, and if'n I was to git down in that hole and git to liftin' that brick offa your back, you wouldn't do nothin' but bite me."

Ol' Brer Snake just hissed.

"Maybe not. Maybe not. Maaaaaaaybe not."

Brer Possum said, "I ain't sure 'bout you at all. I jist don't know. You're a-goin' to have to let me think about it."

So ol' Brer Possum thought—he thought high, and he thought low—and jist as he was thinkin', he looked up into a tree and saw a dead limb a-hangin' down. He climbed into the tree, broke off the limb, and with that ol' stick, pushed that brick offa Brer Snake's back. Then he took off down the road.

Brer Possum thought he was away from ol' Brer Snake when all at once he heard somethin'.

"Help me, Brer Possum."

Brer Possum said, "Oh, no, that's him agin."

But bein' so kindhearted, Brer Possum turned around, went back to the hole, and stood at the edge.

"Brer Snake, was that you a-callin' me? What do you want now?"

Ol' Brer Snake looked up outa the hole and hissed.

"I've been down here for a mighty long time, and I've gotten a little weak, and the sides of this ol' hole are too slick for me to climb. Do you think you can lift me outa here?"

Brer Possum thought.

"Now, you jist wait a minute. If'n I was to git down into that hole and lift you outa there, you wouldn't do nothin' but bite me."

Brer Snake hissed.

"Maybe not. Maybe not. Maaaaaaaybe not."

Brer Possum said, "I jist don't know. You're a-goin' to have to give me time to think about this."

So ol' Brer Possum thought.

And as he thought, he jist happened to look down there in that hole and see that ol' dead limb. So he pushed the limb underneath ol' Brer Snake and he lifted 'im outa the hole, way up into the air, and throwed 'im into the high grass.

TAKE NOTES

Reading Skill 

Write a brief **summary** of the methods Brer Possum uses to protect himself during the two times he helps Brer Snake on this page.

____

____

____

Stop to Reflect 

Why do you think Brer Snake always gives Brer Possum the same response when asked whether he will bite? What does this show about Brer Snake's character?

____

____

____

____

____

Reading Check 

What does Brer Possum do to Brer Snake after he lifts him out of the hole? Underline the sentence that tells you.

TAKE NOTES

Literary Analysis

Stories in the **oral tradition** often use **dialect** to show the way that people speak in a certain area. Write the numbers 1 and 2 next to two complete sentences on this page that use dialect. Rewrite the sentences in your own words below.

____

____

____

____

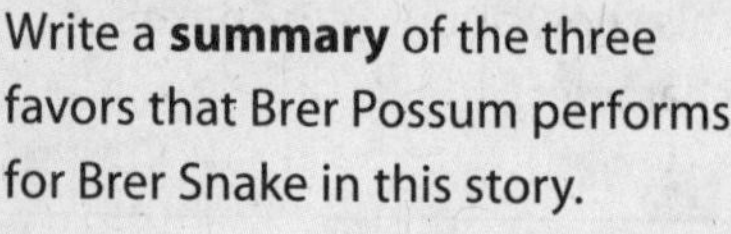

Reading Skill

Write a **summary** of the three favors that Brer Possum performs for Brer Snake in this story.

____

____

____

____

Reading Check 

Why does Brer Snake ask Brer Possum to put him in his pocket? Underline the sentence that tells you.

Brer Possum took off a-runnin' down the road.

Well, he thought he was away from ol' Brer Snake when all at once he heard somethin'.

"Help me, Brer Possum."

Brer Possum thought, "That's him agin."

But bein' so kindhearted, he turned around, went back to the hole, and stood there a-lookin' for Brer Snake. Brer Snake crawled outa the high grass just as slow as he could, stretched 'imself out across the road, rared up,[3] and looked at ol' Brer Possum.

Then he hissed. "I've been down there in that ol' hole for a mighty long time, and I've gotten a little cold 'cause the sun didn't shine. Do you think you could put me in your pocket and git me warm?"

Brer Possum said, "Now you listen here, Brer Snake. I knows you. You's mean and evil and lowdown, and if'n I put you in my pocket you wouldn't do nothin' but bite me."

Brer Snake hissed.

"Maybe not. Maybe not. Maaaaaaybe not."

"No sireee. Brer Snake. I knows you. I jist ain't a-goin' to do it."

But jist as Brer Possum was talkin' to Brer Snake, he happened to git a real good look at 'im. He was a-layin' there lookin' so pitiful, and Brer Possum's great big heart began to feel sorry for ol' Brer Snake.

"All right," said Brer Possum. "You must be cold. So jist this once I'm a-goin' to put you in my pocket."

So ol' Brer Snake coiled up jist as little as he could, and Brer Possum picked 'im up and put 'im in his pocket.

Brer Snake laid quiet and still—so quiet and still that Brer Possum even forgot that he was a-carryin' 'im around. But all of a sudden, Brer Snake commenced to crawlin' out, and he turned and faced Brer Possum and hissed.

Vocabulary Development

pitiful (PIT i fuhl) *adj.* arousing sympathy or pity

3. **rared up** dialect for "reared up."

"I'm a-goin' to bite you."

But Brer Possum said, "Now wait a minute. Why are you a-goin' to bite me? I done took that brick offa your back, I got you outa that hole, and I put you in my pocket to git you warm. Why are you a-goin' to bite me?"

Brer Snake hissed.

"You knowed I was a snake before you put me in you pocket."

And when you're mindin' your own business and you spot trouble, don't never trouble trouble 'til trouble troubles you.

TAKE NOTES

Literary Analysis 

What features of the **oral tradition** are contained in "Brer Possum's Dilemma"?

____

____

____

Reading Check 

What does the snake say he is going to do to Brer Possum? Underline the sentence that tells you.

TAKE NOTES

John Henry

Traditional

John Henry was a lil baby,
Sittin' on his mama's knee,
Said: 'The Big Bend Tunnel on the C. & O. road[1]
Gonna cause the death of me,
Lawd, Lawd, gonna cause the death of me.'

Cap'n says to John Henry,
'Gonna bring me a steam drill 'round,
Gonna take that steam drill out on the job,
Gonna whop that steel on down,
Lawd, Lawd, gonna whop that steel on down.'

John Henry tol' his cap'n,
Lightnin' was in his eye:
'Cap'n, bet yo' las, red cent on me,
Fo' I'll beat it to the bottom or I'll die,
Lawd, Lawd, I'll beat it to the bottom or I'll die.'

Sun shine hot an' burnin',
Wer'n't no breeze a-tall,
Sweat ran down like water down a hill,
That day John Henry let his hammer fall,
Lawd, Lawd, that day John Henry let his hammer fall.

John Henry went to the tunnel,
An' they put him in the lead to drive,
The rock so tall an' John Henry so small,
That he lied down his hammer an' he cried,
Lawd, Lawd, that he lied down his hammer an' he cried.

Literary Analysis 

Poems in the **oral tradition** often have words or phrases that are repeated. Circle the repeated words on this page. What is the effect of this repetition?

____

____

____

Reading Skill 

What is the first important event in this story that you would include in a **summary**?

____

Why is this event important?

____

____

Stop to Reflect 

What qualities do you think a hero should have?

____

____

____

1. **C. & O. road** Chesapeake and Ohio Railroad. The C&O's Big Bend railroad tunnel was built in the 1870s through a mountain in West Virginia.

John Henry started on the right hand,
The steam drill started on the lef'—
'Before I'd let this steam drill beat me down,
I'd hammer my fool self to death,
Lawd, Lawd, I'd hammer my fool self to death.'

John Henry had a lil woman,
Her name were Polly Ann,
John Henry took sick an' had to go to bed,
Polly Ann drove steel like a man,
Lawd, Lawd, Polly Ann drove steel like a man.

John Henry said to his shaker,[2]
'Shaker, why don' you sing?
I'm throwin' twelve poun's from my hips on
down,
Jes' listen to the col' steel ring,
Lawd, Lawd, jes' listen to the col' steel ring.'

Oh, the captain said to John Henry,
'I b'lieve this mountain's sinkin' in.'
John Henry said to his captain, oh my!
'Ain' nothin' but my hammer suckin' win',
Lawd, Lawd, ain' nothin' but my hammer
suckin' win'.'

John Henry tol' his shaker,
'Shaker, you better pray,
For, if I miss this six-foot steel,
Tomorrow'll be yo' buryin' day,
Lawd, Lawd, tomorrow'll be yo' buryin' day.'

John Henry tol' his captain,
'Look yonder what I see—
Yo' drill's done broke an' yo' hole's done choke,
An' you cain' drive steel like me,
Lawd, Lawd, an' you cain' drive steel like me.'

2. **shaker** (SHAY kuhr) *n.* person who sets the spikes and places the drills for a steel-driver to hammer.

TAKE NOTES

Reading Skill 

Reread the bracketed stanza. Write a brief **summary** of the information you learn about John Henry and his wife in this stanza.

Stop to Reflect 

How does summarizing the main events of this poem help improve your understanding of it? Explain.

Reading Check 

What does John Henry tell his shaker will happen if John Henry misses the steel he is driving? Circle the stanza that tells you.

TAKE NOTES

Literary Analysis

Which features of stories in the **oral tradition** are present in this poem?

____

____

____

Reading Skill

Write a **summary** of the events that occur in the poem after John Henry's death.

____

____

____

____

Reading Check

How does John Henry die? Underline the lines that tell you.

The man that invented the steam drill,
Thought he was mighty fine.
John Henry drove his fifteen feet,
An' the steam drill only made nine,
Lawd, Lawd, an' the steam drill only made nine.

The hammer that John Henry swung,
It weighed over nine pound;
He broke a rib in his lef'-han' side,
An' his intrels[3] fell on the groun',
Lawd, Lawd, an' his intrels fell on the groun'.

All the womens in the Wes',
When they heared of John Henry's death,
Stood in the rain, flagged the eas'-boun' train,
Goin' where John Henry fell dead,
Lawd, Lawd, goin' where John Henry fell dead.

John Henry's lil mother,
She was all dressed in red,
She jumped in bed, covered up her head,
Said she didn' know her son was dead,
Lawd, Lawd, didn' know her son was dead.

Dey took John Henry to the graveyard,
An' they buried him in the san',
An' every locomotive come roarin' by,
Says, 'There lays a steel-drivin' man,
Lawd, Lawd, there lays a steel-drivin' man.'

Reader's Response: Which of these folk tales did you enjoy more?

____

Explain, giving two reasons.

____

____

____

3. **intrels** (IN trelz) *n.* dialect for entrails—internal organs.

Brer Possum's Dilemma • John Henry

1. **Infer:** Is Brer Possum meant to look foolish or very kind? Explain.

2. **Deduce:** Why might Brer Possum think it is safe to trust Brer Snake?

3. **Reading Skill:** Complete this timeline to help you **summarize** "John Henry."

Baby John Henry foresees his death.					John Henry is buried.

4. **Literary Analysis:** What story elements in "John Henry" might explain why it has been passed down from generation to generation in the **oral tradition**?

Writing: Writing a Critical Analysis

Write a **critical analysis** to explain how language and idioms affect mood and tone in folk literature. Use this chart to help you list certain dialect or idioms from the stories. Note their meanings. Use your notes to help you write your critical analysis.

Dialect and Folk Idioms	Meaning

Listening and Speaking: Storytelling Workshop

Prepare for a **storytelling workshop**. Select a tale to perform. The following prompts will help prepare you to perform your tale.

- How will you use your voice and body to dramatize the action? Give specific examples of what you will do at different points in the tale.

  ____

  ____

- What informal language or dialect can you add to your performance?

  ____

  ____

- In which parts of the story will you make eye contact? ____________

  ____

Reviews

About Reviews

A **book review** gives a feeling or opinion about a book. You can find book reviews in different places, such as newspapers, magazines, television, or online.

Some book review writers know a great deal about a book's topic or author. Most book reviews have these parts:

- basic information such as author, price, and publisher
- a summary of the book
- opinions about the book's good and bad points
- an opinion about whether the book is worth reading

Reading Skill

Text features organize and highlight information in a written work. When you read, you can **use text features to analyze information,** which will help you understand the text. For example, looking at headings and subheadings will help you identify main ideas. Study the graphic organizer below to learn more about using text features to analyze information.

Structural Features of Book Reviews
• **heading:** large, bold text that identifies the book being reviewed • **byline:** a line that shows who wrote the review • **introduction:** an opening section that briefly describes the book being reviewed or provides information that is useful for context • **conclusion:** a closing section that sums up the book's contents and the reviewer's opinion of it

TAKE NOTES

Text Structure

A book review includes basic information about a book. You can use this information to find the book. Circle the title, editor, publisher, and publication date for *A Life in Letters*. Why would these pieces of information be useful to a reader?

____

____

Vocabulary Builder

Multiple-Meaning Words The verb *penned* has more than one meaning. *Penned* can mean "wrote a note or a letter with a pen." It can also mean "prevented a person or an animal from leaving an enclosed area." What does *penned* mean in the first paragraph?

____

____

Cultural Understanding

The United States Postal Service began in 1775 when Benjamin Franklin was appointed the first Postmaster General. Postage stamps were introduced in 1847. Packages began traveling through the mail in 1913.

A Life in Letters

Book Review
by Zakia Carter

Zora Neale Hurston:
A Life in Letters.

Edited by Carla Kaplan
Doubleday; October 2002;
896 pages

Within days of having *Zora Neale Hurston: A Life in Letters* in my possession, I was inspired to devote the total of my lunch hour to selecting beautiful blank cards and stationery, a fine ink pen and a book of stamps. By the end of the day, I had penned six letters, the old-fashioned way, to friends and relatives—something I haven't done since summer camp. In our haste to save time, we check our inboxes with an eagerness that was once reserved for that moment before pushing a tiny silver key into a mailbox door. E-mail has replaced paper and pen, so much so that the U.S. Postal Service is losing business. But the truth of the matter is, folks will neither salvage nor cherish e-mail as they might a handwritten letter.

And so *A Life in Letters* is a gift. It includes more than 500 letters and postcards written by Zora Neale Hurston over four decades. The 800-plus-page collection reveals more about this brilliant and complex woman than perhaps the entire body of her published works combined, including her notoriously unrevealing autobiography, *Dust Tracks on the Road*. Amazingly, the urgency and immediacy (typos and all) we associate with e-mail can also be found in Zora's letters. She writes to a veritable who's who in American history and society, including Langston Hughes, Carl Van Vechten, Charlotte Osgood Mason, Franz Boas, Dorothy West and W.E.B. Du Bois among others, sometimes more than once or twice a day. In these, her most intimate writings, Zora comes to life.

While we are familiar with Zora the novelist, essayist, playwright and anthropologist, *A Life in Letters* introduces us to Zora the filmmaker; Zora the Barnard College undergrad and Columbia University student; Zora the two-time Guggenheim fellow; Zora the chicken specialist; Zora the thrice-married wife; and Zora the political pundit. Zora's letters are at times flip, ironic, heart-breaking and humorous. They are insightful, biting and candid as journal entries. One can only wish for responses to Zora's words, but the work is not incomplete without them.

A treasure trove of information, in addition to the annotated letters, a chronology of Zora's life, a glossary of the people, events, and institutions to which she refers in her letters, and a thorough bibliographical listing are generously included by editor Carla Kaplan. Each decade of writing is introduced by an essay on the social, political, and personal points of significance in Zora's life. Kaplan's is a fine, well edited and utterly revealing work of scholarship into the life of one of the greatest and often most misunderstood American writers. In many ways, *A Life in Letters* is, in fact, a long love letter for Zora. It is a reminder to salvage and cherish what should not be forgotten and an admonishment to write what you love on paper.

—Zakia Carter is an editor at Africana.com.

TAKE NOTES

Vocabulary Builder

Uncommon Terms Find the word *pundit* in the first full paragraph on this page. *Pundit* means "someone who knows a lot about a particular subject." About what subject does the author believe Zora knows a lot?

____

Vocabulary Builder

Idioms Read the first sentence of the bracketed paragraph. The phrase *a treasure trove of information* means "a large collection of important facts and details." What parts of *A Life in Letters* make up the *treasure trove of information?*

____

____

____

____

Comprehension Builder 

Summarize the main points of this book review.

____

____

____

____

____

Thinking About the Book Review

1. The reviewer says that there is some information in *A Life in Letters* that is not in Hurston's other books. What kind of information would not be found in other books?

2. A **book review** gives an opinion about a book. Some readers know Hurston only as a novelist and storywriter. What is in the review that might surprise these readers?

TALK ABOUT IT Reading Skill

3. What information does the heading of this review provide?

4. How does the author organize the first complete paragraph on page 389?

WRITE ABOUT IT Timed Writing: Summary (20 minutes)

Summarize the **review**. Include the author's main points and opinions. Use this chart to get started.

What does Carter think about *A Life in Letters?*	
What does Carter think readers will gain from reading *A Life in Letters?*	

Ellis Island • from Out of the Dust

Reading Skill

Setting a purpose for reading helps you focus your attention as you read a literary work. When you read about people from a different time and place, for example, your purpose might be to learn about their view of the world and the problems they faced.

One way to set a purpose for reading is to **ask questions** about the topic of the work. Use a "K-W-L" chart. Fill in the first two columns before you begin to read. The second column identifies your purpose. If you can fill in the last column after reading, you have achieved your purpose.

K	W	L
What I already **k**now about the topic	Questions that explore what I **w**ant to know	Answers that show what I **l**earned

Literary Analysis

The **cultural context** of a literary work is the social and historical environment in which the characters live. Major historical events, such as bad economic times or the outbreak of war, can shape people's lives in important ways. Understanding the effects of such events can give you insight into characters' attitudes and actions.

As you read, look for details that show how characters respond to cultural and historical events.

from Out of the Dust

Karen Hesse

Summaries "Out of the Dust" includes three poems. The speaker in "Debts" describes the faith her father has that it will rain again. "Fields of Flashing Light" describes a dust storm on the prairie. In "Migrants," people leave their dried-up farms behind.

 Writing About the Big Question

Are yesterday's heroes important today? In *Out of the Dust,* Hesse explores the responses of ordinary people to the destructive effects of a long drought and an economic depression. Complete these sentences:

Courage can come from unexpected places. One person that others might not consider heroic, but I do, is ______________________ because ____.

Note-taking Guide

Use this chart to list the ways that dust and drought affect the people in each of the three poems.

Effects of Dust and Drought		
Debts	Fields of Flashing Light	Migrants

Debts

Daddy is thinking
of taking a loan from Mr. Roosevelt and his
men,[1]
to get some new wheat planted
where the winter crop has spindled out and
died.
Mr. Roosevelt promises
Daddy won't have to pay a dime
till the crop comes in.

Daddy says,
"I can turn the fields over,
start again.
It's sure to rain soon.
Wheat's sure to grow."

Ma says, "What if it doesn't?"

Daddy takes off his hat,
roughs up his hair,
puts the hat back on.
"Course it'll rain," he says.

Ma says, "Bay,
it hasn't rained enough to grow wheat in
three years."

Daddy looks like a fight brewing.

He takes that red face of his out to the barn,
to keep from feuding with my pregnant ma.

TAKE NOTES

Activate Prior Knowledge

Describe a time when bad weather had a negative effect on your life.

Reading Skill

Setting a purpose for reading helps you focus your attention as you read a literary work. Read the title and the first stanza of this poem. What will your purpose be in reading this poem?

Literary Analysis

The **cultural context** of a literary work is the social and historical environment in which the characters live. What clues does this page of the poem give you about its **cultural context**? Underline three words and/or phrases that tell you.

Vocabulary Development

feuding (FYOOD ing) *v.* quarreling; fighting

1. **. . . . a loan from Mr. Roosevelt and his men** In 1933, President Franklin D. Roosevelt began a series of government programs, called the New Deal, to help Americans suffering from the effects of the Great Depression. Among these programs were government loans to help Dust Bowl farmers.

TAKE NOTES

Reading Check 

In "Debts," what does Daddy do for a living? Underline the answer in the text.

Reading Skill 

What **purpose** for reading might the title "Fields of Flashing Light" give you?

Literary Analysis

The **cultural context** of a story can shape the way its characters think and behave. What does the narrator do in the first stanza of "Fields of Flashing Light"?

How is the narrator's action shaped by the cultural context of the poem?

I ask Ma
how,
after all this time,
Daddy still believes in rain.

"Well, it rains enough," Ma says,
"now and again,
to keep a person hoping.
But even if it didn't
your daddy would have to believe.
It's coming on spring,
and he's a farmer."

March 1934

Fields of Flashing Light

I heard the wind rise,
and stumbled from my bed,
down the stairs,
out the front door,
into the yard.
The night sky kept flashing,
lightning danced down on its spindly legs.

I sensed it before I knew it was coming.
I heard it,
smelled it,
tasted it.
Dust.

While Ma and Daddy slept,
the dust came,
tearing up fields where the winter wheat,
set for harvest in June,
stood helpless.
I watched the plants,
surviving after so much drought and so much
wind,

Vocabulary Development

spindly (SPIND lee) *adj.* long and thin

drought (drowt) *n.* lack of rain; long period of dry weather

I watched them fry,
or
flatten,
or blow away,
like bits of cast-off rags.
It wasn't until the dust turned toward the house,
like a fired locomotive,
and I fled,
barefoot and breathless, back inside,
it wasn't until the dust
hissed against the windows,
until it ratcheted the roof,
that Daddy woke.

He ran into the storm,
his overalls half-hooked over his union suit.[2]
"Daddy!" I called. "You can't stop dust."

Ma told me to
cover the beds,
push the scatter rugs against the doors,
dampen the rags around the windows.
Wiping dust out of everything,
she made coffee and biscuits,
waiting for Daddy to come in.

Sometime after four,
rubbing low on her back,
Ma sank down into a chair at the kitchen table
and covered her face.
Daddy didn't come back for hours,
not
until the temperature dropped so low,
it brought snow.

Ma and I sighed, grateful,
staring out at the dirty flakes,
but our relief didn't last.

2. union suit type of long underwear, common in the 1930s, that combines a shirt and leggings in one garment.

TAKE NOTES

Literary Analysis 

Vocabulary can help you understand the **cultural context** of a text. Circle the words on this page that help you know that this poem takes place in a rural setting in the early part of the twentieth century.

Stop to Reflect 

How would a dust storm such as the one described here affect your life?

____

____

____

____

Reading Skill 

To **set a purpose for reading,** someone might ask the question, "What happens during a dust storm?" Underline words that describe the dust storm. Then, explain the effects in your own words below.

____

____

____

____

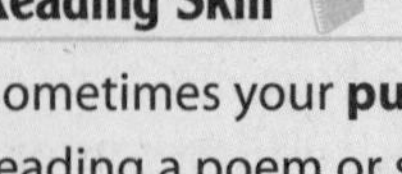

TAKE NOTES

Reading Skill

Sometimes your **purpose** for reading a poem or story may be informational. What details about the Dust Bowl are in the last stanza of "Fields of Flashing Light?"

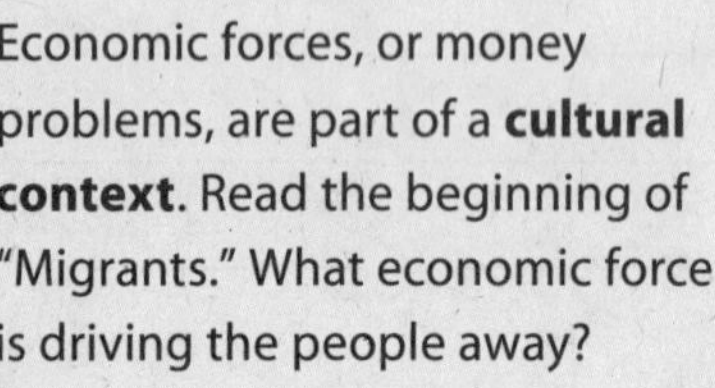

Literary Analysis

Economic forces, or money problems, are part of a **cultural context**. Read the beginning of "Migrants." What economic force is driving the people away?

Reading Check 

What are the people in "Migrants" fleeing? Underline the answer in the text.

The wind snatched that snow right off the
fields,
leaving behind a sea of dust,
waves and
waves and
waves of
dust,
rippling across our yard.

Daddy came in,
he sat across from Ma and blew his nose.
Mud streamed out.
He coughed and spit out
mud.
If he had cried,
his tears would have been mud too,
but he didn't cry.
And neither did Ma.

March 1934

Migrants

We'll be back when the rain comes,
they say,
pulling away with all they own,
straining the springs of their motor cars.
Don't forget us.

And so they go,
fleeing the blowing dust,
fleeing the fields of brown-tipped wheat
barely ankle high,
and sparse as the hair on a dog's belly.

We'll be back, they say,
pulling away toward Texas,
Arkansas,
where they can rent a farm,
pull in enough cash,
maybe start again.

Vocabulary Development

sparse (spahrs) *adj.* thinly spread and small in amount

We'll be back when it rains,
they say,
setting out with their bedsprings and
mattresses,
their cookstoves and dishes,
their kitchen tables,
and their milk goats
tied to their running boards[3]
in rickety cages,
setting out for
California,
where even though they say they'll come back,
they just might stay
if what they hear about that place is true.

Don't forget us, they say.
But there are so many leaving,
how can I remember them all?

April 1935

Reader's Response: Which poem did you find the most powerful?

What did you like most about it? Is there anything you would change about it?

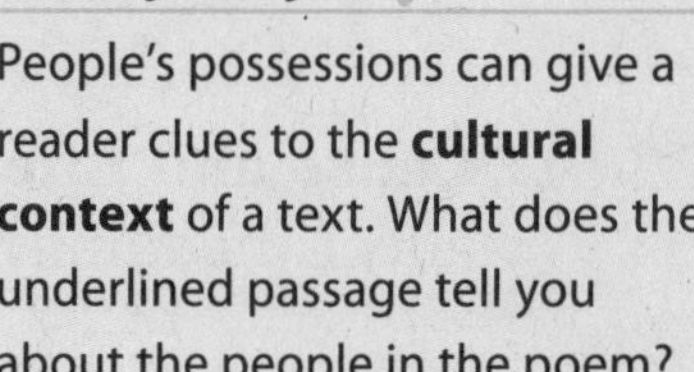

Literary Analysis 

People's possessions can give a reader clues to the **cultural context** of a text. What does the underlined passage tell you about the people in the poem?

Reading Skill 

Read the bracketed passage. Write a **purpose for reading** question that is answered by these lines.

Reading Check

Where are the neighbors going? Circle the answer in the text.

Vocabulary Development

rickety (RIK uht ee) *adj.* weak; likely to break

3. **running boards** steps, or footboards, that ran along the lower part of each side of a car. Running boards were common on cars of the 1930s.

from Out of the Dust

1. **Cause and Effect:** How might the storm in "Fields of Flashing Light" affect the family's income?

2. **Speculate:** In "Migrants," the family's neighbors move. What effects might their decision have on the people who stay behind?

3. **Reading Skill:** What **purpose** did you set for reading the three poems?

4. **Literary Analysis:** Complete this chart by explaining what each detail from the poems from "Out of the Dust" tells you about the poems' **cultural context**. Remember that the cultural context is the social and historical environment in which the characters live.

Detail	Ways of Life and Attitudes
Dust blew away crops, covering items and people.	
Ma and Pa do not cry when their wheat crop is destroyed.	
Pa decides to plant again, but other families decide to move away.	

Writing: Writing a Research Proposal

Write a short **research proposal** for a report on how the Dust Bowl affected farmers in the 1930s. A research proposal is an outline or description of information you plan to research. Complete these steps to help you organize your proposal.

Title of the report: ______________________________

List at least two sources for your report: ______________________________

____

____

Explain what you will describe first in your report: ______________________________

____

Explain what you will describe last in your report: ______________________________

____

Research and Technology: Letter

Use the following chart to list ideas for your **letter**. Imagine what you might experience on a long trip from Oklahoma to California.

Experiences	How I Felt
What Did I See?	
What Did I Do?	

Ellis Island

Joseph Bruchac

Summary The poet imagines his Slovak grandparents as they arrive in the United States. Their first stop in the land of their dreams was Ellis Island in New York. He then writes of his Native American grandparents. He points out that they had always lived in America. Their way of life was destroyed when the Europeans came.

Writing About the Big Question

Are yesterday's heroes important today? In "Ellis Island," Joseph Bruchac writes of the conflicting feelings the famous immigrant processing station awakens in him. Complete this sentence:

Many people view the accomplishments of their immigrant ancestors with pride because ____

____.

Note-taking Guide

Some of the phrases in the poem are hard to understand. They use words that paint pictures and stand for other things. Use this graphic organizer to record some of the hidden messages.

the red brick of Ellis Island	the island of the tall woman	green as dreams and meadows	nine decades the answerer of dreams
↓	↓	↓	↓
The building at Ellis Island is made of red bricks.			

Ellis Island

1. **Interpret:** What does the speaker mean by the phrase "native lands within this nation"?

2. **Analyze:** How does the speaker's dual ancestry influence his feelings toward Ellis Island?

3. **Reading Strategy:** What **purpose** did you set for reading "Ellis Island"?

4. **Literary Analysis:** Complete this chart by explaining what each detail from "Ellis Island" reveals about the poem's **cultural context**—the living conditions and attitudes of immigrants and Native Americans in the late 1800s.

Detail	Cultural Conditions and Attitudes
Immigrants were kept in quarantine before entering the United States.	
Immigrants dreamed of owning their own land.	
Native American lands were invaded "when the earth became owned."	
Native American had "knowledge of the seasons in their veins."	

Writing: Research Proposal

Write a short **research proposal** for a report on immigrants' experiences as they passed through Ellis Island in the 1890s and early 1900s. A research proposal is an outline or description of information you plan to research. Complete these steps to help you organize your proposal.

Title of the report: ______________________________

List at least two sources for your report: ______________________________

____

____

Explain what you will describe first in your report: ______________________________

____

Explain what you will describe last in your report: ______________________________

____

Use your observations to help you get ideas for a research proposal.

Research and Technology: Letter

Write a **letter** to a friend back home as if you are an immigrant at Ellis Island. Use the list below to help you choose what information to include in your letter.

- Where I am coming from: ______________________________
- Reasons for leaving the "old country": ______________________________
- What the journey to America was like: ______________________________
- What I felt when I first saw land: ______________________________
- How I was treated when I arrived: ______________________________

Choice: A Tribute to Martin Luther King, Jr. • An Episode of War

Reading Skill

When you **set a purpose for reading**, you determine your focus before reading. After you have set a purpose, **adjust your reading rate** according to that goal.

- When you read to learn new information, read *slowly* and carefully. After completing a difficult passage, take time to think about what you have just read. Reread, if necessary.
- When you read for entertainment, you can read more *quickly*. You might still choose to reread or linger over certain passages, but studying the text is less important.

The chart shows examples of reading rates. Fill in the blanks in the empty chart to show your reading plan for the selections.

Source	Magazine article on rock star	Source	Biography of John F. Kennedy	Source	
Purpose	Entertainment	Purpose	Research report	Purpose	
Reading Rate	Read quickly to find interesting details.	Reading Rate	Read slowly, selecting facts for your report.	Reading Rate	

Literary Analysis

An **author's influences** are the cultural and historical factors that affect his or her writing. To identify an author's influences:

- Read biographical information to learn about an author's important life experiences and cultural background.
- When reading, note any details in the work that show cultural values or attitudes. In addition, note references to historical events and figures or cultural influences that might have shaped the author's outlook and values.

Choice: A Tribute to Martin Luther King, Jr.

Alice Walker

Summary The author describes Dr. King's successes with the civil rights movement. She explains how Dr. King inspired African Americans to appreciate their heritage.

Writing About the Big Question

Are yesterday's heroes important today?

In "Choice," Alice Walker recalls the tremendous influence of Martin Luther King, Jr. on herself and her community. Complete this sentence:

A figure from the past, besides King, who continues to influence people today is ______________________________ because ______________________________.

Note-taking Guide

Use this diagram to recall the reasons that Alice Walker looks up to Martin Luther King, Jr.

He was not afraid to be arrested for his beliefs.

Why Alice Walker looks up to Martin Luther King, Jr.

Choice: A Tribute to Martin Luther King, Jr.

Alice Walker

This address was made in 1973 at a Jackson, Mississippi, restaurant that had refused to serve people of color until forced to do so by the civil rights movement a few years before.

My great-great-great-grandmother walked as a slave from Virginia to Eatonton, Georgia—which passes for the Walker ancestral home—with two babies on her hips. She lived to be a hundred and twenty-five years old and my own father knew her as a boy. (It is in memory of this walk that I choose to keep and to embrace my "maiden" name, Walker.)

There is a cemetery near our family church where she is buried; but because her marker was made of wood and rotted years ago, it is impossible to tell exactly where her body lies. In the same cemetery are most of my mother's people, who have lived in Georgia for so long nobody even remembers when they came. And all of my great-aunts and -uncles are there, and my grandfather and grandmother, and, very recently, my own father.

If it is true that land does not belong to anyone until they have buried a body in it, then the land of my birthplace belongs to me, dozens of times over. Yet the history of my family, like that of all black Southerners, is a history of dispossession. We loved the land and worked the land, but we never owned it; and even if we bought land, as my great-grandfather did after the Civil War, it was always in danger of being taken away, as his was, during the period following Reconstruction.[1]

My father inherited nothing of material value from his father, and when I came of age in the early sixties I awoke to the bitter knowledge that in order just to continue to love the land of my birth, I was expected to leave it. For black people—including my parents—had learned a long time ago that to stay willingly in a beloved but brutal place is to risk losing the love and being forced to acknowledge only the brutality.

1. **Reconstruction** (1865–1877) period following the American Civil War when the South was rebuilt and reestablished as part of the Union.

TAKE NOTES

Activate Prior Knowledge 

Describe a person you admire who leads, or has led, a fight for an important cause. What qualities do you admire in this person?

Reading Skill 

When you **set a purpose for reading**, you decide what to focus on when you read a literary work. Scan this page of text, including the italicized introductory paragraph. What do you think your purpose will be in reading this text?

Given this purpose, what **reading rate** will you set for this essay?

Reading Check 

How does Walker describe the history of her family and all black Southerners? Circle the word she uses.

TAKE NOTES

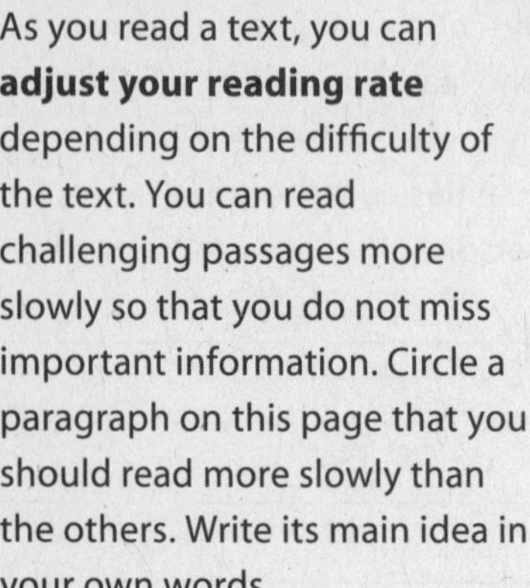

Reading Skill

As you read a text, you can **adjust your reading rate** depending on the difficulty of the text. You can read challenging passages more slowly so that you do not miss important information. Circle a paragraph on this page that you should read more slowly than the others. Write its main idea in your own words.

____

____

____

Literary Analysis

An **author's influences** are events from history and aspects of culture that affect his or her writing. Which historical figures mentioned on this page have influenced Walker?

____

____

____

Reading Check 

What does Walker say she watched her brothers and sisters do? Underline the answer.

It is a part of the black Southern sensibility that we treasure memories; for such a long time, that is all of our homeland those of us who at one time or another were forced away from it have been allowed to have.

I watched my brothers, one by one, leave our home and leave the South. I watched my sisters do the same. This was not unusual; abandonment, except for memories, was the common thing, except for those who "could not do any better," or those whose strength or stubbornness was so colossal they took the risk that others could not bear.

In 1960, my mother bought a television set, and each day after school I watched Hamilton Holmes and Charlayne Hunter[2] as they struggled to integrate—fair-skinned as they were—the University of Georgia. And then, one day, there appeared the face of Dr. Martin Luther King, Jr. What a funny name, I thought. At the moment I first saw him, he was being handcuffed and shoved into a police truck. He had dared to claim his rights as a native son, and had been arrested. He displayed no fear, but seemed calm and serene, unaware of his own extraordinary courage. His whole body, like his conscience, was at peace.

At the moment I saw his resistance I knew I would never be able to live in this country without resisting everything that sought to disinherit me, and I would never be forced away from the land of my birth without a fight.

He was The One, The Hero, The One Fearless Person for whom we had waited. I hadn't even realized before that we had been waiting for Martin Luther King, Jr., but we had. And I knew it for sure when my mother added his name to the list of people she prayed for every night.

I sometimes think that it was literally the prayers of people like my mother and father, who had bowed

Vocabulary Development

sensibility (sen suh BIL uh tee) *n.* moral, artistic, or intellectual outlook

2. **Hamilton Holmes and Charlayne Hunter** students who made history in January 1961 by becoming the first two African Americans to attend the University of Georgia.

down in the struggle for such a long time, that kept Dr. King alive until five years ago.[3] For years we went to bed praying for his life, and awoke with the question "Is the 'Lord' still here?"

The public acts of Dr. King you know. They are visible all around you. His voice you would recognize sooner than any other voice you have heard in this century—this in spite of the fact that certain municipal libraries, like the one in downtown Jackson, do not carry recordings of his speeches, and the librarians chuckle cruelly when asked why they do not.

You know, if you have read his books, that his is a complex and revolutionary philosophy that few people are capable of understanding fully or have the patience to embody in themselves. Which is our weakness, which is our loss.

And if you know anything about good Baptist preaching, you can imagine what you missed if you never had a chance to hear Martin Luther King, Jr., preach at Ebeneezer Baptist Church.

You know of the prizes and awards that he tended to think very little of. And you know of his concern for the disinherited: the American Indian, the Mexican-American, and the poor American white—for whom he cared much.

You know that this very room, in this very restaurant, was closed to people of color not more than five years ago. And that we eat here together tonight largely through his efforts and his blood. We accept the common pleasures of life, assuredly, in his name.

But add to all of these things the one thing that seems to me second to none in importance: He gave

TAKE NOTES

Literary Analysis

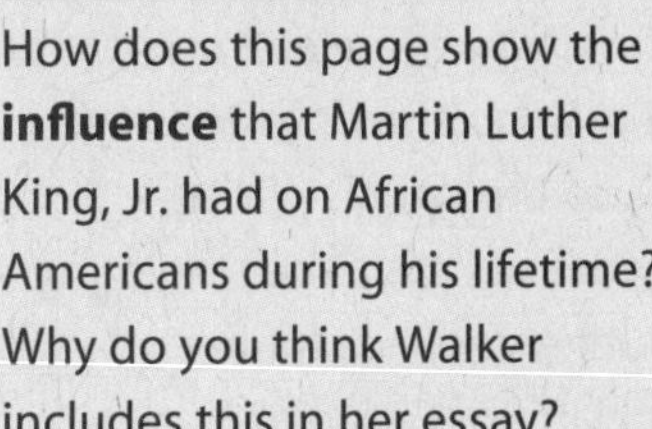

How does this page show the **influence** that Martin Luther King, Jr. had on African Americans during his lifetime? Why do you think Walker includes this in her essay?

Reading Skill

How does this page help you meet the **purpose** you set for reading?

Reading Check 

Dr. King was a leader in the civil rights movement. What other work did he do? Underline the sentence that tells you.

Vocabulary Development

revolutionary (rev uh LOO shuh ner ee) *adj.* favoring or bringing about sweeping change

disinherited (dis in HEHR it id) *n.* people who have been deprived of their rights as citizens

3. **until five years ago** Dr. Martin Luther King, Jr., was assassinated on April 4, 1968.

us back our heritage. He gave us back our homeland; the bones and dust of our ancestors, who may now sleep within our caring *and* our hearing. He gave us the blueness of the Georgia sky in autumn as in summer; the colors of the Southern winter as well as glimpses of the green of vacation-time spring. Those of our relatives we used to invite for a visit we now can ask to stay. . . . He gave us full-time use of our woods, and restored our memories to those of us who were forced to run away, as realities we might each day enjoy and leave for our children.

He gave us continuity of place, without which community is ephemeral.[4] He gave us home. *1973*

Reader's Response: What impresses you the most about Walker's tribute to Martin Luther King, Jr.? Explain.

4. **ephemeral** (i FEM uhr uhl) *adj.* short-lived; fleeting.

TAKE NOTES

Literary Analysis

Cultural values are an important part of an **author's influences**. How do the details Walker provides on this page tell you about her feelings for her homeland of Georgia?

Reading Skill

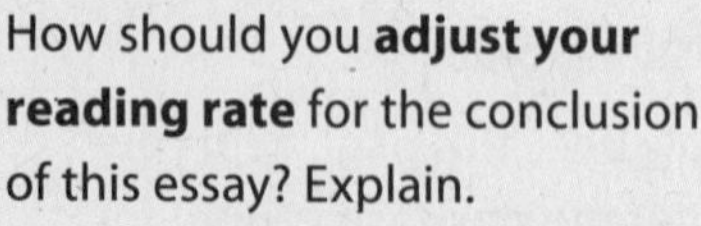

How should you **adjust your reading rate** for the conclusion of this essay? Explain.

Stop to Reflect

Is Walker's message relevant to modern readers? Give specific examples from the text to support your answer.

Choice: A Tribute to Martin Luther King, Jr.

1. **Connect:** What is important about the place where Walker gives her speech?

2. **Interpret:** What did Walker realize about Martin Luther King, Jr. when she first saw him on television?

3. **Reading Skill:** If you were writing a report on Dr. King's accomplishments as a civil rights leader, would this speech be a useful source of information for that **purpose**? Why or why not?

4. **Literary Analysis:** Complete the chart below to show how the **author's influences** affect her writing.

	Influences	Effect on Her Portrayal of Dr. King
Time and place of Walker's birth		
Walker's cultural background		
Major news events		

Writing: Speech

A **speech** is meant to be read aloud to a group. Prepare a speech for the dedication of a local monument to Martin Luther King, Jr. Your speech should celebrate Dr. King's accomplishments and leadership in the civil rights movement. Use your notes from the prompts to write your speech.

- List three of Dr. King's values: ____________________

  ____

- Explain three reasons why Dr. King should be remembered: ____________________

  ____

  ____

  ____

- Explain why Dr. King's ideas are still important today: ____________________

  ____

  ____

Research and Technology: Newspaper Article

Use the following chart to record information for your **newspaper article**. Remember that a newspaper article answers the questions *who, what, where, when,* and *how.*

Information about King	
Quotes from King, Walker, and Others	

An Episode of War

Stephen Crane

Summary A Civil War lieutenant is shot by a stray bullet. The other soldiers are worried for him. The doctors and medical staff act as if he is a bother. The lieutenant is ashamed that he was not shot in battle. His arm is removed. The lieutenant tells his family that missing an arm does not really matter.

Writing About the Big Question

Are yesterday's heroes important today? "An Episode of War" explores various reactions to the wounding of a soldier, including those of the soldier himself. Complete this sentence:

The concept of heroism (is/is not) outdated in our times because ________

____.

Note-taking Guide

Use this chart to record the attitudes of the different characters in "An Episode of War."

Characters	Attitudes	Reasons for Attitudes
Lieutenant		
Other soldiers	awed and sympathetic	
Surgeon		
Lieutenant's family		

An Episode of War

1. **Analyze:** How does the manner in which he was wounded make you sympathize with the lieutenant?

2. **Interpret:** Why do you think the lieutenant tells his family, "I don't suppose it matters so much as all that"?

3. **Reading Skill:** Would this be an appropriate text to read for the **purpose** of writing a research report on Civil War leadership? Explain.

4. **Literary Analysis:** Complete the chart below to evaluate the effect of the **author's influences** on his writing. Refer to the author biography on page 1016 in the textbook to help you.

	Influences	Effect on "An Episode of War"
Crane's Interests		
Crane's Research		

Writing: Speech

Prepare a **speech** for the dedication of a local Civil War memorial. The memorial will honor those who died or were injured in the war. Begin by answering these questions:

- When did the Civil War take place? ____________________
- Did any Civil War battles take place near your community? __________

  If so, where and when? ____________________
- Did people in your community fight for the Union or the Confederacy?

  ____
- Why do you think those who fight in the Civil War, on either side, deserve to be honored?

  ____

  ____

Use your notes to help you write your speech.

Research and Technology: Newspaper Article

Write a **newspaper article** about the experience and cost of fighting in the Civil War. Make up statements that might have been made by the lieutenant in "An Episode of War."

What do you think the lieutenant would say about the kind of men with whom he served?	
What do you think the lieutenant would say about military hospitals?	
How do you think the lieutenant felt about having to live the rest of his life without an arm?	

Use the quotations from your chart in your newspaper article.

Transcripts

About Transcripts

Transcripts are written records of speech. They use the exact words of the speakers. Transcripts provide a complete record of what was said at an event. They do not include opinions or rewording. People use transcripts to record:

- radio or television shows
- trials or government hearings
- interviews or oral histories
- debates or speeches

Reading Skill

Analyze the treatment, scope, and organization of ideas to help you understand information in a transcript. The treatment reveals the purpose of the piece of writing. The purpose of a transcript is to record what was said during an event. The scope of the transcript includes the entire record of what was said by all participants at an event. The scope can be broad and cover lots of topics. It can also be narrow and cover a specific subject. The organization of a transcript follows the questions and comments of the participants in the order in which they were spoken.

Checklist for Evaluating Treatment, Scope, and Organization

- ☐ Has the author addressed the topic in a way that is neutral or biased?
- ☐ Does the author cover different sides of an issue or only one?
- ☐ Does the author present ideas in a logical sequence?
- ☐ Are details organized in a way that enhances the author's points?

Build Understanding

Knowing these words will help you read this transcript.

paralyzed veterans (PAR uh lyzd VET uhr uhnz) *n.* people who have been in the military and now have arms and/or legs that cannot move

paraplegics (par uh PLEE jiks) *n.* people who have both legs paralyzed

spinal cord injuries (SPY nuhl KORD IN juh reez) *n.* damage to the nerves that run from the brain down the back

MORNING EDITION,
NATIONAL PUBLIC RADIO

November 11, 2003

PROFILE: **World War II veterans who founded the Paralyzed Veterans of America.**

BOB EDWARDS, **host:** This is MORNING EDITION from NPR News. I'm Bob Edwards.

In February of 1947, a small group of World War II veterans gathered at Hines VA Hospital near Chicago. The fact that they were there at all was considered extraordinary. The men were paralyzed, living at a time when paraplegia was still an unfamiliar word and most people with spinal cord injuries were told they would die within a few years. But these wounded veterans had other ideas, so they came from hospital wards across the country to start a national organization to represent veterans with spinal cord injuries. Today on Veterans Day, NPR's Joseph Shapiro tells their story.

JOSEPH SHAPIRO **reporting:** The logo of the Paralyzed Veterans of America looks a bit like the American flag, except that it's got 16 stars, one for each of the men who started the PVA when they gathered at that first convention nearly 57 years ago. Today only one of those 16 paralyzed veterans is still alive. His name is Ken Seaquist. He lives in a gated community in Florida. . . . It's there that Seaquist sits in his wheelchair and flips through some yellowed newspaper clippings . . .

MR. KEN SEAQUIST: Oh, here it is. OK.

SHAPIRO: . . . until he finds a photo. . . . The picture shows that convention. It was held in a veterans hospital just outside Chicago. A large room is filled with scores of young men in wheelchairs. Others are in their pajamas and hospital beds, propped up on white pillows.

TAKE NOTES

Text Structure 

You can use the text structure to understand transcripts. Look at the heading on this transcript. Circle the date the program aired and the name of the program. What was the program about on this day?

____

____

Comprehension Builder 

Reading transcripts can be confusing. Different people are involved, but you cannot see any of them. So, you have to keep them straight by looking at their names. You also have to remember how each person is involved in the discussion. Explain how each person below is involved in this radio show.

Bob Edwards: ______________

Joe Shapiro: ______________

Ken Seaquist: ______________

TAKE NOTES

Text Structure 

The names of the speakers stand out in the formatting of the text. Circle the names of the three people who are talking on this page.

Note that a person's full name is given the first time the person talks. After the first time, names are written in shorter ways. Underline the names of a person who is talking for the first time on this page.

Vocabulary Builder

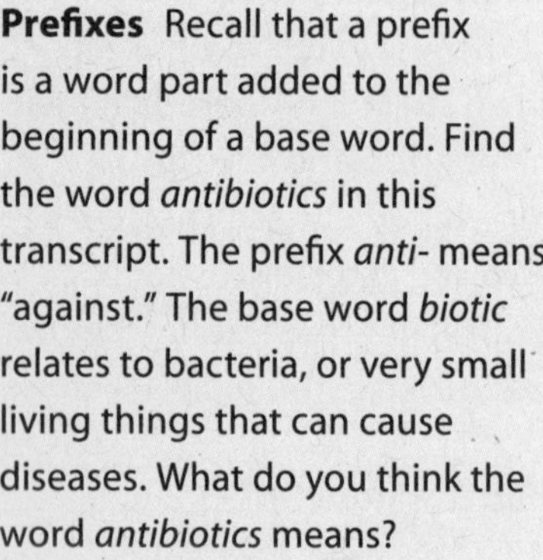

Prefixes Recall that a prefix is a word part added to the beginning of a base word. Find the word *antibiotics* in this transcript. The prefix *anti-* means "against." The base word *biotic* relates to bacteria, or very small living things that can cause diseases. What do you think the word *antibiotics* means?

____

____

Cultural Understanding

The president that Shapiro refers to is President Franklin D. Roosevelt. He was president of the United States from 1933–1945. He is the only president to serve four terms in office.

MR. SEAQUIST: There's Bill Dake. He came with us and then Mark Orr. Three of us came in the car from Memphis. Mark had one good leg, his right leg, and he was the driver of the car.

SHAPIRO: Ken Seaquist was a tall, lanky 20-year-old in an Army mountain ski division when he was wounded in Italy. He was flown back to the United States to a veterans hospital in Memphis. He came back to a society that was not ready for paraplegics.

MR. SEAQUIST: Before the war, people in our condition were in the closet. They never went out hardly. They didn't take them out.

SHAPIRO: Few people had ever survived for more than a few years with a spinal cord injury. Infections were common and deadly. But that was about to change. David Gerber is a historian at the University at Buffalo. He's written about disabled veterans.

MR. DAVID GERBER (UNIVERSITY AT BUFFALO): With the development of antibiotics, which came into general use in World War II, there were many healthy spinal cord-injured veterans who were able to survive and begin to aspire to have a normalized life.

SHAPIRO: Gerber says neither the wounded veterans, nor the world around them at that time knew what to make of men who were seen as having gone from manly warriors to dependent invalids.

MR. GERBER: The society is emphatically not ready for them, and nor is the medical profession. To this extent, it was often the paralyzed veterans themselves who were pioneers in the development of a new way of life for themselves.

SHAPIRO: Seaquist and the others set out to overcome the fear and pity of others. After Seaquist was injured, he never heard from his girlfriend. His mother's hair turned white in a matter of months. People stared when he went out in public. It was a time when a president with polio felt he had to hide the fact that he used a wheelchair. Beyond attitudes, there was a physical world that had to change. When Seaquist arrived at the Memphis hospital, he could not get off the ward. There were steps in the way.

MR. SEAQUIST: They had no idea of what they had to do for wheelchairs. So when we got there, they had to put in all these long ramps and this is what we were talking about. The ramping and just to get around the hospital and get out ourselves, you know; not having somebody help us all the time. We were an independent bunch.

SHAPIRO: There were about 2,500 soldiers with spinal cord injuries, most of them living in military hospitals around the country. Pat Grissom lived at Birmingham Hospital in California. He would become one of the first presidents of the PVA, but he was unable to travel from California to Chicago for that first convention. Grissom, too, had come back from war with little hope for his future.

MR. PAT GRISSOM: I just suppose that we were going to live the rest of our lives either in the hospital or go to an old soldiers home. We were just going to be there taking medicine and if you got sick, they would try to take care of you and you'd have your meals provided and your future was the hospital or the old soldiers home.

SHAPIRO: At Birmingham Hospital, Grissom met a doctor who was about to become a pioneer in the new field of spinal cord medicine. Dr. Ernst Bors did a lot to improve the physical care of paraplegics. He also pushed the men at Birmingham to set goals for their lives, to go back to school, get jobs and marry. Bors and the veterans at Birmingham Hospital were the subject of a Hollywood film, *The Men.* The realistic and sympathetic portrayal helped the American public better understand paralyzed veterans. In the film, the kindly doctor in a lab coat is based on Bors. He urges on a wounded soldier in a white T-shirt, played by a young Marlon Brando.

TAKE NOTES

Fluency Builder 

When people speak, they may not use grammatically correct language. Read the sentence spoken by Mr. Seaquist that begins "The ramping and." Rewrite the entire sentence using grammatically correct language. You may need to incorporate ideas from other sentences in the paragraph.

____

____

____

Now, read the entire paragraph aloud.

Vocabulary Builder 

Proper Nouns A proper noun names a specific person, place, or thing. Proper nouns begin with capital letters. Read the paragraph beginning "SHAPIRO: There were about." Circle the proper nouns in this paragraph.

Comprehension Builder 

How did injured soldiers' lives change due to the influence of Dr. Ernst Bors? Summarize the changes on the lines below.

____

____

____

____

Text Structure

Read the bracketed passage. How is this passage different from the rest of the **transcript?**

Cultural Understanding

Long ago, all cars had manual transmissions. The driver had to change gears frequently while driving, in the same way that you might change gears on a bicycle while riding uphill. The automatic transmission changed gears when necessary without any action by the driver. *Oldsmobile* is a manufacturer of cars.

(Soundbite of The Men)

MR. MARLON BRANDO: Well, what am I going to do? Where am I going to go?

Unidentified Actor: Into the world.

MR. MARLON BRANDO: I can't go out there anymore.

Unidentified Actor: You still can't accept it, can you?

MR. MARLON BRANDO: No. What did I do? Why'd it have to be me?

Unidentified Actor: Is there an answer? I haven't got it. Somebody always gets hurt in the war.

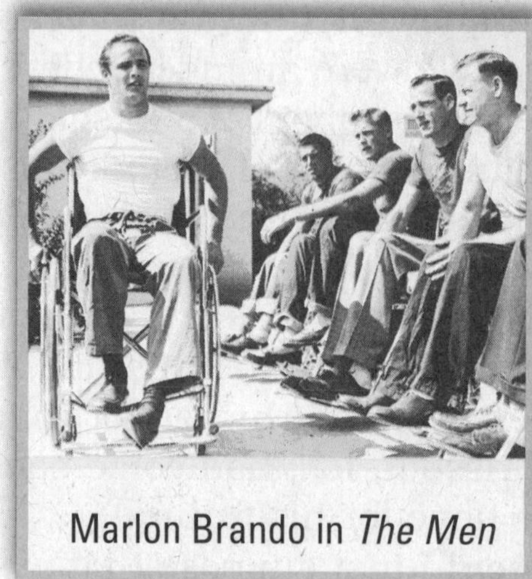

Marlon Brando in *The Men*

SHAPIRO: For Grissom and the other paralyzed veterans, there was something else that helped them go out into the world, a new technology. The introduction of automatic transmission meant that a car could be modified with hand controls for the gas and brakes. Pat Grissom.

MR. GRISSOM: Oldsmobile came up with the hydromatic drive and they put on hand controls and they sent people out to start giving driving lessons to us and we started having visions of saving up enough money to get a car and then things were looking better all the time.

SHAPIRO: Ken Seaquist says driving opened up all kinds of possibilities, from going out to a restaurant with a bunch of friends to romance.

MR. SEAQUIST: In Memphis, we had—our favorite place was called the Silver Slipper and they welcomed us with open arms and we had maybe 10, 12 wheelchairs going with our dates. Generally it

Car modified with hand controls

was our nurses that we dated, 'cause, you know, we couldn't get out anywhere. We took the girls with us, you know. Eventually I married one of them.

SHAPIRO: Seaquist and his wife quickly had two daughters. And with a young family, he had to find work. He went to school and became a landscape architect. Ken Seaquist stopped seeing himself as an invalid and became a man with a future. So in 1947, he and the other founders of the PVA met in Chicago to put together a collective voice to express their dreams and what they needed to accomplish them. They came up with a slogan to get others to join, 'Awaken, gentlemen, lest we decay.' Ken Seaquist explains what it meant.

MR. SEAQUIST: If they forget us, we're going to decay. We're going to be left in the closet. We've got to get out there and speak out, getting things done so we can roll around this country and have access to the whole country.

SHAPIRO: The PVA quickly won some important legislative victories in Washington: money for paralyzed veterans to modify automobiles and houses, money for medical care. Later they would help push for laws that would make buildings and streets accessible to wheelchair users. The PVA has continued to advocate for veterans with spinal cord injuries through every war since World War II.

Joseph Shapiro, NPR News.

TAKE NOTES

Fluency Builder 

With a partner, take turns reading aloud the first speech by Shapiro on this page. Read his words as though you were a radio announcer.

Comprehension Builder 

Why did Mr. Seaquist and others found the PVA? Underline the sentences that tell the answer.

Vocabulary Builder

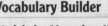

Multiple-Meaning Words The verb *push* can mean "move a person or thing by pressing with your hands." It can also mean "try to persuade someone to accept or do something." What meaning does the verb have in the bracketed passage?

____

____

Thinking About the Transcript

1. Why were veterans of World War II more likely to survive their injuries?

2. Why did the veterans form the Paralyzed Veterans of America?

TALK ABOUT IT Reading Skill

3. How does the organization of the transcript help you identify the comments by the veterans?

4. Describe the scope of the information presented in this transcript. Is the scope broad or narrow? Explain.

WRITE ABOUT IT Timed Writing: Explanation (20 minutes)

Paralyzed veterans face many stereotypes. Write a paragraph explaining why stereotyping can be hurtful.

- Identify examples of stereotypes from the transcript.

- Use these examples to explain why stereotyping can hurt people.

The exercises and tools presented here are designed to help you increase your vocabulary. Review the instruction and complete the exercises to build your vocabulary knowledge. Throughout the year, you can apply these skills and strategies to improve your reading, writing, speaking, and listening vocabulary.

The following list contains common word roots with meanings and examples. On the blank lines, write other words you know that have the same roots. Write the meanings of the new words.

Root	Meaning	Example and Meaning	Your Words	Meanings
-brev-	brief; short	*brevity:* the quality of lasting for a short time		
-cede-	go	*recede:* move or go away or move or go back		
-dict-	say or tell	*predict:* tell what might happen next		
-fac-	make	*factory:* place where things are made		
-fer-	bring; carry	*reference:* something you say or write that mentions another person or thing, something that brings or carries more information		
-ject-	throw	*eject:* push or throw out with force		
-manu-	hand	*manual:* operated or done by hand		

Root	Meaning	Example and Meaning	Your Words	Meanings
-phon-	hearing; sound	*telephone:* a device that brings sound over long distances		
-port-	carry	*support:* carry or hold something up		
-scrib-	write	*scribble:* write something quickly in a messy way		
-sequ-	follow	*consequence:* effect that follows a cause		
-similis-	same	*similar:* alike in some way		
-spec-	look; see	*inspect:* look carefully at something		
-sum-	take; use	*assumption:* something that you think is true or take as true		
-tele-	far; distant	*telescope:* instrument that makes distant objects look larger		
-vali-	strong; worth	*valid:* true, based on strong reasons or facts		
-ver-	truth	*verify:* make sure something is true		

The following list contains common prefixes with meanings and examples. On the blank lines, write other words you know that begin with the same prefixes. Write the meanings of the new words.

Prefix	Meaning	Example and Meaning	Your Words	Meanings
anti-	against	*antisocial:* not liking to meet and talk to people; against friendliness		
aud-	hearing; sound	*auditorium:* a room for hearing concerts or speeches		
con-	with; together	*concur:* agree with		
de-	down; from	*decrease:* become less		
dis-	not	*disorganized:* not organized		
in-	without; not	*incapable:* not able		
inter-	between	*intermission:* short period of time between the parts of a play or concert		
ir-	without; not	*irregular:* not regular		

Prefix	Meaning	Example and Meaning	Your Words	Meanings
mis-	wrong; bad	*misspell:* spell wrong; spell incorrectly		
multi-	many	*multicolored:* having many colors		
non-	without; not	*nonfat:* without fat		
ob-	against	*obstacle:* something that works against another, something that makes it difficult for you to succeed		
post-	after	*post-test:* a test given after instruction		
pre-	before	*preview:* look before		
re-	again	*remake:* make again		
sub-	below, under	*submarine:* a ship that moves under the ocean		
super-	above; over	*superior:* better than another		
un-/an-/a-	not	*unbelievable:* not believable		

The following list contains common suffixes with meanings and examples. On the blank lines, write other words you know that have the same suffixes. Write the meanings of the new words.

Suffix	Meaning	Example and Meaning	Your Words	Meanings
-able/-ible	able to be	*movable:* able to be moved		
-al	relating to	*financial:* relating to money		
-ance/-ence	act of; state of; quality of	*assistance:* act of giving help		
-ate	make	*motivate:* make someone feel eager to do something		
-en	make	*weaken:* make something less strong		
-er/-or	one who	*actor:* person who acts		
-ful	filled with	*joyful:* filled with happiness		
-hood	state or quality of	*manhood:* the state of being an adult male		

Suffix	Meaning	Example and Meaning	Your Words	Meanings
-ic	like; pertaining to	*heroic:* like a hero; brave		
-ish	resembling	*foolish:* not sensible		
-ist	one who	*violinist:* person who plays the violin		
-ize/-yze	make	*publicize:* make public; tell people about		
-less	without	*powerless:* without power		
-ly	in a way	*quickly:* done in a short amount of time		
-ment	act or quality of	*excitement:* feeling of being excited		
-ness	state or quality of	*kindness:* friendly and caring behavior		
-ous	having; full of	*famous:* having fame; known and recognized by many people		
-sion/-tion	act or process of	*persuasion:* act of convincing someone		

Use a **dictionary** to find the correct spelling, the meaning, the pronunciation, and the part of speech of a word. The dictionary will show you how the plural is formed if it is irregular. You can also find the word's history, or *etymology*, in a dictionary. Etymology explains how words change, how they are borrowed from other languages, and how new words are invented, or "coined."

Here is a sample entry from a dictionary. Notice what it tells about the word. Then, follow the instructions.

> **lemon** (lem´ ən) ***n.*** [ME *lymon* < MFr *limon* < Ar *laimūn* < Pers *līmūn*] **1** a small, egg-shaped, edible citrus fruit with a yellow rind and a juicy, sour pulp, rich in ascorbic acid **2** the small, spiny, semitropical evergreen citrus tree (*Citrus limon*) bearing this fruit **3** pale yellow **4** [slang] something, esp. a manufactured article, that is defective or imperfect

1. Circle the *n.* in the dictionary entry. It stands for *noun.* Write what these other parts of speech abbreviations mean: *v.* __________, *adv.* __________, *adj.* __________, *prep.* __________.

2. Underline the origins of the word *lemon.* ME stands for Middle English, Ar stands for Arabic, and Pers. stands for Persian. What do you think MFr stands for? __________

3. Put a box around the pronunciation.

4. How many noun definitions does the entry have? __________

5. Which definition is slang? __________

6. Which definition of *lemon* is used in the following sentence? __________

   The car that my dad bought turned out to be a lemon.

Activity: Use a dictionary to learn about the origins of these words.

Activity: Use a dictionary to learn about the origins of these words.

1. literature ________ / ________ / ________
pronunciation main part of speech original language(s)

________ / ________
1st meaning other meanings

____

____

____

____

2. language ________ / ________ / ________
pronunciation main part of speech original language(s)

________ / ________
1st meaning other meanings

____

____

____

Activity: Look up each of the following words in a dictionary. Then, write a definition of the word and a sentence using the word.

moment ________

____

popular ________

____

remedy ________

____

blur ________

____

lazy ________

____

Use these word study cards to break big words into their parts. Write the word at the top of the card. Then, divide the word into its prefix, root, and suffix. Note that not all words have prefixes and suffixes. List the meaning of each part of the word. Next, find three words with the same root and write them on the card. Finally, write the word's part of speech and its definition. Use a dictionary to help you. One example has been done for you.

Word: invisible

Prefix	**Root**	**Suffix**
in: not	**vis:** see	**ible**-able to be

Root-related Words

1. vision
2. revise
3. visibility

Definition: invisible *adj.* not able to be seen

Word:

Prefix	**Root**	**Suffix**

Root-related Words

1.
2.
3.

Definition:

Word:

Prefix **Root** **Suffix**

Root-related Words
1.
2.
3.

Definition:

Word:

Prefix **Root** **Suffix**

Root-related Words
1.
2.
3.

Definition:

Word:

Prefix **Root** **Suffix**

Root-related Words
1.
2.
3.

Definition:

achieve (uh CHEEV) *v.* succeed; accomplish
analyze (AN uh lyz) *v.* study the parts of something
anticipate (an TIS uh payt) *v.* look forward to; expect
determine (dee TER muhn) *v.* figure out
establish (uh STAB lish) *v.* show or prove
formulate (FAWR myoo layt) *v.* make a statement; form an idea
intention (in TEN shuhn) *n.* purpose; goal
modify (MAHD uh fy) *v.* change
predict (pree DIKT) *v.* make a logical assumption about future events
revise (ri VYZ) *v.* correct, improve, or change

A. True/False For each of the following, mark T or F to indicate whether the italicized vocabulary word has been used correctly in the sentence. If you have marked F, correct the sentence by using the word properly.

1. _____ If you *modify* your answer, you leave it exactly the same as it is.
2. _____ You can *predict* how a story will end by paying attention to the author's clues.
3. _____ Based on reliable evidence, the scientist will *formulate* a new theory.
4. _____ Rita *anticipates* the trip that she went on last week.
5. _____ Most students *achieve* their goals in school by failing tests.
6. _____ When you *analyze* a story, you look at the plot details.
7. _____ Roger uses the blinker on his car to *determine* where he is going to turn.
8. _____ When you *revise* an essay, you usually try to make it incorrect.
9. _____ The author's *intention* is to bore readers.
10. _____ Use facts to *establish* what is true.

B. Use each word pair in an original sentence that illustrates the meaning of the academic vocabulary word.

achieve/goal ______________________________

____

analyze/situation ______________________________

____

anticipate/party ______________________________

____

determine/truth ______________________________

____

establish/rules ______________________________

____

formulate/idea ______________________________

____

intention/persuade ______________________________

____

modify/answer ______________________________

____

predict/conclusion ______________________________

____

revise/errors ______________________________

____

aspect (AS pekt) *n.* the specific part that you are observing or studying
conclude (kuhn KLOOD) *v.* decide by reasoning
differentiate (dif uhr EN shee ayt) *v.* show how things are different
evidence (EV uh duhns) *n.* facts that serve as clues or proof
examine (eg ZAM uhn) *v.* study carefully
indicate (IN di kayt) *v.* show; hint at
infer (in FER) *v.* draw conclusions based on facts
logical (LAHJ i kuhl) *adj.* reasonable; sensible
similar (SIM uh luhr) *adj.* alike
unique (yoo NEEK) *adj.* having nothing that is similar or equal

A. True/False For each of the following, mark T or F to indicate whether the italicized vocabulary word has been used correctly in the sentence. If you have marked F, correct the sentence by using the word properly.

1. ____ It is *logical* to think that monkeys can fly.
2. ____ What can you *infer* about the main character from the way he dresses?
3. ____ Ben can *differentiate* between books by describing how they are the same.
4. ____ Two pens that look exactly alike are *unique.*
5. ____ The left blinker in the car is used to *indicate* a left turn.
6. ____ Jason found *evidence* to support his theory.
7. ____ Facts *examine* the author's purpose.
8. ____ What can you *conclude* from the details in the story?
9. ____ *Examine* the tent carefully for leaks.
10. ____ How *similar* was the movie version to the book?

B. Use each word pair in an original sentence that illustrates the meaning of the academic vocabulary word.

aspect/character ______________________________

____

conclude/detail ______________________________

____

differentiate/novels ______________________________

____

evidence/prove ______________________________

____

examine/details ______________________________

____

indicate/correct ______________________________

____

infer/details ______________________________

____

logical/answer ______________________________

____

similar/traits ______________________________

____

unique/characteristic ______________________________

____

accurate (AK yuh ruht) *adj.* free from error; correct; exact
bias (BY uhs) *n.* unfair preference or dislike for someone or something
cite (SYT) *v.* refer to an example or fact as proof
credible (KRED uh buhl) *adj.* believable; reliable
focus (FOH kuhs) *n.* the central point of a work
focus (FOH kuhs) *v.* concentrate on one thing
imply (im PLY) *v.* hint at; suggest
implied (im PLYD) *adj.* suggested
pertinent (PERT uhn uhnt) *adj.* relevant; having a connection
suggest (suhg JEST) *v.* show indirectly; imply
support (suh PORT) *v.* provide evidence to prove or back up an idea
topic (TAHP ik) *n.* the subject

A. Code Name Use the code to figure out each vocabulary word. Each letter is represented by a number or symbol. This exercise will help you learn how to spell and recognize the vocabulary words.

%	5	•	*	2	#	!	7	^	&	9	¶	£	$	3	¥	+	=	?	÷	4	¢	6	§	«	ç
a	b	c	d	e	f	g	h	i	j	k	l	m	n	o	p	q	r	s	t	u	v	w	x	y	z

1. # 3 • 4 ? ________________
2. ¥ 2 = ÷ ^ $ 2 $ ÷ ________________
3. ^ £ ¥ ¶ ^ 2 * ________________
4. % • • 4 = % ÷ 2 ________________
5. • = 2 * ^ 5 ¶ 2 ________________
6. ? 4 ¥ ¥ 3 = ÷ ________________
7. ÷ 3 ¥ ^ • ________________
8. 5 ^ % ? ________________
9. • ^ ÷ 2 ________________
10. ? 4 ! ! 2 ? ÷ ________________

B. Answer each question. Then, explain your answer.

1. Would drama be a good *topic* for a science paper? ______________________

   ____

2. If an answer is *accurate*, are there mistakes in it? ______________________

   ____

3. When you are trying to *focus* on homework, is it a good idea to watch television? ______________________

   ____

4. If a suggestion is *implied*, is it generally stated aloud? ______________________

5. Would a *pertinent* comment have anything to do with the topic being discussed? ______________________

   ____

6. Would you expect someone with a *bias* to always be fair? ______________________

   ____

7. Is it a good idea to *support* your ideas with facts and examples? ______________________

   ____

8. If someone you knew told a lot of lies, would she be *credible*? ______________________

   ____

9. If an article *suggests* that there is life on Mars, would it be directly stated? ______

   ____

10. If the author *cites* the work of someone else, does she mention the work? ______

    ____

adapt (uh DAPT) *v.* change something to make it more suitable
clarify (KLAR uh fy) *v.* explain; make clearer
confirm (kun FERM) *v.* make certain; prove to be correct
context (KAHN tekst) *n.* text surrounding an unfamiliar word
convey (kuhn VAY) *v.* carry meaning; communicate
emphasize (EM fuh syz) *v.* stress
reflect (ri FLEKT) *v.* mirror an image; express or show
restate (ree STAYT) *v.* express the same idea in a different way
restatement (ree STAYT muhnt) *n.* expressing the same idea in different words
synonymous (si NAHN uh muhs) *adj.* having the same, or nearly the same, meaning

A. Completion Complete each sentence that has been started for you. Your sentence completion should be logical and illustrate the meaning of the vocabulary word in italics.

1. Some words that are *synonymous* with happy are ______________________

____

2. The teacher tried to *clarify* ______________________________

____

3. A smile can *convey* ______________________________________

____

4. A writer might *adapt* a story to ___________________________

____

5. It is a good idea to *restate* a poem so that ____________________

____

6. You can *confirm* a fact by _______________________________

____

7. If you look at the *context* surrounding an unfamiliar word, you may be able to

____

____

8. One way to *emphasize* an important idea in writing is to ____________

____

9. A good reason for a *restatement* of an idea is ______________________________

____

10. A restatement should *reflect* ______________________________

____

B. Using the word pair, write an original sentence that illustrates the meaning of the academic vocabulary word.

reflect/image ______________________________

____

convey/meaning ______________________________

____

emphasize/main point ______________________________

____

restate/words ______________________________

____

adapt/story ______________________________

____

synonymous/words ______________________________

____

restatement/idea ______________________________

____

confirm/report ______________________________

____

context/unfamiliar ______________________________

____

clarify/difficult ______________________________

____

assumption (uh SUMP shuhn) *n.* something one supposed to be true, without proof
connect (kuh NEKT) *v.* show how things are related
consequence (KAHN si kwens) *n.* result; outcome
evaluate (ee VAL yoo ayt) *v.* judge; determine the worth or strength of something
factor (FAK tuhr) *n.* something that helps bring about a result
impact (IM pakt) *n.* the power to produce changes or effects
influence (IN floo uhns) *n.* ability to affect results
rational (RASH uhn uhl) *adj.* based on reason; logical
reaction (ree AK shuhn) *n.* response to an influence or force
valid (VAL id) *adj.* based on facts and strong evidence; convincing

A. Completion Complete each sentence that has been started for you. Your sentence completion should be logical and illustrate the meaning of the vocabulary word in italics.

1. One *consequence* of a heavy rain might be ______________________________

____

2. Do not make *assumptions* if ______________________________________

____

3. A *valid* conclusion would ____

____

4. A strange *reaction* to a scary movie would be ________________________

____

5. One *factor* in success in school is ___________________________________

____

6. A *rational* reason to go to bed early is ______________________________

____

7. If you *connect* all the facts, you will ________________________________

____

8. One way that teachers *evaluate* students is ___________________________

____

9. The event that has had the biggest influence on my life so far is ______________________________

10. Books can have an impact on ______________________________

B. Using the academic word pair, write an original sentence that illustrates the meaning of the words.

factor/influence ______________________________

consequence/impact ______________________________

reaction/rational ______________________________

assumption/valid ______________________________

evaluate/connect ______________________________

critique (kri TEEK) *v.* write a critical essay or review
disorganized (dis OHR guh nyzd) *adj.* not arranged in a logical order
essential (uh SEN shuhl) *adj.* necessary
extract (ek STRAKT) *v.* deduce; obtain
focus (FOH kuhs) *v.* direct one's attention to a specific part of something
identify (y DEN tuh fy) *v.* recognize; find and name
organized (OHR guh nyzd) *v.* arranged in a logical order
revise (ri VYZ) *v.* change; adjust
sequence (SEE kwuhns) *n.* order
skim (SKIM) *v.* read quickly, skipping parts of the text

A. True/False For each of the following, mark T or F to indicate whether the italicized vocabulary word has been used correctly in the sentence. If you have marked F, correct the sentence by using the word properly.

1. ____ A telephone book should be *organized* in alphabetic order.
2. ____ If you *skim* a book, you read every single word.
3. ____ When you *revise* an essay, you should not change anything.
4. ____ We will *identify* the dishes after dinner.
5. ____ Please, *critique* my essay for me before I turn it in.
6. ____ A dictionary is an *essential* tool for an English student.
7. ____ If something is out of *sequence*, it is in the correct order.
8. ____ A *disorganized* desk would be very neat and orderly.
9. ____ If you are supposed to *focus* on a reading, you should sit in a quiet place.
10. ____ To *extract* important information from a text, only read every other word.

B. Answer each question. Then, explain your answer.

1. Is a television *essential* for life in the United States? ____________________
____

2. How would you *extract* information from an encyclopedia? ____________________
____

3. Will a *disorganized* summary help you remember key ideas? ____________________
____

4. Should words in a dictionary be *organized* in order of importance? ____________
____

5. What would be a logical *sequence* for events in a story? ____________________
____

6. Why might you *revise* your essay? ____________________
____

7. If you were asked to *skim* a magazine article, would you read it slowly and carefully? ____________________
____

8. Could you *critique* a novel without reading it? ____________________
____

9. If you are asked to *focus* on a sentence, should you flip through the whole book? ____________________
____

10. If you were asked to *identify* the main character in a story, what would you do?
____

Use this page to write down academic words you come across in other subjects, such as social studies or science. When you are reading your textbooks, you may find words that you need to learn. Following the example, write down the word, the part of speech, and an explanation of the word. You may want to write an example sentence to help you remember the word.

dissolve *verb* to make something solid become part of a liquid by putting it in a liquid and mixing it

The sugar *dissolved* in the hot tea.

Use these flash cards to study words you want to remember. The words on this page come from Unit 1. Cut along the dotted lines on pages V25 through V32 to create your own flash cards or use index cards. Write the word on the front of the card. On the back, write the word's part of speech and definition. Then, write a sentence that shows the meaning of the word.

lurking	burdened	finery
innumerable	preliminary	descendants
virtuous	retribution	unobtrusively

verb ready to spring out, attack; existing undiscovered The man was *lurking* in the shadows so we did not see him.	*adjective* too numerable to be counted There are *innumerable* stars in the desert sky.	*adjective* moral; upright A *virtuous* man respects the rights of others.
adjective weighted down by work, duty, or sorrow The old man seemed to be *burdened* with worry.	*adjective* introductory; preparatory The dinner began with a *preliminary* appetizer.	*noun* punishment for wrongdoing The victim wanted *retribution* from the man who robbed him.
noun fancy clothing and accessories The girls felt glamorous in their borrowed *finery*.	*noun* children, grandchildren, and continuing generations The old man willed all of his possessions to his many *descendants*.	*adverb* without calling attention to oneself She slipped out of the room *unobtrusively*.

Use these flash cards to study words you want to remember. Cut along the dotted lines on pages V25 through V32 to create your own flash cards or use index cards. Write the word on the front of the card. On the back, write the word's part of speech and definition. Then, write a sentence that shows the meaning of the word.

Use a fold-a-list to study the definitions of words. The words on this page come from Unit 1. Write the definition for each word on the lines. Fold the paper along the dotted line to check your definition. Create your own fold-a-lists on pages V35 through V38.

sinister

compliance

tangible

impaired

rigorous

inexplicable

celestial

exertion

maneuver

ascent

Fold In ←

Write the word that matches the definition on each line.
Fold the paper along the dotted line to check your work.

threatening harm or evil ____________________

agreement to a request ____________________

able to be perceived by the senses ____________________

made weaker or less useful ____________________

very harsh or strict ____________________

not possible to explain ____________________

heavenly ____________________

energetic activity; effort ____________________

series of planned steps ____________________

the act of climbing or rising ____________________

Fold In ←

VOCABULARY FOLD-A-LIST

Write the words you want to study on this side of the page. Write the definitions on the back. Then, test yourself. Fold the paper along the dotted line to check your definition.

Word: ______________________________

____

Word: ______________________________

____

Word: ______________________________

____

Word: ______________________________

____

Word: ______________________________

____

Word: ______________________________

____

Word: ______________________________

____

Word: ______________________________

____

Word: ______________________________

____

Word: ______________________________

____

Fold In ←

Write the word that matches the definition on each line.
Fold the paper along the dotted line to check your work.

Definition: ________________

Definition: ________________

Definition: ________________

Definition: ________________

Definition: ________________

Definition: ________________

Definition: ________________

Definition: ________________

Definition: ________________

Definition: ________________

Fold In ←

COMMONLY MISSPELLED WORDS

The list on these pages presents words that cause problems for many people. Some of these words are spelled according to set rules, but others follow no specific rules. As you review this list, check to see how many of the words give you trouble in your own writing. Then, add your own commonly misspelled words on the lines that follow.

abbreviate
absence
absolutely
abundance
accelerate
accidentally
accumulate
accurate
ache
achievement
acquaintance
adequate
admittance
advertisement
aerial
affect
aggravate
aggressive
agreeable
aisle
all right
allowance
aluminum
amateur
analysis
analyze
ancient
anecdote
anniversary
anonymous
answer
anticipate
anxiety
apologize
appall
appearance
appreciate
appropriate
architecture
argument
associate
athletic
attendance
auxiliary
awkward
bandage
banquet
bargain
barrel
battery
beautiful
beggar
beginning
behavior
believe
benefit
bicycle
biscuit
bookkeeper
bought
boulevard
brief
brilliant
bruise
bulletin
buoyant
bureau
bury
buses
business
cafeteria
calendar
campaign
canceled
candidate
capacity
capital
capitol
captain
career
carriage
cashier
catastrophe
category
ceiling
cemetery
census
certain
changeable
characteristic
chauffeur
chief
clothes
coincidence
colonel
column
commercial
commission
commitment
committee
competitor
concede
condemn
congratulate
connoisseur
conscience
conscientious
conscious
contemporary
continuous
controversy
convenience
coolly
cooperate
cordially
correspondence
counterfeit
courageous
courteous
courtesy
criticism
criticize
curiosity
curious
cylinder
deceive
decision
deductible
defendant
deficient
definitely
delinquent
dependent
descendant
description
desert
desirable
dessert
deteriorate
dining
disappointed
disastrous
discipline
dissatisfied
distinguish
effect
eighth
eligible
embarrass
enthusiastic
entrepreneur
envelope
environment
equipped
equivalent
especially
exaggerate
exceed
excellent
exercise
exhibition
existence
experience
explanation
extension
extraordinary
familiar
fascinating
February
fiery
financial
fluorescent

foreign
fourth
fragile
gauge
generally
genius
genuine
government
grammar
grievance
guarantee
guard
guidance
handkerchief
harass
height
humorous
hygiene
ignorant
immediately
immigrant
independence
independent
indispensable
individual
inflammable
intelligence
interfere
irrelevant
irritable
jewelry
judgment
knowledge
lawyer
legible
legislature
leisure
liable
library
license
lieutenant
lightning
likable
liquefy
literature
loneliness
magnificent
maintenance
marriage
mathematics
maximum
meanness
mediocre
mileage
millionaire
minimum

minuscule
miscellaneous
mischievous
misspell
mortgage
naturally
necessary
neighbor
neutral
nickel
niece
ninety
noticeable
nuisance
obstacle
occasion
occasionally
occur
occurred
occurrence
omitted
opinion
opportunity
optimistic
outrageous
pamphlet
parallel
paralyze
parentheses
particularly
patience
permanent
permissible
perseverance
persistent
personally
perspiration
persuade
phenomenal
phenomenon
physician
pleasant
pneumonia
possess
possession
possibility
prairie
precede
preferable
prejudice
preparation
previous
primitive
privilege
probably
procedure

proceed
prominent
pronunciation
psychology
publicly
pursue
questionnaire
realize
really
recede
receipt
receive
recognize
recommend
reference
referred
rehearse
relevant
reminiscence
renowned
repetition
restaurant
rhythm
ridiculous
sandwich
satellite
schedule
scissors
secretary
siege
solely
sponsor
subtle
subtlety
superintendent
supersede
surveillance
susceptible
tariff
temperamental
theater
threshold
truly
unmanageable
unwieldy
usage
usually
valuable
various
vegetable
voluntary
weight
weird
whale
wield
yield

When you are reading, you will find many unfamiliar words. Here are some tools that you can use to help you read unfamiliar words.

Phonics

Phonics is the science or study of sound. When you learn to read, you learn to associate certain sounds with certain letters or letter combinations. You know most of the sounds that letters can represent in English. When letters are combined, however, it is not always so easy to know what sound is represented. In English, there are some rules and patterns that will help you determine how to pronounce a word. This chart shows you some of the vowel digraphs, which are combinations like *ea* and *oa*. Two vowels together are called vowel digraphs. Usually, vowel digraphs represent the long sound of the first vowel.

Vowel Diagraphs	Examples of Usual Sounds	Exceptions
ee and *ea*	steep, each, treat, sea	head, sweat, dread
ai and *ay*	plain, paid, may, betray	plaid
oa, *ow*, and *oe*	soak, slow, doe	now, shoe
ie and *igh*	lie, night, delight	friend, eight

As you read, sometimes the only way to know how to pronounce a word with an *ea* spelling is to see if the word makes sense in the sentence. Look at this example:

The water pipes were made of *lead.*

First, try out the long sound "ee." Ask yourself if it sounds right. It does not. Then, try the short sound "e." You will find that the short sound is correct in that sentence.

Now try this example.

Where you *lead*, I will follow.

Word Patterns

Recognizing different vowel-consonant patterns will help you read longer words. In the following sections, the V stands for "vowel" and the C stands for "consonant."

Single-syllable Words

CV – go: In two-letter words with a consonant followed by a vowel, the vowel is usually long. For example, the word *go* is pronounced with a long *o* sound.

In a single-syllable word, a vowel followed only by a single consonant is usually short.

CVC – got: If you add a consonant to the word *go*, such as the *t* in *got*, the vowel sound is a short *o*. Say the words *go* and *got* aloud and notice the difference in pronunciation.

Multi-syllable words

In words of more than one syllable, notice the letters that follow a vowel.

VCCV – robber: A single vowel followed by two consonants is usually short.

VCV — begin: A single vowel followed by a single consonant is usually long.

VCe — beside: An extension of the VCV pattern is vowel-consonant-silent *e*. In these words, the vowel is long and the *e* is not pronounced.

When you see a word with the VCV pattern, try the long vowel sound first. If the word does not make sense, try the short sound. Pronounce the words *model, camel,* and *closet*. First, try the long vowel sound. That does not sound correct, so try the short vowel sound. The short vowel sound is correct in those words.

Remember that patterns help you get started on figuring out a word. You will sometimes need to try a different sound or find the word in a dictionary.

As you read and find unfamiliar words, look the pronunciations up in a dictionary. Write the words in this chart in the correct column to help you notice patterns and remember pronunciations.

Syllables	Example	New words	Vowel
CV	go		long
CVC	got		short
VCC	robber		short
V/CV	begin open		long long
VC/V	closet		short

MNEMONICS

Mnemonics are devices, or methods, that help you remember things. The basic strategy is to link something you do not know with something that you *do* know. Here are some common mnemonic devices:

Visualizing Create a picture in your head that will help you remember the meaning of a vocabulary word. For example, the first four letters of the word *significance* spell *sign.* Picture a sign with the word *meaning* written on it to remember that significance means "meaning" or "importance."

Spelling The way a word is spelled can help you remember its meaning. For example, you might remember that *clarify* means to "make clear" if you notice that both *clarify* and *clear* start with the letters *cl.*

To help you remember how to spell certain words, look for a familiar word within the difficult word. For example:

Believe has a *lie* in it.

Separate is *a rat* of a word to spell.

Your *principal* is your *pal.*

Rhyming Here is a popular rhyme that helps people figure out how to spell *ei* and *ie* words.

i before ***e*** — except after ***c*** *or when sounding like* ***a*** *as in neighbor and weigh.*

List words here that you need help remembering. Work with a group to create mnemonic devices to help you remember each word.

List words here that you need help remembering. Work with a group to create mnemonic devices to help you remember each word.

COMMUNICATION STRATEGIES

Use these sentence starters to help you express yourself clearly in different classroom situations.

Expressing an Opinion

I think that ______________________________

I believe that ______________________________

In my opinion, ______________________________

Agreeing

I agree with ______________ that ______________

I see what you mean.

That's an interesting idea.

My idea is similar to ______________'s idea.

My idea builds upon ______________'s idea.

Disagreeing

I don't completely agree with you because ______________

My opinion is different than yours.

I got a different answer than you.

I see it a different way.

Reporting a Group's Ideas

We agreed that ______________________________

We decided that ______________________________

We had a different approach.

We had a similar idea.

Predicting

I predict that ______________________________

I imagine that ______________________________

Based on ______________ I predict that ______________

Paraphrasing

So you are saying that ______________________________

In other words, you think ______________________________

What I hear you saying is ______________________________

Offering a Suggestion

Maybe we could ______________________________

What if we ______________________________

Here's something we might try.

Asking for Clarification

I have a question about that.

Could you explain that another way?

Can you give me another example of that?

Asking for a Response

What do you think?

Do you agree?

What answer did you get?

Cut out each bookmark to use as -a handy word list when you are reading. On the lines, jot down words you want to learn and remember. You can also use the bookmark as a placeholder in your book.

TITLE

Word	Page #

TITLE

Word	Page #

TITLE

Word	Page #

Cut out each bookmark to use as -a handy word list when you are reading. On the lines, jot down words you want to learn and remember. You can also use the bookmark as a placeholder in your book.

TITLE

Word **Page #**

TITLE

Word **Page #**

TITLE

Word **Page #**

Use these cards to record words you want to remember. Write the word, the title of the story or article in which it appears, its part of speech, and its definition. Then, use the word in an original sentence that shows its meaning

Word: ______________________ Page ______________________

Selection: ______________________

Part of Speech: ______________________

Definition: ______________________

____

My Sentence ______________________

____

Word: ______________________ Page ______________________

Selection: ______________________

Part of Speech: ______________________

Definition: ______________________

____

My Sentence ______________________

____

Word: ______________________ Page ______________________

Selection: ______________________

Part of Speech: ______________________

Definition: ______________________

____

My Sentence ______________________

____

Use these cards to record words you want to remember. Write the word, the title of the story or article in which it appears, its part of speech, and its definition. Then, use the word in an original sentence that shows its meaning

Word: ______________________ Page ______________________

Selection: ______________________

Part of Speech: ______________________

Definition: ______________________

____

My Sentence ______________________

____

Word: ______________________ Page ______________________

Selection: ______________________

Part of Speech: ______________________

Definition: ______________________

____

My Sentence ______________________

____

Word: ______________________ Page ______________________

Selection: ______________________

Part of Speech: ______________________

Definition: ______________________

____

My Sentence ______________________

____

Using the Personal Thesaurus

The Personal Thesaurus provides students with the opportunity to make connections between words academic words, familiar words, and even slang words. Students can use the Personal Thesaurus to help them understand the importance of using words in the proper context and also avoid overusing words in their writing.

Use the following routine to foster frequent use of the Personal Thesaurus.

1. After students have read a selection or done some writing, have them turn to the Personal Thesaurus.
2. Encourage students to add new entries. Help them to understand the connection between their personal language, which might include familiar words and even slang, and the academic language of their reading and writing.
3. Call on volunteers to read a few entries aloud. Point out that writers have many choices of words when they write. Help students see that audience often determines word choice.

N

nice

admirable

friendly

agreeable

pleasant

cool

phat

A

B

C

D

E

F

G

H

I

J

K

L

M

N

O

P

Q

R

S

T

U

V

W

X

Y

Z

(Acknowledgments continued from page ii)

Dramatic Publishing
From *Anne Frank & Me* by Cherie Bennett with Jeff Gottesfeld. Copyright © 1997 by Cherie Bennett. Printed in the United States of America. Used by permission. CAUTION: Professionals and amateurs are hereby warned that *Anne Frank & Me,* being fully protected under the copyright Laws of the United States of America, the British Empire, including the Dominion of Canada, and all other countries of the Universal Copyright and Berne Conventions, are subject to royalty. All rights, including professional, amateur, motion picture, recitation, lecturing, public reading, radio and television broadcasting, and the rights of translation into foreign languages, are strictly reserved. All inquiries regarding performance rights should be addressed to Dramatic Publishing, 311 Washington St., Woodstock, IL 60098. Phone: (815) 338-7170. All rights reserved. Used by permission.

Florida Holocaust Museum
Florida Holocaust Museum Press Release from *www.flholocaustmuseum.org.* Copyright © Florida Holocaust Museum, 2001, 2005; All rights reserved. Used by permission.

Richard Garcia
"The City is So Big" by Richard Garcia from *The City Is So Big.*

Harcourt, Inc.
"Choice: A Tribute to Martin Luther King, Jr." by Alice Walker from *In Search Of Our Mothers' Gardens: Womanist Prose.* Copyright © 1983 by Alice Walker. "For My Sister Molly Who in the Fifties" from *Revolutionary Petunias & Other Poems,* copyright © 1972 and renewed 2000 by Alice Walker. This material may not be reproduced in any form or by any means without the prior written permission of the publisher. Used by permission of Harcourt, Inc.

HarperCollins Publishers, Inc.
From *An American Childhood* by Annie Dillard. Copyright © 1987 by Annie Dillard. Used by permission of HarperCollins Publishers.

The Estate of Dr. Martin Luther King, Jr. c/o Writer's House LLC
"The American Dream" by Dr. Martin Luther King, Jr. from *A Testament Of Hope: The Essential Writings Of Martin Luther King, Jr.* Copyright © 1961 Martin Luther King Jr.; Copyright © renewed 1989 Coretta Scott King. Used by arrangement with The Heirs to the Estate of Martin Luther King Jr., c/o Writers House as agent for the proprietor New York, N.Y.

Alfred A. Knopf, Inc.
"The 11:59" by Patricia C. McKissack from *The Dark Thirty* by Patricia McKissack illustrated by Brian Pinkney, copyright © 1992 by Patricia C. McKissack. Illustrations copyright © 1992 by Brian Pinkney. Used by permission of Alfred A. Knopf, a division of Random House, Inc.

Liveright Publishing Corporation
"Runagate Runagate" Copyright © 1966 by Robert Hayden, from *Collected Poems of Robert Hayden,* edited by Frederick Glaysher. This selection may not be reproduced, stored in a retrieval system, or transmitted in any form or by any means without prior written permission of the publisher. Used by permission of Liveright Publishing Corporation.

Robert MacNeil
"The Trouble with Television" by Robert MacNeil condensed from a speech, *November 1984 at President Leadership Forum, SUNY.* Copyright © 1985 by Reader's Digest and Robert MacNeil. Used by permission of Robert MacNeil.

Eve Merriam c/o Marian Reiner
"Thumbprint" from *A Sky Full of Poems* by Eve Merriam. Copyright © 1964, 1970, 1973, 1986 by Eve Merriam. Used by permission of Marian Reiner.

N. Scott Momaday
"New World" by N. Scott Momaday from *The Gourd Dancers.* Used with the permission of Navarre Scott Momaday.

National Public Radio
"Profile: World War II veterans who founded the Paralyzed Veterans of America" from *National Public Radio, November 11, 2003.* Copyright © 2005 National Public Radio. Used by permission. All rights reserved.

Naomi Shihab Nye
"Words to Sit in, Like Chairs" by Naomi Shihab Nye from 911: The Book of Help. "Hamadi" by Naomi Shihab Nye from America Street. Used by permission of the author, Naomi Shihab Nye.

Harold Ober Associates, Inc.
"Cat!" by Eleanor Farjeon from *Poems For Children.* Copyright © 1938 by Eleanor Farjeon, renewed 1966 by Gervase Farjeon. Used by permission of Harold Ober Associates Incorporated. All rights reserved.

Oxford University Press, Inc.
"Summary of The Tell-Tale Heart" by James D. Hart from *The Oxford Companion To American Literature.* Copyright © 1983. Used by permission of Oxford University Press, Inc. www.oup.co.uk.

Pantheon Books, a division of Random House Inc.
"Coyote Steals the Sun and Moon" by Richard Erdoes and Alfonso Ortiz from *American Indian Myths and Legends,* copyright © 1984 by Richard Erdoes and Alfonso Ortiz.

Pearson Prentice Hall
"The War in Vietnam" from *The American Nation* by Dr. James West Davidson and Dr. Michael B. Stoff. Copyright © 2003 by Pearson Education, Inc., publishing as Prentice Hall. Used by permission.

G.P. Putnam's Sons
"Describe Somebody," and "Almost a Summer Sky" from *Locomotion* by Jacqueline Woodson, copyright © 2003 by Jacqueline Woodson. Used by permission of G.P. Putnam's Sons, A Division of Penguin Young Readers Group, A Member of Penguin Group (USA) Inc., 345 Hudson Street, New York, NY 10014. All rights reserved.

Marian Reiner, Literary Agent
"Concrete Mixers" by Patricia Hubbell from *8 A.M. Shadows.* Copyright © 1965 Patricia Hubbell. Copyright renewed © 1993 Patricia Hubbell. Used by permission of Marian Reiner on behalf of the author.

Reprint Management Services - A/R
"Hands-free Law Won't Solve the Problem" by Mike Langdon Nov. 14, 2006 from *http://www.mercurynews.com/mld/mercurynews/business/column.* Copyright 2007 San Jose Mercury News. Used by permission.

Maria Teresa Sanchez
"Old Man" by Ricardo Sanchez from *Selected Poems.* Used by permission of Maria Teresa Sanchez for the Estate of Dr. Ricardo Sanchez.

Savannah International Trade & Convention Center
Savannah Belles Ferry Schedule from *http://www.catchacat.org.* Copyright © 2007 Chatham Area Transit Authority. All Rights Reserved. Used by permission.

Scholastic Inc.
From *Out of the Dust* ("Debts", "Fields of Flashing Light" and "Migrants") by Karen Hesse. Published by Scholastic Press/Scholastic Inc. Copyright © 1997 by Karen Hesse. "An Hour with Abuelo" from *An Island Like You: Stories of the Barrio* by Judith Ortiz Cofer. Published by Orchard Books/Scholastic Inc. Copyright © 1995 by Judith Ortiz Cofer. Used by permission of Scholastic Inc.

Argelia Sedillo
"Gentleman of Rio en Medio" by Juan A.A. Sedillo from *The New Mexico Quarterly, A Regional Review, Volume IX, August, 1939, Number 3.*

Sprint
Instructions for an Answering Machine from *Sprint User's Manual for Tapeless Digital Answering System with Time/Day SP-818.* Used by permission of Sprint.

The Society of Authors
"Silver" by Walter de la Mare from *The Complete Poems of Walter de la Mare 1901–1918.* Used by permission of The Literary Trustees of Walter de la Mare and the Society of Authors as their representative.

Thomson Higher Education
"Summary of The Tell-Tale Heart" from *Short Story Criticism: Criticism Of The Works Of Short Fiction Writers, Short Story Criticism Vol 34 34th Edition* by Anna Sheets Nesbitt (Editor). Copyright © 1999. Used with permission of Gale, a division of Thomson Learning: www.thomsonrights.com.

Estate of Jackie Torrence
"Brer Possum's Dilemma" retold by Jackie Torrence from *Homespun: Tales From America's Favorite Storytellers.* Copyright © 1988 by Jackie Torrence, published in Homespun: Tales from America's Favorite Storytellers by Jimmy Neil Smith. Used by permission of author.

Vallejo Baylink
Baylink Ferry Schedule and Logo from *http://www.baylinkferry.com.* Copyright © 2007. Used by permission.

Vital Speeches of the Day
From Sharing in the American Dream by Colin Powell from *Vital Speeches, June 1, 1997, V63 N16, P484(2).* Used by permission of Vital Speeches of the Day.

W. W. Norton & Company, Inc.
"Water Names" from *Hunger* by Lan Samantha Chang. Copyright © 1998 by Lan Samantha Chang. Used by permission of W. W. Norton & Company, Inc.

Walker & Company
"The Baker Heater League" by Patricia and Frederick McKissack from *A Long Hard Journey: The Story of the Pullman Porter.* Copyright © 1989 by Patricia and Frederick McKissack. Used with permission of Walker & Company.

Water Taxi, Inc.
Fort Lauderdale Water Taxi™ Schedule from *http://www.watertaxi.com.* Copyright © 2002–2007 Water Taxi, Inc. All Rights Reserved. Used by permission.

Richard & Joyce Wolkomir
"Sun Suckers and Moon Cursers" by Richarad and Joyce Wolkomir. Copyright © 2002 by Richard & Joyce Wolkomir. Used with the authors' permission.

Note: Every effort has been made to locate the copyright owner of material reproduced on this component. Omissions brought to our attention will be corrected in subsequent editions.

PHOTO AND ART CREDITS

Cover: *False Start*, 1959, oil on canvas, Johns, Jasper (b.1930)/Private Collection, Lauros/ Giraudon;/www.bridgeman.co.uk/Cover art © Jasper Johns/Licensed by VAGA, New York, NY; **4:** Hulton Archive/Getty Images Inc.; **9:** Courtesy of Diane Alimena; **20:** Jeff Greenberg/PhotoEdit; **33:** New York State Historical Association, Cooperstown, New York; **37:** Paul Fusco/Magnum Photos, Inc.; **44:** Pearson Education/PH School Division; **47:** © Charles E. Rotkin/CORBIS; **48:** © Charles E. Rotkin/CORBIS; **49:** © Charles E. Rotkin/CORBIS; **53:** Pearson Education; **60:** Getty Images; **64:** Corel Professional Photos CD-ROM™; **67:** Corel Professional Photos CD-ROM™; **68:** © Daryl Benson/Masterfile; **71:** The Granger Collection, New York; **74:** Charles Krebs/CORBIS; **75:** ©Daryl Benson/Masterfile; **76:** The Granger Collection, New York; **77:** Prentice Hall; **81:** Courtesy National Archives, photo no. (542390); **90:** © Peter Frischmuth/argus/Peter Arnold, Inc.; **104:** California Department of Parks & Recreation; **108:** © Ulf Sjostedt/FPG International Corp.; **112:** Courtesy of the Library of Congress; **120:** Courtesy of the Library of Congress; **124:** Courtesy of the Library of Congress; **129:** SuperStock; **138:** Dianna Sarto/CORBIS; **142:** Sid Grossman (1913–1955), Photographer, Reprinted by permission of the Museum of the City of New York, Gift of the Federal Art Project, Work Projects Administration; **149:** Pure Pleasure, Pat Scott/The Bridgeman Art Library, London/New York; **153:** Image courtesy of the Advertising Archives; **158:** NASA; **167:** Getty Images; **173:** Harriet Tubman Quilt made by the Negro History Club of Marin City and Sausalito, CA, 1951, 120 x 96 inches, cotton appliqued. Designed by Ben Irvin. Gift of the Howard Thurman Educational Trust to the permanent collection of the Robert W. Woodruff Library, Atlanta University Center, Atlanta, GA; **177:** Paul Conklin/PhotoEdit; **180:** Bettmann/ CORBIS; **186:** Courtesy National Archives, photo no. (NWDNS-200-HN-PO-5); **190:** Bettmann/CORBIS; **195:** Jon Feingersh/CORBIS; **202:** Courtesy of the Library of Congress; **206:** Hulton Archive/Getty Images Inc.; **212:** NASA; **216:** Norman Chanistockphoto.com; **223:** Playground, P.J. Crook/ The Bridgeman Art Library, London/New York; **231:** Getty Images; **237:** Anne-Marie Weber/ CORBIS; **241:** Bruce Forster/Getty Images; **246:** *t.* StockFood; **246:** *b.l.* Eising Food Photography/StockFood America—All rights reserved.; **246:** *b.r.* Snowflake Studios Inc./ StockFood America—All rights reserved.; **246:** background Getty Images; **247:** Corel Professional Photos CD-ROM™; **247:** background Getty Images; **254:** USDA Photo; **263:** Pearson Education; **267:** *The Magpie*, 1869, Claude Monet, Reunion des Musées Nationaux/Art Resource, NY; **276:** *Crawling Turtle II*, Barry Wilson/SuperStock; **285:** Courtesy of Pensacola Little Theatre; **292:** Photofest; **300:** Lon C. Diehl/PhotoEdit; **302:** Lon C. Diehl/Photoedit; **305:** Copyright ANNE FRANK-Fonds, Basle/Switzerland; **347:** The Granger Collection, New York; **351:** Courtesy of the Florida Holocaust Museum; **356:** Kevin Schafer/CORBIS; **362:** Random House Inc.; **364:** Corel Professional Photos CD-ROM™; **370:** Warren Bolster/Getty Images; **374:** Paul & Lindamarie Ambrose/Getty Images; **377:** Illustration from "Count Your Way Through Mexico" by Jim Haskins; illustrations by Helen Byers. Illustrations copyright ©1989 by Carolrhoda Books, Inc.; **388:** Random House Inc.; **392:** AP/Wide World Photos; **400:** Felix Zaska/ CORBIS; **404:** AP/Wide World Photos; **411:** Art Resource, NY; **417:** Bettmann/CORBIS; **390:** Bettmann/CORBIS; **391:** Richard Oliver/ CORBIS; **446:** Richard Oliver/CORBIS